Lebanon

Siona Jenkins
Ann Jousiffe

LONELY PLANET PUBLICATIONS
Melbourne • Oakland • London • Paris

LEBANON

Tripoli
Bustling medieval souqs dominated by a Crusader castle

Qadisha Valley
Lush, isolated and dotted with ancient monasteries and hermits' caves

Byblos
Impressive archaeological remains in one of the world's most ancient towns

Afqa Grotto
Sacred cavern where Adonis and Aphrodite had their first kiss

Beirut
Vibrant city being rapidly rebuilt

Jebel Sannine
Home to Lebanon's favourite ski resorts of Faraya and Faqra

Baalbek
Site of one of ancient Rome's most lavish temples

Zahlé
Open-air restaurant and wine centre of Lebanon

SYRIA

MEDITERRANEAN SEA

BEIRUT

Homs

Tell Nabi Mend

Lake Qattineh

Nabi Mend

Qoubayet

Charbiné

Hermel

Hermel Pyramid

Al-Qaa

Akkar al-Atiqa

Akkar

Abboudiye

Aarida

Amrit

Halba

Qubbet al-Baddawi

Zgharta

Al-Mina

Tripoli (Trablous)

Qalamoun

Enfe

Chekka

Balamand

Amioun

Ehden

Bcharré

Barzoun & Hasroun

The Cedars

Qornet as-Saweda (3090m)

Horsh Ehden Nature Reserve

Qadisha Valley

Jebel Tannourine

Aaqoura

Laklouk

Qartaba

Douma

Masnaqa

Rachana

Qubba

Batroun

Byblos (Jbail)

Amchit

Jounieh

Beit Mary

Brummana

Bikfaya

Ajaltoun

Jeita Grotto

Nahr al-Kalb

Nahr Ibrahim

Adonis Valley

Afqa Valley

Afqa Grotto

Fagra

Faraya Mzaar

Jebel Sannine (2628m)

Qanat Bakiche

Baskinta

Kesrouane

Metn

Zaarour

Furzol

Zahlé

Niha

Rayak

Rayak

Baalbek

Bekaa Valley

Anti-Lebanon Range

Talat Musa (2669m)

Mt Lebanon Range

Nahr al-Aasi (Orontes River)

Deir Mar Maroun

Nahr Abu Moussa

Nahr Abu Ali

Nahr al-Kabir

Moussalayha Castle

To Krak des Chevaliers

To Krak des Chevaliers

35°40'E

34°40'N

34°20'N

34°00'N

S Y R I A

ELEVATION

	2500 m
	2000 m
	1500 m
	1000 m
	500 m
	0

Aanjar
Majestic remains of the Middle East's only Umayyad fortified city

DAMASCUS

Beiteddine
Magnificent Ottoman-era palace

Chtaura

Aanjar
Masnaa

Majdel Aanjar

Qabb Elias

Aamiq Swamp

Jebel ash-Sheikh (Mt Hermon) (2814m)

Deir al-Qamar
Beiteddine
Baadine

Chouf Cedar Reserve

Hasbaya

Khiam

Qula

Moukhtara

Jezzine

Quneitra

Golan Heights

Nahr Litani

Damour

Joun

Khirbin

Temple of Echmoun

Nabatiye
Marjeyun

Beaufort Castle

Kiryat Shmona

Jordan River

Sidon
Picturesque fishing port with labyrinthine old souqs

Sidon (Saida)
Maghdouche

Ghaziye

Bint Jbayl

Tibnin

Tyre
Major centre in ancient Phoenicia and home to one of the world's largest Roman hippodromes

Sarafand

Qana

Tomb of Hiram

I S R A E L   &   T H E
P A L E S T I N I A N
T E R R I T O R I E S

Tyre (Sour)

Mansoura

Nahariya

33°40'N

33°20'N

Lebanon
2nd edition – January, 2001
First published – February, 1998

Published by
Lonely Planet Publications Pty Ltd ABN 36 005 607 983
90 Maribyrnong St, Footscray, Victoria 3011, Australia

Lonely Planet Offices
Australia Locked Bag 1, Footscray, Victoria 3011
USA 150 Linden St, Oakland, CA 94607
UK 10a Spring Place, London NW5 3BH
France 1 rue du Dahomey, 75011 Paris

Photographs
All the images in this guide are available for licensing from
Lonely Planet Images.
email: lpi@lonelyplanet.com.au

Front cover photograph
A Lebanese car license plate (Paul Doyle)

ISBN 1 86450 190 1

text & maps © Lonely Planet 2001
photos © photographers as indicated 2001

Printed by Colorcraft Ltd, Hong Kong

Contents – Text

1

Contents – Maps

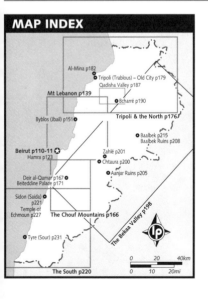

MAP INDEX

Al-Mina p182
Tripoli (Trablous) – Old City p179
Qadisha Valley p187
Mt Lebanon p139
Bcharré p190
Byblos (Jbail) p151
Tripoli & the North p176
Baalbek p215
Baalbek Ruins p208
Beirut p110-11
Hamra p123
Zahlé p201
Chtaura p200
Aanjar Ruins p205
Deir al-Qamar p167
Beiteddine Palace p171
Sidon (Saida) p221
Temple of Echmoun p227
The Chouf Mountains p166
The Bekaa Valley p198
Tyre (Sour) p231

0   20   40km
0   10   20mi

The South p220

The Authors

Siona Jenkins

In 1989, Siona Jenkins went to Cairo for six months of Arabic language training after completing her Masters degree in Middle Eastern Studies. Eleven years on, she's still there. A freelance journalist who writes for the *Irish Times* and just about anyone else who pays on time, she has also appeared in or helped produce three documentaries on Egypt. Siona's previous work for Lonely Planet includes co-authoring the *Egypt* guide and updating the Egypt chapter of *Africa* and the *Egyptian Arabic phrasebook*. She is passionate about the desert, Middle Eastern politics and her son, Leo.

Ann Jousiffe

A London-based freelance writer and photographer Ann has travelled widely around the Mediterranean, North Africa and the Middle East pursuing her love of ancient ruins and deserts. She has a strange affinity with the letter L – lives in London and the Languedoc, writes about Lebanon and Libya and her hobbies are loafing around museums and lager drinking. Her current 'work in progress' is a book about Libya.

FROM SIONA

While I was in Lebanon, what seemed like an army of people patiently answered less-than-informed questions, shared their favourite places or extended a warm, very Lebanese welcome that instantly made this visitor feel right at home. So, in no particular order, I would like to thank Karim Shaer for his fascinating forays around Beirut; Clement and Jean Pierre for showing me the Jord; Nada Khoury and Youssef for discussing Saida and soap over *halloumi* and Kefraya; Kamal Mousawak for deliciously demonstrating a perfect tabouleh and other tips on Lebanese cuisine; Dr Helga Seeden for generously donating papers as well as her time; Rosemary Sayegh for helping to untangle the civil war and Emily Nasrallah for feeding me chicken soup and discussing her novels. Thanks also to Faris and Zeina Sayegh for getting me started on so many tracks, to Peter Speetjens for his environmental articles, Karim Jisr for explaining conservation, Tracy Kitzman for firsthand hiking tips, and Chris Hack, Ed McBride and Ann Ranahan for helping out a fellow hack. Johnny & Cyn Farah cannot be thanked enough for their generous hospitality, nor can Warren Singh-Bartlett for patiently answering last-minute queries when he could have been in Paradise. Last but not least I would like to thank Leo for being such a trooper.

This Book

The first edition of this book was written by Ann Jousiffe. This second edition was thoroughly researched and revised by Siona Jenkins.

From the Publisher
This book was edited in Lonely Planet's Melbourne office by Julia Taylor with assistance from Bethune Carmichael, Justin Flynn and Michelle Glynn. Sonya Brooke coordinated the mapping and design. Trudi Canavan, Sarah Jolly, Indra Kilfoyle and Sonya Brooke drew the illustrations and Maria Vallianos designed the cover. Quentin Frayne organised the Language chapter. Thanks to Camilia Saad for checking and correcting the script of Arabic place names.

Acknowledgments
Many thanks to the following travellers who used *Lebanon* and wrote to us with helpful hints, useful advice and interesting anecdotes about travelling in Lebanon.

Alan Keohane, Alexander Styhre, Alida Lehnort, Andrew Jamieson, Andrew Radford, Andrzej Bielecki, Andy Thomas, Arne Stapnes, B Manger, Bjarke Petersen, Colin McKinnon, DJ Graham, Damien Galanaud, David Siddhartha Patel, Emily Peckham, Ernst Lessan, Evan Petrelis, Fareed Abou-Haidar, Frank Boizard, Godfrey Fowler, Helen Craven, Inge & Peter Haechler, Iris McKinley, Isabel Durack, Jamil van der Linde, Jedidiah J Palosaari, Jenny Hodge, Joanne Brais, John Brinkley, Jonathan Harris, Captain Jorma Sormunen, Joshua Taylor Barnes, Jun Nakabayashi, Kathryn Dally, Keiran Donovan, Kenneth Morton, Knut Aalborg, Maha DeMaggio, Martin Williams, Mary Findell, Matevz Zgaga, Matthias Hanke, Michael Carroll, Michel Thomas, Mike & Gillian Finnie, Neal Bierling, Nick Tyldesley, Pascal C Leverd, Patrick Kennen, Patrick Wullaert, Paul Werne, Pim Santegoeds, R Kalia, Richard Tanner, RJ Collie, Dr Stephen Buston-Xhignesse, Steve Dodson, Susan Gill, Thomas Kramer, Todd Hilton, Tom Roche, Tony Bonnaud, Trine L Carstensen, Vassili B Lebedev, Vatsala Mamgain, W Stockl-Manger, Walid Chahine, Wassim El Chemeitelli, William Habib, Yuval Ronen, Yvonne Doris and Zahid Ali.

Foreword

ABOUT LONELY PLANET GUIDEBOOKS

The story begins with a classic travel adventure: Tony and Maureen Wheeler's 1972 journey across Europe and Asia to Australia. Useful information about the overland trail did not exist at that time, so Tony and Maureen published the first Lonely Planet guidebook to meet a growing need.

From a kitchen table, then from a tiny office in Melbourne (Australia), Lonely Planet has become the largest independent travel publisher in the world, an international company with offices in Melbourne, Oakland (USA), London (UK) and Paris (France).

Today Lonely Planet guidebooks cover the globe. There is an ever-growing list of books and there's information in a variety of forms and media. Some things haven't changed. The main aim is still to help make it possible for adventurous travellers to get out there – to explore and better understand the world.

At Lonely Planet we believe travellers can make a positive contribution to the countries they visit – if they respect their host communities and spend their money wisely. Since 1986 a percentage of the income from each book has been donated to aid projects and human rights campaigns.

Updates Lonely Planet thoroughly updates each guidebook as often as possible. This usually means there are around two years between editions, although for more unusual or more stable destinations the gap can be longer. Check the imprint page (following the colour map at the beginning of the book) for publication dates.

Between editions up-to-date information is available in two free newsletters – the paper *Planet Talk* and email *Comet* (to subscribe, contact any Lonely Planet office) – and on our Web site at www.lonelyplanet.com. The *Upgrades* section of the Web site covers a number of important and volatile destinations and is regularly updated by Lonely Planet authors. *Scoop* covers news and current affairs relevant to travellers. And, lastly, the *Thorn Tree* bulletin board and *Postcards* section of the site carry unverified, but fascinating, reports from travellers.

Correspondence The process of creating new editions begins with the letters, postcards and emails received from travellers. This correspondence often includes suggestions, criticisms and comments about the current editions. Interesting excerpts are immediately passed on via newsletters and the Web site, and everything goes to our authors to be verified when they're researching on the road. We're keen to get more feedback from organisations or individuals who represent communities visited by travellers.

> Lonely Planet gathers information for everyone who's curious about the planet – and especially for those who explore it first-hand. Through guidebooks, phrasebooks, activity guides, maps, literature, newsletters, image library, TV series and Web site we act as an information exchange for a worldwide community of travellers.

Research Authors aim to gather sufficient practical information to enable travellers to make informed choices and to make the mechanics of a journey run smoothly. They also research historical and cultural background to help enrich the travel experience and allow travellers to understand and respond appropriately to cultural and environmental issues.

Authors don't stay in every hotel because that would mean spending a couple of months in each medium-sized city and, no, they don't eat at every restaurant because that would mean stretching belts beyond capacity. They do visit hotels and restaurants to check standards and prices, but feedback based on readers' direct experiences can be very helpful.

Many of our authors work undercover, others aren't so secretive. None of them accept freebies in exchange for positive write-ups. And none of our guidebooks contain any advertising.

Production Authors submit their raw manuscripts and maps to offices in Australia, USA, UK or France. Editors and cartographers – all experienced travellers themselves – then begin the process of assembling the pieces. When the book finally hits the shops, some things are already out of date, we start getting feedback from readers and the process begins again …

WARNING & REQUEST

Things change – prices go up, schedules change, good places go bad and bad places go bankrupt – nothing stays the same. So, if you find things better or worse, recently opened or long since closed, please tell us and help make the next edition even more accurate and useful. We genuinely value all the feedback we receive. Julie Young coordinates a well travelled team that reads and acknowledges every letter, postcard and email and ensures that every morsel of information finds its way to the appropriate authors, editors and cartographers for verification.

Everyone who writes to us will find their name in the next edition of the appropriate guidebook. They will also receive the latest issue of *Planet Talk*, our quarterly printed newsletter, or *Comet*, our monthly email newsletter. Subscriptions to both newsletters are free. The very best contributions will be rewarded with a free guidebook.

Excerpts from your correspondence may appear in new editions of Lonely Planet guidebooks, the Lonely Planet Web site, *Planet Talk* or *Comet*, so please let us know if you *don't* want your letter published or your name acknowledged.

Send all correspondence to the Lonely Planet office closest to you:

Australia: Locked Bag 1, Footscray, Victoria 3011
USA: 150 Linden St, Oakland, CA 94607
UK: 10A Spring Place, London NW5 3BH
France: 1 rue du Dahomey, 75011 Paris

Or email us at: talk2us@lonelyplanet.com.au

For news, views and updates see our Web site: www.lonelyplanet.com

HOW TO USE A LONELY PLANET GUIDEBOOK

The best way to use a Lonely Planet guidebook is any way you choose. At Lonely Planet we believe the most memorable travel experiences are often those that are unexpected, and the finest discoveries are those you make yourself. Guidebooks are not intended to be used as if they provide a detailed set of infallible instructions!

Contents All Lonely Planet guidebooks follow roughly the same format. The Facts about the Destination chapters or sections give background information ranging from history to weather. Facts for the Visitor gives practical information on issues like visas and health. Getting There & Away gives a brief starting point for re-searching travel to and from the destination. Getting Around gives an overview of the transport options when you arrive.

The peculiar demands of each destination determine how sub-sequent chapters are broken up, but some things remain constant. We always start with background, then proceed to sights, places to stay, places to eat, entertainment, getting there and away, and getting around information – in that order.

Heading Hierarchy Lonely Planet headings are used in a strict hierarchical structure that can be visualised as a set of Russian dolls. Each heading (and its following text) is encompassed by any preceding heading that is higher on the hierarchical ladder.

Entry Points We do not assume guidebooks will be read from beginning to end, but that people will dip into them. The tradi-tional entry points are the list of contents and the index. In addition, however, some books have a complete list of maps and an index map illustrating map coverage.

There may also be a colour map that shows highlights. These highlights are dealt with in greater detail in the Facts for the Visitor chapter, along with planning questions and suggested itin-eraries. Each chapter covering a geographical region usually begins with a locator map and another list of highlights. Once you find something of interest in a list of highlights, turn to the index.

Maps Maps play a crucial role in Lonely Planet guidebooks and include a huge amount of information. A legend is printed on the back page. We seek to have complete consistency between maps and text, and to have every important place in the text captured on a map. Map key numbers usually start in the top left corner.

Although inclusion in a guidebook usually implies a recommen-dation we cannot list every good place. Exclusion does not necessarily imply criticism. In fact there are a number of reasons why we might exclude a place – sometimes it is simply inappropriate to encourage an influx of travellers.

Introduction

High mountains and deep valleys; minuscule bikinis and head-to-toe *chadors*; exquisite Graeco-Roman ruins and pockmarked high-rises; poverty and extraordinary wealth: whether it's the drama of the landscape or the powerful mixture of sects and traditions, Lebanon lives up to its tourist-brochure cliche as a land of contrasts.

Forget the 15 years of civil war and destruction; the Lebanese, famed for their commercial skill, great food and appreciation of a good party, might not be able to turn back the clock and regain their status as the Middle East's decadent commercial centre overnight, but they're trying.

Tourism is an integral part of this drive to put the civil war behind them, and all the ingredients are here to make their plan a success. Geographically, Lebanon is as diverse as it is possible to imagine in a country so small. In an area less than half the size of Wales, there is a Mediterranean coast with ancient cities and very modern beaches, the soaring Mt Lebanon Range with popular ski resorts and alpine scenery, and the Bekaa Valley, an agricultural plain bound in by a second mountain range. Presiding over them all is Beirut, once the Paris of the Middle East, which became a synonym for modern anarchy, and is now a vibrant, cosmopolitan city bent on a comeback.

Culturally, too, there is diversity: throughout the country Christian and Islamic heritage and architecture are mixed with the remains of earlier civilisations. All the great conquering peoples of antiquity have left signs of their presence in the form of well-preserved monuments. Apart from the Phoenicians, there are relics from the Egyptians, Greeks, Romans, Byzantines, Arabs, Ottoman Turks, Crusaders and latterly the French, who had a mandate over Lebanon until independence in 1946.

Until 2000, Israel's continued occupation of the south kept foreign visitors away. Now that the soldiers have gone, it's the perfect time to visit before the country becomes too popular – as it surely will in years to come.

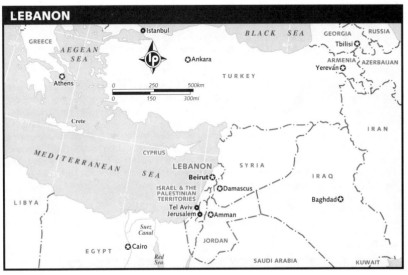

Facts about Lebanon

HISTORY

Although the modern state of Lebanon has only existed since 1946, its territory boasts a history as long as it is eventful and complex. This is the biblical 'land of milk and honey' and, over the millennia, conquerors have been attracted to its abundant natural resources, safe anchorages and strategic coastal mountains.

The shores of Lebanon attracted settlers from about 10,000 BC. Simple early settlements from this period evolved into more complex villages over time and eventually, around 3000 BC, into prototype cities. (The layers of development can be seen most clearly in the modern excavations at Byblos.) By 4000 BC these settlements had started to use copper, although only in a decorative way, and ceramics had become fairly sophisticated.

Phoenicians

By around 2500 BC the coast was colonised by the people who later became known as the Phoenicians. A Semitic race, probably related to the Canaanites who had settled in the coastal lowlands from about 3000 BC, the Phoenicians became one of the most influential cultures of the region. They dominated the sea with their superior vessels and navigational skills and are thought to have created the first real alphabet – a remarkable breakthrough which paved the way for the great works of literature of the early Greeks and the rest of the classical civilisations.

However, despite their innovations and skills as artisans and traders, the Phoenicians never became unified politically, and instead remained independent city-states along the Lebanese shore. Gebal (Byblos, later Jbail) and Tyre (Sour) were the most important of these cities, followed by Sidon (Saida) and Berytus (Beirut). The name Phoenicia was given to this collection of city-statelets by the Greeks.

As traders, rather than soldiers, the Phoenicians were always vulnerable to invasion and conquest, and for centuries were

Phoenician Alphabet

The Phoenicians were crucially important to the development of the alphabet. Their language, a variant of 'north-west' Semitic, was very close to Hebrew and Moabite. The earliest Phoenician inscription that has survived is on King Hiram's sarcophagus found at Byblos, dating from the 11th century BC.

Until the alphabet was invented, writing was restricted to scribes who could learn the complicated hieroglyphic and cuneiform scripts. Hieroglyphs were pictorial representations of whole words or ideas in quite involved symbols. Cuneiform script was made up of wedge-shaped characters from which this writing system was named – the Latin word *cuneus* means 'wedge'.

Trade was no doubt the 'mother of invention' that saw the development of the much simpler 22-letter alphabet. It was a writing system that was less complicated and quicker to write than the hieroglyphic and cuneiform scripts. The Phoenicians took this alphabet with them throughout the Mediterranean. The Greeks soon adopted the system and it is from Greek that Latin and subsequently all European written language is descended.

Herodotus, the 5th-century BC Greek historian and the 'father of history', wrote that the alphabet was introduced into Greece by Cadmus and his Phoenician followers. The Greeks did not, according to Herodotus, call the new letters 'alphabet' but *phoinikia grammata* – Phoenician letters. The modern term 'phonetic' comes from this revolutionary idea of assigning symbols to corresponding sounds.

controlled and culturally influenced by whichever regional powerbroker was in ascendancy. From 2334 to 2279 BC, the Akkadians burst out of the Euphrates Valley in Mesopotamia and occupied the Mediterranean, under the leadership of Sargon of Akkad. Around 2100 BC the Amorites, Semitic tribes from the deserts to the east and south, conquered Phoenicia, followed about 300 years later by the warlike Hyksos from Western Asia, and then, in the 16th century BC, by the Egyptians. Egyptian rule lasted for the next four centuries and its traces are clearly visible in the religious artefacts that remain from the period.

During the 14th century BC the Hittites (from Anatolia) invaded from the north, gradually breaking Egypt's control of the region. It was not until after this invasion that the Phoenicians enjoyed the period of independence that fostered a golden age of sea trading, exploration and colonisation, and which gave rise to their historical fame. From Tyre, Sidon and the other Phoenician cities, sailors went forth into the Mediterranean and spread both their cultural ideas and their goods.

Their success in exploration and navigation was dependent upon a large amount of what today would be called industrial espionage. New routes and safe harbours were anxiously sought. If a Phoenician captain thought his ship was being followed, he would risk being shipwrecked rather than reveal a secret anchorage. These safe havens were dotted around the coast and provided safe overnight camps and supplies of food and water for the ships.

Phoenician colonies spread throughout the Mediterranean from Utica and Carthage in North Africa to Gades (Cadiz) in southern Spain. Voyages of exploration took them as far south as India where their cultural influence has been identified. One school of thought believes that some traders made it as far north as Cornwall in southern England to buy tin. Another posits that the Phoenicians may have managed to carry out the first circumnavigation of Africa, leaving via the ancient canal connecting the Nile to the Red Sea and returning via the Mediterranean.

A Shipwreck at Cape Gelidonya

In the early 1960s archaeologists excavated one of the oldest shipwrecks in the world in the waters around Cape Gelidonya (the 'Cape of the Swallows') off the coast of Turkey near Bodrum. The ship, lying in approximately 30m of water, turned out to be a Phoenician trader that had sunk around 1200 BC as it carried a cargo of bronze and copper ingots to Greek metalworkers. The ingots, cast in the four-handled 'oxhide' shape common to the period, had been loaded on board at ancient Alashiya in Cyprus, which was probably the ship's last major port of call.

As it was navigating a stretch of water described by the Roman writer Pliny as 'extremely dangerous to mariners', the ship's nine- to 12m-long hull struck a reef of jagged rocks. Thanks to its cargo, it sank like a stone.

Stone relief of a Phoenician trading ship with single mast, carved on a sarcophagus found at Sidon in the 2nd century AD.

Apart from their trading skills, the Phoenicians were also talented manufacturers. One of their most famous, and lucrative, products was the highly prized purple dye that they extracted from the murex shell. In addition, they produced some of the finest metalwork, glass and textiles in the world at the time. Sidon, in particular, was famed for the quality of its goods.

The Phoenicians absorbed various cultural and religious influences from the peoples with whom they came into contact. Their pantheon of gods greatly resembled that of the Semitic peoples of Mesopotamia. They worshipped Baal, 'the Lord of Heaven', who represented the sun, and Ashtoreth, the Assyrian Astarte, their 'Great Mother'. Ashtoreth originally represented the moon, but later became the goddess of nature, and was worshipped with orgiastic rites. Melkart, the god of the cities (later called Heracles by the Greeks), and Dagon, god of the fishes, were also worshipped. The legend of Adonis, or Tammuz, flourished in Phoenicia, and has a potent resonance throughout all the subsequent religions of the area, even to this day. It is a classic tale of life, death and rebirth symbolised by the passing seasons (see the boxed text 'Lovers Forever' in the Mt Lebanon chapter, as well as the boxed text 'Mythology' in the 'Architecture of Lebanon' special section later in this chapter).

However, despite the supposed glories of Phoenician civilisation, there are few traces left today. Most information we have about the period comes from literary sources, including the Bible and from a number of Greek authors, such as Homer and Herodotus. Physical remains are limited to artefacts, such as King Hiram's sarcophagus, the 11th century BC king of Byblos, and a few architectural remnants in coastal cities such as Byblos and Tyre.

Phoenician ascendancy began to wane when, in the 9th century BC, they came under the conquering boot of the Assyrian king Ashurnasirpal II, and was forced to pay heavy tributes. Byblos was not annexed and was left in a state of relative autonomy, as was the island of Tyre, but the other cities and their surrounding areas suffered. The Phoenicians' exclusive hold on trade in the Mediterranean had been broken.

Following the fall of Nineveh in 612 BC, Assyrian rule was replaced by that of the Neo-Babylonians. Attempts at rebellion failed and it was only the conquest of Babylonia by the Persians in 539 BC that rid Phoenicia of the Babylonian yoke.

The Phoenicians regarded the Persians as liberators at the time and Phoenicia temporarily became one of the most prosperous provinces in the Persian Empire. Neverthe-

less, various movements to assert independence occurred over the next two centuries. The most serious rebellion took place in 346 BC, led by King Tennes of Sidon, who destroyed the provincial governor's palace and sacked the royal park. Artaxerxes Ochus brutally put down the rebellion and burnt Sidon to the ground, killing 40,000 people, including King Tennes, in the process.

Shortly afterwards Persian rule came to an end in Phoenicia, when Alexander the Great swept through the Middle East in a sequence of brilliant military triumphs. (See the boxed text 'Alexander the Great' in The South chapter for more details.)

Greeks & Romans

In 333 BC Alexander's army inflicted a decisive defeat on the Persians at the Battle of Issus. The main cities of Phoenicia (Aradus, Byblos and Sidon) submitted immediately, opening their gates to the conquering hero. Tyre, however, chose to resist. After a lengthy siege that last for months and destroyed much of the city, Tyre finally fell in 332 BC. The city was rebuilt as a Macedonian fortress and colonised by the Greeks.

The dominant culture of the region now became Greek. The essence of Phoenicia slipped away, giving way to new customs, laws and religious practices. After the death of Alexander in 323 BC, his empire was parcelled up among his generals, with the three strongest – Ptolemy, Seleucus and Antigonus – taking the main prizes. Phoenicia came under the dominance of Ptolemy I, along with Egypt and part of Palestine, while Seleucus took Babylonia and Antigonus took Asia Minor and Macedonia. The next century saw much squabbling between the Seleucids and the Ptolemies over control of Palestine and Phoenicia. On several occasions the Seleucids tried to force their claim unsuccessfully. In 198 BC they finally succeeded under Antiochus III.

Antiochus III tried to spread his influence westwards into the Mediterranean, but was held in check by the emerging new power emanating from Rome. Alexander the Great's empire had fragmented and although Greek thought and culture was a great civilising force in the world, the Romans were gaining the upper hand as a military force.

In 188 BC Antiochus' army was decisively beaten after a three-year campaign by the Romans and he was forced to concede all his territories in Asia Minor. In 64 BC Pompey the Great conquered Phoenicia. The country, along with Palestine, became part of the Roman province of Syria. Berytus (Beirut) became an important new centre of power under Herod the Great, who was appointed governor and ruled from 40 to 4 BC. Despite his reputation as a tyrant, who during his later life was reputed to be mentally unstable, this was a rare period of peace and prosperity referred to as the Pax Romana.

Baalbek became an important centre for worship during this time. It was known as 'Heliopolis', a Greek word meaning 'City of the Sun'. The great temples were built or enlarged from the earlier buildings and displayed all the splendour and might of the Roman Empire. Both Heliopolis and Berytus were made official colonies by the first emperor of Rome, Augustus.

Culturally the people began to merge more in with their Syrian neighbours, replacing Canaanite with Aramaic as their everyday language. The Romanisation of the temples saw the decline of the Phoenician and Greek pantheon and the corresponding rise of their Roman counterparts.

But the splendour of the Roman Empire was not to last. By AD 250 the Goths began to invade Europe; the first of successive waves of tribes which would ultimately destroy Rome and split the empire. From the east, the Sassanians from Persia attacked Syria, putting further pressure on the Roman administration. The temples of Baalbek were barely finished before they became redundant as the Roman Empire fell apart and the old religion with it.

Christianity & Byzantium

Meanwhile Christianity was the new rising religious force in the region. St Paul passed through Lebanon on one of his journeys in the 1st century, but it is thought to have been the apostle St Peter who began to sow the seeds of Christianity among the locals.

These early Christians were affiliated to the Patriarch of Antioch (modern Antakya in southern Turkey). A legend from these early days is that one of the first pontiffs to the see of Rome was Lebanese. His name was Anicetus and he became pope around AD 157. He was martyred between AD 161 and 168 and later canonised.

The new religion gathered momentum, and eventually the Roman emperors themselves adopted Christianity. In AD 324 Emperor Constantine moved the capital of the empire to Byzantium on the shores of the Bosphorus. The city was renamed Constantinople (modern Istanbul). This shifted the focus away from Italy, which was in turmoil, and by the end of the 4th century, the Roman Empire was officially split into west and east. The area of what is now Lebanon became part of the Eastern Roman Empire (Byzantine Empire), which gathered in strength and importance as Rome withered and declined. Blending the refined influences of Hellenistic culture with that of Christianity, the Byzantines adopted a strict orthodoxy.

Byzantium's lasting effect on what was to become Lebanon had its roots in the great church schisms of the 5th century. At this time, fierce debate was raging about whether or not Christ had both a divine and a human nature. Monophysites denied the double nature and their view became eastern orthodoxy for a time. In AD 451, however, the decision was reversed at the Council of Chalcedon. Most Syrian Christians accepted the new decree and formed the Melchite Church. The majority of Monophysites, however, refused to accept the decision of the Council of Chalcedon. For almost 200 years the controversy raged. In the mid-7th century, a compromise solution, the Monothelite Doctrine, proposed that Christ had two natures but only a single divine will. The idea was rejected by both the Monophysites and Eastern Christians. However, a small group of Syrian Christians broke away from the mainstream and embraced Monothelitism. They became known as the Maronites.

The term Maronite may have originated from a hermit, St Maron, or from the group's first patriarch, John Maroun. The group was persecuted for its break with orthodoxy by Justinian II and took refuge in the rugged mountains of north Lebanon, where its followers remained, isolated and fiercely protective of their sect, for centuries.

In the meantime, buffeted by frequent raids from the east, and riven by inter-Christian dissent, Byzantium's hold on the area was weakening. Just around the corner was a new force, this time from the south, that would change the face of the Middle East forever.

The Arabs & the Crusaders

During the 7th century a new religion swept Arabia: Islam. The prophet Mohammed was born in about 570 in Mecca, in western Arabia. In the year 610 he began to receive a series of divine revelations from God. These lengthy revelations were committed to memory and subsequently written down to form the holy book of Islam, the Quran. Mohammed gathered a huge following and, after his death in Medina in 632, his followers, led by their caliph, or spiritual leader, formed a conquering force the like of which had not been seen since Alexander the Great.

In 636 this formidable army won a decisive victory at the Battle of Yarmouk, which marks the modern border between Jordan and Syria. Conquest of most of Syria followed and the Byzantine forces retreated towards Anatolia. Within 20 years of Mohammed's death, Muslim Arab armies had taken Palestine, Syria, Egypt, Persia and parts of what is now Afghanistan. Within a century they controlled an empire stretching from the Atlantic to India. In the area around Mt Lebanon they faced little resistance; many local people regarded themselves as being liberated from the Byzantine tyranny and welcomed the newcomers.

Under Mohammed's successors, the focus of power quickly shifted from Medina to Damascus in Syria. In 658 Mu'awiyah, the military governor of Syria and a distant relation of the Prophet, became caliph and established the first of the great Muslim dynasties, the Umayyads, which reigned for about a century.

In 750, a coup, led by a former slave, overthrew the Umayyads and a new dynasty,

the Abbasids, took power. In an effort to dissociate themselves with the Umayyads, they moved their capital to Baghdad. With this shift of power, the bilad ish-Sham (the area of modern Syria, Lebanon and Palestine) went into a decline. The new capital was far from Levantine (and therefore Byzantine) influences and the cultural pool from which the Abbasids drank was far more eastern.

After 820, Abbasid control of the vast Muslim empire began to loosen and although Abbasid descendants continued to hold the title of caliph, political control was seized by regional strongmen and dynasties. Lebanon and Syria were ruled by a succession of small Egyptian-based dynasties between the mid-ninth and tenth centuries.

Then, in 973, the Fatimids, a Shiite dynasty from North Africa, took the Egyptian capital and ruled most of bilad ish-Sham for the next century. Their relatively brief period of ascendancy had a lasting effect on the area, however. Not only were they Shiite Muslims, as opposed to the Sunni (or 'orthodox') Abbasids, but they were from a heterodox Shiite sect known as the Ismailis. Like ordinary Shiites, they believed that their Imams, or leaders, were descendants of the prophet Mohammed, and were divine and infallible. But when the Fatimid Caliph al-Hakim declared himself to be the earthly incarnation of God in 1016, only a small group of Syrian Ismailis, led by Hakim's prime minister, became his followers. They based themselves in the area south of Mt Lebanon and formed the sect that later became known as the Druze.

The Fatimids soon began to weaken and by the second half of the 11th century the government in Egypt was crumbling. In 1074 the Seljuks, Turkish tribal leaders loyal to the by now puppet caliph in Baghdad, but based in Persia, wrested power from the Fatimids and restored Sunni Islam's ascendancy in Syria. A viceroy ruled from Aleppo but upon his death his sons divided the territory (including what is now Lebanon), one ruling from Aleppo, the other from Damascus, ushering in a period of petty dynastic rule and struggle.

It was into this fragmented political maelstrom that the Crusaders launched their bid to 'liberate' the Holy Land – Jerusalem being the prime objective. The Seljuk Turks had moved northwards and taken Armenia, Azerbaijan and part of Anatolia (Asia Minor). The Byzantine emperor, together with the Greek Orthodox Church, felt trapped and appealed to the Pope for help. In 1095 Pope Urban II saw an opportunity to establish Rome's primacy in the east and called for a Christian force to fight this holy war.

The Crusaders joined the Byzantine army and besieged Antioch, then marched down the Syrian and Lebanese coast before turning towards Jerusalem. Jerusalem fell in 1099 after a six-week siege. Within a short time, they had established four states in the Middle East. Northern Lebanon came under the County of Tripoli and the southern area under the Kingdom of Jerusalem.

The Maronites rallied around the new Christian rulers and, foreshadowing events that would take place almost one thousand years later, welcomed the Crusaders as saviours from their Muslim overlords. By 1180, they even entered into formal union with Rome, renouncing monothelitism and adopting some Latin rites. At the same time, the Muslims around Mt Lebanon, whether Sunni, Shiite or Druze, threw in their lot with the hopelessly divided Turkic Muslim dynasties in Damascus and Aleppo.

The Muslim reconquest began in 1144 when Zengi, the founder of a short-lived Kurdish dynasty from Mosul (in modern Iraq), wiped out the Edessa. Within a few years he and his successor, Nureddin (Nur ad-Din), reduced the principality of Antioch to a sliver

Saladin

The figure of Saladin (1138–93), a Muslim leader during the Crusades, has come down to us through numerous books, films and poems. He figured most notably in Sir Walter Scott's book *The Talisman* as a chivalrous warrior. In many ways he epitomised the idea of a paragon of princely virtue. Rather fittingly his name means 'Righteousness of the Faith'.

Saladin was born in Tikrit in modern Iraq to Kurdish parents. At the young age of 14 he joined other members of his family (the Ayyubids) in the service of Nureddin, ruler of Aleppo and Damascus. He then went to fight with the Fatimids of Egypt against the Crusaders based in Palestine and distinguished himself in three expeditions. He then revitalised the Egyptian economy and reorganised the military.

After Nureddin's death in 1174, Saladin expanded his power throughout the Middle East and allied the armies of Damascus, Mosul and Aleppo under his command. He turned his attentions to routing the Crusaders from Jerusalem and other parts of the Holy Land, which he did in the decisive Battle of Hittin, in 1187. In response the Europeans launched the Third Crusade to win back Jerusalem.

SARAH JOLLY

Saladin eventually concluded an armistice with King Richard I of England that allowed the Crusaders to reconstitute their kingdom but left Jerusalem in Muslim hands. Saladin's descendants ruled Egypt and parts of Syria and Palestine, until the rise of the Mamluks slave-soldier dynasties in 1250.

of land along the coast. The tide was turning for the Crusaders.

Nureddin placed his general, Saladin (Salah ad-Din), in the Fatimid court in Cairo. Saladin took control of Egypt in his own right in 1171 and went on to head the Muslim armies that reconquered Jerusalem in 1187, followed by Palestine and later Beirut. Over the next century, Saladin's dynasty, the Ayyubids, squeezed the Crusaders into a small corner. The Muslim army was held at bay by the Third Crusade, which clung to the coastal strip for another century. But finally Antioch and Jaffa fell in 1268, Tripoli in 1289 and Acre in 1291.

The Mamluks & the Ottomans

The Ayyubids ruled bilad ish-Sham, Egypt, western Arabia and parts of Yemen until they were in turn overthrown in 1261. Power then fell into the hands of the Mamluks, originally slave soldiers who took over from their Ayyubid masters and ruled Egypt and Syria for the best part of 300 years.

The Mamluks were, like so many conquerors after them, drawn into Mt Lebanon's growing sectarian divisions. The Maronites in the north maintained their contacts with Rome and the newly emerging Italian republics. Despite being staunch Sunni Muslims, the Mamluks allied themselves with Druze chieftains, the Tanukhs, who enrolled as cavalry officers in a special Mamluk regiment. The slave soldiers were less tolerant with the large numbers of Shiites who lived in the strategic mountain region of Kesrouane, between Beirut and Tripoli, and, after quelling a number of rebellions in the area, brought in Sunni Turkoman settlers to keep watch.

In 1453, a once obscure Turkish dynasty, the family of Osman – rendered in English as 'Ottoman' – conquered Constantinople, bringing to an end the remnants of Byzantine rule. In a swift, phenomenally successful territorial expansion, they took over a large swathe of the Balkans and bilad ish-Sham. They later extended their rule over most of Arabia, North Africa and Iraq, taking with them the caliphate (after the last Abbasid conveniently died in captivity),

thus reunifying Sunni Islam's political and spiritual leadership.

In the area of Mt Lebanon, the Ottomans' arrival on the scene in 1516 saw the re-emergence of the Turkomans in Kesrouane after a period of obscurity. A Turkoman dynasty, the Assafs, ruled the area and favoured the Maronites, who gradually began to settle in the region.

The transition was not as smooth for the Druze in the Chouf. Deprived of their Mamluk allies, the Tanukh emirs were overshadowed by chieftains from the Maan family. Repeated Maan rebellions were brutally quelled by the Ottomans, who wanted firm control of the mountains to ensure that there was no danger of infiltration by the Persian Safavid dynasty, which was allied with Syria's Shiites. Once they had subdued the Maans, the Ottomans co-opted the rebellious Druze dynasty in 1590 by appointing one member, Fakhreddine (Fakhr ad-Din al-Maan II), as their local governor, or emir.

Talented and ambitious, Fakhreddine was to eventually prove as unruly in office as he was in opposition (see the boxed text 'Fakhreddine' in The Chouf Mountains chapter). He took firm control over Beirut (which included Kesrouane) and Sidon, as well as the Chouf. In return for his allegiance and obvious ability to control the area, in 1605 the Ottomans increased his mandate to include large parts of Palestine and most of the area that is now Lebanon. However, he had greater aims, and stretched his rule into what is now Jordan and well into Syria. He also unified for the first time the territory that would become modern Lebanon. His ambition became his downfall and after repeatedly challenging the authority of his paymasters, he was captured in a mountain hide-out and taken to Istanbul, where he was killed in 1633.

After his removal, the Ottomans barely managed to keep administrative and military control over the Kesrouane and Chouf Mountains, and over the restive Shiites further to the south. In 1667 they found a new local ally to do their bidding in Fakhreddine's grand nephew, Ahmad Maan. He was awarded an emirate that was annually renewable and encompassed the Chouf and Kesrouane, but excluded the coastal towns. When he died without an heir in 1697, the emirate passed to the Shihab family, Sunni descendants of the Maans through the female line.

Despite the family connection, the Shihab were from outside the Chouf and, while they cultivated alliances with the main Druze families (in particular the Jumblatts), they sought their main political support from the steadily increasing Maronite population. In the second half of the 18th century they began to convert to Christianity and by 1770 all Shihab emirs were Maronite.

The Shihabs gradually extended their emirate and consolidated their political power by ruthlessly disposing of local rivals while at the same time carefully maintaining good relations with their Turkish overlords, the pashas (provincial governors) of Tripoli, Sidon and Damascus. Shihab power reached its apogee under Bashir II, a ruthless, skilled leader who assumed power in 1788. By 1821, he controlled the heartland of Mt Lebanon, reconsolidating the territory first united by Fakhreddine.

Emir Bashir Shihab II, a powerful, unifying figure in pre-Independence Lebanon

His skilful consolidation of power continued until he threw in his lot with the Egyptian leader Mohammed Ali, whose son Ibrahim occupied Syria in 1832. European powers, alarmed that a change in the balance of power would upset their commercial interests, came to the aid of the Ottomans and helped drive out Ibrahim. Emir Bashir was captured and sent into exile in 1840, bringing to an end the rule of Lebanese emirs.

After three years of unsuccessful direct rule, the Ottomans divided Mt Lebanon into two administrative regions, or *qa'im maqamiyats* – one Druze, the other Maronite – under the supervision of the pashas of Sidon and Beirut. Relations between Christians and Druze had already been troubled before the downfall of the Shihabs and the new arrangement only increased the tensions. Not only did the area assigned to the Druze have a Christian majority, but economic turmoil, brought about by the influx of European industrial goods on the Syrian market, was having increasing social fallout. Bouts of open warfare between the Christians and Druze became increasingly common. In 1858 stirrings of class warfare were added to the mixture when, at the urging of their clergy, Maronite peasants in Kesrouane rebelled against local Druze leaders, expelling them from the area. Their success encouraged the Maronites of the Chouf to do the same. However, the Druze in the Chouf got wind of the plans and preempted the revolt in 1860 by massacring some 11,000 Christians.

Alarmed at the violence, France, self-appointed protector of fellow Catholics, sent troops to Beirut and ended the conflict. Under European pressure, the Ottomans reorganised Mt Lebanon into a single administrative unit, called a *mutasarrifa*, which was under the control of a Christian Ottoman governor and guaranteed by the European powers. An elected council, representing the various Lebanese communities in proportion to their numbers, was appointed to advise and assist the governor.

Under the new system, Lebanon stabilised and prospered. Beirut, in particular, became an important centre for trade between Europe and the Arab world. Foreign missions established a number of schools, including the American University of Beirut (AUB), and the country gained a reputation as an academic and cultural centre in the Ottoman Empire. The establishment of a publishing industry stimulated a revival in Arabic literature. Up to this point, the Turkish Ottomans had been accepted as guardians of Islamic culture and political dogma, but now there was a revival of Arab nationalism.

Colonial Rule

In 1920 France was awarded the mandate for Syria and Mt Lebanon by the newly formed League of Nations. Later that year, the French governor, under pressure from the Maronites, enlarged the territory of the Ottoman mutasarrifa to include the coastal cities of Tyre, Sidon, Beirut, Tripoli, the Bekaa Valley and the Akkar region, to form 'Greater Lebanon'. Its flag was the French tricolour imprinted with a cedar tree (this was later changed to the current red and white background).

Apart from ignoring the wishes of almost half of 'Greater Lebanon', for whom anything connected to France was inevitably tinged with colonial exploitation and oppression, the French attempt to create a Lebanese nation fell foul of growing Arab nationalist sentiment, which held that Arabs should live in a greater Arab homeland, rather than arbitrarily drawn nation states. For the Maronites, who looked towards Europe and, in many cases, preferred to bypass several hundred years of history and call themselves Phoenician, Arab nationalism was a threat. But the fact remained that 'Lebanon' had never existed, except as an ancient geographical term for the mountains between the Mediterranean and Syria; even Mt Lebanon was little more than an Ottoman administrative term. Most inhabitants of Greater Lebanon referred to themselves as Syrian.

However, scant attention was paid to the opposition and in 1926 the French and their Maronite allies drew up and passed a new constitution, sowing the seeds of Lebanon's troubled future. The document formalised a largely symbolic power-sharing formula, but Maronites still managed to secure a virtual monopoly on positions of power and Sunni Muslims boycotted the constitution. It was suspended in 1932. In the same year, the country's first-and-only census was carried out, confirming a slight Christian majority. In 1936, the Franco-Lebanese treaty was signed, promising eventual independence for Lebanon; the following year a new constitution was drawn up but not ratified by the French.

During WWII, Lebanon fell under Vichy control but Free French and British troops landed in 1941 and declared Lebanon a free and independent state. In reality, though, French troops and administrators ensured that France was still in control. Nationalist sentiment against the French led the various religious and political factions to come together in 1943 and draw up the Lebanese National Covenant, an unwritten agreement dividing power along sectarian lines on the basis of the 1932 census. The president was to be Maronite, the prime minister a Sunni Muslim, and the speaker of the house a Shiite. Parliamentary seats were divvied-up between Christians and Muslims on a ratio of six to five. The Maronites were also given control of the army, with a Druze chief of staff. In return, the Maronites were to renounce their special relationship with Europe and acknowledge Lebanon as an Arab country.

When, in November 1943, the fledgling Lebanese government of President Bishara al-Khouri went a step further and passed legislation removing all references to French Authority in the constitution, the French retaliated by arresting the president, and members of his cabinet, and suspending the constitution. Britain, the US and the Arab states supported the Lebanese cause for independence, and in 1944 the French began the transfer of all public services to Lebanese control, followed by the withdrawal of French troops. Independence was declared in 1946.

Independence

Bringing the nascent state's diverse and mutually suspicious sectarian groups together was no easy task, but in the early days after independence, the government of President al-Khouri struggled to make the National Covenant work. However, although the agreement was an effective short-term compromise, as a long-term solution to the country's diverse mixture of religious and economic interests it was too weak. It enshrined confessionalism, or division of power along sectarian lines, as the basis of the republic, guaranteeing that the interests of the community would ultimately win out over those of nation.

Soon after it came into being, the country was hit with major political and economic challenges. In 1948 the devaluation of the French franc (to which the Lebanese currency was tied) damaged the country's economy. The same year saw the last act of colonialism in the area, when the British oversaw the partition of its Palestine Mandate and promptly withdrew. In the war that followed, Jewish forces flooded into Palestinian areas and evicted thousands before establishing the State of Israel. About 140,000 Muslim and Christian Palestinian refugees flooded into Lebanon, welcomed at first (when it was thought their stay would be temporary), but nonetheless upsetting the confessional balancing act. Then, in 1950, economic ties with Syria were cut, placing further strain on the economy.

Increasing support for the burgeoning Arab nationalist movement, which was sweeping the region, also had a destabilising effect. In 1951, the Sunni prime minister, Riad al-Solh, was assassinated by Syrian nationalists and, the following year, growing unrest led to the resignation of the government. The new president, Camille Chamoun, was an avowedly pro-Western Maronite who added fuel to the fire. He assumed power in 1952, the same year as Egypt's revolution. When Egyptian president Gamal Abdel Nasser, widely seen as a leftist, and therefore pro-Soviet, revolutionary by the West, nationalised the Suez Canal in 1956, Chamoun supported the attempted Israeli/British/French invasion of Egypt. The rest of the Arab world, still smarting from colonial domination, was behind Nasser.

Chamoun's disregard for the principles of the National Covenant and insensitivity to the feelings of non-Christian Lebanese precipitated the country's biggest crisis yet in 1958. The previous year he had enthusiastically signed the Eisenhower Doctrine. This Cold War document allowed the USA to 'use armed forces to assist any nation or group of nations in the Middle East requesting assistance against armed aggressors from any country controlled by international communism'. It was roundly rejected by all other Arab countries, and even pushed some of them closer to the Soviet Union. In 1958 Arab Nationalist fervour reached its peak when Egypt and Syria united as the United Arab Republic. Chamoun immediately announced that Lebanon would not join, inflaming Arab nationalist sentiment still more.

When Chamoun then won parliamentary elections, amid widespread allegations of fraud and with the likely help of the CIA, he tried to change the constitution and allow himself a second term as president. Violence that had been simmering in the background broke out throughout the country, pitting pro-Western Maronites against their largely (but not entirely) Muslim pro-Arab nationalist opponents. A panicked Chamoun requested American help and in July 1958, some 15,000 American marines landed on the shores in Beirut, creating an uproar in the Cold War world.

Chamoun was forced out of office thanks to his mismanagement, and the chief of staff, Fouad Chehab, a moderate, replaced him. He presided over the withdrawal of the American troops and appointed Rashid Karami, leader of the Muslim insurrectionists in the north, to the post of prime minister, ushering in a brief period of calm in which Lebanon's economy appeared to flourish. However, the prosperity was largely concentrated in Beirut and along the coast. The hinterland was neglected, with virtually no industry, a burgeoning population growth and extreme poverty. Chehab did try to moderate the extremes slightly, presiding over improvements in public services and infrastructure, and winning widespread respect and popularity in Beirut, but the poor of the countryside saw little change in their existence.

Chehab's successor, Charles Helou, who came to power in 1964, attempted, less successfully, to continue the reforms. But this was the freewheeling 1960s, for which Lebanon is still famous. The economy appeared to be booming and the fact that the government did little to redistribute the spoils or pay attention to the dispossessed did not bother the rich Lebanese who partied with the international jet set at the Casino du Liban.

The Six Day War & the Palestinians

Lebanon may not have sent troops to fight in the 1967 war but, along with the rest of the Middle East, was profoundly affected by the conflict. After their arrival on the Lebanese scene in 1948, the Palestinians had initially had a sympathetic reception. Urban middle-class Palestinians were able to participate in the laissez-faire economy and some Christians were even granted Lebanese citizenship. The rest were given basic housing in UN-run camps. But as time wore on, the Palestinian presence became a threat to Lebanon's increasingly shaky National Covenant. To the pro-Western Maronites, the presence of the Palestinians, who were sympathetic to the anti-colonial doctrines of Nasserism and Arab Nationalism, strengthened Lebanon's Arab Nationalist challenge to their power. Gradually, restrictions were imposed on the ability of Palestinians to work or move around. Under President Chehab, army intelligence posts were established inside the camps to try and control Palestinian political activity.

The humiliating loss of what remained of Palestine in 1967 radicalised the Palestinians, thousands of whom had been languishing in hope of return to their homes for almost twenty years. This, and the fresh influx of refugees into Lebanon, Jordan and Syria, turned Palestinian camps throughout the Middle East into de facto centres of guerrilla resistance to the Israeli occupation. Well armed and increasingly radical, the guerrillas had the sympathy of many ordinary Arabs, who identified with the humiliation of their position. Arab governments, while helpful on the surface, saw in the Palestinians a po-

tential threat to their own less-than-open regimes and cracked down on the guerrilla activities. The Lebanese government was too weak to impose such restrictions. As a result, an increasing number of guerrilla attacks were launched from Lebanon.

Israeli forces retaliated with attacks across the border in May 1968. Events escalated in December of the same year when an Israeli airliner was machine-gunned at Athens airport. Two days later the Israelis launched an attack on Beirut airport and destroyed 13 Lebanese passenger aircraft – a clear warning not to allow any further attacks from Lebanese soil.

In 1968 and 1969 Lebanese forces clashed violently with Palestinians, who demanded to be independent in the matter of camp security and to be free to launch attacks across the border into Israel. But Lebanon's weak army was no match for the guerrillas and under pressure from Lebanese Muslims, the government signed the Cairo Agreement with the Palestine Liberation Organization (PLO), in which most of the Palestinians' demands were met and the camps were moved away from civilian towns to protect civilians from injury during reprisal raids.

Maronite opposition to the Cairo Agreement was immediate. The right-wing Christian Phalange party (formed in the 1930s by a member of the Gemayel clan) began to arm and train its young men in Maronite mountain strongholds around the Qadisha Valley. In March 1970, fighting broke out in the streets of Beirut between Palestinian guerrillas and Phalangists. Tensions rose still further in September, when, after heavy fighting, the Jordanian army drove Palestinian guerrillas out of their country. Following their defeat in what became known as Black September, the guerrillas flocked into Lebanon where they continued their attacks into Israel with scant regard to the effect on the local, mainly Shiite population, who were displaced by Israeli retaliatory attacks and migrated to the rapidly growing slums around Beirut.

The increased power of the Palestinians, coupled with the shift in relative numbers of the Muslim and Christian populations in

Lebanon, destabilised the balance of power set out by the National Covenant. The government was losing control and the country became increasingly factionalised in the jockeying for power that followed. Groups armed themselves and formed private militias along religious/political (and clan/tribal) lines. The fiercely militant Maronite president, Suleiman Franjieh, who came to power in 1970, did little to prevent the dangerous build-up.

Underlying all this were the old political tensions between the pro-Western Maronites and the pro-Arab nationalist Muslims. A loose grouping of left-wing Arab nationalists and Muslims, led by Kamal Jumblatt, formed the National Movement and allied with the Palestinians to push for constitutional reforms that would break the existing guarantees of Maronite power. The Phalange, complaining that the Palestinian resistance had now become a magnet for radicals who threatened the National Covenant – and therefore the security of the country – developed close ties with the Israelis to try and rid the country of the Palestinians. The Israelis armed the Phalange and used them as their proxies to try and destroy the Palestinian nationalist movement in Lebanon. Waves of violent confrontation began to escalate, pitting the Lebanese army and Phalange militia against the Palestinians and the militias of the National Movement. Although Lebanon avoided direct involvement in the October War in 1973, Israel's intensified reprisals against Palestinian attacks following the conflict only exacerbated the intensity of the clashes.

The Civil War

Although violence was already becoming commonplace in Lebanon, it is generally agreed that the civil war began on 13 April 1975 when Phalangist gunmen attacked a bus in the Beirut suburb of Ain al-Rummaneh and massacred 27 of its Palestinian passengers. Tit-for-tat killings and the spiral into anarchy intensified. When four Christians were found shot dead in a car in December 1975, Phalangists stopped all cars around Beirut and checked identity cards,

before slitting the throats of any Muslims they found. Muslim militias soon followed suit with Christians. By the end of the day, known as Black Saturday, some 300 people were dead. A month later, the Phalange led other militias in the siege and massacre of Palestinian refugees in the camps of Qarantina and Tell al-Zaatar. The Palestinians responded by attacking the town of Damour, just south of Beirut, and massacring most of its Christian inhabitants.

Fighting continued and Beirut was soon partitioned between the Christian East and Muslim West along the infamous 'Green Line' and the rest of the country was likewise controlled area by area along lines marked out by the various religious sects. This state of affairs would last throughout the 17-year civil war, although loyalties would change and sides would re-form many times.

Syrian Intervention In 1976, the Syrians, alarmed at the prospect of partition of Lebanon and possible Israeli occupation in the event of a Maronite victory, tried to end the fighting. By May there were an estimated 40,000 Syrian troops in the country. Initially sympathetic to the National Movement and the Palestinian cause, disagreements with the National Movement's leader, Kamal Jumblatt, caused them to switch sides and they moved through the country trying to crush the Palestinian guerrilla groups, hoping to install a pro-Syrian government. As a staunch Arab Nationalist power, the Syrian alliance with the Maronites was roundly condemned by other Arab countries and later that year the Arab League brokered a ceasefire. An Arab peace-keeping force, the Arab Deterrent Force (ADF) was established, but most of its troops were Syrian and it was largely ineffective. The violence continued and in March 1977 Kamal Jumblatt was assassinated, probably by the Syrians. This led to a series of massacres of Christian villagers by Druze in the Chouf Mountains.

Israeli Invasions Continued Palestinian attacks on Israel in March 1978 gave the Israelis the pretext to launch an attack on southern Lebanon in an effort to destroy the

PLO and its bases in Lebanon. Following demands for withdrawal by the Security Council, the UN formed the United Nations Interim Force in Lebanon (Unifil) to oversee the withdrawal and 'restore international peace'. (It remained an 'interim' force for a further 22 years.) The Israeli forces withdrew, but instead of handing over to Unifil, they created their own militia, the South Lebanon Army (SLA), installed a pro-Israeli Christian, Saad Haddad as its head, and proclaimed the area south of the Litani River 'Free Lebanon'.

Meanwhile, fighting between the Syrian ADF soldiers and Christian militiamen flared up in Beirut. By 1981 the Syrians had switched allegiance, again, and joined with the Palestinians to lay siege to the Phalange-controlled town of Zahlé in the Bekaa. Worried by Phalange links to the Israelis, their presence in the Bekaa was too close for Syrian comfort. Tensions were further heightened when Israel shot down two Syrian helicopters in one of its frequent raids against the Palestinians. The Syrians placed missiles in the Bekaa Valley, and the two countries appeared to be on the brink of all-out war. However, the Phalange withdrew and an American-brokered cease-fire came into force.

As with more than 150 other cease-fires during the first eight years of the war, this one proved to be short-lived. Although the Palestinians by and large adhered to it, Israel's right-wing government was determined to crush the PLO once and for all. In the view of Israel's generals, its very existence was fanning the flames of Palestinian nationalism in the occupied territories of the West Bank and Gaza, making the Palestinians there unwilling to negotiate with their occupiers. So, on 6 June 1982, after an exchange of small attacks with the Palestinians, the Israeli army marched into Lebanon, one contingent pushing the Syrians out of the Bekaa Valley, the rest sweeping northward until they reached Beirut. The invasion was accompanied by a devastating bombing campaign that laid waste large parts of Tyre, Sidon, Damour, Nabatiye. This was the beginning of Operation Peace in Galilee.

About a week after the invasion began, the Israelis began their siege of West Beirut, where the PLO leadership was based. In the coming two months, the city was subject to an almost continuous bombardment with deadly suction bombs, cluster bombs and phosphorus shells. The city was devastated and the overwhelming majority of the 18,000 dead and 30,000 injured were civilians. On 21 August, following an American-brokered agreement, the PLO left Beirut under multinational supervision. Two days after their evacuation, which many took to be a sign that the Maronites had won the war, Phalange-leader Bashir Gemayel was, with Israeli help, elected president.

Sabra & Shatila Three weeks later a huge bomb was placed outside Phalange headquarters, killing Bashir and 60 of his supporters. Responsibility for the attack was never claimed, but many suspect that Israel, who found their ally to be less than amenable to their interference in Lebanon, may have had a role in it. The following day Israeli forces moved into West Beirut, in violation of the American-sponsored agreement. Three

Bashir Gemayel was killed in 1982 after less than one month as president.

days later, Israel's Phalange allies, bent on revenge for Bashir's assassination, entered the Palestinian refugee camps of Sabra and Chatila, on the outskirts of Beirut, to root out 'terrorists'. In a brutal two-day rampage of rape and murder, the militia (which may also have had help from Saad Haddad's SLA) killed as many as 2000 Palestinians, mostly women and children.

An Israeli inquiry later found that, despite the denials of the defence minister, Ariel Sharon, Israeli troops were fully aware of what their Phalange allies were doing. Not only were they stationed around the camp, they offered logistical help, lending bulldozers for the digging of mass graves and even dropping flares through the night so the Phalange could better find their targets.

News of the massacres shocked the world and international condemnation was swift. Multinational peace-keeping forces, comprised of French, British, American and Italian troops returned to Beirut and tried, unsuccessfully, to keep the peace.

Multinational Forces Following the arrival of the peacekeepers, Bashir Gemayel's brother, Amin, was elected president, although at first he controlled little more than Beirut and part of Mt Lebanon. The Israelis had pulled back to a position a few miles south of Beirut, and occupied the south, while the north of the country was dominated by the Syrians. In both these areas the fighting continued.

In Tripoli, PLO leader Yasser Arafat, who'd returned to Lebanon with a much smaller group of fighters, was engaged in fierce fighting with other Syrian-supported Lebanese and breakaway Palestinians. Palestinian refugee camps were once again pawns in the game for political supremacy. Both they and the city of Tripoli were ravaged in the fighting. In December 1983, under multinational-force protection, Arafat left Lebanon again, this time for Tunis.

Fighting also raged in the Chouf Mountains. Inhabited by Druze and Christians, the area had been relatively peaceful throughout the war. It was now occupied by the Israelis, who brought in Phalangist militiamen in 1982. Phalangist harassment of Druze civilians led to reprisals that escalated into widespread sectarian violence. The government threatened to bring in the army but the Druze refused, fearing that the troops would side with the Phalangists. The fighting threatened to engulf Beirut when Druze leader, Walid Jumblatt, shelled Beirut airport and attacked Lebanese army positions in the city. At this moment, the Israelis pulled out of the mountains. The army joined with the Phalangists against the Druze (who were helped by the Shiite militia, Amal). The Druze had the upper hand until the Americans, in their Cold War fervour, claimed that they were in fact acting for the Syrians, under the orders of Moscow. American warships then bombarded Druze positions. Shortly after yet another cease-fire was negotiated.

The Americans were becoming increasingly bogged down in the war. When the multinational forces arrived, Beirut, for a time, appeared to be safe, even as the areas around it were paralysed by fighting. However, the Americans were increasingly seen to favour the Israelis and the severely compromised government of Amin Gemayel, and opposition to them and the other peacekeepers grew. Any lingering illusions that the multinational force would bring an end to the war were brutally shattered when in April, 1983, the American embassy was destroyed by a powerful blast that left 63 dead and 100 wounded. Although the Americans stayed on, the simultaneous attacks by suicide bombers on the US and French military headquarters in Beirut the following October, which left 265 marines and 56 French soldiers dead, shook their resolve and paved the way for their retreat. It followed in February 1984.

The Shiite Renaissance Responsibility for the attacks on the Americans and French was claimed by a little known organisation called Islamic Jihad. This was later discovered to be the armed wing of a radical, Iranian-backed Shiite group known as Hezbollah, or 'party of God', a new – but soon to be famous – actor in the ever-growing cast of players in the civil war. The Shiites had always been Lebanon's poor.

They were largely excluded from the Sunni-Maronite power struggles and ignored by the government. Concentrated in the south, they had borne the brunt of Israeli retaliatory attacks for Palestinian raids, had suffered brutal repression at the hands of Israeli occupiers and their Lebanese proxies, and been turned into destitute refugees stuck in shanty towns around Beirut. With Syrian approval, Iranian Revolutionary Guards stationed themselves in the Bekaa Valley and began to train and preach to the disaffected. They provided fertile ground for Hezbollah's message of overthrowing Western imperialism, in the form of what they saw as the pro-Israeli Americans and the anti-Muslim Phalange. The organisation's effectiveness, and willingness to sacrifice its own in suicide bombings, turned it into a feared fighting force. Its reputation grew against a backdrop of growing factional fighting and attempts to push out the Israelis.

In 1984 it began to use one of Lebanon's most chilling militia tactics, kidnapping. Although Lebanese were often targeted by one militia or another and either held for ransom or killed, several high-profile abductions of Westerners, such as CIA bureau chief William Buckley (who was tortured and killed) and AP bureau chief Terry Anderson (later released), resulted in widespread press coverage and the exodus of most Westerners.

Battle of the Camps Brutal in its treatment of Shiites and Palestinians in the south and relentlessly targeted by guerrilla fighters and suicide bombers, Israel was gradually removing its troops and handing control to Haddad's SLA. It was also arming other Christian militias to do its bidding. In early 1985 the last Israeli troops withdrew, preserving for themselves a self-proclaimed 'security zone' along the border. The SLA controlled the area, with the help of a few Israeli soldiers.

Once the Israelis withdrew, the militias that it had encouraged clashed with Druze and Shiite militias around Sidon in the south, while in West Beirut, fighting continued between Sunni, Shiite and Druze militias. Amid the confusion, the PLO began to filter back into Lebanon, leading to more fighting around the camps. The attacks were led by the Shiite Amal militia, worried that the return of the Palestinian fighters would lead to Israeli intervention and yet more suffering for the people in the south. Vicious fighting continued through 1985 and 1986, laying waste the already battered Palestinian camps and inflicting thousands of casualties.

In the summer of 1986, the Syrians returned to West Beirut and their numbers increased over the coming months. As the most influential foreign power in Lebanon, Damascus was able to institute an uneasy cease-fire, but although the Syrians were able to lift the siege of the camps in Beirut over the following winter (and then keep tight control over them to prevent the re-establishment of the PLO), the camps in South Lebanon remained under Amal control until the beginning of 1988.

Aoun & the Taif Accord Although real power now lay in the hands of the militias, the government still technically existed. By September 1988 Amin Gemayel's term of office was due to expire, but, due to militia violence, deputies trying to vote for a new president were unable to reach the parliament. With only hours to go until his term was up, Gemayel appointed his chief of staff, General Aoun, to head an interim military government. Aoun's staunchly anti-Syrian stance was dimly viewed in Damascus and the Syrians opposed his appointment, as did the Americans. Gemayel also appointed three Christian and three Muslim officers to serve under Aoun, but the Muslims refused to take up their posts. Instead, Selim al-Hoss, Gemayel's Muslim former prime minister, formed his own rival government in West Beirut. By the end of 1988, it appeared that the partition of the country into Muslim and Christian ministates had finally come to pass.

Perhaps inevitably, violence between Christian and Muslim militias once again raged across the Green Line that bisected Beirut. Aoun was determined to drive the Syrians from Lebanon and the fighting continued for most of the coming year. Once again, other countries became involved. France began supplying humanitarian aid to both sides, but given its traditional friendship with the Maronites, the move was viewed by suspicion by the Muslims. Aoun angered the Syrians still more by receiving arms from Iraq, Syria's implacable enemy.

A serious attempt to negotiate a peace settlement finally came in the autumn of 1989. Diplomatic efforts by a committee consisting of Morocco's King Hassan, King Fahd of Saudi Arabia and President Chadli of Algeria proposed a comprehensive cease-fire and a meeting of the parliament to discuss a 'Charter of National Reconciliation', which, while retaining the confessional-based distribution of power in the government, attempted to even out the balance. On 23 September the cease-fire was implemented and the national assembly met in Taif, Saudi Arabia. With some minor amendments the charter, known as the Taif Accord, was formally ratified on 5 November 1989 despite General Aoun's opposition. René Mouawad was elected president, but only 17 days later was assassinated by opponents of the agreement. Parliament, fearing this would trigger yet another round of war, immediately appointed Elias Hrawi to take his place.

Aoun continued to oppose the agreement and fighting once more broke out, this time between Aoun and rival Christian militias who disagreed with his stance. Fighting also broke out between Hezbollah and Amal militias, first in Beirut, then in the south.

Nevertheless, in August 1990 the National Assembly voted to amend the constitution to adopt the reforms of the Taif Accord. When Syria supported the American-led military campaign in the Gulf War, the US allowed Syrian troops to join with the Lebanese army in getting rid of General Aoun, who had barricaded himself in the presidential palace in Baabda. At the end of September a blockade was imposed on the palace. This was followed by a Syrian offensive that defeated the renegade general and, with the exception of the still-occupied south, led to the first period of lasting peace in Lebanon for fifteen years.

Later in the same year, Syria formalised its dominance over Lebanese affairs with the signing of the Treaty of Brotherhood, Co-operation and Co-ordination, followed in 1992 by a defence pact. Although they had a mixed reception, both agreements held. According to the Taif Accord, Syrian forces were to withdraw from Lebanon, but while they began to pull out in March 1992, the withdrawal was only partial and the Syrian army is still present today.

The Post-War Period

Even with peace shakily restored, the many militias remained armed and in March 1991 the delicate process of disarming and extending government authority over the country began. The Syrian and Lebanese army jointly gained control of most of Lebanon's territory. The south, occupied by Israel through the SLA militia, was an exception. Palestinian bases remained around Sidon, and Hezbollah fighters were allowed to keep their arms in order to fight the occupation.

Violence continued to flare along the southern border, with tit-for-tat mortar attacks punctuated by Israeli offensives in June 1991 and 1992. The latter was yet another attempt to destroy Palestinian and Hezbollah bases, and displaced as many as 300,000 Lebanese.

By mid-June 1992, all Western hostages who were still alive in Lebanon had been released and the following October the country's first parliamentary elections in twenty years took place. Despite a boycott by much of the Christian community, Rafiq Hariri, a Lebanese-born Saudi entrepreneur, became the new prime minister of Lebanon. He also assumed the post of finance minister and set about rebuilding the shattered country.

As he embarked on the reconstruction program, Hariri also tried to redress the imbalance brought about by the Christian boycott of the elections and in 1994 attempted to bring more Christians into the government. He was blocked by both the Syrians and by President Hrawi, and offered his resignation. He was reappointed after Syrian mediation, but the same events were repeated in 1995.

While Beirut and the north of the country was rebuilt, the south suffered from

Rafiq Hariri supervised Lebanon's reconstruction.

Hezbollah battles and Israeli attacks. In March 1995 a senior Hezbollah official was assassinated by a rocket attack on his car near Tyre. In response to counter attacks from the Hezbollah, Israel launched another campaign, Operation Grapes of Wrath, in April 1996. This was a combined land-sea-air offensive, ostensibly aimed at Hezbollah positions, but it extended far beyond the south and involved attacks on Lebanon's painstakingly rebuilt infrastructure, destroying Beirut's power station and blockading ports. The attack was clearly intended to pressure the Lebanese government to act against the Hezbollah. It was during this attack that the Qana Massacre took place (see the boxed text 'Bitter Wine from the Grapes of Wrath' in The South chapter).

Although both sides initially respected the agreement, Israel once again launched attacks, bombing Beirut's power stations in 1999, while Hezbollah continued its hit-and-run guerrilla attacks on the SLA and on Israel's northern border. Sustained losses led to increased calls within Israel for a withdrawal, and on 24 May 2000, the Israeli army finally withdrew from the south.

The withdrawal was celebrated within Lebanon. Members of Hezbollah, which had already transformed itself from a fanatic, suicide-bombing group into an efficient political party, with popular and well-managed social welfare programs, became heroes overnight. However, many Lebanese questioned how the power vacuum would be filled. The death of Syrian President Hafez al-Assad only a few days after the withdrawal increased the uncertainty. Even with the international border between Lebanon and Israel demarcated, the fate of relations between the two countries remains dependent on peace talks between Syria and Israel. Moreover, at least 350,000 Palestinians remain in Lebanon, unwelcome by most Lebanese and subject to severe hardship. Their presence will continue to be a destabilising factor, one that is unlikely to be removed until Israel and the Palestinian Authority agree on their fate.

President Hrawi was replaced by Emile Lahoud following presidential elections in Otober 1998. Prime Minister Hariri was replaced in 1998 by Selim al-Hoss, but was poised for a return to power in elections held in September 2000.

GEOGRAPHY

Lebanon is one of the world's smallest countries with an area of only 10,452 sq km, but within its borders are several completely diverse geographical regions. There is a very narrow, broken, coastal strip on which the major cities are situated. This stretches 225km from the Israeli border in the south at Naqoura to Nahr al-Kabir at the northern border with Syria. There are many rivers which flow into the Mediterranean.

Inland, the Mt Lebanon Range rises steeply with a dramatic set of peaks and ridges – the highest, Qornet as-Sawda, reaches over 3000m south-east of Tripoli. South of Beirut are the Chouf Mountains, which get progressively lower in altitude as you head south. The unusual feature of this mountain range is its nonporous layer of rock, which forces water to the surface at a high altitude and in big enough quantities to produce large springs at up to 1500m. This means that in addition to an abundance of picturesque waterfalls, Lebanon has cultivation in unusually high places.

The Mt Lebanon Range gives way steeply to the Bekaa Valley, 150km from end to end, which, although low in comparison to the mountain peaks, is still 1000m above sea level. Flanked on both sides by mountains, the Bekaa Valley lies in a rain shadow and is considerably more arid than the rest of the country; nevertheless, it is the major agricultural area, producing wine, vegetables and, until recently, cannabis.

The Anti-Lebanon Range to the east of the Bekaa Valley forms a natural border with Syria and rises in a sheer arid massif from the plain. The highest peak in the range is Jebel ash-Sheikh (Mt Hermon) at 2814m.

CLIMATE

With such a diverse topography, it is not surprising that the weather varies quite considerably from region to region. Broadly speaking, Lebanon has three different climate zones – the coastal strip, the mountains and the Bekaa Valley.

The coastal strip has cool, rainy winters and hot Mediterranean summers from June to the end of September. The Mt Lebanon Range can concentrate the summer heat and humidity on the coast to a stifling degree. During the spring (March to May) and autumn (October until mid-December) the weather on the coast is warm and dry with the occasional shower. October and April can see very heavy rainfall – Beirut has more rainfall than Manchester in the UK, but only half the number of rainy days.

The mountains have a typical alpine climate. Fresh breezes keep the summer heat comfortable – which is why many people head there to escape the oppressive heat of Beirut during the summer months. There is heavy winter snow, which lasts from December to May on the higher peaks. At certain times of year you can stand on the warm coast and look inland at snow-covered peaks. The brochure cliches are true: it is indeed possible to go skiing in the morning and swimming in the afternoon, although few people actually do it. The main roads and those up to the ski stations are kept open during the winter months, but

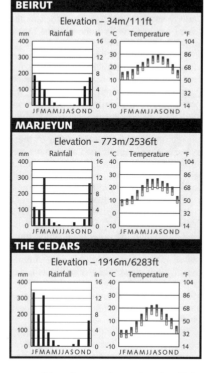

some of the minor roads are closed until the thaw.

The Bekaa Valley has hot, dry summers and cold, dry winters with snow and frost. The valley is set between two parallel mountain ranges and the wind can blow fiercely, especially in winter.

ECOLOGY & ENVIRONMENT

Ravaged by 15 years of anarchy, decades of unfettered building and weak state control, Lebanon's environment has suffered throughout much of the 20th century and remains extremely fragile.

During the war, massive damage was inflicted by bombs. Trees were cut for fuel or simply destroyed in the cross-fire, adding to Lebanon's already considerable soil-erosion problem. Illegal quarries, which continue to operate, proliferated. Much of the country was mined. (Paradoxically, this actually protected some areas.) Much of the Chouf was reportedly mined by the Druze and now has the country's largest nature reserve. The total absence of any basic services throughout the war meant that solid waste was dumped throughout the country. According to environmentalists, during the years of conflict militias were making money by accepting toxic waste from Europe, which was dumped in the sea or in coastal areas. Although the worst of these excesses have been cleaned up with the creation of massive landfill sites, continued lack of environmental awareness and inadequate waste disposal means that most water sources are polluted and garbage is a common site along riverbeds and valleys, especially near built-up areas. By the mid-1990s Lebanon did not have a single functioning waste-water treatment plant, and raw sewage was pouring out to sea. A number of plants have been rehabilitated, and new ones are being built, but offshore water quality remains a concern. Dumping of medical waste, particularly along the coast, also continues to be a serious problem.

Just as damaging to the environment is the huge amount of unplanned – and even planned – development, particularly along the coast. High-rise buildings were constructed on inappropriate mountain sides and landfill poured into the sea to create marinas or private beaches. Although this was most serious during the war, particularly along the coast north of Beirut, corruption and vested interests continue to dominate zoning.

A further problem, also related to state impotence, is agricultural mismanagement, which has led to overuse of pesticides on most of the country's farms.

In the recently liberated south, the land is littered with mines and unexploded ordnance (see the boxed text 'Warning' in The South chapter). However, in the eyes of many environmentalists, the occupation has saved the area. Beaches to the south of Tyre remain unspoiled and there has been no interest in 'developing' an area that was so unstable. As in the Chouf, the mines have prevented encroachment on the countryside.

However, this may now change. Rumours that the beaches have already been parcelled out to developers could result in the same ugly, ill-planned sprawl that has destroyed much of Lebanon's northern coastline. Ominously, the ministerial committee formed to look at reconstruction and development of the south in the aftermath of the withdrawal did not even include a representative of the Ministry of the Environment.

Although Beirut is on the coast and has strong sea breezes, air pollution is a major problem. There are some 1.5 million cars in Lebanon and a huge proportion of them are driven in Beirut.

Against this litany of woes there are positive signs, however. The fact that a Ministry of the Environment even exists is a step in the right direction, even though it is weak and rarely consulted by other ministries. More encouraging is the establishment of a number of environmental organisations in Lebanon. Greenpeace has an office in Beirut, and a growing number of local environmentalist groups, such as Greenline (www.greenline.org.lb), a volunteer organisation that promotes environmental awareness and conservation, are actively fostering grass-roots opposition to the worst excesses of planning. In May 2000, this included a campaign to prevent private developers from taking over one of the country's few remaining public beaches, Tam-Tam Beach near Byblos.

Environmental tourism is also having a positive effect. Trekking and other adventure-travel organisations are rapidly growing in Lebanon (for more information see Activities in the Facts for the Visitor chapter) and promoting environmental concerns to thousands of Lebanese and some foreign visitors each year. The establishment of an ecolodge in the mountains near Hermel (see The Bekaa Valley chapter for details) is another sign of growing environmental consciousness.

There are also campaigns under way to promote awareness of the dangers of pesticide use. Some restaurants in Beirut are now trying to use organic produce and farmers are being taught alternatives to chemical pesticides and fertilisers.

FLORA & FAUNA
Flora

The most famous flora in Lebanon – the cedar tree – is now found on only a few mountaintop sites, notably at Bcharré and near Barouk in the Chouf Mountains. These lonely groves are all that remain of the great cedar forests that in biblical times once covered vast areas of the country. Nevertheless, there are some sites where new trees are being planted. Of course it will take centuries before new forests look anything like their predecessors. (For more information, see the boxed text 'The Cedar Tree' in the Tripoli & the North chapter.)

In spite of widespread deforestation before, during and after the war, Lebanon is still the most densely wooded of all the Middle Eastern countries. Many varieties of pine, including Aleppo pine, flourish on the mountains, in addition to juniper, oak, beech and cypress. In spring there is an abundance of wildflowers on the hills and mountains, including the indigenous Lebanon violet.

Much of the coastal land is cultivated with fruit trees, such as oranges, lemons, medlars, bananas and olives. In the Bekaa Valley most of the arable land is given over to agriculture, including wine production.

In Beirut many of the magnificent, mature palm trees that once lined the Corniche were blown up during the civil war. Replanting schemes are taking place, but it will be 20 years or more before tall palms sway in the Beirut breeze again.

Fauna

Lebanon has a huge variety of bird life, in part due to its location as a resting place for many species as they migrate between Africa and Europe/Asia. Some 135 species of bird have been observed off the Lebanese coast while, further out, at the Palm Islands Reserve, over 300 have been seen. A variety of nesting birds make their homes on the islands, including the mistle thrush, tern, broad-billed sandpiper, osprey and various types of finch.

The Bekaa Valley is another extremely important migratory stop for millions of birds, including the stork, which passes through every April, as well as hoopoes, red-rumped swallows, buzzards, golden eagles and kestrels.

Lebanon's love affair with the car is echoed by its obsession with guns. On almost any mountain track in the country you will find spent bullet shells – not from the war, but from hunters. Hunting, combined with pollution, has had a huge negative affect on Lebanon's wildlife, but thanks to conservation efforts over the past decade, some species are returning. Wolves, wild boar, ibex and gazelle remain endangered species in Lebanon, but they have been sighted in the Chouf Cedar Reserve, along with wild cats, porcupines, badgers, foxes and squirrels.

Marine life has also been given a boost by the establishment of the Palm Islands Reserve. Mediterranean turtles, which had disappeared from the Lebanese coast, have begun nesting there, while the waters around the island have become an important nursery for fish.

National Parks & Nature Reserves

Although there are a total of 31 areas in Lebanon that are protected by ministerial decrees, only in the country's three nature reserves is conservation actually being practised. They are the main hope for the future of the country's threatened flora and fauna. The reserves are overseen by the Protected Areas Directorate at the Ministry of the Environment and receive funding from a variety of NGOs and international organisations, as well as the government.

Chouf Cedar Reserve This is Lebanon's largest nature reserve, it covers over 50,000 hectares – some 5% of the country's entire area. Established in 1996, it is the best managed and easiest to visit of the three reserves, and boasts six cedar forests, including three that contain old-growth cedars. A huge variety of flora and fauna, including a number of endangered species, are found here and, like the other reserves, it contains areas used as resting places for migratory birds. For more information, see The Chouf Mountains chapter.

Horsh Ehden Nature Reserve This reserve is situated 35km from Tripoli and 100km from Beirut in the northern stretch of the Mt Lebanon Range, just 3km from the summer resort of Ehden. The reserve is a unique natural habitat supporting rare indigenous trees and plants, including the Cicilian fir, Lebanese violet, Ehden milk vetch and dozens of others. It also provides a habitat for rare birds and butterflies, and is the last natural archetype of Lebanon's ancient indigenous forests. For more information, see the Tripoli & the North chapter.

Palm Islands Reserve Incorporating Palm Island, Sanani Island and Ramkine Island, the reserve lies 5km off the coastal city of Tripoli. Its area covers 5 sq km of land and sea and is an important nesting place for marine birds as well as turtles and Mediterranean monk seals. For more information, see the Tripoli & the North chapter.

GOVERNMENT & POLITICS

Lebanon has been an independent, sovereign republic since 1946. The constitution, which was first drawn up in 1926, also says that there is no state religion and that personal freedom and freedom of the press are guaranteed and protected. In reality, confessionalism permeates government, and continues to be one of Lebanon's biggest challenges (see the History section earlier in this chapter).

The legislative power of the country lies in the National Assembly, which has 128 members and holds two three-month sessions a year. Elections to the National Assembly normally take place every four years and every Lebanese over the age of 21 has the right to vote. There is no secret voting in the assembly chamber; all votes have to be public, either by show of hands or standing and sitting.

The head of state is an elected president with a nonrenewable term of six years. Government powers are distributed along confessional lines: the president must be a Maronite, the prime minister a Sunni Muslim and the speaker of the house a Shiite Muslim. The religion of the government's 30 ministers is also laid down in the constitution and must be in proportion to the size of the respective religious communities. The prime beneficiaries of the new postwar system have been the Shiites, represented by Amal and Hezbollah. Estimated to be the largest single ethnic group in Lebanon, they were under-represented in Lebanese politics before the war.

In an effort to dilute the powers of the president, the 1990 Taif Accord strengthened the role of the prime minister and speaker, thus turning the executive into a troika of sorts. The president needs the prime minister to co-sign most decisions and he cannot appoint a prime minister without the approval of the National Assembly.

But while the multiparty system appears to be working, behind-the-scenes meddling by Syria means that the government cannot be called truly democratic. In the 1996 National Assembly elections, Syria's desire to keep Hezbollah in check resulted in a far smaller representation than predicted for the party. Pro-Syrian politicians, such as the head of the Progressive Socialist Party, Walid Jumblatt, and Amal leader Nabih Berri, strengthened their political positions. The current president, Emile Lahoud is careful to toe Damascus' line, particularly on the peace process and relations with Israel. Student demonstrations calling for Syrian withdrawal from Lebanon were forcefully quelled by riot police in May 2000. Whether there will be any change in this cautious pro-Syrian policy with the withdrawal of Israel from the south and the death of Hafez al-Assad remains to be seen.

ECONOMY

Lebanon has always been famous for its laissez-faire capitalism and minimal government interference. Before the war Beirut was a regional banking centre and had a thriving tourist industry. Not surprisingly, the civil war destroyed all this, shattering the economy as dramatically as it destroyed the country's infrastructure. The Lebanese pound went from a stable LL2.50 to the US dollar in 1975 to a low, immediately after the war, of LL2800 to the US dollar. At this time, inflation was running at 200%. Taxation, barely collected before the war, was nonexistent and the government all but bankrupt.

Rebuilding the economy and infrastructure was Rafiq Hariri's priority when he became president in 1992. A Saudi-borne billionaire businessman, his background was seen as an asset to the Herculean task of getting Lebanon back on the road to prosperity. He secured loans from the World Bank, the European Union and a number of Arab Gulf States and then, in 1993, established the Council for Development & Reconstruction (CDR). The council drew up an ambitious 10-year, US$13 billion (later raised to US$18.1 billion) plan for the reconstruction of Lebanon's infrastructure. Hariri also established Solidére, a private company that was to plan and implement the rebuilding of Beirut's destroyed downtown area.

The rebuilding frenzy stimulated the economy and Lebanon appeared to boom. Hariri was unable to reform the inefficient and bloated bureaucracy that he inherited, so he simply bypassed it, appointing his own men or creating his own organisations (such as the CDR). Opposition to this was muted while the economy seemed to thrive, but a growing authoritarian streak, seen in a curtailment of press freedom and banning of public demonstrations in the mid-1990s led to increased criticism. Nevertheless, Hariri stabilised the currency and most major infrastructure projects were completed.

By 1997, however, Lebanon's apparently flourishing economy had slowed down. In 1998, Emile Lahoud was elected president and later in the year, Hariri was replaced by the low-key Selim al-Hoss, who had been prime minister in the 1980s. Under their leadership the government launched an austerity program that was in contrast to the flamboyant spending that characterised the Hariri reconstruction. Lebanon's foreign debt was spiralling (currently about 40% of the budget goes towards debt service) and continued Israeli attacks on the country were costing millions in damage, as well as depressing the slowly recovering tourist trade. Many reconstruction projects were stopped or slowed down, ostensibly to investigate corruption allegations, but also because the state could simply no longer finance them. The government has since embarked on a privatisation program and is planning to introduce value-added tax. In the meantime, other sectors of the economy continue to have mixed results. The agricultural sector, which accounts for 12% to 15% of Lebanon's GDP, suffered hugely during the war and now finds itself in trouble. Farmers do not have easy access to credit, they lost markets during the war years and now find themselves undercut by cheaper products from neighbouring countries. Grapes (used for winemaking) and potatoes are the primary, and most successful crops, but a variety of vegetables and citrus fruit are also grown.

The tourist industry, which used to be one of Lebanon's main currency-earners, has suffered too, largely due to political uncertainty in the region. Nevertheless, the future could be rosy. Although the majority of the country's visitors are of Lebanese origin, the number of non-Lebanese visiting the country each year has increased by an average of about 10%. Like the rest of the economy, this will likely improve if political stability is maintained.

POPULATION & PEOPLE

The thorny question of confessional balance and politics means that no census has been held in Lebanon since 1932. However, the United Nations estimates the population to be about 3,500,000, of which half are concentrated in Beirut. This makes Lebanon the most densely populated Middle Eastern country with about 306 people per sq km.

An estimated 150,000 people were killed during the civil war and some 1.5 million lost their homes, a staggering number in such a small country. Lebanon has always had a high level of emigration but the civil war exacerbated the trend. There are now an estimated 10 million Lebanese (or people of Lebanese descent) around the world. Famous for their business acumen, they are the country's most successful export, but most maintain close ties to their homeland and an estimated 40,000 have resettled since the end of the war.

The majority of Lebanon's population is Muslim. Although it is not reflected in the political arena, Shiite Muslims are the single largest group, comprising an estimated 35% of the population. Sunni Muslims make up an estimated 22% of the population. Shiite Lebanese have traditionally been the poorest section of the population and have been concentrated in the south of the country and in parts of the Bekaa Valley. The Sunnis have traditionally been liberal urban dwellers.

While often described as Muslim, the Druze are considered heretical in mainstream Islam. They comprise some 5% of the total population and are concentrated around the Chouf Mountains.

Christian Lebanese are divided into a bewildering array of sects and denominations. The Maronites are by far the most significant, both in terms of numbers and influence. They make up about 21% of the total population. The other Christians are Greek Orthodox, Greek Catholic, Armenian Orthodox, Armenian Catholic, Chaldean Catholic, Syrian Catholic, Roman Catholic and Protestant, and account for some 14% of the total population.

Ethnically, the overwhelming majority of Lebanese (about 95%) are classified as Arab, but even this seemingly simple statement is fraught with political implications. Many Christian Lebanese distance themselves from their Arab past, preferring to call themselves 'Phoenicians'. In fact, Lebanon's many conquerors have left their mark on the ethnic make-up of the people and the Lebanese are a Semitic melange. Egyptians, Hittites, Assyrians, Greeks and Arabs, among others, have all contributed to the gene pool.

Armenians are Lebanon's largest ethnic minority. They fled here to escape the WWI genocides in Turkey and now have Lebanese nationality. They comprise about 4% of the population, and a large number are concentrated around Borj Hammoud, at the eastern edge of Beirut.

The Palestinians also fled to Lebanon, but their status remains uncertain. About 350,000 Palestinians live in Lebanon – many have been here for more than 50 years – but their presence is barely tolerated by the majority of Lebanese. Their complex role in the civil war and their potential for destabilising the country's confessional balance means they are unwanted in Lebanon. Their country no longer exists, so they have no nationality, thus no passport, and cannot travel. Trapped in Lebanon, they face severe restrictions on the types of work they can do, are largely dependent on handouts from the UN Relief & Works Agency (UNRWA) and, in the overwhelming majority of cases, live in appalling conditions. They are the tragic victims of more than a century of foreign meddling in the region. Some Lebanese politicians have openly said that they want to make the lives of Palestinians so miserable that they will leave, although quite where they are supposed to go remains a mystery. In the meantime, they wait in their camps for Israel and the Palestine Authority to negotiate their future in final status peace talks.

For all its emigration and relatively high unemployment (currently standing at about 20%, according to some estimates), Lebanon plays host to a large number of foreign workers. Egyptians, Sri Lankans, Filipinos and Ethiopians carry out much of Lebanon's menial labour. But by far the majority of workers are Syrian, and they are the labourers on construction sites and in fields all over the country.

EDUCATION

Lebanon boasts one of the highest literacy rates in the Middle East, at well over 90%. Only five years of primary school is mandatory, but children stay through at least part of secondary school. State schools have a poor reputation and, in 1997, over 50% of Lebanese students were privately educated. At the end of secondary school, most students obtain the Lebanese Baccalaureate, which is similar to its French equivalent. Because of the large number of private institutions using British or American curriculums, some students also leave secondary school with British or American qualifications.

There are 21 universities in Lebanon, of which seven are considered 'premier league'. Only one, the Lebanese University, is state-funded. The American University of Beirut (AUB), which has pupils of all sects,

charré, the Qadisha Valley's main town

The beautiful Qadisha Valley is a hiker's paradise.

he golden light of a Mediterranean sunset bathes the city of Jounieh.

The fertile Bekaa Valley, one of ancient Rome's breadbaskets, is now a major wine-producing region.

Wildflowers, seen here in Beirut's Raouché area, flourish throughout Lebanon in the spring.

The spectacular Pigeon Rocks are Beirut's best-known natural feature.

was established by American missionaries in the 19th century and is arguably the most respected academic institution in the country.

ARTS

Lebanon has a very lively arts scene, both traditional and contemporary. In the summer almost every village has a festival in which both traditional music and dance play a part. For more information on Lebanon's larger festivals, see the boxed text 'Lebanon's Festivals' in the Facts for the Visitor chapter.

Dance

The national dance, the *dabke*, is an energetic, five-step folk dance performed at weddings and celebrations throughout the country. People join hands and are led by a 'master' dancer who stands in front. The dance is a staple of the spectacles in large, tourist-oriented restaurants and hotels, where dancers wear the traditional costume of the mountains and the dances portray aspects of village life. Far more fun is when a spontaneous dabke erupts at a wedding or social occasion, and people just form circles and start to move.

Carácalla is the closest thing Lebanon has to a national dance troupe, although it combines elements of theatre as well. Founded by Ahmed Caracalla, the choreographer of the Baalbek Festival in the 1960s, the group's performances are inspired by oriental dance, but combine opera, dance and theatre. With colourful costumes and musicals based on sources as diverse as Shakespeare and modern Lebanese novelists, they can be seen at some of Lebanon's summer festivals, and sometimes perform at the Casino du Liban.

With their gyrating hips and spangled bikinis, belly-dancers are one of the Middle East's famous sights. No matter that these days many are not even Arab. They can be found at large Lebanese restaurants in Beirut and, of course, the super nightclubs that cater to Gulf Arabs and tourists.

Music

In most Middle Eastern countries, music is everywhere. You will hear it blasted from shop doorways, from street traders' cassette decks, from the interiors of passing cars or wafting from the balconies of apartment

Oriental Dancing

This ancient form of dance, known in the east as *raks sharki* and to the world as belly-dancing, sums up the eastern nightclub experience. The dance is characterised by its sensual hip movements and graceful arm movements – and also by the skimpy costumes worn by the practitioners. When Westerners first saw this dance performed, they were struck by its erotic quality and this image has stayed with the dance ever since. Not surprisingly really – Europe in the 18th century had no equivalent dance and the degree of nudity involved in oriental dancing must have been shocking to Christian Europeans of that time.

Professional belly-dancers can earn a fortune for a single performance. Others make do with large denomination notes tucked into their costume as a tribute from their appreciative audience. The top dancers are usually Egyptian, although you come across dancers from just about every country you can think of.

The origins of the dance are lost in history. Some scholars think they come from the professional dancers of medieval Spain. Others think belly-dancing has a connection with pagan fertility dances performed in temples. These days the dance is performed as entertainment in clubs and restaurants and still plays an important role at traditional weddings. The belly-dancer who performs at weddings represents the transition from virgin bride to sensual woman.

If you find yourself confronted by a gyrating torso at a club, etiquette requires that you place a rolled or folded banknote into the bra or waistband of the dancer without too much physical contact. The belly-dancer will then move on to another table and repeat the performance.

blocks. In taxis it's not uncommon to have to ask the driver to turn the music down.

After WWII, Lebanese music experienced a major resurgence that focused on Arabic, as opposed to Turkish, music. There are many contemporary Lebanese singers and musicians. The most famous is Fairouz (though she rarely performs today); her long, soulful songs have made her a legend not only in Lebanon but throughout the Arab world (see the boxed text 'Fairouz'). Her son, Ziad, is a renowned experimental jazz performer.

Lebanon's many festivals mean the world's biggest names in music can be heard live here – if your visit coincides with the festival dates. The Bustan Festival, which concentrates on classical music, usually takes place in February, while the remainder run through the summer. (For further details, see the boxed text 'Lebanon's Festivals' in the Facts for the Visitor chapter.)

The Classical Style Tonality and instrumentation aside, Arabic classical music differs from that of the west in one big respect: the orchestra is there primarily to back a singer. The all-time favourite voice of classical Arabic music is Egyptian-born songstress Umm Kolthum, who was at her peak in the 1940s and 50s – the golden age of Arab music – but whose voice remains ubiquitous on radios and cassette decks throughout the Middle East today.

The Arab orchestra is a curious cross-fertilisation of East and West. Western-style instruments such as violins and many of the wind and percussion instruments predominate, next to such local species as the oud and tabla. The sounds that emanate from them are anything but Western. There is all the mellifluous seduction of Asia in the backing melodies, the vaguely melancholic, languid tones you would expect from a sun-drenched and heat-exhausted Middle Eastern summer.

The 1950s gave rise to a pantheon of stars that notably included Fairouz. Today her popularity in Lebanon even surpasses that of Umm Kolthum.

Fairouz

A Lebanese torch singer with a voice memorably described as 'silk and flame in one', Fairouz has enjoyed star status throughout the Arab world since recording her first performances in Damascus in the 1950s. Along with her writers, the Rahbani brothers, Fairouz embraced a wide range of music forms from flamenco to jazz and during the 1960s and 70s became the perfect embodiment of freewheeling Beirut when it was still called 'Paris of the Middle East'. During the civil war she became a symbol of hope for national unity and an icon for the Lebanese identity (though, in disgust, she sat out the fighting in Paris). At the end of the hostilities, in 1994, she returned to give a concert to 40,000 in downtown Beirut. Now in her late 60s, she has resettled in her homeland, living in the hills above Beirut.

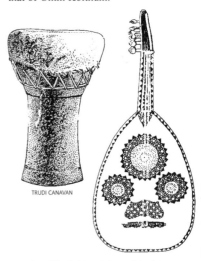

TRUDI CANAVAN

The tabla (left) and the oud (right), two important instruments in an Arabic orchestra

Arabic Fusion A popular musician who marries classical Arabic music with contemporary sounds is Marcel Khalifé, who hails from Amchit, near Byblos. An oud player with a cult following throughout the world, many of his songs have a controversial political side, such as a composition for the dead of Sabra and Shatila.

Other Lebanese musicians who fuse Arabic and contemporary sounds include Rabih Abou-Khalil, whose CDs can be found in the West, as well as in Beirut, and Charbel Rouhana, who composes new-age type music based on traditional Arabic sounds.

Pop Characterised by a clattering, hand-clapping rhythm overlaid with synthesised twirlings and a catchy, repetitive vocal, the first Arabic pop music came out of Cairo in the 1970s. As the Arab nations experienced a population boom and the mean age decreased, a gap in popular culture had developed that the memory of the greats couldn't fill. Enter Arabic pop. The blueprint for the new youth sound (which became known as *al-jeel*, from the word for generation) was set by Egyptian Ahmed Adawiyya, the Arab world's first 'pop star'. But to unattuned ears, the Arabic pop of the 1980s is far from appealing. It's cheesy and one dimensional and much of it sounds like it came reprogramed out of a Casio keyboard – hunt down a copy of the excruciating 'Lo Laki' by Ali Hameida, which was played everywhere nonstop for several years after its release in 1988. It's like an up-tempo, electronic version of the Chinese water torture.

During the 1990s, there was a calculated attempt to create a more upmarket sound. Tacky electronics were replaced with moody pianos, Spanish guitars and thunderous drums. Check out Amr Diab, whose heavily produced songs have made him the best-selling artist ever in the Arab world (achieved with his 1996 album *Nour al-Ain*).

Diab is Egyptian but in recent years the Egyptians have been beaten at their own game and many of the current biggest-selling artists come from elsewhere. Heading the current crop of megastar singers are Majida al-Rumi of Lebanon and Iraq-born Kazem al-Saher. Recent Lebanese additions to the scene also include The 4 Cats, Lebanon's sultry answer to the Spice Girls, whose album *Leil Nahar* melds Arab and Western pop. Or Diana Haddad, who has produced

six albums and sings in a variety of Arabic dialects (to listen to their music, or that of other Lebanese pop musicians, check out the Web site www.musicoflebanon.com).

The Live Music Scene Sadly, it's very difficult to see live music almost anywhere in the Middle East. While Beirut has one of the liveliest arts scenes in the region, there are few live-music clubs that play Arabic music. Other than at Lebanon's festivals, such as Baalbek or Beiteddine, your best chance of catching a performance is at a wedding or party, which is where nearly all Arab singers and musicians get their start.

Anyway, when it comes to Arabic pop, its true home is not on stage but on cassette. Artists have traditionally had little regard for production values and the music is slapped down in the studio and mass-produced on cheap tapes in their thousands. Few people can afford quality tape decks anyway, so who cares about the quality of sound? Shopkeepers are usually only too happy to play cassettes before you buy, although at only a dollar or two a pop you can afford to take risks.

Literature

For such a small country, Lebanon has produced an enormous number of literary figures. Beirut has had a flourishing publishing industry since the 19th century and continues to be a regional publishing centre.

The following is a (highly personal) selection of Lebanese writers whose works have been translated into English.

Etel Adnan *Sitt Marie Rose* may be a slight volume but is probably the best novel about the civil war. It's hard to find (although there are rumours that it is to be reprinted in Beirut), so grab it if you can get your hands on it.

Tawfiq Yusuf Awwad Awwad's most famous novel, *Death in Beirut*, foreshadows the civil war with the story of a Shiite village girl who makes the journey to Beirut to attend university just after the 1967 war. The author was tragically killed by a shell in 1989.

Khalil Gibran This famous 19th-century mystical writer/poet/painter, whose book *The Prophet* has rather unfairly become cast as a hippy favourite, wrote a number other works too, and remains a national cultural hero in Lebanon. (See the boxed text 'Khalil Gibran' in the Tripoli & the North chapter for more on the man and his work.)

Tony Hanania London-based Lebanese writer Tony Hanania's *Unreal City* is an occasionally surreal story of the young scion of a feudal family from the south who leaves for England. Returning to his war-torn country, he eventually falls in with Hezbollah fighters in his search for meaning amid the anarchy.

Amin Maalouf Based in Paris, Amin Maalouf writes in French and has written a number of fiction and nonfiction works. His two most famous are *Leo the African* and *Samarkand*, both epic but readable historical fiction that, like his *Crusades Through Arab Eyes*, give Western readers a glimpse into an exotic, bygone world. Highly recommended.

Emily Nasrallah Emily Nasrallah stayed in Beirut for most of the civil war, but many members of her family left for Canada. Her themes tend to dwell on the familial and cultural dislocation that accompanied the conflict. *Flight Against Time* is probably her best-known novel, while *Fantastic Strokes of Imagination* is a collection of short stories.

Nabil Salih Nabil Salih writes historical fiction in the Amin Maalouf vein. *Outremer* is the story of intolerance and love set against the brutality of the Crusades.

Hanan al-Shaykh Another foreign-based writer, Hanan al-Shaykh lives in London but writes mostly about Lebanon and largely with a feminist slant. Her *Story of Zahra* is a harrowing, unputdownable account of the civil war. *Beirut Blues* is slightly less successful, but very readable nonetheless.

Architecture

There are still a few examples of traditional architecture in Beirut, but many of the old buildings have suffered the same redevelopment fate as in the rest of the Mediterranean. Beirut's old houses are usually large and airy with a courtyard garden, a terrace overgrown with vines and large, arched windows, often inset with coloured glass. The style is a mix of Italian influence and Arabic layout. There are about five of them left on the Corniche in Ain al-Mraisse, Beirut, and one or two in the backstreets near the American University of Beirut. A few more are hidden in the backstreets of Achrafiye.

Most buildings constructed since the 1960s have been rather brutish concrete blocks, although there are one or two modernist gems that could be wonderful, if they are sympathetically restored. In the Beirut Central District, many of the buildings were too damaged by the war to be saved, and reconstruction is being done in the 'spirit' of the original. Those buildings that could be salvaged are being painstakingly restored.

In the regions, styles vary; some villages have red-tiled roofs, others a more Middle-Eastern, flat-roofed style. In the north, Tripoli has a wealth of medieval and Islamic architecture, and a fine collection of 18th-century merchants' houses can be seen in the small town of Amchit, north of Byblos. Deir al-Qamar, in the Chouf, is an extremely well-preserved village, with some beautiful 18th- and 19th-century villas and palaces. Beiteddine, also in the Chouf, is a melange of Italian and traditional Arab architecture, although it is more remarkable for its lavish interiors than any architectural innovation.

For more information on Lebanese architectural styles, see 'The Architecture of Lebanon'.

Painting

Lebanon's first art school, the Academie Libanais des Beaux-Arts, was established in 1937 and twenty years later AUB established its Department of Fine Arts. The two institutions nurtured a growing artistic community. In the 1950s and 60s a number of galleries opened to showcase its art, and the private Sursock Museum, in Achrafiye, also began to show new artists.

In the 1960s a group of artists and scholars, headed by Jenine Rubeiz, formed Dar al-Fan (literally, 'place of art') to provide a forum for artists to gather and discuss their work. Jenine Rubeiz is still involved in the art scene and runs one of Beirut's most respected galleries. By the 1970s Lebanese artists were winning international acclaim. However, with the civil war, the artistic community was scattered.

[Continued on page 49]

THE ARCHITECTURE
OF LEBANON

Although the present state of Lebanon was not created until 1946, the region has been inhabited from prehistoric times. A rich and fascinating architectural record survives in a relatively small area, making it a dizzying destination for enthusiasts of architecture and history. Most of the notable architectural examples are from Greek and Roman times through until the Byzantine and Islamic periods. However, there are remains of early Stone Age structures, as well as the buildings of the most well-known occupants of the region – the Phoenicians.

Neolithic to Iron Age (5000–1200 BC)

Evidence at Byblos indicates that Stone Age villagers lived in round huts, which had hard-packed, crushed limestone floors. Several settlements in the Byblos archaeological site reveal these types of floors, which can still be seen today, albeit with difficulty as that area of the site is overgrown.

With the advent of metal tools the villagers could better exploit the nearby forests, and timber beams began to be used for roof construction. At first these timber-roofed rooms were long and narrow, a reflection of the fact that the people of the time didn't have the technology to process the timber to the required size. Later, as the necessary technology developed, the rooms became squarer and the architecture took on increasing complexity.

As political organisation and social complexity arose from cultural stabilisation, architecture became increasingly focused on producing public rather than domestic works.

Phoenician (1200–550 BC)

Phoenician culture was primarily focused on the sea and trade. Little architecture remains intact from this time, partially because settlements were located on the coast and subsequently demolished during countless sea-based invasions, and also because most of their main cities, eg, Sidon, Tyre and Beirut, continue to be occupied to this day.

Title Page: Remnants of a Corinthian arch frame a remarkably intact entablature and colonnnade at Baalbek. This vista leads into one of the main axes of the temple compound. (Photo: Bethune Carmichael)

Top: Pottery from the Neolithic age (Illustration Trudi Canavan)

Left: Known locally as 'Nebuchadnezzar's Tablet', this cuneiform script can be found carved on a rock on a mountain road near Hermel.

BETHUNE CARMICHAEL

The legacy of the Phoenicians is somewhat hard to pinpoint, as much of their culture has since been overlayed with the artefacts of countless other civilisations. They did, however, develop settlements around ports that took on interesting defensive designs. Urban plans, rather than individual architectural examples, are the best legacy we have of the Phoenicians.

The typical Phoenician town was divided in two: a maritime town sited on a promontory with an island offshore; and an inland town separated from the maritime one by gardens. Good examples of this are at Sidon and at Tyre, which, in plan, retain their Phoenician flavour to this day.

Phoenician cities were quite compact and the houses were multi-storey, with small square windows and balustrades supported by miniature palm columns. Strabo, the Greek historian and geographer, has left a description of these houses, pointing out that the houses in Tyre were higher than those in Rome itself.

The Phoenicians laid out their cities in a grid pattern and surrounded them with defensive walls. They also took pains to ensure that their cities had access to more than one harbour. At Sidon this double-harbour strategy (which virtually guaranteed they had a wind to sail out on) is still evident.

The Phoenician ruins of Byblos, once an important trading city, have been largely obliterated by later Roman and Crusader occupation. However, architectural knowledge and influence obtained from Egyptian trading contact are evident in the ruins, particularly the Obelisk Temple at Byblos. The temple complex at Baalbek, specifically the Temple of Bacchus, also exhibits the design and craftsmanship of Phoenician stonemasons, whose skill was also used in the construction of the Temple of Solomon in Jerusalem. Other temples of the region (such as the Temple of Echmoun near Sidon) retain evidence of their Phoenician origins, although they have been much altered by later cultures.

Greeks & Romans (333 BC–AD 300)

After Alexander swept through the region, the small Phoenician kingdoms succumbed to Greek influence and strong waves of migration. The Hellenising effect resulted in the incorporation of Greek architectural styles into the local idiom. The main coastal trading ports became predominantly Hellenic, while the isolated inland outposts developed more hybrid styles.

The Greeks introduced three orders of architecture: the Doric, Ionic and Corinthian.

These different orders (which are basically a system of design) are best distinguished by their respective temples and columns. The orders arose from stylistic developments in the earlier Classical period, and were a means of architectural production that prescribed the form and design of buildings (usually civic and religious) and also their siting and layout.

THE ARCHITECTURE OF LEBANON

Mythology

Lebanon has countless temples and sanctuaries. While many have been left in ruins and others turned into Christian churches, most still reflect their original purpose. The gods and goddesses of the ancient Middle East evolved into Greek, and later, Roman equivalents. Even the Christian holy family has some echo of the role played by older gods. To unravel some of the names of deities, which crop up again and again in Lebanon, here is a brief guide.

Ashtoreth/Astarte/Ishtar

Ashtoreth is the supreme female divinity of the Phoenicians, known by the Babylonians as Ishtar and the Greek and Romans as Astarte. They symbolise the female principle in all her aspects, just as Baal symbolised maleness. She was the Great Mother, goddess of fertility and queen of heaven. Astarte was later identified with a number of Greek goddesses: Selene, the moon goddess, Artemis, the goddess of nature and Aphrodite, the goddess of love and beauty. Astarte is most famous for her love of the youth Tammuz. The story also features in Greek mythology as the story of Aphrodite and Adonis.

Bel/Baal

Bel was the supreme god of the Babylonians and the name Bel is the Chaldean form of Baal. The name literally means 'lord' (as it still does in Hebrew). Bel presided over the air and was associated astrologically with the planet Jupiter, which, in astral mythology, is connected to the productive power of nature.

Dagon/Dagan

Dagon is the second most important god after El, the supreme god. He is the recognised god of crop fertility and is also the legendary inventor of the plough. He is also known as the god of the fishes.

Echmoun/Asklepios/Aesculapius

Echmoun is the principal god of the city of Sidon and is associated with

TRUDI CANAVAN

Left: Wooden figurine of Ashtoreth from Kamid al-Loz.

Ionic and Corinthian are the main orders to be seen in the ruins of Lebanon. The origins of the Ionic order are contentious, although some say the capitals (column tops) were inspired by the shape of rams horns and nautilus shells. Certainly the mathematical purity of these shapes

Mythology

healing. Echmoun began as a mortal youth from Berytus (Beirut). Astarte fell in love with him but to escape from her, he mutilated himself and died. She brought him back to life in the form of a god. He was still primarily a god of healing and is identified with the Greek Asklepios, the god of medicine, and the Roman god Aesculapius.

El

El is the father of all gods except Baal. In Phoenician texts he is described as the creator of the earth. El is usually represented as an old man with a long beard and, often, two wings.

Melkart/Heracles

Melkart, later called Heracles by the Greeks, is the god of cities. He is specifically the patron god of Tyre.

Resheph/Reshef

Resheph is the god of the plague, and of burning and destructive fire. Usually represented with a shield and lightning rod, he is also seen as a war god. He later became the Babylonian god Nergal.

Tammuz/Adonis

Adonis was a beautiful youth loved by both Aphrodite and Persephone, queen of the underworld. When he was slain by a wild boar, Aphrodite pleaded with Zeus to restore him. Zeus agreed that Adonis should spend the winter months with Persephone in Hades and the summer months with Aphrodite. His story is the allegory of nature's death and rebirth every spring.

TRUDI CANAVAN

Zeus/Jupiter/Jove

Zeus is the ruler of the gods and the son of Saturn (who he overthrew). Jupiter is identified with the Greek Zeus and was worshipped as the god of thunder and lightning. He is also the guardian of law, defender of truth and protector of justice.

Right: Stele of Baal, discovered at Ugarit.

held wonder for the classical Greeks, yet the columns used throughout the Levant in previous centuries were of similarly shaped forms, such as the lotus columns of Egypt and the lily-shaped capitals used in Canaanite temple architecture.

Wrapped in a carved garland of foliage, the Corinthian capitals are the most decorative of all. The famous author of architectural treatises, Vitruvius, recounts the fabled origins of the Corinthian capital. Callimachus, a famous Athenian bronze sculptor, obtained the idea for the capital from watching the growth of the native acanthus plant through an upturned basket. This basket, weighted down with a tile to keep it in place, was appropriately located upon the grave of a Corinthian maiden and intended to protect the offerings piously placed upon the grave. The fortuitous result of this was a beautifully sculpted plant honouring the dead beauty.

That a whole style of architecture, still observable in the construction of buildings to this century, developed from this chance growth is somewhat fantastical. The vegetation of the region has always been of influence in architecture and, as with the Ionic, Egyptian columns are also thought to have informed the advent of the Corinthian order. (But thanks anyway Vitruvius for a great story.) There are examples of Corinthian columns at the temple ruins in Faqra. Corinthian columns were also incorporated into the design of the Great Mosque in Sidon.

Roman architecture can be seen as a further development from the ground rules of the Greek orders, but was more widespread and permanent. After Antiochus' armies were decisively beaten, and after victories by Pompey the Great, the whole of Asia Minor became part of the Roman Empire. Under Republican Rome, architectural developments filtered down and meshed with the still strong Hellenistic flavour of the region. Notable Roman architecture, usually religious, was adapted to accommodate cultural and religious differences and the persistence of cults, which were still popular.

Below: List of details

1 Entablature
2 Column
3 Cornice
4 Frieze
5 Architrave
6 Capital
7 Shaft
8 Base
9 Plinth
10 Triglyph
11 Metope
12 Abacus
13 Echinus
14 Flute
15 Arris
16 Fascia
17 Volute
18 Fillet
19 Dentils

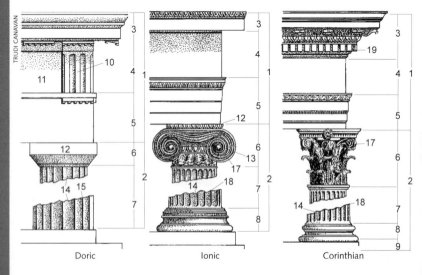

TRUDI CANAVAN

Doric   Ionic   Corinthian

Roman temples differed from Greek ones in several respects: the stylobate (the sub-structure or upper level on which the building rested) was substituted with an elevated podium and instead of having stairs that ran around the temple, the Romans built just one flight, on the entrance facade. The typically Greek colonnade became increasingly decorative and was sometimes set into the cella (the hall containing the cult image) of the temple itself.

The Romans were also more concerned with imposing their style on the environment. They further developed the gridded urban design strategies inherited from the Greeks, and the architecture was far more experimental in its forms and use of materials then anything previously. The Romans borrowed the Greek orders of architecture, but added two of their own: the Composite and the Tuscan. Although they didn't invent it, they also made good use of the arch, as it suited their desire for space and monumentality. They generally modified and enlarged existing Greek buildings, embellishing them further with the wealth of the Roman Empire. As Lebanon experienced something of a building boom under the Romans, their architectural ideals are much in evidence.

The Roman passion for order and harmony was reflected in their town planning. Two main roads, the *decumanus maximus* (usually east/west) and the *cardo maximus* (usually north/south), intersected near the city centre, where the forum and amphitheatre could also usually be found. Important roads like these were invariably colonnaded. The layout divided the city into four quarters, the whole being enclosed within the city walls. This system can be seen at many of Lebanon's ruined sites, and also many contemporary cities that have their origins in Roman times, such as Beirut (Berytus under the Romans) and Baalbek, both of which became important administrative and trading centres under Imperial Rome. The Romans ensured the cities were well endowed with temples and other public buildings, including hippodromes and monumental arches. Most have long since been lost, their existence known only from coins struck at the time and from descriptions in contemporary documents. Remains of Roman baths, or thermae, have survived under the Grand Seraglio plateau in Beirut.

Other historical sites in Lebanon have many examples of Roman architecture: a theatre in Batroun; a temple in Majdel Aanjar; and a necropolis in Dakweh. A good example of a Roman theatre can be found in Byblos. Unlike the Greeks, who took advantage of natural slopes when building their theatres, the Romans didn't excavate but instead built on level ground. Walls formed a continuous barrier around the stage and seating. As they didn't use a chorus, the orchestra (reached through a series of vaulted passages) formed part of the auditorium.

A typical example of a hippodrome, that was lined with tiers of seats along each side, has survived in a reasonably intact state at Tyre. One end of the hippodrome was curved while the opposite end was squared off so the chariots could enter and draw up for the start.

PATRICK SYDER

Arguably the most important Roman remains in Lebanon are at Baalbek: the gigantic columns of the Temple of Jupiter; the well-preserved Temple of Bacchus (some claim it's the Roman world's finest example of a Corinthian building); and the circular Temple of Venus. Although their invention of concrete allowed the Romans to build gigantic structures elsewhere, at Baalbek they achieved the same effect using mortarless stone, exemplifying their brilliant craftsmanship. With lavish carving and innovative designs, these temples are perfect examples of both the earlier strictness of design under Republican Rome, and the comparative excesses of the later Imperial Roman architecture, where colour, carving and previously unseen architectural developments in space and form (such as the Temple of Venus) pre-empt the excesses of the Baroque, which was to surface in Europe centuries later. These ruins, well preserved and on a monumental scale, are among the most impressive in existence. They were also built to last; the substructure at Baalbek contains some of the largest single blocks of stone to be found in the world.

Early Christian, Byzantine, Arab & Crusader (AD 324–1300)

The decline of the Roman Empire saw much of the grand architecture in Lebanon gradually crumble – a central administration no longer held sway, trading centres waned and state religions dissolved. Much of the finery was plundered, destroyed, or systematically disassembled by locals for new building stock. The adoption of Christianity (previously an underground cult for three centuries) by the Romans under Constantine provided a new use for the temples and many were gradually modified to accommodate this new religious practice, which required devotion to one God rather than many different deities. Constantine moved the centre of the church to Byzantium (then renamed it Constantinople), and Rome continued to wither as the centre of power moved to the east.

Top: Tyre features the world's largest and best-preserved hippodrome. I is 480m long and seatec 20,000 spectators.

Early Christians used the synagogue until their numbers grew and Jewish ties were severed. With the new liturgical practices of baptism, and the necessity to accommodate large numbers of people in a sacred space, the early Christians needed a new architectural style. The Roman model of the basilica (a hall for the administration of justice) was adopted as the basis for church design. These churches were typically orientated on an east/west axis – a long hall terminated in an apse at the east end. Aisles on either side of the nave were separated by colonnades, using the classical orders. Recognisable church motifs developed from fountains, triumphal arches and other Roman architectural elements. The floors were covered with brilliant mosaics; the tesserae consisting of brightly glazed tiles, semi-precious stones and coloured glass (a feature also copied from the Romans). An example of such a mosaic, found by the British in Beirut in 1918, is now in the American University of Beirut Museum, with more early mosaics being uncovered as Beirut rebuilds. In recent years further discoveries have been made: a mosaic from a Byzantine shopping colonnade on the northern side of the decumanus maximus and a mosaic uncovered in the souqs, which features a musing (in Greek) on the nature of jealousy.

As Christianity developed and liturgical practices became more ritualised, so the designs of early Christian churches developed and experimented with other forms, gradually abandoning the basilica as the sole model appropriate for religious architecture. The flourishing culture around Constantinople, the mystical melting pot bridging Europe and the East, provided a fervent locale for exotic, decorative influence in regional architecture. It was, however, the incorporation of the dome, fundamental to the enclosure of large spaces, that changed the design of churches remarkably. There is contention as to whether the Pantheon in Rome, or smaller domed structures (such as the Temple of Minerva Medica in Rome) were the responsible architectural models. Liturgically, an emphasis shifted from elongated spaces to centralised spaces, with a strong vertical axis that could correspond with the popular Christian ideals of heaven and god being above. The development of the dome gave birth to a whole new model of church, which spread throughout the Holy Land and particularly Eastern Europe. Characterised by this new spatial understanding through the inventive use of domes, arches and columns, Byzantine architecture had evolved. There are many examples of early Christian and Byzantine churches in Lebanon, most notably in Beirut, Sidon, Qartaba, Enfe, Beit Mary and Tyre.

Only one site, Aanjar, bears the imprint of the Damascus-based Umayyad dynasty, whose influence waxed and waned between the 7th and 8th centuries AD. At first glance Aanjar seems almost Roman, laid out as it is in a square grid, with two 20m-wide thoroughfares and enclosed within walls punctuated by four towers. Arcades of shops once lined the main roads; elsewhere are Roman-style baths, mosques and at least two palaces. The only other remnant of Umayyad rule in Lebanon is in Baalbek where a small mosque remains just outside the main temple complex.

Under the call of Pope Urban II in 1095, the First Crusade set out to recapture the Holy Lands from Muslim occupation. From this and subsequent incursions into the region by vast armies originating in the West, a string of Crusader castles exists, in varying degrees of ruin. Fine construction and strategic siting provided an effective defence mechanism for many of the castles, which withstood battle and siege over centuries. An elaborate system of communication, combining signalling and the use of carrier pigeons, enabled the Crusaders to unify their coastal defences. Crusaders used ancient temple columns in the walls to strengthen them and make undermining by enemies more difficult, as can be seen at Byblos.

Typically, 12th-century Crusader castles, such as the one at Byblos, featured a rectangular, two-storeyed donjon (the place of final retreat), which in the case of Byblos was accessed by a ladder to a first-floor door. Staircases to the upper storeys were cut into the walls, which are 4m thick. The castle at Byblos was defended from five towers (placed at the four corners of an almost square bailey), each with arrow slits to allow flanking fire. It was built on the site of the old acropolis soon after the town was captured (in 1104) and boasts some impressively large blocks of stone, although these were almost certainly 'liberated' from more ancient structures nearby.

The castle at Tripoli, built by Raymond de Saint-Gilles, was designed to put the local population under military and economic pressure. Like the castle in Byblos, it consisted of a rectangular, two-storeyed donjon; rectangular towers project gently from the outer walls. At Sidon the Crusaders built their castle on the small island just offshore from the promontory where the Phoenicians before them had built their city. The Mamluks destroyed it. The Arabs rebuilt it. Unsurprisingly, it shows a mixture of styles and add-ons. In true Crusader fashion, ancient masonry was recycled by the Crusaders; the colonnades built into the outer walls are still in evidence.

PAUL DOYLE

Left: Ruins of Sidon's Sea Castle, a 12th-century offshore fort

The Crusaders also left behind churches at their strategic coastal locations, such as St John's in Tyre. Beirut Cathedral (now a mosque) has an impressive barrel vault and curved apses. The Church of St John the Baptist in Byblos (still in use by the Maronites) was built in Romanesque style around 1116.

Ottoman to Colonial Rule (AD 1300 to French Mandate)

After several attempts, the Crusaders' power finally succumbed to the Mamluks who took control of most of the region by the late 13th century. The remnants of the Byzantine Empire were later united and under Süleyman the Magnificent, the Ottoman Empire reached its golden age. It was during these years that the most impressive Islamic architecture was constructed, as the waves of Islamic conquest that had tried to grasp the region for centuries finally took hold. Just as temples were converted to churches by the Byzantines, so churches were converted to mosques by the Muslims – the 13th-century Great Mosque in Sidon was originally a church built by the Hospitallers of St John.

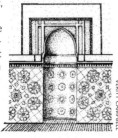

A mosque, which is symmetrical and usually square or rectangular, is generally built around an open courtyard with one or more *iwan* (covered halls) leading from it. A mosque must also have a mihrab (a vaulted niche in a wall), which indicates the direction of prayer. Mihrabs can be simple or elaborate. On the right side of the mihrab is the minbar – a pulpit usually raised above a staircase. Most mosques also have a *kursi*, a wooden stand for holding the Quran. The most visible, although not obligatory, element of a mosque is the minaret or tower from which the call to prayer is made. A minaret can be plain or ornate and usually distinguishes one mosque from another and mosques from other buildings in an Islamic town.

The Muslims also left a legacy of khans and caravanserais and other evidence of trade and commerce. Examples of khans, a cross between a market, an inn and a stable (usually two storeyed), can be found in the Old City in Tripoli and in Sidon. Earmarked for possible reconstruction is the khan that once stood in the souqs of Beirut, until it was destroyed during the war.

The Beiteddine Palace is a great example of early 19th-century Lebanese architecture. Conceived by Italian architects, it incorporates traditional Arab and Italian baroque motifs. All the buildings have arcades along their facades. The gate opens onto a vast 60m-long courtyard, walled on three sides only and a double staircase leads to an inner courtyard

Top: A minbar, the pulpit from which the sermon is delivered in a mosque.

Bottom: A mihrab, a niche in the wall of a mosque that indicates the direction of Mecca.

VERITY CAMPBELL

with a central fountain. The private *hammams* (bathing rooms) are intricately ornamented, and the reception rooms and inner court are decorated with rich wall panels, painted ceilings and mosaics.

In Beirut are the remnants of Ottoman rule (such as the Grand Seraglio, built in 1853 as the barracks for the Turkish army) and the imprint of the French Mandate. The French swept clear a swathe of the medieval town and rearranged the streets in a star shape, placing the parliament building at its centre. The streets themselves were sometimes modelled on those in Paris; Maarad St, for example, was modelled on Rue de Rivoli.

Brett Moore & Christine Niven

BETHUNE CARMICHAEL

Left: Tripoli's Hammam al-Jadide was built in 1740 by Asaad Pasha al Azem, governor of Damascus.

Top: Tyre's partially restored Corinthian colonnade

Middle: The design of the tetrapylon at Aanjar reflects the Roman influence which shaped the Middle East's only surviving Umayyad town.

Bottom: Set against the backdrop of the Anti-Lebanon Range, a Corinthian colonnade at Aanjar offers a glimpse of a bygone era.

BETHUNE CARMICHAEL

BETHUNE CARMICHAEL

BETHUNE CARMICHAEL

PAUL DOYLE

Top: A huge, triple-bay triumphal arch stands at the entrance to the Roman town in Tyre.

Middle: Intricate stone detail at Baalbek (left) and Ehden (right)

Bottom: Phoenician ramparts have been uncovered at Byblos on both sides of the Crusader castle entrance

[Continued from page 36]

As with the rest of the country, the art scene has re-established itself with vigour since the end of the war and there is a thriving artistic community in Beirut. Although some critics maintain that the enthusiasm of the artists is not always warranted, many Lebanese have exhibited internationally.

Apart from Khalil Gibran, famous 20th-century artists include the painters Hassan Jouni, Moustafa Farroukh and Mohammed Rawas. Some of the better-known contemporary painters include Marwan Rechmawi, Bassam Kahwaji, Amin al-Basha, Helen Khal and Etel Adnan (who, like Gibran, is also a writer – see Literature earlier).

Sculpture

Many of the galleries in Beirut exhibit sculpture as well as painting. One of the current stars is Salwa Raodash Shkheir.

A permanent display of sculpture can be seen at the house of the Basbous brothers in Rachana village, to the north of Beirut. The brothers are all established sculptors and you can informally visit their workshops and galleries there. Their larger works line the streets nearby and attract quite a few visitors, especially at the weekend. (See Rachana in the Mt Lebanon chapter for details.)

Beirut's most famous sculpture is the bronze monument at the Place des Martyrs. It suffered a lot of damage during the fighting, and although it was initially decided to leave the statue as a reminder of the destructiveness of the war, it is now being restored and will be hidden from public view until the underground parking lot upon which it will sit is completed.

Cinema

The civil war brought Lebanon's cinema industry to a virtual halt. Most film makers were forced to work outside the country and their work was seldom shown in Lebanon. Some of the well-known film-makers who continued working throughout the war include Maroun Baghdadi (who won an award at the Cannes Film Festival), Roger Assaf, Samir Nasri and Mohammed Sweid.

Since then, Lebanon has begun to produce some notable postwar films, many of which have been shown at international festivals. One of the stars of the Lebanese film community is Jocelyn Saab, who lives in Paris. During the war she made 15 documentaries in Lebanon. They were backed with European finance and only seen in the West or Japan. Her feature-length film, *Once Upon a Time In Beirut*, uses a montage of footage from prewar Beirut to further the plot. The footage dates from 1914 to 1975 and comes from over 300 different films.

In 1998, *West Beirut* won critical acclaim both inside and outside Lebanon. Directed by Ziad Duweyri, a cameraman for American director Quentin (*Reservoir Dogs*) Tarantino, the film tells the story of a teenager living in West Beirut during the first year of the war. Poignant yet humorous, it struck a chord with audiences around the world.

Also in 1998, Mai Masri made a highly acclaimed documentary *Children of Shatila* which looks at the history of the notorious camp through the eyes of children. The film was nominated for the Amnesty International Award.

War was also the theme of Ghassan Shalhab's feature *Beyrouth Fantome*, which tells the story of a former militiaman who returns to the city in the late 1980s after a 10-year absence.

Autour de la Maison Rose, a Lebanese/French/Canadian co-production directed by Joana Hadjithomas and Khalil Joreige is another recommended recent production.

Lebanon currently has four film schools and six TV stations, but the film industry has yet to recover from the war. Most young film-makers complain that because there is no state funding it is impossible to get films made. Still, Beirut is the production centre for advertising and films from all over the Arab world, with high production values and plenty of talent – all signs of a hopeful future. Two annual film festivals, the Beirut Film Festival and Docudays, a documentary festival, are also helping put the country's film industry back on the international scene.

Theatre

With only a limited number of venues and a virtual absence of funding, young theatre artists find it difficult to get a start in Beirut (where most theatres are based). Nevertheless, a small corps of young performers and writers is emerging. Prominent Lebanese playwrights, who include Roger Assaf, Jalal Khoury and Issam Mahfouz, are trying to encourage younger artists, and a revitalised Lebanese theatre is gradually emerging.

The Beirut Theatre in Ain al-Mraisse puts on high quality performances, often experimental works by young actors and playwrights. It also hosts foreign productions and is a likely place to find high-quality English- or French-language theatre.

Al-Medina Theatre and the Piccadilly Theatre are two other performance venues based in West Beirut, both of which show plays primarily in Arabic. In Achrafiye, Theatre Monot tends to show French-language productions. The Casino du Liban is another venue, although this tends more towards spectacles rather than plays. The Caracalla dance troupe (whose performances often veer into theatre) often perform here.

The AUB campus has a theatre, which sometimes performs plays in English, although the quality of the productions can vary wildly.

Other kinds of live entertainment abound. There has been a revival of the nightclub cabaret scene in a big way. It is probably flattering to include these shows under this heading, but if scantily clad dancing girls and variety acts are your sort of thing, then there is no shortage of options.

SOCIETY & CONDUCT
Traditional Culture

The Lebanese, in common with the rest of the Middle East, place a great importance on family life. In villages and small towns you often come across extended family networks where everyone seems to be related to everyone else. Most family occasions, such as weddings, funerals and christenings, are often large celebrations involving the whole community. Behind this jovial exterior is the reality that, in a place where

social programs are virtually nonexistent, the family is also an employer, an insurance policy, a day-care centre and an obligation.

In most societies, it is in attitudes towards women and the family that tradition comes to the fore, and Lebanon is no different. Despite the outwardly liberal attitudes, women are supposed to be virgins when they get married, as much for the honour of the family as their own reputation. As in most other Arab countries, women cannot pass Lebanese nationality on to their children, so if a woman is married to a non-Lebanese her children do not automatically become Lebanese, even if they are born and brought up in Lebanon. This is a huge problem in cases of divorce, or when a foreign spouse dies, or if a Lebanese woman marries a Palestinian.

Marriage is another area where tradition betrays what appears to be a free and modern reality. In spite of all the problems that religion and sectarianism have caused, it is still not possible to get a civil marriage in Lebanon. Seventeen sects are recognised by the state and the religious leaders of each sect have absolute authority on matters of marriage, divorce and inheritance. If a couple is not religious or are from different religious backgrounds, they have to have a civil ceremony abroad. Even though the Lebanese government doesn't recognise the marriage itself, the Lebanese courts will handle divorce and inheritance in the law of the country where the marriage took place. As many as 22% of Lebanese marriages involve civil ceremonies performed abroad. The location of choice is nearby Cyprus. An attempt to change the law and allow civil marriage as an option saw a rare coming together of clerics from all sects, who united together in their opposition to what they called a 'secular virus' that was 'equal to adultery'.

Dos & Don'ts

The Lebanese are extremely liberal in matters of dress, especially in Beirut, where you often see women wearing the latest Western fashions, including miniskirts. In the more conservative Muslim areas, it is more a matter of courtesy than necessity to cover up, but by doing so, you will avoid any unwelcome stares and unpleasantness. This applies to men as well as women. When visiting a mosque, it is necessary for women to wear a headscarf – some mosques even provide you with a hooded cloak.

Given the complex loyalties and political affiliations of the various religious groups, which culminated in the civil war, it would be unwise to get into any heavy political debates about the merits, or otherwise, of the various 'sides'. Although people from all the communities are very friendly towards foreigners, there is still a lot of resentment and prejudice lurking beneath the surface.

RELIGION

About 60% of Lebanon's population is Muslim and 40% Christian. The largest Muslim group is the Shiite (Shia) sect, followed by the Sunni and the Druze. The largest Christian group is the Maronite sect, followed by the Greek Orthodox, the Greek Catholic, the Syrian Catholic, the Chaldean Catholic, Protestant and the Orthodox churches.

Islam

Islam was founded in the early 7th century AD by the Prophet Mohammed, who was born around AD 570 in Mecca. The basis of Islam is a series of divine revelations in which the voice of the archangel Gabriel revealed the word of God to Mohammed. His first revelation happened quite late in his life, at the age of 40. These revelations continued throughout his life and were originally committed to memory and then written down. This text forms the Quran (the name meaning literally 'recitation'), which also came to establish the form of written Arabic for centuries. Great care is taken not to change one single dot of the holy Quran – the speech of God – and foreign translations are never described as Qurans, only interpretations.

Mohammed's teachings were not an immediate success. He started preaching in 613, three years after the first revelation, but could only attract a few dozen followers. Having attacked the ways of Meccan life – especially the worship of idols – he also made many enemies. In 622 he and his followers retreated to Medina, an oasis town some 360km from Mecca. It is this Hejira, or migration, which marks the beginning of the Muslim calendar.

In Medina, Mohammed quickly became a successful religious, political and military leader. After several short clashes with the Meccans, he finally gathered 10,000 troops and conquered his home town, demolishing the idols worshipped by the population and establishing the worship of the one God.

Mohammed died in 632, but the new religion continued its rapid spread, reaching all of Arabia by 634, Egypt, Palestine, Syria, Lebanon and what is now Iraq and western Iran by 642, and most of Iran and Afghanistan by 656. This remarkable wave of conquests was achieved by Mohammed's successors, the caliphs (or Companions of Mohammed) of which there were four. By the end of the 7th century, the Muslims had reached across North Africa to the Atlantic, and having consolidated their power, invaded Spain in 710.

Sunnis & Shiites Not long after the death of Mohammed, Islam suffered a major schism that divided the faith into two main sects: the Sunnis and the Shiites. The split arose over disputes about who should succeed Mohammed, who had died without an heir. The main contenders were Abu Bakr, who was father of Mohammed's second wife Ayesha and the Prophet's closest companion, and Ali, who was Mohammed's cousin and husband to his daughter Fatima. They both had their supporters, but Abu Bakr was declared the first caliph, an Arabic word meaning 'successor' or 'lieutenant'.

Ali finally became the fourth caliph following the murder of Mohammed's third successor, Uthman. He in turn was assassinated in 661 after failing to bend to the military governor of Syria, Mu'awiyah. A relative of Uthman, Mu'awiyah had revolted against Ali over the latter's alleged involvement in Uthman's killing and set himself up as caliph.

Ali's supporters continued to hold fast to their belief in the legitimacy of his line and became known as the *shi'a* (Shiites) or 'partisans of Ali'. They believe in 12 imams (spiritual leaders), the last of whom will one day appear to create an empire of the true faith.

The Sunnis are followers of the succession from the caliph.

The Faith A great number of people in the conquered countries converted to Islam. This is simply achieved by a profession of faith in front of two witnesses (the shahada). This is the first of the Five Pillars of Islam, the five tenets which guide Muslims in their daily life:

Shahada (The Profession of Faith) 'There is no God but Allah and Mohammed is his prophet'. *'La il-laha illa Allah Mohammed rasul Allah.'* This is the fundamental tenet of Islam and is often quoted at events such as births and deaths. The first part is used as an exclamation good for any time of life or situation.

Salat (The Call to Prayer) This is the obligation to pray in the direction of Mecca five times a day, when the muezzins call the faithful to prayer from the minarets. Prayers can be performed anywhere if a mosque is not available and Muslims often travel with a prayer mat and pray at the side of the road or anywhere else for that matter. The midday prayers on Friday are the most important of the week and are roughly equivalent to attending Sunday Mass for Catholics.

Zakat (The Giving of Alms to the Poor) This was a fundamental part of the social teaching of Islam. It has become formalised in some states into a tax, which is used to help the poor. In other countries it is a personal obligation to give and is a spiritual duty rather than the Christian idea of charity.

Sawm (Fasting) Ramadan, the ninth month of the Islamic calendar, commemorates the month when the Quran was revealed to Mohammed. In a demonstration of Muslims' renewal of faith, they are asked to abstain from sex and from letting *anything* pass their lips from dawn to dusk for an entire month.

Haj (Pilgrimage) The pilgrimage to Mecca is the ultimate profession of faith for the devout Muslim. Ideally, the pilgrim should go to Mecca during the last month of the year, Zuul-Hijja, to join with Muslims from all over the world in the pilgrimage and subsequent feast. On the pilgrimage the pilgrim wears a white seamless robe and walks around the Kaaba, the black stone in the centre of the Grand Mosque, seven times. The returned pilgrim can be addressed as *haji*.

To Muslims, Allah is the same God as the Christian and Jew worship. Adam, Abraham, Noah, Moses and Jesus are all recognised as prophets. Jesus is not recognised as the son of God. According to Islam, all these prophets partly received the word of God, but only Mohammed received the complete revelations.

Islamic Holidays The principal Islamic holidays are tied to the lunar Hejira calendar. The word 'Hejira' refers to the flight of the prophet Mohammed from Mecca to Medina in AD 622, which marks the first year of the calendar (year 1 AH). The calendar is about 11 days shorter than the Gregorian (Western) calendar, meaning that Islamic holidays fall 11 days earlier each year. See also the boxed text 'Islamic Holidays' in the Facts for the Visitor chapter.

Ras as-Sana This means New Year's Day, and is celebrated on the first day of the Hejira calendar year, 1 Moharram.

Ashura This is the day of public mourning observed by the Shiites on 10 Moharram. It commemorates the assassination of Hussein ibn Ali, grandson of the prophet Mohammed and pretender to the caliphate, which led to the permanent schism between Sunnis and Shiites.

Moulid an-Nabi This is a lesser feast celebrating the birth of the prophet Mohammed on 12 Rabi' al-Awal. For a long time this was not celebrated at all in the Arab world.

Ramadan & Eid al-Fitr Most Muslims take part in the fasting that characterises the holy month of Ramadan. It is a time when the faithful are called upon as a community to renew their relationship with God. Ramadan was the month in which the Quran was first revealed. From dawn until dusk Muslims are expected to abstain from eating, drinking, smoking and sex. Those who are engaged in heavy physical work, travellers or nursing mothers are considered exempt, although they are expected to make up the fast at a later time. At sunset there is the *iftar*, or breaking of the fast. It is also a time for prayers. Both things often happen in the local mosque; praying followed by an animated picnic. Non-Muslims are not expected to observe the fast, but it is good manners not to eat and smoke in public. In any case, most restaurants and cafes would be closed during the day.

The end of Ramadan is marked with Eid al-Fitr, the Festival of Breaking the Fast, which lasts for at least three days and often longer. Generally, everything shuts down during this holiday.

Haj & Eid al-Adha The haj, or pilgrimage to Mecca, is the fifth pillar of Islam and it is the duty of all Muslims to perform at least one haj in their lifetime. The traditional time for the haj is during the month of Zuul-Hijja, the 12th month of the Muslim year.

The high point of the pilgrimage is the visit to the Kaaba, the construction housing the stone of Ibrahim in the centre of the haram, the sacred area into which non-Muslims are forbidden to enter. The pilgrims, dressed only in a plain white robe, circle the Kaaba seven times and kiss the black stone. This is only one of a series of acts of devotion carried out by pilgrims.

The haj culminates in the ritual slaughter of a lamb (in commemoration of Ibrahim's sacrifice) at Mina. This marks the end of the pilgrimage and the beginning of Eid al-Adha, or Feast of Sacrifice. Throughout the Islamic world the act of sacrifice is repeated and the streets of towns and cities seem to run with the blood of slaughtered sheep. It is customary to give part of the sheep to the poor. The holiday runs from 10 to 13 Zuul-Hijja.

The Druze

The Druze are one of the religious curiosities of the Middle East. Originally an offshoot of Islam, they have diversified so much from mainstream Islam that they are often considered to constitute a whole separate religion. The majority of Druze live in Lebanon, but there are also large numbers in Syria and a few in Israel.

Their origins stem from the Fatimid Ismailis, a branch of Shiite Islam. The Druze believe that God incarnated himself in men at various times and that his last, and final, incarnation was Al-Hakim bi Amrillah, the sixth Fatimid caliph who died in AD 1021. Al-Hakim declared himself to be the incarnation of God in Cairo in AD 1016 and by 1017 the idea grew into a movement, primarily due to the zeal of Hasan al-Akhram, an Ismaili missionary who proclaimed his divinity.

After the murder of al-Akhram in 1018, Hamzah ibn Ali ibn Ahmad became the leader and major founder of the new sect. He became vizier (minister) to Al-Hakim and made many converts, especially in Syria. The third founding member of the sect, from which its name derives, is Mohammed ibn Ismail al-Darazi. He was an Ismaili teacher who went to Cairo around 1017. He taught that the divine spirit, embodied in Adam, passed down to Ali and from him through the imams to Al-Hakim. Al-Darazi disappeared – his followers say he withdrew secretly to Syria. In 1021 Al-Hakim also disappeared (possibly assassinated).

The laws laid down by Hamzah are still considered binding by the Druze today. Briefly they are as follows:

1   Veracity in dealing with each other
2   Mutual protection and assistance
3   Renunciation of other religions
4   Belief in the divine incarnation of Al-Hakim
5   Contentment with the works of God
6   Submission to God's will
7   Dissociation from unbelievers

They believe in reincarnation and that there are a fixed number of souls in existence. Druze tenets also include the belief that Al-Hakim and Hamzah will reappear, conquer the world and establish justice.

The Druze gather for prayer meetings on Thursday evening, not in mosques, but in inconspicuous halls outside Druze villages. Outsiders are not permitted to attend and the rites remain highly secretive.

Christianity

Around 40% of the population in Lebanon is Christian. There are many different churches and rites representing the three main branches of Christianity – Eastern Orthodox,

Catholic and Protestant – but the main Christian sect in Lebanon is Maronite, a Roman Catholic church of eastern origin.

Maronite Church The Maronite church traces its origins back to the 4th century AD and to the monk, St Maro (also called St Maron) who chose a monastic life on the banks of Nahr al-Aasi (Orontes River) in Syria. It is said that 800 monks joined his community and began to preach the gospel in the surrounding countryside. After his death, his followers built a church over his tomb, which was destined to become an important sanctuary. Later, a monastery grew around the church. This became a centre from which early missionaries set out to convert the people.

The Byzantine emperor Heraclius visited the monastery in 628 to discuss his new ideas for mending the rifts in Christianity. His new doctrine was that of monothelitism, according to which the will of Jesus Christ, both divine and human, was defined as one and indivisible. The Western orthodoxy later condemned this idea as heretical. But the Syrians of Lebanon remained attached to monothelitism, which grew to be identified with their national and religious aspirations. This led to their isolation from both the orthodox and Jacobite sections of the Lebanese community.

Two major events charted the course of the Maronites. Firstly, the Arab conquest put an end to Christian persecutions of heretical groups. Secondly, serious differences led to the expulsion of the Patriarch of Antioch, and the Maronites elected their own national patriarch at the end of the 8th century who took the title Patriarch of Antioch and the East – a title still held today.

During the Crusades, the Maronites were brought back into contact with the Christian world and the Church of Rome. A gradual process of Romanisation took place, but the church still worshipped in Syriac (a dialect of Aramaic spoken in Syria) and maintained its own identity. Today the Maronite sect is considered a branch of Roman Catholicism.

Eastern Orthodox Church This branch of Christianity is well represented in Lebanon. There are many Greek and Armenian Orthodox Churches as well as a small Syrian Orthodox community.

Greek Orthodox has its liturgy in Arabic and is the mother church of the Jacobites (or Syrian Orthodox), who broke away in the 6th century. Syrian Orthodox uses only Syriac, which is closely related to Aramaic, and was the language of Christ. Armenian Orthodox (also known as the Armenian Apostolic Church) has its liturgy in classical Armenian and is seen by many to be the guardian of the national Armenian identity.

Catholic The Catholic churches come under the jurisdiction of Rome. The largest such group in Lebanon are the Maronites, but many other Catholic rites are represented. There are Greek Catholics (also know as Melchites), who come under the patriarch of Damascus; Syrian Catholics who still worship in Syriac; and Armenian Catholics whose patriarch lives in Beirut. There is also a small community of Catholics who worship in the Chaldean rite or the Latin rite. The Middle East-based patriarchs are often responsible for the worldwide members of their churches.

LANGUAGE

Arabic is the official language of Lebanon. French is widely spoken in the area, but any effort to communicate with the locals in their own language will be well rewarded. No matter how far off the mark your pronunciation or grammar might be, you'll often get the response (usually with a big smile), 'Ah, you speak Arabic very well!'. These days English is also widely spoken in business circles, especially in Beirut. See the Language chapter at the back of the book for the basics in Arabic.

Facts for the Visitor

SUGGESTED ITINERARIES

If you only have time to visit one place in Lebanon, it should be Baalbek, Lebanon's number one archaeological attraction. It is possible to see all of Lebanon's main sites in one week, but two would be better if you don't want to feel rushed.

One Week

A good circuit (in summer) is to head north to Byblos, a must see for its ruins and picturesque port. On the way, don't miss the enormous and surreal-looking Jeita Grotto. Then head on to Tripoli, with its dramatic Crusader castle and fine Islamic monuments in the Old City district. Spend a night and another day exploring. After your second night in Tripoli, head up to the Qadisha Valley to Bcharré (don't miss the famous Cedars) and over the mountains to the Bekaa Valley's Baalbek. Spend a night there seeing the magnificent temples and then make your way back to Beirut, where you can either spend your remaining time in the city, or make it your base for a day trip to the Chouf Mountains to see the picturesque village of Deir al-Qamar and the lavish Beiteddine Palace.

Two Weeks

For a leisurely two-week holiday, you could add a trip from Byblos to the Afqa Grotto, in the beautiful Adonis Valley. After Tripoli, spend a day exploring the Qadisha Valley between Tripoli and Bcharré. From Baalbek you could go to Zahlé, stopping to taste some wine at one of the Bekaa's vineyards and then moving on to have lunch at one of the town's riverside restaurants. On the way back across Mt Lebanon to Beirut, stop at the Umayyad ruins of Aanjar. From Beirut, head down to Sidon and explore its souqs and ruins. From there you can go on to Tyre and its ancient sites. Tyre can be a good base to explore the newly liberated south. From there you can go to the Chouf and spend a day hiking through the cedar reserve. Then back to Beirut to sample the city's vibrant nightlife.

PLANNING

When to Go

Lebanon is a year-round destination depending on what activities you want to pursue. It is becoming increasingly popular as a winter sports destination. There are six ski resorts in the Mt Lebanon range and the ski season extends from November to May. (See the boxed text 'Ski Resorts at a Glance' later in this chapter.) Away from the slopes, winter tends to be cold and often rainy. Although larger hotels have heating, smaller ones may not and can be very uncomfortable.

The most beautiful time of the year to visit Lebanon is spring. During April and May the weather can be warm enough for swimming and the entire country is carpeted with flowers. If your timing is just right, you may be able to live the cliche and catch the end of the ski season while being able to sunbathe on the coast. If you can't make the spring, aim for mid-September through to November, between the intense heat of summer and the cloud and damp of winter.

For real worshippers of the sun, temperatures soar from June to the middle of September. However, if you want to do anything other than sit by a pool or on a beach, it can be uncomfortable. The coast can be extremely humid, the interior is hot and dry.

What Kind of Trip?

Lebanon is ideally suited to an archaeological sightseeing tour. The country is small and easy to get around, and there are several outstanding sites.

For the more adventurous, the rugged mountains offer scope for a range of outdoor activities. Hiking, mountain biking, rafting or skiing are all options. An increasing number of ecolodges and camping resorts are opening and private camping is often possible with permission from local owners.

Maps

Lonely Planet's *Jordan, Syria & Lebanon travel atlas* has detailed coverage of the whole country. For Beirut, the continuing reconstruction means that many maps are not entirely accurate but the best is by GEOprojects, which is available in most Lebanese bookshops. There is also a reasonably up-to-date map published by the Ministry of Tourism and it is free if you go to the tourist information offices.

A good commercial map is published by All Prints of Beirut and is available for about US$3 in most of the bookshops. It is also available from Stanfords travel bookshop in London for UK£6.95. This is the most recent map of the country and there is a good city map of Beirut on the reverse. English and French versions are available.

What to Bring

There is very little that you cannot buy in Beirut so don't laden yourself down with duty-free goods and toiletries – these things are cheaper in Beirut anyway. The only exception is high SPF sunblock, which can be difficult to find and is very expensive.

Clothing depends on the season. Even in May you will need a jacket for the evenings or for trips up to the mountains, but from June onwards you can travel much more lightly. The heat can be quite intense in high summer and good sunglasses and a hat are essential to avoid sunstroke.

If you are visiting in winter, a waterproof coat is a good idea and you might even consider a pair of waterproof boots. You will certainly need a heavy sweater of some kind. The most useful thing you can pack at any time of the year is a sturdy pair of walking boots or, at the very least, a good pair of running shoes; you will almost certainly find yourself walking over some rugged terrain at some point in your trip.

Remember that if you intend to partake of Beirut's famed nightlife you will have to dress the part: Lebanese tend to see foreigners as hopelessly scruffy and doormen at some of the trendier clubs and restaurants are merciless.

Lebanon is riddled with caves, grottoes and dark churches, so a torch (flashlight) will be very useful on any number of occasions, including the occasional power fail-

ures. If you are sleeping in Beirut, a pair of earplugs will help cut down the constant noise from traffic and construction. Beirut's ongoing rebuilding has also created a severe dust problem. If you are sensitive to dust, bring a good eye-drop solution with you and a pair of sunglasses. For medical items, see the Health section later in this chapter.

RESPONSIBLE TOURISM

It may seem perverse to talk about responsible tourism in a country where most of the damage to the environment has been caused by war and anarchic development. Even more so when many Lebanese seem oblivious to the effect of the paper and plastic bags that they throw from their car windows as they drive through some of the country's spectacular landscapes. But the fragility of the country's environment makes it all the more important that you do your part. Many areas of the country are still relatively pristine and a bit of common sense will minimise the impact of your visit. Do not leave any garbage behind. Take care with matches and cigarettes, especially in summer and autumn – Lebanon's forests have already been denuded and a careless match could burn the fragile seedlings that have sprouted in recent years. Stick to trails wherever you find them and, in the words of the folks at the Chouf Cedar Reserve, 'Take only memories, leave only footprints'.

TOURIST OFFICES
Local Tourist Offices

The main tourist information office (☎ 01-343 073, fax 340 945, 343 279), 550 Rue Banque du Liban (PO Box 11-5344), is in the Hamra district of Beirut, in the same building as the Ministry of Tourism.

There are also tourist offices in Byblos (☎ 09-540 325), near the Crusader castle; in Zahlé's Chamber of Commerce building (☎ 08-802 566, fax 803 595); and in Tripoli (☎ 06-433 590), on the roundabout with the large 'Allah' sign in Arabic. An office is planned for Sidon but at the time of writing was not yet complete.

Tourist Offices Abroad

There are currently only two Lebanese tourist offices outside Lebanon: one in Paris, the other in Cairo. However, you can get brochures and information from the offices of the national airline, Middle East Airlines (MEA), and from Lebanese diplomatic missions. They have a set of regional brochures of the main archaeological sites, many with useful maps of the ruins.

You can contact the tourist offices in the following countries:

Egypt (☎/fax 02-393 7529) 1 Sharia Talaat Harb (Midan Tahrir), Cairo
France (☎ 01 43 59 10 36, 01 43 59 12 13/4, fax 01 43 59 11 99) 124 Rue Faubourg St Honoré, Paris 75008

VISAS & DOCUMENTS
Passport

All nationalities must have a valid passport to enter Lebanon. It pays to be aware if your passport is about to expire or is nearly full. Most foreign embassies in Lebanon can issue replacement passports to their nationals, but it is better to get a new passport before you leave home if you think you are going to need one.

It is also a good idea to keep your passport on you at all times when travelling around Lebanon. There are still a lot of Lebanese and Syrian army checkpoints, although they rarely ask to see your ID these days. However, if you are stopped and you don't have any ID, it will create delays and hassles.

Visas

All nationalities need a visa to enter Lebanon. Nationals of Australia, Austria, Belgium, Canada, Denmark, Finland, France, Germany, Greece, Ireland, Italy, Japan, Luxembourg, Netherlands, Norway, Portugal, South Korea, Spain, Sweden, Switzerland, the UK, the USA and GCC countries can get a tourist or business visa upon arrival at Beirut airport. Visa stamps are sold at a window on the right, just before passport control. This will be validated at the clearly marked desk against the hall's right-hand wall. A stamp for a two-week visa costs $15; for up to three months it costs US$34.

Visas can be obtained in advance at any Lebanese embassy or consulate; you'll need two passport-size photographs and usually a letter of recommendation from your employer to say that you are returning to your job. They are valid for three months and cost about US$20 for a single-entry visa and US$40 for a multiple-entry visa (useful if you're planning to visit Syria from Lebanon and return to Beirut). They are usually issued the next day but can sometimes take longer.

When planning your trip, keep in mind Lebanese visas are not available in Damascus; however, visas are now available at all points of entry in Lebanon, so if you come from Syria it is now possible to get a visa at the border. Note that you cannot get a visa to enter Syria from Lebanon. Only passport holders from countries that have no Syrian consulate may obtain visas at the Syrian border, so if you want to travel overland, make sure you have a valid Syrian visa before you go to Lebanon.

If you have an Israeli stamp in your passport, or have stamps from Egyptian or Jordanian crossing points, you will be refused entry into Lebanon.

Re-Entry Visas If you want your visa in advance, re-entry visas are available at the *maktab amn al-aam* or general secur-ity office, a block to the west of the Cola taxi and bus stand in Beirut. The office is on the 2nd floor and is open from 8 am to 1 pm daily, except Sunday. The staff speak English. If you know in advance that you are going to need a re-entry visa, it is a lot less hassle to ask for a multiple-entry visa in your country of origin.

Visa Extensions Visas can be extended for a further three months at no charge at the maktab amn al-aam. A second extension of three months is possible and costs about US$20. Allow a day or two for processing.

Travel Insurance

A travel insurance policy to cover theft, loss and medical problems is a good idea. Some policies offer lower and higher medical expense options; the higher ones are chiefly for countries such as the USA which have extremely high medical costs. There is a wide variety of policies available, so check the small print and work out what you need.

Some policies specifically exclude 'dangerous activities', which can include scuba diving, motorcycling, even trekking. A locally acquired motorcycle licence is not valid under some policies.

You may prefer a policy which pays doctors or hospitals directly rather than you having to pay on the spot and claim later. If you have to claim later, make sure you keep all documentation. Some policies ask you to call back (reverse charges) to a centre in your home country where an immediate assessment of your problem is made.

Check that the policy covers ambulances or an emergency flight home. It's also a good idea to make a copy of your policy, in case the original is lost.

Driving Licence & Permits

If you intend to drive in Lebanon, you should obtain an International Driving Permit (IDP) from your local automobile association before you leave home – you'll need a passport photo and a valid licence. Third-party insurance is not mandatory, but strongly recommended for your own protection. For more information on driving in Lebanon, see the Getting Around chapter.

Hostel Cards

Although there are as yet no youth hostels in Lebanon, Campus Travel on Rue Makhoul, near the American University of Beirut, represents the International Youth Hostel Association in Lebanon. If hostels do open in Lebanon, they may be able to issue cards. Contact them by phone at ☎ 01-744 588.

Student & Youth Cards

ISIC cards can be obtained at Campus Travel but they are of little use in Lebanon. Student discounts at archaeological sites and museums are only available to Lebanese students or children under 12.

Copies

All important documents (eg, passport data page and visa page, credit cards, travel insurance policy, air/bus/train tickets, driving licence etc) should be photocopied before you leave home. Leave one copy with someone at home and keep another with you, separate from the originals.

It is also a very good idea to store details of your travel documents in Lonely Planet's free online Travel Vault in case you misplace the photocopies. Your password-protected Travel Vault is accessible online anywhere in the world. Create it at www.ekno.lonely planet.com

EMBASSIES & CONSULATES

It's important to realise what your own embassy – the embassy of the country of which you are a citizen – can and can't do to help you if you get into trouble. Generally speaking, it won't be much help in emergencies if the trouble you're in is remotely your own fault. Remember that you are bound by the laws of the country you are in. Your embassy will not be sympathetic if you end up in jail after committing a crime locally, even if such actions are legal in your own country.

In genuine emergencies you might get some assistance, but only if other channels have been exhausted. For example, if you need to get home urgently, a free ticket home is unlikely – the embassy would expect you to have insurance. If you have all your money and documents stolen, it might assist with getting a new passport, but a loan for onward travel is out of the question.

Some embassies used to keep letters for travellers or have a small reading room with home newspapers, but these days the mail holding service has usually been stopped and even newspapers tend to be out of date.

Lebanese Embassies & Consulates

Visas are available at all Lebanese foreign missions, including the following:

Australia
  Embassy: (☎ 02-6295 7378, fax 6239 7024)
  27 Endeavour St, Red Hill, ACT 2603
  Consulate: (☎ 02-9361 5449, fax 9360 7657)
  Level 5, 70 William St, Sydney, NSW 2000
  Issues visas to NSW residents only.

Consulate: (☎ 03-9529 4588) 117 Wellington St, Windsor, Vic 3181. Issues visas to Victorian residents only.

Canada
Embassy: (☎ 613-236 5825, fax 232 1609) 640 Lyon St, KIS 3Z5 Ottawa, Ontario
Consulate: (☎ 514-276 2638, fax 276 0090) 40 Chemin Côte Ste Catherine, H2V-2A2-PQ, Montreal 153

Egypt
Embassy: (☎ 02-738 2823/5, fax 738 2818) 22 Mansour Mohamed St, Zamalek, Cairo
Consulate: (☎ 03-484 6589) 64 Rue de la Liberté, Alexandria

France
Embassy: (☎ 01 40 67 75 75, fax 01 40 67 16 42) 3 Villa Copernic, Paris 75016
Consulate: (☎ 04 91 71 50 60, fax 04 91 77 26 75) 424 Rue Paradis, Marseille 13008

Germany
Embassy: (☎ 4930-474 9860, fax 474 9866) Berlinerstrasse 126–127, 13187 Berlin

Italy
Embassy: (☎ 06-844 05 21, fax 841 17 94) Via Giacomo Carissimi 38, Rome 00198
Consulate: (☎ 02-86 45 45 40, fax 72 00 04 68) 26 Via Larga, Milan 20122

Jordan
Embassy: (☎ 592 9111/4, fax 592 2333) Sharia Mohammed Ali Bdeir, Abdoun, Amman

Netherlands
Embassy: (☎ 070-365 8906, fax 362 0779) 2 Frederick St, The Hague 2514

Spain
Embassy: (☎ 01-345 1370, fax 345 5631) 178 Paseo de la Castellana, 28046 Madrid

Turkey
Embassy: (☎ 312-446 7487, fax 446 1033) 44 Kizculesi Sokak, Çankaya, Ankara
Consulate: (☎ 212-236 1365, fax 227 3373) Tesvikiye Caddesi, Sary Apt 134/1, 80200 Tesvikiye, Istanbul

UK
Embassy: (☎ 020-7229 7265/6, fax 7243 1699) 21 Palace Gardens Mews, London W8 4RA
Consular Section: (☎ 020-7727 6696) 15 Palace Gdns Mews

USA
Embassy: (☎ 202-939 6300, fax 939 6324) 2560 28th St NW, Washington DC 20008
Consulate: (☎ 213-467 1253, fax 467 2935) Suite 510, 7060 Hollywood Blvd, Los Angeles, CA 90028
Consulate: (☎ 212-744 7905/6, fax 794 1510) 9 East 76th St, NYC, NY 10021

Embassies & Consulates in Lebanon

Embassies and consulates in Lebanon include the following:

Australia (☎ 01-374 701, fax 374 709) Farra Bldg, Rue Bliss, Ras Beirut
Canada (☎ 04-521 163/4/5) Coolrite Bldg, Jal al-Dib
Egypt (☎ 01-862 932, 867 917) Rue Thomas Edison, Ramlet al-Bayda
France (☎ 01-616 730/5) Mar Takla, Hazmieh
Germany (☎ 04-914 444) Mataileb, Rabieh
Italy (☎ 01-340 225/6/7) Cosmides Bldg, Rue Makdissi, Hamra
Jordan (☎ 05-922 500/1) Rue Elias Helou, Baabda
Netherlands (☎ 01-204 663) Achrafiye
Spain (☎ 05-464 120/1, fax 352 448) Palace Chehab, Hadath
Turkey (☎ 04-520 929) Tobi Bldg, Rue 3, Zone II, Rabieh
UK (☎ 04-417 007, 405 070, 403 640) Villa Tohmeh, Rue no 8, Rabieh
USA (☎ 04-417 774, 403 300, fax 407 112) Antelias

CUSTOMS

There is no problem bringing most items into Lebanon, such as cameras, videos or computers, and there is no censorship of books and magazines. Duty-free allowances are 400 cigarettes and one bottle of spirits or 200 cigarettes and two bottles of spirits.

MONEY
Currency

The currency in Lebanon is the Lebanese lira (LL), known locally as the Lebanese pound. The currency suffered from galloping inflation during the war and low denomination coins (piastres) are now virtually worthless. There are LL250 and LL500 coins still in circulation.

The notes are of the following denominations: 50, 100, 250, 500, 1000, 5000, 10,000, 20,000, 50,000 and 100,000, but you will rarely need anything smaller than 1000. US dollars are accepted virtually everywhere and the two are virtually interchangeable (for this reason both US$ and LL prices are given in this book). The standard rate of exchange is US$1 = LL1500. Many shops and restaurants display prices only in US dollars, however they will give you your change in either currency.

Exchange Rates

Exchange rates are subject to frequent change, although the fluctuations are less extreme than they used to be. At the time of writing, the exchange rates were:

country	unit		lira
Australia	A$1	=	LL880
Canada	C$1	=	LL1019
euro	€1	=	LL1373
France	10FF	=	LL2093
Germany	DM1	=	LL702
Japan	¥100	=	LL1382
Jordan	JD1	=	LL2134
Syria	S£10	=	LL340
Turkey	TL100,000	=	LL23
UK	UK£1	=	LL2279
USA	US$1	=	LL1513

Exchanging Money

Cash If you're travelling with US dollars you only need to exchange a small amount into lira for tipping, service taxis and the like. Avoid bringing US$100 bills – because there are so many forgeries, people are unwilling to take them. Stick to US$50 and US$20 and also US$1 bills for tipping and small items. Also keep in mind that worn or torn US notes may not be accepted.

Most banks will exchange cash if it is in British pounds or US dollars. There are many banks in the capital and all but the smallest village has at least one bank.

If you are changing other currencies, you may need to go to one of the private exchange shops. There are many of these on and around Rue Hamra in Beirut, and all the smaller towns have at least one exchange shop. You may find it a problem changing money in some of the smaller places.

Before using moneychangers try to find out what the current exchange rates are. Either ask at a bank or check the previous day's closing exchange rates in the local newspapers. The rate you'll be offered will never be the same as the published rate, as it includes the moneychanger's commission, but you can always bargain with them to

bring the rate closer to it. If you're not happy with the rate offered by one moneychanger, try another one. The commission varies from 3% to 5% for changing currency.

There is no black market in Lebanon.

Travellers Cheques Travellers cheques may be a smart way to change money, but they can be time-consuming, depending on the bank or currency exchange shop you find yourself in. Fees are US$1 per US$50, US$2 per US$100 and US$3 per US$1000 and so on.

ATMs There are ATMs throughout the country and all dispense cash in either US dollars or Lebanese pounds. If you have a card, they are the way to go. Keep some extra cash with you as insurance, though; periodic power cuts can mean that the ATM could be down when you need it.

Credit Cards Credit cards are accepted by almost all hotels with two or more stars, mid-range restaurants and many shops. They will not be accepted by budget hotels and restaurants. Cash advances are easily available in most banks, although transactions are far quicker at ATMs.

International Transfers There are Western Union offices in almost all major towns in Lebanon and they can arrange international transfers. For more information, contact them at their Beirut headquarters (☎ 01-391 000).

Security

Although Lebanon is certainly not a major crime area, it still pays to be circumspect when carrying money. If you are carrying a lot of cash around, it is always a good idea to use a moneybelt or one of those inside-the-shirt fabric wallets that hang around your neck. Always buy these in a flesh colour so they don't show through your clothing. As for travellers cheques, always keep your receipt for these in a separate part of your luggage.

It also pays to keep an emergency stash of money hidden away – say US$100 hidden under the innersole of your shoe or in a plastic film container in your toiletries bag – to help you out of dire straits.

Costs

Lebanon is quite expensive by Mediterranean and Middle East standards. If you are on a seriously low budget, you may find your choices limited. It is possible, though, with careful spending, to live on US$15 to US$25 per day. To spend less than that is possible, but difficult.

The main item of expense is accommodation. There are very few hotels in the budget range and most are pretty basic. Most of these will set you back from US$10 to US$20 per night (hardly cheap for those used to Middle Eastern prices) but there are some for as little as LL5000 per night. Many of these bargains are basic places that house Syrian workers – single women should steer clear. Keep in mind also that many hotels do not make a reduction for singles, so it is much cheaper if you are travelling with a friend. One thing to look out for is the service charge, which is often 16%, and can bump up your hotel bill. It is best to ask beforehand whether 'service' is included.

Cheap food is not so much of a problem. There are sandwich and snack bars all over Lebanon. They all serve the same repertoire of fillings and are usually substantial and very tasty. A sandwich will cost from LL750 to LL2000 and some places serve Lebanese 'pizzas' for about LL1500. Sit-down restaurants are more expensive, but the cheaper variety often serve a simple lunch or dinner for around US$5 to US$10. Some restaurants offer a fixed-price menu for lunch or dinner which can be a good deal.

Organised sightseeing costs depend on the luxury of the transport and whether lunch or dinner is included. The price also depends on how many people book at once; the more, the cheaper. On average a one-day coach tour with lunch should cost US$45, but there are cheaper options. Most monuments cost about LL6,000 to enter, but many have no charge at all.

The good news is that transport around Beirut and to other parts of the country is cheap, especially if you use buses. Fares within the centre of Beirut are only LL500 and to the regions from LL1000 to LL3000 depending on the distance. Service taxis ply the routes where buses do not run and are also a bargain, ranging from LL1000 to LL10,000 depending on the distance travelled. If you want to visit more remote regions, cars can be rented for as little as US$20 per day.

Tipping & Bargaining

Tipping is considered normal for service in Lebanon, even though most restaurants add a service charge to the bill (often 16%). Even so it is expected that you leave a tip of 5% to 10% on top of that. Wages for workers are very low and, in real terms, getting lower all the time with the devaluation of the lira. Waiters therefore rely on tips to supplement their incomes.

It is often possible to negotiate a better price at hotels and, occasionally, in restaurants and shops. Tourism is still shaky and hotels are often anxious to fill their rooms, especially in the low season. Prices can drop as much as 40% from the rack rate.

Prices for taxis are also negotiable. The service routes have set fares, but the moment you try to hire a private taxi, the price quoted (often in dollars) climbs steeply. The solution is to ask the price before getting in the taxi and, if you are not happy, find another taxi.

POST & COMMUNICATIONS

Lebanon's postal service has recently been privatised and is set to improve dramatically over the coming years. For the moment, though, few Lebanese use it unless they have no other choice. There are no public post boxes in Lebanon, and you have to go to a post office to buy stamps or send anything. It is recommended that you send your mail from Beirut to avoid delays. Some people claim that the post office at the American University of Beirut is the most reliable for sending mail, if you can get access.

Postal Rates

It's the same price to send a postcard or letter. To Europe it costs LL1250 and to Australia and the USA it's LL1500. Parcels to Europe and the USA cost LL30,000 for 1kg and LL65,000 for 5kg. To Australia it costs LL35,000 for 1kg and LL100,000 for 5kg.

Letters can take anything from five to 21 days to reach Europe, North America or Australia – if they arrive at all. Most Lebanese use courier services for sending parcels. DHL has a Beirut office on Rue Banque du Liban and its counterpart is Federal Express (☎ 01-345 385) which is on Rue Emile Edde.

Receiving Mail

Receiving mail from around the world generally takes several weeks and there are no poste restante facilities. American Express (AmEx) provides a mail-holding service for people using its travellers cheques; letters can be sent to AmEx, Bloc C, Gefinor Centre, Beirut. If you know the hotel in which you'll be staying, the staff will keep your incoming mail for you if you let them know that you are expecting letters.

Telephone

Gone are the postwar days when making a phone call involved trying five or six numbers and crossing one's fingers. Most Lebanese, if they can afford it, use cell phones, and have the dubious distinction of clocking up more minutes per month than almost any other country in the world. Cell phone coverage extends throughout the country, with only one or two remote areas falling outside the network area. Calling to or from a cell phone costs about US$0.06 per minute. Getting a cell phone costs at least US$250 to US$300 but you can rent them through the larger car rental agencies for about US$6 per day, plus a deposit and call charges. (See Rental under Car & Motorcycle in the Getting Around chapter for details of car rental companies.) If you have your own Global System for Mobile (GSM) phone, you can get a chip with a prepaid line of 220 units for about US$60 from any of the hundreds of mobile phone dealers throughout the country. Service lasts for 30 days, although you can receive calls for a further five days. If you want extra call units you can buy cards for US$22, US$33 and US$44.

While the state telephone system works well enough, there are few pay phones.

When you do locate one, local calls cost LL250 or LL500 depending on the length of the call (whereas local calls from a private phone within the same area code cost LL30 for the first minute and then LL20 per subsequent minute). Local phone calls from corner shops and private offices can cost as much as LL1000, LL2000 if you're dialling outside the local dialling area.

International calls are expensive and are usually made through private phone offices, large hotels or *centrales* (government-run phone offices). The latter is the cheapest option but they are often crowded. To make a call you must fill out a slip of paper with the number(s) you require and wait until you are called. You pay at the desk when your calls are complete. The minimum charge for an international call is for three minutes. From the centrale, calls cost LL2100 per minute to the UK, the USA and Europe. Peak time in Lebanon is from 7 am to 10 pm, and tariffs drop by about one-third outside these hours.

Despite the government's objections that it is undercutting their phone system, many Internet cafes offer Net2phone, telephone calls via the Internet, which is a far cheaper way of making international calls.

Lebanon's country code	☎ 961
Cell phone code	☎ 03
Information	☎ 120
Cellular directory inquiries	☎ 01-200 100
Calls to Syria code	☎ 02
(international dialling prefix is unnecessary)	

Fax

Fax machines are quite widely used and most hotels, except for the very smallest, seem to have a fax machine. Many of the private bureaus also have fax machines. You can often get a hotel to send a fax for you even if you are not staying there. They charge commercial rates but they are not usually too exorbitant. The three-minute minimum call applies. From a hotel, faxes are charged at the same rate as phone calls.

Email & Internet Access

There has been an Internet explosion in Lebanon during the past four years. The country now has at least 15 Internet service providers (ISPs) and cybercafes are easily found in most towns. Connections are frustratingly slow. However, rapid expansion in the telecommunications sector means that digital lines will likely be widespread in the near future. Three reputable ISPs are:

Cyberia (☎ 01-744 101) www.cyberia.net.lb
Libancom (☎ 01-877 202) www.libancom.com.lb
Terranet (☎ 01-577 511) www.terr.net.lb

Start-up fees begin at about US$25 and most have monthly fees of anything from US$12.99 to US$30 for unlimited service. Major ISPs, AOL (www.aol.com) and CompuServe (www.compuserve.com) have dial-in nodes in Lebanon; download a list of the numbers before you leave home.

If you plan to carry your notebook or palmtop computer with you, remember that Lebanon's electricity supply is unstable, and power surges pose a real risk to your equipment. Most Lebanese run their appliances off voltage regulators, which are far too cumbersome for travelling. Ensure that your adaptor can handle higher than 220 volts (most laptop adaptors can take up to 240 volts) and don't leave the computer plugged in any longer than necessary.

Also, keep in mind that your PC-card modem may or may not work once you leave your home country – and you won't know for sure until you try. If you're not sure, the safest option is to buy a reputable 'global' modem before you leave home. Lebanon tends to have USA-style phone sockets, so check to see if you need an adaptor. For more information on travelling with a portable computer, see www.teleadapt.com or check out www.warrior.com.

There are Internet cafes in all Lebanese cities and many smaller towns. Most charge between LL3000 and LL5000 per hour. For specific cafes, check the information section in each town. If you have don't have a Web-based email service, remember that you'll need your incoming (POP or IMAP) mail server name, your account name and your password. Your ISP or network supervisor will be able to give you these. It pays to be-

come familiar with the process of doing this before you leave home. A final option is to open a free eKno Web-based email account online at www.ekno.lonelyplanet.com. You can then access your mail from anywhere in the world from any Internet-connected machine running a standard Web browser.

INTERNET RESOURCES

The World Wide Web is a rich resource for travellers. You can research your trip, hunt down bargain air fares, book hotels, check on weather conditions or chat with locals and other travellers about the best places to visit (or avoid!).

Cyberia The home page of the popular cyberia ISP has articles from the *Daily Star*, entertainment listings, up-to-date weather reports and useful links to other Lebanon sites.
www.cyberia.net.lb

Daily Star Excellent source of daily news from Beirut's high-quality English daily.
www.dailystar.com.lb

Home Page This is a Lebanon-based home page including the Lebanon white pages, the republic's national anthem, cultural groups, radio and TV services.
www.geocities.com/vienna/4320

Lebanon Embassy The official home page for the Lebanon Embassy in the USA. It has useful visa and travel news and good links to other Lebanon-related sites.
www.embofleb.org

Lebanon's Ministry of Tourism This is the ministry's official home page. It has facts about the country, history, accommodation and travel information.
www.lebanon-tourism.gov.lb

Lebanon Online This informative site has news, culture, business and a chat room, and also links to other Middle East pages.
www.lebanon-online.com

Lonely Planet This is Lonely Planet's own award-winning site, containing destination updates, recent travellers letters and a useful travellers bulletin board. Here you'll find succinct summaries on travelling to most places on earth, postcards from other travellers and the Thorn Tree bulletin board, where you can ask questions before you go or dispense advice when you get back. You can also find travel news and updates to many of our most popular guidebooks, and the subWWWay section links you to the most useful travel resources elsewhere on the Web.
www.lonelyplanet.com.au

BOOKS

Most books are published in different editions by different publishers in different countries. As a result, a book might be a hardcover rarity in one country while it's readily available in paperback in another. Fortunately, bookshops and libraries search by title or author, so your local bookshop or library is best placed to advise you on the availability of the following recommendations.

The following is a small and by no means exhaustive list for recommended reading.

Lonely Planet

If you're heading to other countries in the region, Lonely Planet also publishes guides to Lebanon's neighbours, *Syria* and *Israel & the Palestinian Territories* as well as *Turkey*, *Iran* and *Egypt*. Travellers contemplating a longer swing through the region should also check out the *Middle East*, with chapters on all Middle Eastern countries, including Lebanon, and *Istanbul to Cairo,* an overland guide with a chapter on Lebanon. Lonely Planet's *Jordan, Syria & Lebanon travel atlas* is a great companion to this guide. There is also an *Egyptian Arabic phrasebook*. For help with those all-important travel photos, check out *Travel Photography: A Guide to Taking Better Pictures* by internationally renowned travel photographer, Richard I'Anson. It's full colour throughout and designed to take on the road.

Guidebooks

Not surprisingly the travel guide market dried up during the war and there are very few up-to-date guides to refer to. Although local guides are starting to be published, most are publicity-style listings.

At Home in Beirut by Charlotte Hamaoui & Sylvia Palamoudian. A newly published practical guide to living in Beirut and covers everything from clearing shipments through customs to wedding etiquette to driving in Lebanon.
Lebanon: An Insider's Guide by Blair Kuntz. A newly published guide with reasonably extensive coverage of the country.
The Middle East This volume is part of a series published back in 1967 by Hachette and still available in some Beirut bookshops. It has an interesting section on Lebanon and is particularly detailed on the ancient sites; ignore the useless practical information.
A Miracle In Stone: Baalbeck by Michel Harriz. A small paperback guide with the stated aim of helping 'the intelligent observer...understand the meaning of the mystical and symbolic aspects of cults and temples where blood sacrifices, wine orgies, and free love were means of experiencing oneness with the gods...' Available near the temple entrance.

Travel

David Roberts R.A. 1796–1864: A Biography by Katherine Sim. An interesting account of the life and travels of this orientalist artist who popularised the image of the decadent Arab throughout 19th century Europe.
Freya Stark in the Levant by Malise Ruthven. Charts the travels of this well-known Middle Eastern explorer with reproductions of many of her black-and-white photographs from the 1930s to the 1950s.
From the Holy Mountain by William Dalrymple. The acclaimed British writer follows in the footsteps of a 6th-century monk in an effort to reveal the state of Christianity in the modern Middle East. The brilliantly written section on Lebanon manages to be both hilarious and disturbing. Highly recommended.
The Hills of Adonis by Colin Thubron. A lucid and insightful account of his travels just before the civil war, weaving ancient religious beliefs and modern politics into a fascinating tale.
The Nun of Lebanon – The Love Affair of Lady Hester Stanhope & Michael Bruce by Ian Bruce (ed). The collected letters of the famous woman from Joun and her lover. Her biography *Lady Hester Stanhope* by Frank Hamel is also worth reading.
Touring Lebanon by Philip Ward. Published in 1971. Other old travel books worth tracking down include: *Baalbek Caravans* by Charis Waddy (this can be found in some Beirut bookshops) and *Smelling the Breezes: A Journey Through High Lebanon* by Ralph & Molly Izzard.

Pre-20th Century History

Arab Historians of the Crusades by Francesco Gabrieli (ed) and *The Crusades Through Arab Eyes* by Amin Maalouf. Both books use Arab chroniclers to give a different perspective on the crusade.
An Arab-Syrian Gentleman and Warrior in the Period of the Crusades: The Memoires of Usamah ibn Munqidh by Philip K Hitti (trans). A

ide the Omari Mosque, Beirut

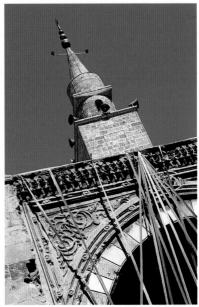

Archway of the Bab es-Saray Mosque, Sidon

ayer flags above a mosque in Sidon

The luxurious *hammam* inside Beiteddine Palace

Throughout Lebanon, from Beirut (top & bottom right) to the Bekaa Valley's Deir al-Qamar (top le
and Beiteddine Palace (bottom left & middle right), you will find wonderful carving and mosaic wo

Syrian nobleman's delightful observations of boorish crusader behaviour in medieval Egypt, Syria and Lebanon.

A History of the Arab Peoples by Albert Hourani. A good place for background of Middle Eastern history, religion and culture.

Lebanon in History by Philip K Hitti. Written by a respected scholar, this is a good historical survey.

The Phoenicians by Donald Harden. A comprehensive and authoritative study of the famed ancients.

Contemporary History & Politics

As one would expect, most contemporary history books examine the civil war and/or its historical roots. Much of this is harrowing reading, but anyone visiting Lebanon should try to read at least one book about the civil war, as understanding the major forces at play in the country during the last two decades will provide a better insight to the people and culture.

Beirut Reborn: The Restoration & Development of the Central District by Angus Gavin. A glossy look at the postwar redevelopment of Beirut's downtown.

Beseiged: A Doctor's Story of Life and Death in Beirut by Dr Chris Giannou. A harrowing account of the three-year siege of the Shatila refugee camp by a Canadian surgeon who saved hundreds of lives in the face of impossible conditions.

A House of Many Mansions – The History of Lebanon Reconsidered by Kamal Salibi. Looks at the root causes of the civil war in the light of a re-examination of Lebanese history. Salibi's *Crossroads to Civil War*, which concentrates on the period from 1958 to 1976 is also most highly recommended.

Lebanon – Death of a Nation by Sandra Mackey. An account of the war and its causes. It also elaborates on the misunderstanding between the Middle East and Western nations.

Lebanon: The Fractured Country by David Gilmour. A well-respected book examining the early stages of the war and the events leading up to its outbreak.

Pity the Nation: Lebanon at War by Robert Fisk. This personal and highly readable account by *The Independent*'s respected Middle East correspondent chronicles the events from 1975 and is one of the best books on the civil war.

Projecting Beirut: Episodes in the Construction and Reconstruction of a Modern City Peter Rowe & Hashim Sarkis (ed). Describes the reconstruction of the city.

Too Many Enemies: The Palestinian Experience in Lebanon by Rosemary Sayigh. This book, by a long-time Beirut resident, is invaluable to understanding the complex position of the Palestinians in Lebanon, both before, during and after the war.

Tribes With Flags: A Journey Curtailed by Charles Glass. Describes the author's kidnapping and subsequent release. See also *An Evil Cradling*, a sensitive and literate account of a Beirut kidnapping by Irish teacher and former captive, Brian Keenan.

Cookbooks

L'Art Culinaire Libanais by George Rayes. The cooking bible for Lebanese women. It is published in Beirut by Librairie Antoine.

A New Book of Middle Eastern Cookery by Claudia Roden. A classic of the region's cooking and includes historical background as well as recipes from Morocco to Iran.

A Taste of Lebanon by Mary Salloum. Another more recent offering that gives a good basic background of Lebanese cuisine.

General

Eternal Beirut by R Stetie. Another big picture book, which does a nice job of covering many facets of the city.

Lebanon by Fluvio Roiter. One of the better coffee-table books about Lebanon. It has exquisite colour plates of prewar Lebanon, its heritage and people, but it is expensive at US$75.

Lebanon: Pictures of Our Heritage A beautiful, three-volume series with a book each on public buildings, religious architecture and old homes.

NEWSPAPERS & MAGAZINES

Imported newspapers and magazines are available from the major bookshops. European papers arrive about one day late and publications from further afield a couple of days late. The most popular and easily obtainable are: the *Independent, The Times, Le Monde, Le Figaro* and the *International Herald Tribune.* Of the international news weeklies, *Time, Newsweek, Economist, Le Point, Paris Match* and *Der Spiegel* are all on sale at most bookstalls in Beirut. It is not easy to find international publications in other Lebanese cities.

Agenda Culturelle (☎ 01-369 242) A French bi-weekly guide to Beirut's art scene. Usually sold by subscription only, it is useful and worth begging off someone.

Beirut Review A quarterly literary publication that is published in English and available at some of the better bookshops in Beirut.

Emerging Lebanon An annual survey of economic and political developments in Lebanon. Published in magazine format, it is well written and informative and contains an enormous amount of information that is useful for non-business oriented types too.

Femme and **Prestige** Both locally published French glossies which comprise a mixture of personality profiles and in-depth travel features with photo spreads.

Lebanon Opportunities A monthly business magazine that covers real estate, finance, business and the economy.

L'Orient-le Jour The *Daily Star*'s French equivalent. It has up-to-date listings for local cinema and theatre performances. There are also the French-language weeklies *Magazine* and *La Revue du Liban.*

Saveur A French-language monthly that specialises in food and travel in Lebanon and throughout the world. If you're a foodie and read French this is worth a look.

The Daily Star Lebanon's high-quality English-language daily newspaper. It is particularly good for features on Lebanon and there are rumours that it is about to be included in the *Herald Tribune* empire.

The Guide An extremely useful glossy monthly with extensive but selective listings of bars, cafes, restaurants, shops, films, theatres and other cultural events.

RADIO & TV

The anarchy of the civil war meant that anyone who had a transmitter could set up a radio or TV station. Militias fought one another through the airwaves just as viciously as on the ground and at one time there were as many as 200 radio stations and 50 TV stations. Now the broadcast media is regulated again and there are six local television stations: Télé-Liban, Future TV, Lebanese Broadcasting Corporation (LBC), Murr Television (MTV), Al-Manar and NBN. Most hotels have satellite TV with the usual staples of international offerings. Program listings for local TV can be found in the *Daily Star* and *L'Orient-le Jour.*

Radio stations have also been regulated but you can still find almost any type of music you want, from Arabic classics to the latest techno, and almost everything in between, with presenters in Arabic, French and English.

You can pick up BBC World Service in English on 1323 kHz or 72 kHz, its Arabic service, broadcasts around the clock on 639 kHz.

VIDEO SYSTEMS

If you want to watch a video, Lebanon uses the PAL system. The various systems in use worldwide (PAL, NTSC and SECAM) are incompatible with each other. Tapes from one system will not play on another without a costly conversion.

PHOTOGRAPHY & VIDEO
Film & Equipment

Unless you want an obscure brand, you won't have any trouble buying film or video tapes in Lebanon; Kodak, Agfa and Fuji are the most widely available brands. Good-quality colour transparency films are available in Beirut and the larger towns, and occasionally in tourist shops at historical sites (but watch the expiry date). Processing is widely available for colour negative films (C41 process) both in Beirut and around the country in fast turnover labs. There are also a few E6 labs which process colour transparencies. The overall quality is quite good. The cost of processing in Lebanon is about LL4000 for negative film and about LL16,000 for transparency film.

The cost of film and video tape is reasonable. A regular 36-exposure print film costs from LL6500 to LL8500 and a slide film is LL15,000 (which sometimes includes processing). Black and white film is harder to find and to process, so it is better to bring your own and have it processed when you return home. A VHS tape costs LL10,000, Super VHS costs LL25,000 and Hi-8 is LL30,000.

Many camera shops have a one-hour or same-day processing and printing service – LL10,000 for a 36-exposure film – and they can be found in the main towns. You also shouldn't have too much trouble finding spare parts for the main makes of camera, such as Nikon, Pentax, Olympus and Canon. Check out Kamera (for Olympus and Canon) and Lord Camera Shop in Rue Hamra, next door to the Horseshoe Restaurant in Beirut. Other towns usually have at least one camera shop. There is no problem getting even unusual batteries for cameras in most places.

Technical Tips
Lebanon is very photogenic with its dramatic landscapes and clear Mediterranean light. Dust can be a problem when taking your camera around Beirut and it is a good idea to keep it wrapped in a plastic bag even inside a camera bag. Take a soft lens brush and some camera wipes with you to prevent grit and dust getting inside the works. A flash gun is useful if you want to photograph the interiors of dark churches and mosques.

The best times to shoot are in the morning until 10 am and the afternoon between 4 pm and sunset. If you can't avoid around noon, use a warm filter and avoid unflattering shadows by shooting people in the shade, perhaps with a white reflector (even a T-shirt will do) bouncing the light back onto their faces.

If you feel in need of further help, *Travel Photography: A Guide to Taking Better Pictures* is written by internationally renowned travel photographer, Richard I'Anson. It's full colour throughout and designed to take on the road.

Restrictions
You should have no problems taking photographs anywhere in Lebanon, with the exception of military areas. If you happen to be near an army checkpoint, go up to the soldiers first and explain to them what you want to photograph. They usually won't object. Do not, however, try and take shots of the soldiers themselves. Nor should you point your camera at buildings occupied by Syrian soldiers or any other military installations unless you've been given express permission.

Airport Security
X-ray machines are generally safe to pass film through, but if you are going on a multiflight trip, ask for film to be hand searched to avoid the accumulative effects of x-ray exposure. If you are worried about your film,

invest in lead-lined film pouches, which protect your film from any harmful rays.

TIME
Lebanon is two hours ahead of GMT/UTC during winter (October to March) and three hours ahead during the summer (April to September) when daylight saving is used.

When it is noon in Lebanon, it is:

city	time
Los Angeles	2 am
New York/Montreal	5 am
London	10 am
Moscow	1 pm
Melbourne/Sydney	7 pm

ELECTRICITY
Lebanon has now standardised its electricity supplies to 220V and mains power has been restored. Two-pin plugs are used. There are still power cuts in Lebanon, but most hotels and large buildings have backup generators. After the Israelis bombed Beirut and Tripoli's power stations in 1999, many private houses and businesses reconnected to neighbourhood generators but that doesn't mean you will have an uninterrupted supply so it is a good idea to have a torch (flashlight) with you.

If you have brought electronic goods, such as small stereos or computers, remember that because of the weak supply, the voltage in Lebanon can be extremely erratic. Most Lebanese run appliances on voltage regulators or some type of surge protector. If you don't want to buy one of these (easily available at hardware shops but cumbersome for travelling with), remember not to leave anything plugged in to the mains unless absolutely necessary.

WEIGHTS & MEASURES
Lebanon uses the metric system. See the conversion tables inside the back cover of this book.

LAUNDRY
Most neighbourhoods in the capital and major towns have dry-cleaners which offer a one- or two-day service. Some also offer

a laundry service, but there are no laundromats. Most hotels have their own laundry service or, if not, they can direct you to the nearest one.

TOILETS

By Middle Eastern standards Lebanese toilets are generally very clean. You will find a mixture of Western-style upright toilets and the squat 'Turkish' variety, although the latter are usually only found at very cheap hotels and restaurants or in public conveniences (which should be avoided except in dire emergency). It's perfectly acceptable for men to urinate outside but women should be circumspect. Lebanon is small enough that you are almost always close enough to a decent hotel or restaurant that will let you use their facilities. Remember to keep paper tissues or toilet paper with you as they're often absent.

HEALTH

Travel health depends on your predeparture preparations, your daily health care while travelling and how you handle any medical problem that does develop. While the potential dangers can seem quite frightening, in reality few travellers experience anything more than an upset stomach.

Predeparture Planning

Immunisations Plan ahead for getting your vaccinations: some of them require more than one injection, while some vaccinations should not be given together. Note that some vaccinations should not be given during pregnancy or to people with allergies – discuss this with your doctor.

It is recommended you seek medical advice at least six weeks before travel. Be aware that there is often a greater risk of disease with children and during pregnancy.

Discuss your requirements with your doctor, but vaccinations you should consider for this trip include the following (for more details about the diseases themselves, see the individual disease entries later in this section). Carry proof of your vaccinations, especially yellow fever, as this is needed for entry into Lebanon if you are coming from an infected area.

Medical Kit Check List

Following is a list of items you should consider including in your medical kit – consult your pharmacist for brands available in your country.

- ☐ **Aspirin or paracetamol (acetaminophen in the USA)** – for pain or fever
- ☐ **Antihistamine** – for allergies, eg, hay fever; to ease the itch from insect bites or stings; and to prevent motion sickness
- ☐ **Cold and flu tablets, throat lozenges and nasal decongestant**
- ☐ **Multivitamins** – consider for long trips, when dietary vitamin intake may be inadequate
- ☐ **Antibiotics** – consider including these if you're travelling well off the beaten track; see your doctor, as they must be prescribed, and carry the prescription with you
- ☐ **Loperamide or diphenoxylate** –'blockers' for diarrhoea
- ☐ **Prochlorperazine or metaclopramide** – for nausea and vomiting
- ☐ **Rehydration mixture** – to prevent dehydration, which may occur, for example, during bouts of diarrhoea; particularly important when travelling with children
- ☐ **Insect repellent, sunscreen, lip balm and eye drops**
- ☐ **Calamine lotion, sting relief spray or aloe vera** – to ease irritation from sunburn and insect bites or stings
- ☐ **Antifungal cream or powder** – for fungal skin infections and thrush
- ☐ **Antiseptic (such as povidone-iodine)** – for cuts and grazes
- ☐ **Bandages, Band-Aids (plasters) and other wound dressings**
- ☐ **Water purification tablets or iodine**
- ☐ **Scissors, tweezers and a thermometer** – note that mercury thermometers are prohibited by airlines
- ☐ **Sterile kit** – in case you need injections in a country with medical hygiene problems; discuss with your doctor

---

Diphtheria & Tetanus Vaccinations for these two diseases are usually combined and are recommended for everyone. After an initial course of three injections (usually given in childhood), boosters are necessary every 10 years.

Hepatitis A Hepatitis A, the most common travel-acquired illness, exists in all Middle Eastern countries, but can easily be prevented by vaccination. Hepatitis A vaccine (eg, Avaxim, Havrix 1440 or VAQTA) provides long-term immunity (possibly more than 10 years) after an initial injection and a booster at six to 12 months. Alternatively, an injection of gamma globulin can provide short-term protection against hepatitis A – for two to six months, depending on the dose given. It is not a vaccine, but ready-made antibodies collected from blood donations. It is reasonably effective and, unlike the vaccine, it is protective immediately, but because it is a blood product, there are current concerns about its long-term safety. Hepatitis A vaccine is also available in a combined form, Twinrix, with hepatitis B vaccine. Three injections over a six-month period are required, the first two providing substantial protection against hepatitis A.

Hepatitis B Endemic in all Middle Eastern countries, travellers who should consider vaccination against hepatitis B include those on a long trip, as well as those going to places where blood transfusions may not be adequately screened or where sexual contact or needle sharing is a possibility. Vaccination involves three injections, with a booster at 12 months. More rapid courses are available if necessary.

Rabies Vaccination should be considered by those who will spend a month or longer in Lebanon, especially if they are cycling, handling animals, caving or travelling to remote areas, and for children (who may not report a bite). Pretravel rabies vaccination involves having three injections over 21 to 28 days. If someone who has been vaccinated is bitten or scratched by an animal, they will require two booster injections of vaccine; those not vaccinated require more.

Typhoid Vaccination against typhoid may be required if you are travelling for more than a couple of weeks in most parts of Asia, Africa, Central and South America and Central and Eastern Europe. It is now available either as an injection or as capsules to be taken orally. A combined hepatitis A/typhoid vaccine was launched recently but its availability is still limited – check with your doctor to find out its status in your country.

Yellow Fever A yellow fever vaccine is now the only vaccine that is a legal requirement for entry into Lebanon for travellers coming from an infected area (parts of Africa and South America). You may have to go to a special yellow fever vaccination centre.

Health Insurance

Make sure that you have adequate health insurance. See Travel Insurance under Visas & Documents earlier this chapter for details.

Travel Health Guides

There are a number of books on travel health, including:

CDC's Complete Guide to Healthy Travel The US Centers for Disease Control & Prevention recommendations for international travel

Staying Healthy in Asia, Africa & Latin America by Dirk Schroeder. Probably the best all-round guide to carry, as it's compact but very detailed and well organised

Travellers' Health by Dr Richard Dawood. Comprehensive, easy to read, authoritative and also highly recommended, although it's rather large to lug around

Where There is No Doctor by David Werner. A very detailed guide intended for someone, such as a Peace Corps worker, going to work in an underdeveloped country, rather than for the average traveller

Travel with Children by Maureen Wheeler. Includes advice on travel health for young children

There are also a number of excellent travel health sites on the Internet. From the Lonely Planet homepage, www.lonelyplanet.com, there are links at www.lonelyplanet.com/health/health.htm/h-links.htm, to the World Health Organization, Centers for Diseases Control & Prevention in Atlanta, Georgia, and to the Stanford University Travel Medicine Service.

Other Preparations

Make sure you are healthy before you start travelling. If you are going on a long trip make sure your teeth are OK. If you wear glasses remember to take both a spare pair and your prescription.

If you require a particular medication take an adequate supply, as it may not be available locally. Take part of the packaging showing the generic name rather than the brand, which will make getting replacements easier. It is also a very good idea to have a legible prescription or letter from your doctor to show that you legally use the medication in order to avoid any problems at customs.

Basic Rules

Food There is an old colonial adage which says: 'If you can cook it, boil it or peel it you can eat it...otherwise forget it'. Vegetables and fruit should be washed with purified water or peeled where possible. Beware of ice cream as it might have melted and been refrozen; if there's any doubt (eg, a power cut in the last day or two), steer well clear. Shellfish such as mussels, oysters and clams should be avoided as well as undercooked meat, particularly in the form of mince. Steaming does not make shellfish safe for eating.

If a place looks clean and well run and the vendor also looks clean and healthy, then the food is probably safe. In general, places that are packed with travellers or locals will be fine, while empty restaurants are questionable. The food in busy restaurants is cooked and eaten quite quickly with little standing around and is probably not reheated.

Water The number one rule is *be careful of the water* and especially ice. If you don't know for certain that the water is safe, assume the worst. Reputable brands of bottled water or soft drinks are generally fine, although in some places bottles may be refilled with tap water. Only use water from containers with a serrated seal – not tops or corks. Take care with fruit juice, particularly if water may have been added. Tea or coffee should be OK, since the water should have been boiled.

Water Purification The simplest way of purifying water is to boil it thoroughly. Vigorous boiling should be satisfactory; however, at high altitude water boils at a lower temperature, so germs are less likely to be killed. In these environments, boil the water for longer.

Consider purchasing a water filter for a long trip. There are two main kinds of filter. Total filters take out all parasites, bacteria and viruses and make water safe to drink. They are often expensive, but they can be more cost effective than buying bottled water. Simple filters (which can even be a nylon mesh bag) take out dirt and larger foreign bodies from the water so that chemical solutions work much more effectively; if water is dirty, chemical solutions may not work at all. It's very important when buying a filter to read the specifications, so that you know exactly what it removes from the water and what it doesn't. Simple filtering will not remove all dangerous organisms, so if you cannot boil water it should be treated chemically. Chlorine tablets will kill many pathogens, but not some parasites like giardia and amoebic cysts. Iodine is more effective in purifying water and is available in tablet form. Follow the directions carefully and remember that too much iodine can be harmful.

Medical Problems & Treatment

Self-diagnosis and treatment can be risky, so wherever possible seek medical help. Although we do give treatment dosages in this section, they are for emergency use only. Medical advice should be sought before administering any drugs.

An embassy or consulate can usually recommend a good place to go for such advice. So can five-star hotels, although they often recommend doctors with five-star prices. (This is when that medical insurance really comes in useful!)

Note that antibiotics should be administered only under medical supervision. Take only the recommended dose at the prescribed

Everyday Health

Normal body temperature is up to 37°C (98.6°F); more than 2°C (4°F) higher indicates a high fever. The normal adult pulse rate is 60 to 100 per minute (children 80 to 100, babies 100 to 140). As a general rule the pulse increases about 20 beats per minute for each 1°C (2°F) rise in fever.

Respiration (breathing) rate is also an indicator of illness. Count the number of breaths per minute: Between 12 and 20 is normal for adults and older children (up to 30 for younger children, 40 for babies). People with a high fever or serious respiratory illness breathe more quickly than normal. More than 40 shallow breaths a minute may indicate pneumonia.

intervals and use the whole course, even if the illness seems to be cured earlier. Stop immediately if there are any serious reactions and don't use the antibiotic at all if you are unsure that you have the correct one. Some people are allergic to commonly prescribed antibiotics such as penicillin; carry this information (eg, on a bracelet) when travelling.

Medical Services in Lebanon

There are sophisticated medical facilities available in Lebanon. Most doctors have graduated overseas and speak English or French, but they are almost all private (and expensive). The best facilities tend to be in Beirut and the most highly recommended hospital in the country is the American University of Beirut Hospital. See the Medical Services and Emergency section in the Beirut chapter for more details.

There are pharmacies in almost every town and most drugs are widely available and can be bought over the counter, generally at the same price as in Europe. Although it is usually unnecessary, you should check expiry dates before buying; drug dumping is a common problem in the Middle East. Pharmacists are usually very helpful and knowledgeable about the drugs they sell and most speak English or French.

Environmental Hazards

Jet Lag Jet lag is experienced when a person travels by air across more than three time zones (each time zone usually represents a one-hour time difference). It occurs because many of the functions of the human body (such as temperature, pulse rate and emptying of the bladder and bowels) are regulated by internal 24-hour cycles. When we travel long distances rapidly, our bodies take time to adjust to the 'new time' of our destination, and we may experience fatigue, disorientation, insomnia, anxiety, impaired concentration and loss of appetite. These effects will usually be gone within three days of arrival, but to minimise the impact of jet lag:

- Rest for a couple of days prior to departure.
- Try to select flight schedules that minimise sleep deprivation; arriving late in the day means

you can go to sleep soon after you arrive. For very long flights, try to organise a stopover.
- Avoid excessive eating (which bloats the stomach) and alcohol (which causes dehydration) during the flight. Instead, drink plenty of non-carbonated, nonalcoholic drinks such as fruit juice or water.
- Avoid smoking.
- Make yourself comfortable by wearing loose-fitting clothes and perhaps bringing an eye mask and ear plugs to help you sleep.
- Try to sleep at the appropriate time for the time zone you are travelling to.

Sunburn Whether on the coast or in the mountains you can get sunburnt surprisingly quickly, even through cloud. Use a sunscreen, a hat and a barrier cream for your nose and lips. Calamine lotion or a commercial after-sun preparation are good for mild sunburn. Protect your eyes with good-quality sunglasses, particularly if you will be near water, sand or snow.

Prickly Heat Prickly heat is an itchy rash caused by excessive perspiration trapped under the skin. It usually strikes people who have just arrived in a hot climate. Keeping cool, bathing often, drying the skin and using a mild talcum or prickly heat powder or resorting to air-conditioning may help.

Heat Exhaustion Dehydration and salt deficiency can cause heat exhaustion. Take time to acclimatise to high temperatures, drink sufficient liquids and do not do anything too physically demanding.

Salt deficiency is characterised by fatigue, lethargy, headaches, giddiness and muscle cramps; salt tablets may help, but adding extra salt to your food is better.

Anhidrotic heat exhaustion is a rare form of heat exhaustion that is caused by an inability to sweat. It tends to affect people who have been in a hot climate for some time, rather than newcomers, and it can progress to heatstroke. Treatment involves removal to a cooler climate.

Heatstroke This serious, occasionally fatal, condition can occur if the body's heat-regulating mechanism breaks down and the body temperature rises to dangerous levels.

Long, continuous periods of exposure to high temperatures and insufficient fluids can leave you vulnerable to heatstroke.

The symptoms are feeling unwell, not sweating very much (or at all) and a high body temperature (39° to 41°C or 102° to 106°F). Where sweating has ceased, the skin becomes flushed and red. Severe, throbbing headaches and lack of coordination will also occur, and the sufferer may be confused or aggressive. Eventually the victim will become delirious or convulse. Hospitalisation is essential, but in the interim get victims out of the sun, remove their clothing, cover them with a wet sheet or towel and then fan continually. Give fluids if they are conscious.

Hypothermia Too much cold can be just as dangerous as too much heat. If you are trekking at high altitudes or simply taking a long bus trip over mountains, particularly at night, be prepared. You should always be prepared for cold, wet or windy conditions even if you're just out walking or hitching.

Hypothermia occurs when the body loses heat faster than it can produce it and the core temperature of the body falls. It is surprisingly easy to progress from very cold to dangerously cold due to a combination of wind, wet clothing, fatigue and hunger, even if the air temperature is above freezing. It is best to dress in layers; silk, wool and some of the new artificial fibres are all good insulating materials. A hat is important, as a lot of heat is lost through the head. A strong, waterproof outer layer (and a 'space' blanket for emergencies) are essential. Carry basic supplies, including food containing simple sugars to generate heat quickly and fluid to drink.

Symptoms of hypothermia are exhaustion, numb skin (particularly toes and fingers), shivering, slurred speech, irrational or violent behaviour, lethargy, stumbling, dizzy spells, muscle cramps and violent bursts of energy. Irrationality may take the form of sufferers claiming they are warm and trying to take off their clothes.

To treat mild hypothermia, first get the person out of the wind and/or rain, remove their clothing if it's wet and replace it with dry, warm clothing. Give them hot liquids – not alcohol – and some high-kilojoule, easily digestible food. Do not rub victims, instead allow them to slowly warm themselves. This should be enough to treat the early stages of hypothermia. The early recognition and treatment of mild hypothermia is the only way to prevent severe hypothermia, which is a critical condition.

Motion Sickness Eating lightly before and during a trip will reduce the chances of motion sickness. If you are prone to motion sickness try to find a place that minimises movement – near the wing on aircraft, close to midships on boats, near the centre on buses. Fresh air usually helps; reading and cigarette smoke don't. Commercial motion-sickness preparations, which can cause drowsiness, have to be taken before the trip commences. Ginger (available in capsule form) and peppermint (including mint-flavoured sweets) are natural preventatives.

Infectious Diseases

Diarrhoea Simple things like a change of water, food or climate can all cause a mild bout of diarrhoea, but a few rushed toilet trips with no other symptoms is not indicative of a major problem.

Dehydration is the main danger with any diarrhoea, particularly in children or the elderly as dehydration can occur quite quickly. Under all circumstances *fluid replacement* (at least equal to the volume being lost) is the most important thing to remember. Weak black tea with a little sugar, soda water, or soft drinks allowed to go flat and diluted 50% with clean water are all good. With severe diarrhoea a rehydrating solution is preferable to replace minerals and salts lost. Commercially available oral rehydration salts (ORS) are very useful; add them to boiled or bottled water. In an emergency you can make up a solution of six teaspoons of sugar and a half teaspoon of salt to 1L of boiled or bottled water. You need to drink at least the same volume of fluid that you are losing in bowel movements and vomiting. Urine is the best guide to the adequacy of replacement – if you have small amounts of concentrated urine, you need to drink more.

Keep drinking small amounts often. Stick to a bland diet as you recover.

Gut-paralysing drugs such as loperamide or diphenoxylate can be used to bring relief from the symptoms, although they do not actually cure the problem. Only use these drugs if you do not have access to toilets (eg, if you *must* travel). Note that these drugs are not recommended for children under 12 years.

In certain situations antibiotics may be required: diarrhoea with blood or mucus (dysentery), any diarrhoea with fever, profuse watery diarrhoea, persistent diarrhoea not improving after 48 hours and severe diarrhoea. These suggest a more serious cause of diarrhoea and in these situations gut-paralysing drugs should be avoided.

In these situations, a stool test may be necessary to diagnose what bug is causing your diarrhoea, so you should seek medical help urgently. Where this is not possible the recommended drugs for bacterial diarrhoea (the most likely cause of severe diarrhoea in travellers) are norfloxacin 400mg twice daily for three days or ciprofloxacin 500mg twice daily for five days. These are not recommended for children or pregnant women. The drug of choice for children would be co-trimoxazole with dosage dependent on weight. A five-day course is given. Ampicillin or amoxycillin may be given in pregnancy, but medical care is necessary.

Two other causes of persistent diarrhoea in travellers are giardiasis and amoebic dysentery.

Giardiasis This is caused by a common parasite, *Giardia lamblia*. Symptoms include stomach cramps, nausea, a bloated stomach, watery, foul-smelling diarrhoea and frequent gas. Giardiasis can appear several weeks after you have been exposed to the parasite. The symptoms may disappear for a few days and then return; this can go on for several weeks.

Amoebic dysentery Caused by the protozoan *Entamoeba histolytica*, amoebic dysentery is characterised by a gradual onset of low-grade diarrhoea, often with blood and mucus. Cramping abdominal pain and vomiting are less likely than in other types of diarrhoea, and fever may not be present. It will persist until treated and can recur and cause other health problems.

You should seek medical advice if you think you have giardiasis or amoebic dysentery, but where this is not possible, tinidazole or metronidazole are the recommended drugs. Treatment is a 2g single dose of tinidazole or 250mg of metronidazole three times daily for five to 10 days.

Fungal Infections Hot-weather fungal infections are most likely to occur on the scalp, between the toes or fingers (athlete's foot), in the groin (jock itch or crotch rot) and on the body (ringworm). You get ringworm (which is a fungal infection, not a worm) from infected animals or by walking on damp areas, like shower floors.

To prevent fungal infections wear loose, comfortable clothes, avoid artificial fibres, wash frequently and dry carefully. If you do get an infection, wash the infected area daily with a disinfectant or medicated soap and water, and rinse and dry well. Apply an antifungal powder like the widely available Tinaderm. Try to expose the infected area to air or sunlight as much as possible and wash all towels and underwear in hot water as well as changing them often and letting them dry in the sun.

Typhoid Typhoid fever is a dangerous gut infection caused by contaminated water and food. Medical help must be sought.

In its early stages sufferers may feel they have the flu on the way, as early symptoms are a headache, body aches and a fever which rises a little each day until it is around 40°C (104°F) or more. The victim's pulse is often slow relative to the degree of fever present – unlike a normal fever where the pulse increases. There may also be vomiting, abdominal pain, diarrhoea or constipation.

In the second week the high fever and slow pulse continue and a few pink spots may appear on the body; trembling, delirium, weakness, weight loss and dehydration may occur. Complications such as pneumonia, perforated bowel or meningitis may occur.

Hepatitis Hepatitis is a general term for inflammation of the liver. It is a common disease caused by several different viruses and they differ in the way that they are transmitted. The symptoms are similar in all forms of the illness, and include fever, chills, headache, fatigue, feelings of weakness and aches and pains, followed by loss of appetite, nausea, vomiting, abdominal pain, dark urine, light-coloured faeces, jaundiced (yellow) skin and yellowing of the whites of the eyes. People who have had hepatitis should avoid alcohol for some time after the illness, as the liver needs time to recover.

Hepatitis A Transmitted by contaminated food and drinking water. You should seek medical advice, but there is not much you can do apart from resting, drinking lots of fluids, eating lightly and avoiding fatty foods.
Hepatitis B Has almost 300 million chronic carriers throughout the world. It is spread through contact with infected blood, blood products or body fluids (eg, through sexual contact, unsterilised needles and blood transfusions, or contact with blood via small breaks in the skin). Other risk situations include shaving, tattoo or body piercing with contaminated equipment. The symptoms of hepatitis B may be more severe than type A and the disease can lead to long term problems such as chronic liver damage, liver cancer or a long term carrier state.
Hepatitis C & D These are spread in the same way as hepatitis B and can also lead to serious long-term complications.
Hepatitis E Transmitted in the same way as hepatitis A; it can be particularly serious in pregnant women.

There are vaccines against hepatitis A and B, but there are currently no vaccines against the other types of hepatitis. Following the basic rules about food and water (hepatitis A and E) and avoiding risk situations (hepatitis B, C and D) are important preventative measures.

HIV/AIDS Infection with the human immunodeficiency virus (HIV) may lead to acquired immune deficiency syndrome (AIDS), which is a fatal disease. Any exposure to blood, blood products or body fluids may put the individual at risk. The disease is often transmitted through sexual contact or dirty needles – vaccinations, acupuncture, tattooing and body piercing can be potentially as dangerous as intravenous drug use. HIV/AIDS can also be spread through infected blood transfusions.

If you do need an injection, ask to see the syringe unwrapped in front of you, or take a needle and syringe pack with you.

Fear of HIV infection should never preclude treatment for any serious medical conditions.

Intestinal Worms These parasites are most common in rural, tropical areas. Tapeworms may be ingested on food such as undercooked meat. Infestations may not show up for some time, and although they are generally not serious, if left untreated some can cause severe health problems later. Consider having a stool test when you return home to check for these and determine the appropriate treatment.

Sexually Transmitted Infections (STIs) HIV/AIDS and hepatitis B can be transmitted through sexual contact – see the relevant sections earlier for more details. Other STIs include gonorrhoea, herpes and syphilis; sores, blisters or rashes around the genitals and discharges or pain when urinating are common symptoms. In some STIs, such as wart virus or chlamydia, symptoms may be less marked, especially in women. Chlamydia infection can cause infertility in men and women before any symptoms have been noticed. Syphilis symptoms eventually disappear completely but the disease continues and can cause problems in later years. While abstinence from sexual contact is the only 100% effective prevention, using condoms is also effective. The treatment of gonorrhoea and syphilis is with antibiotics. The different STIs each require specific antibiotics.

Cuts, Bites & Stings
Bedbugs & Lice Bedbugs live in various places, but particularly in dirty mattresses and bedding. Spots of blood on bedclothes or on the wall around the bed are signs that it's time to find another hotel. Bedbugs leave itchy bites in neat rows. Calamine lotion or Stingose spray may help.

All lice cause itching and discomfort. They make themselves at home in your hair (head lice), your clothing (body lice) or in your pubic hair (crabs). You catch lice through direct contact with infected people or by sharing combs, clothing and the like. Powder or shampoo treatment will kill the lice and infected clothing should then be washed in very hot water.

Bites & Stings Bee and wasp stings are usually painful rather than dangerous. Calamine lotion will give relief or ice packs will reduce the pain and swelling. There are some spiders with dangerous bites but antivenenes are usually available. There are also various fish and other sea creatures which can sting or bite dangerously or which are dangerous to eat. For example, sea urchins, blowfish, fire coral, feathery lionfish, moray eels, turkeyfish, stonefish and triggerfish should all be avoided. Seek local advice before entering unfamiliar water.

Cuts & Scratches Wash well and treat any cut with an antiseptic such as povidone-iodine. Where possible avoid bandages and Band-Aids, which can keep wounds wet. Coral cuts are notoriously slow to heal and if they are not adequately cleaned, small pieces of coral can become embedded in the wound.

Jellyfish In summer, jellyfish are common in the sea off Lebanon. Local advice is the best way of avoiding contact with these sea creatures and their stinging tentacles. Stings from most jellyfish are simply irritating rather than painful. Dousing in vinegar will deactivate any stingers which have not 'fired'. Calamine lotion, antihistamines and analgesics may reduce the reaction and relieve the pain.

Scorpions Scorpion stings are a serious cause of illness and occasionally death in the Middle East, although effective antivenenes are available. Shake shoes, clothing and towels before use. Inspect bedding and don't put hands or feet in crevices where they may be lurking. A sting usually produces redness and swelling of the skin, but there may be no visible reaction. Pain is common, and tingling or numbness may occur. At this stage, cold compresses on the bite and pain relief (eg, paracetamol) are called for. If the skin sensations start to spread from the sting site (eg, along the limb), then immediate medical attention is required.

Snakes To minimise your chances of being bitten always wear boots, socks and long trousers when walking through undergrowth where snakes may be present. Don't put your hands into holes and crevices, and be careful when collecting firewood.

Snake bites do not cause instantaneous death and antivenenes are usually available. Keep the victim calm and still, wrap the bitten limb tightly, as you would for a sprained ankle, and then attach a splint to immobilise it. Then seek medical help, if possible with the dead snake for identification. Don't attempt to catch the snake if there is even a remote possibility of being bitten again. Tourniquets and sucking out the poison are now comprehensively discredited.

Ticks You should always check all over your body if you have been walking through a potentially tick-infested area as ticks can cause skin infections and other more serious diseases. If a tick is found attached, press down around the tick's head with tweezers, grab the head and gently pull upwards. Avoid pulling the rear of the body as this may squeeze the tick's gut contents through the attached mouth parts into the skin, increasing the risk of infection and disease. Smearing chemicals on the tick will not make it let go and is not recommended.

Less Common Diseases
Leishmaniasis This is a group of parasitic diseases transmitted by sandflies, which are found in many parts of the Middle East. Cutaneous leishmaniasis affects the skin tissue causing ulceration. Seek medical advice, as laboratory testing is required for diagnosis and correct treatment. Avoiding sandfly bites is the best precaution. Bites are usually painless, itchy and yet another reason to cover up and apply repellent.

Rabies Rabies is a fatal viral infection found in all Middle Eastern countries and is caused by a bite or scratch by an infected animal. Dogs and cats are noted carriers. Any bite, scratch or even lick from a mammal should be cleaned immediately and thoroughly. Scrub with soap and running water, and then clean with an alcohol or iodine solution. If there is any possibility that the animal is infected, medical help should be sought immediately to prevent the onset of symptoms and death. Even if the animal is not rabid, all bites should be treated seriously as they can become infected or can result in tetanus. A rabies vaccination is now available and should be considered if you are in a high-risk category – eg, if you intend to explore caves (bat bites could be dangerous) or work with animals.

Tetanus This potentially fatal disease is found worldwide. It is difficult to treat but is preventable with immunisation. Tetanus occurs when a wound becomes infected by a germ which lives in the soil and faeces of horses and other animals, so clean all cuts, punctures or animal bites. Tetanus is known as lockjaw, and the first symptom may be discomfort in swallowing, or stiffening of the jaw and neck; this is followed by painful convulsions of the jaw and whole body.

Tuberculosis Although this disease is widespread in many developing countries, it is not a serious risk to travellers. Young children are more susceptible than adults and vaccination is a sensible precaution for children under 12 travelling in endemic areas. TB is commonly spread by coughing or by unpasteurised dairy products from infected cows. Milk that has been boiled is safe to drink; the souring of milk to make yogurt or cheese also kills the bacilli.

Women's Health
Gynaecological Problems Antibiotic use, synthetic underwear, sweating and contraceptive pills can lead to fungal vaginal infections, especially when travelling in hot climates. Fungal infections are characterised by a rash, itch and discharge and can be treated with a vinegar or lemon-juice douche, or with yogurt. Nystatin, miconazole or clotrimazole pessaries or vaginal cream are the usual treatment. Maintaining good personal hygiene and wearing loose-fitting clothes and cotton underwear may help prevent these infections.

Sexually transmitted diseases are a major cause of vaginal problems. Symptoms might include a smelly discharge, painful intercourse and sometimes a burning sensation when urinating. Medical attention should be sought and male sexual partners must also be treated. For more details see the Sexually Transmitted Infections section earlier. Besides abstinence, the best thing is to practise safe sex using condoms.

Pregnancy It is not advisable to travel to some places while pregnant as some vaccinations are not advisable during pregnancy. In addition, some diseases are much more serious during pregnancy and may increase the risk of a stillborn child.

Most miscarriages occur during the first three months of pregnancy. Miscarriage is not uncommon and can occasionally lead to severe bleeding. The last three months should also be spent within reasonable distance of good medical care. A baby born as early as 24 weeks stands a chance of survival, but only in a good modern hospital. Pregnant women should avoid all unnecessary medication, although vaccinations and malarial prophylactics should still be taken where needed. Additional care should be taken to prevent illness and particular attention should be paid to diet and nutrition. Alcohol and nicotine, for example, should be avoided.

WOMEN TRAVELLERS
Women travelling in Lebanon will notice a huge difference in the attitude towards them compared to most other parts of the Middle East. In Beirut it is common to see Lebanese women in the tightest and tiniest of outfits, including micro miniskirts, tight trousers and teeny tank tops. However, if you are travelling alone, you may want to be little more restrained than your Lebanese sisters. As a foreign woman you are per-

ceived by some as outside the protection of male relatives and therefore as fair game for the odd leer and comment.

Having said that, you can wear more or less whatever you want, particularly in Beirut. In the coastal resorts the dress code is also relaxed and bikinis are *de rigeur* on the beach. Going topless is out.

Away from the Beirut and the resorts, and particularly in predominantly Muslim areas, it is sensible to adopt a more conservative style of dress to avoid unwelcome attention. If you are planning to visit any mosques, be sure that your arms and legs are covered and that you take a headscarf with you – some mosques even provide women visitors a black cloak at the door.

If you do find yourself the subject of unwanted attention in the street, the best thing to do is ignore the perpetrators. If they persist, ask them loudly to leave you alone and the chances are they'll be told off by other passers-by.

In the mid-range and top-end hotels the security is usually very good and women need not worry about being hassled. In the budget hotels it might be more of a problem. A few hotels in this book are frequented by Syrian workers and should be avoided by solo women travellers (this is pointed out in the text). As a general rule, do not open your hotel room door unless you know who is there, and when you are alone in your room keep the door locked. In seedy hotels look out for holes in the walls – stuffing tissues into the keyhole and other suspicious holes can thwart any would-be peeping toms.

Women should not get into an unlicensed service taxi if there are no other passengers, especially at night. If a car stops when you are waiting for a taxi and you do not like the look of it, just firmly wave the car away – don't feel pressured into getting in.

For more information about women in Lebanon, see Society & Conduct in the Facts about Lebanon chapter.

GAY & LESBIAN TRAVELLERS

There is a thriving, if clandestine, gay and lesbian scene in Lebanon, largely concentrated in Beirut. Homosexuality is illegal under Lebanese law, so you must be careful. It also pays to be discreet when checking into a double hotel room. As a basic rule, the Muslim areas tend to be more conservative than the Christian ones.

There are no gay venues as such but a number of clubs are known to be frequented by gays. These currently include the famous BO18 in Qarantina, Acid in Sin al-Fil or Amor Y Libertad in Jounieh. Keep in mind that in the shifting Lebanese nightlife scene things change quickly and these may well be passe by the time you read this. There are a few beaches and baths that are also popular gay haunts. For the most up-to-date listings and other tips for gay travellers in Lebanon, check out: www.surf.to/gay.lebanon.

DISABLED TRAVELLERS

Considering the number of people that were disabled during the civil war, it is curious that Lebanon is not more disabled-friendly. Disabled people are rarely seen on the street, which is perhaps not surprising given the difficulties of navigating through the potholes, rubble and anarchic traffic. Buildings and archaeological sites do not have wheelchair ramps and bathrooms are not modified for access. The only exception is the newly constructed downtown area, which has Braille in lifts and wide access doors.

SENIOR TRAVELLERS

The older traveller, who is reasonably fit, will have no trouble with Lebanon. The main historical sites are all quite accessible and can be seen without too much climbing and exertion. The exceptions are the Qadisha Valley, which is very strenuous, and some of the minor ruins in the Bekaa Valley. In summer, it would be more comfortable to stay higher up in the mountain resorts above Beirut – advice that is good for any age.

TRAVEL WITH CHILDREN

The Lebanese love children and bringing along the kids will open doors and guarantee you make new friends. For babies and young children, major brands of disposable nappies and baby foods are easily available. The only thing you will have to watch is the heat in summer – sunhats and maximum protection sun block are an absolute must. High-factor SPF is not always easy to find in Lebanon and can be expensive, so it's probably better to bring your own. See Lonely Planet's *Travel with Children* by Maureen Wheeler for more information.

Finding space for children to run in Beirut is something of a challenge. The public park at Saniyeh is small and can be very crowded on weekends. If you can get past the security guards, the American University of Beirut has beautiful grounds, even if there is no playground as such. A popular destination for Beirutis trying to amuse bored young children is one of the seafront cafes in Ras Beirut. **Raouda**, and the adjacent **Luna Park Funfair**, are both popular choices.

Planet Discovery is a children's science museum on the edge of Beirut's redeveloped downtown. Small but very well organised it centres on the theme of building and has four sections with interactive exhibits based around building structures, physical phenomena, finished houses and a children's village. Demonstrations are in Arabic, English, French and braille. Opening hours are from 9 am to 6 pm weekdays and 10 am to 7.30 pm weekends and holidays. Entrance is LL5000 per person.

Away from town, **Animal Encounter** in Aley, on the road to the Bekaa, is a non-profit shelter for injured and orphaned wild animals and birds. It aims to educate adults and children about Lebanon's fauna and the importance of preserving its natural habitat. Whenever possible the rehabilitated animals are released back into the wild. The centre gets more than 40,000 visitors a year, more than half of whom are school-age children. For more information, call founders Mounir or Diana Abi-Said (☎ 05-558 724 or cell 03-667 355).

Other child-friendly excursions explained in other chapters throughout this book are the Jeita Grotto (see the Mt Lebanon chapter) and Castle Moussa (see the Chouf Mountains chapter).

If it's hot, **Splash Mountain** (☎ 04-531 166), in Ain Saadeh, has water slides and other water games. It's open from 10 am to 6 pm daily. Entrance is LL20,000 for the entire day or LL10,000 from 2 to 6 pm.

If you want to get rid of your little darlings for a few days, La Reserve near the Afqa Grotto (see the Mt Lebanon chapter) runs two **summer camps** for children aged seven to 15. Children participate in a wide variety of activities, including learning about the environment, visiting local archaeological sites and, of course, fun stuff like making mud sculptures, playing games and watching films. In 1999 some 95 children from Lebanon, other Arab countries and Europe signed up. For more information contact La Reserve (☎ 01-498 774/5/6) or check out the Web site: www.lareserve.com.lb.

Many of Beirut's theatre companies put on plays for children. Call Theatre de Beirut (☎ cell 03-506 279) and City Theatre *(masrah al-medina)* (☎ 01-371 962/4) to see if they are showing anything for children. Each year the Children's Touring Theatre takes a play around the country. Call (☎ cell 03-839 891) for dates and venues.

Every July, the Deir al-Qamar Estivalés, takes place in the Chouf Mountains village of Deir al-Qamar. The festival focuses on family and holds a variety of children's activities. See the boxed text 'Lebanon's Festivals' later in this chapter.

There are a few good Lebanon-related children's books on the market. For younger children, *The Houses of Lebanon* by Nayla Audi is a lavish pop-up style book shaped like a house and showing different styles of the rapidly disappearing traditional Lebanese house. *Sami and the Time of the Troubles* by Florence Parry Heide, is the illustrated story of how a young boy and his family cope with the civil war. For older children, *Once Upon a Time In Lebanon* by Roseanne Khalaf is a compilation of three folktales that give a good background to Lebanese culture, while *Dances with Gods* is a collection of myths, mostly dating back to Phoenician times.

USEFUL ORGANISATIONS

For those touring by car or motorcycle, contact the Automobile et Touring Club du Liban (☎ 01-390 645). If you encounter difficulties, call the Tourist Police (☎ 01-343 209). The United Nations Interim Force in Lebanon (Unifil) monitors the Israeli-Lebanese border and can advise about travel in the former occupied zone. Call its office (☎ 01-424 583) for more information.

DANGERS & ANNOYANCES

For a country that was in lost in violent anarchy little more than a decade ago, it is amazing just how safe Lebanon has become. Since the disarming and disbanding of the militias in the early 1990s, it has become possible to travel anywhere day or night without worries about security. There are frequent Lebanese and Syrian army checkpoints on the roads and occasionally you may be required to show your passport. This is usually just a formality but make sure you always carry it with you.

At the time of writing the political situation in Lebanon was uncertain; Israel's pullout from the south was rapidly followed by the death of Syrian president Hafez al-Assad. Whether this will lead to instability remains to be seen. If you are worried, find out if any travel warnings have been issued by your country's foreign ministry.

Currently, the main danger to visitors wandering through the Lebanese countryside are land mines and unexploded ordnance. UN experts estimate that there are more than 100,000 and other explosive devices scattered over the area that was occupied by Israel for 22 years (see boxed text 'Warning' at the beginning of The South chapter). Such was the danger in the immediate aftermath of the withdrawal that Lebanese television was broadcasting daily warnings on the dangers of land mines in the south. Do *not* wander off tracks, particularly in remote areas, and check with locals if you're unsure.

Theft can be a bit of a worry, but random crime is far lower than in most Western cities. Just use common sense: never leave your belongings unattended or money and valuables in your hotel room. Most hotels have a strong box where you can leave your money and valuables. Use moneybelts and avoid showing too much cash.

EMERGENCIES

If you find yourself in an emergency, then it's useful to have the following numbers:

Civil Defence	☎ 125
Emergency Police	☎ 160
Fire Brigade (extension 0)	☎ 175
Red Cross	☎ 145

See Emergency in the Beirut chapter for more telephone numbers.

BUSINESS HOURS

Sunday is the end-of-week holiday in Lebanon. Government offices, including post offices, are open from 8 am to 2 pm Monday to Saturday, except Friday when the opening hours are from 8 to 11 am. However, you'll rarely find anyone at work before 9.30 am. Banks are open from 8.30 am to 12.30 pm Monday to Saturday.

Shops and private businesses open from 9 am to 6 pm Monday to Saturday. Many grocery stores keep later hours and open on Sunday as well. In summer many places close around 3 pm.

PUBLIC HOLIDAYS & SPECIAL EVENTS

Most holidays are religious and, with so many different sects in Lebanon, there are quite a few events to celebrate, including the Feast of Mar Maroun (the patron saint of the Maronites). There are also a number of historical occurrences to commemorate, including Qana Day. Qana Day is the offical day of mourning for the massacre at Qana in 1996 in which 107 Lebanese civilians were killed by Israeli shells at a UN camp.

New Year's Day 1 January
Feast of Mar Maroun 9 February
Easter March/April
Qana Day 18 April
Labour Day 1 May
Martyrs' Day 6 May
Assumption 15 August
All Saints Day 1 November
Independence Day 22 November
Christmas Day 25 December

Islamic Holidays

Because the Islamic, or Hejira, calendar is 11 days shorter than the Gregorian (Western) calendar, Islamic holidays fall about 11 days earlier each year. The 11-day rule is not entirely strict – the holidays can fall from 10 to 12 days earlier. The precise dates are known only shortly before they fall, depending upon the sighting of the moon. See the Language chapter for a listing of the months. The following are the expected dates for the specific Islamic holidays during the lifetime of this book:

Hejira Year	New Year	Prophet's Birthday	Ramadan Begins	Eid al-Fitr	Eid al-Adha
1421	06.04.00	14.06.00	27.11.00	27.12.00	06.03.01
1422	26.03.01	03.06.01	16.11.01	16.12.01	23.02.02
1423	15.03.02	23.05.02	16.11.01	16.12.01	23.02.02
1424	04.03.03	12.05.03	25.10.03	24.11.03	01.02.04
1425	22.02.04	01.05.04	14.10.04	13.11.04	21.01.05
1426	11.02.05	20.04.05	03.10.05	02.11.05	10.01.06

Festivals

In the mid-1950s the town of Baalbek became a fixture on the international performance circuit with the establishment of the annual Baalbek Festival. Legendary performances in front of the spectacular ruins continued until the civil war intervened.

In an attempt to remember culture amid the ravages of war, the Beiteddine Festival was started in 1985. Although it had to close after two seasons, it began again in 1993. Baalbek was resurrected in 1997, and now it seems that no large town in Lebanon is worth its salt without some sort of festival in one of its floodlit ancient sites. All of which is very good news for music and dance lovers. The season kicks off in February with classical music at the Bustan Festival and continues until the end of the summer. In addition, many towns and villages have their own small festivals, which can be anything from local fairs to folkloric performances.

ACTIVITIES
Water Sports

A cursory glance at the Lebanese coastline is enough to show you that long stretches of white sand are not the rule here. Where there might have been nice beaches, an almost solid line of concrete resorts (at least north of Beirut) has carved up the waterfront. But while much of Lebanon's swimming is from rocks or artificial platforms built out on jetties, there are one or two very pleasant public sand beaches. The best can be found in the far south of the country, south of Tyre and near Byblos. There is also a public sandy beach in Beirut, but the cleanliness of the water is highly questionable. All public beaches get crowded on weekends.

The rocky bathing makes for good snorkelling and there are often water sports facilities at the private beach resorts. Water-skiing, windsurfing and sailing are all popular in summer and equipment can be rented from most resorts. There are good swimming pools at almost all the larger hotels and resorts. Expect to pay between US$6 and US$25 per person per day, depending on the level of luxury.

For those who like a bit more activity in the water, rafting is becoming increasingly popular in Lebanon. The Nahr al-Aasi (Orontes River) in the northern Bekaa, and the Nahr Ibrahim, east of Byblos, both swell, as the mountain snow melts in spring, and are ideal for rafting trips. La Reserve (see Afqa Grotto in the Mt Lebanon chapter for more information) arranges rafting courses on the Nahr Ibrahim during spring. Lebanese Adventure and Destination Liban also arrange rafting trips on both rivers (see Organised Tours in the Getting Around chap-

Lebanon's Festivals

Baalbek Festival
The mother of all Lebanese festivals, Baalbek had its first season in 1956, when Jean Cocteau presented *La Machine Infernale*. Rudolf Nureyev, Duke Ellington, Joan Baez and Ella Fitzgerald were just some of the legendary names that appeared in subsequent festival programs. Performances stopped in 1975 with the outbreak of war but resumed in 1997. Watching the musicians and dancers perform against the spectacular backdrop of the Baalbek's Roman temples is an amazing experience. For this year's program, check the Web site: www2.baalbeck.org.lb.

Beiteddine Festival
Started in 1985 by Walid Jumblatt, as war was raging, the festival runs throughout July and August. Performers take the stage in the beautiful 19th-century palace high in the Chouf Mountains and, in 2000, included such legends as Joe Cocker, Jessye Norman and Dame Kiri Te Kanawa. Buses leave from various locations in central Beirut on the evening of the performance. For more information check out the Web site: www.beiteddine.org.lb.

Bustan Festival
Increasingly prestigious classical music festival featuring performers from around the world held annually in February or March. Each year has a different theme and in 2000 it was 'The New Millennium: Rising Stars of the 21st Century'. Hosted by and named after the Hotel al-Bustan in Beit Meri. For more information call the Hotel al-Bustan (☎ 04-972 980/1/2 or cell 03-752 000/9).

Byblos Festival
Officially called the International Byblos Mediterraneo Festival, this is another mixture of classical, jazz and pop music, and concentrating on performers or music from around the Mediterranean. Usually held in August amid the town's spectacular ruins or at the port. For more information, call Eléftériadés Productions (☎ cell 03-640 881).

Tyre Festival
International pop and classical music performed in Tyre's magnificent hippodrome. For more information call festival organiser Nadia Hammoud (☎ cell 03-816 992).

Deir al-Qamar Estivalés
A child-friendly festival that runs on weekends throughout July in the picturesque mountain village. Includes games and activities for children as well as concerts and art shows. Program is published in the local media or on the Web site: www.Cyberia.net.lb in June.

Souq al-Barghout Festival
An annual market held each June in a different location among the restored buildings of Beirut's downtown. Exhibitors sell everything from antiques to hot dogs. An attempt to liven up the revamped city centre after hours, it is open from 4 to 10 pm.

ter for contact information). Hermel, in the northern Bekaa Valley, has a kayaking club that runs courses and trips on the Nahr al-Aasi. Trips usually last from four to seven hours and can accommodate all levels. Contact François Joubert (☎ cell 03-415 580) or Ismail Shahin (✉ ischahin@cyberia.net.lb) for more information.

Skiing
Lebanon may not spring to mind as a ski destination but the country's six ski resorts

Ski Resorts at a Glance

There are six main ski resorts in Lebanon with various grades of difficulty. All have ski equipment hire and instructors on hand. Most also have first-aid teams. Each resort has at least one hotel but Lebanese ski bunnies rent chalets for the season.

The Cedars

Lebanon's oldest and highest resort, 8km from Bcharré, has five lifts, four slopes and the longest season in the country. Altitude: 1850 to 3087m.

Faqra

Private luxury resort 45km from Beirut and skiing is by invitation only. Currently the only Lebanese resort to offer night skiing. Has three lifts and seven slopes. Altitude: 1735 to 2001m.

Faraya Mzaar

Lebanon's largest resort, 54km north-east of Beirut, with 16 lifts, 17 slopes and plenty of four- and five-star hotels. Altitude: 1874 to 2463m.

Laklouk

Located 28km east of Byblos. Less glitzy than Faqra or Faraya, it has nine lifts and nine slopes, including one recently approved for competition by the international ski federation. Altitude: 1650 to 1920m.

Qanat Bakiche

Small resort only 47km from Beirut, with two lifts and six slopes. Altitude: 1904 to 2250m.

Zaarour

Only 35km from Beirut, with two lifts and nine slopes. Altitude: 1651 to 2000m.

are becoming increasingly popular for overseas visitors as well as the Lebanese themselves. All are easily accessible as a day trip from Beirut and the ever fun-loving Lebanese make sure that the apres-ski scene is also worth sampling. The season lasts from November to May, depending on the snow. The mountains are relatively close to the sea, so the air around the slopes is humid. In the mornings, when the air is coldest, this can mean icy conditions; by the afternoon, with the rise in temperature, the snow becomes wetter.

You can take a short package ski holiday from Beirut arranged by some of the local tour operators. These include transfers to and from Beirut and full board at one of the ski hotels. Depending on the package chosen, and the class of hotel, the average costs are around US$80 per day inclusive (although this does not include ski and lift passes). The cost of hiring ski equipment is very reasonable and available at all the resorts – a full kit will cost about US$10 to US$15 per day.

Cross-country skiing and snow-shoeing are less popular but can also be done at the higher altitudes. Equipment can be rented at the resorts. Most of Lebanon's trekking clubs organise snow-shoeing day trips in winter. See the following Trekking section for more information.

The Ministry of Tourism publishes a very useful booklet called *Ski Lebanon*, which details all the ski resorts and facilities. For up-to-date information on the resorts and snow conditions, check www.skileb.com. For more information, see the Mt Lebanon chapter for all resorts except the Cedars, which you will find in the Tripoli & the North chapter.

Trekking

Lebanon has fabulous trekking opportunities in its mountains and gorges. In Horsh Ehden Forest Nature Reserve, near Tripoli, and the Chouf Cedar Reserve, there are well-maintained trails. Other popular areas include the Qadisha Valley, Makmel Park (near the Cedars) and the Adonis Valley.

There are a number of organisations that arrange treks and hikes for Lebanese as well as foreign visitors. Liban Trek is a well-established trekking club that arranges weekend treks throughout Lebanon. It also organises other mountain sports. Greenline arranges treks and day trips into the mountains and countryside of Lebanon that are designed to foster an awareness of Lebanon's

Considerations for Responsible Hiking

Please consider the following tips when hiking and help preserve the ecology and beauty of Lebanon:

Rubbish

Carry out all your rubbish. If you've carried it in, you can carry it out. Don't overlook those easily forgotten items, such as silver paper, orange peel, cigarette butts and plastic wrappers. Empty packaging weighs very little anyway and should be stored in a dedicated rubbish bag. Make an effort to carry out rubbish left by others.

Never bury your rubbish. Digging disturbs soil and ground cover and encourages erosion. Buried rubbish will more than likely be dug up by animals, who may be injured or poisoned by it. It may also take years to decompose, especially at high altitudes.

Minimise the waste you carry out by taking minimal packaging and taking no more food than you will need. Take reusable containers or stuff sacks.

Sanitary napkins, tampons and condoms should also be carried out despite the inconvenience. They burn and decompose poorly.

Human Waste Disposal

Contamination of water sources by human faeces can lead to the transmission of hepatitis, typhoid and intestinal parasites such as giardia, amoebas and roundworms. It can cause severe health risks not only to members of your party, but also to local residents and wildlife.

Where there is a toilet, please use it. Where there is none, bury your waste. Dig a small hole 15cm (six inches) deep and at least 100m (320 feet) from any watercourse. Consider carrying a lightweight trowel for this purpose. Cover the waste with soil and a rock. Use toilet paper sparingly and bury it with the waste. In snow, dig down to the soil; otherwise, your waste will be exposed when the snow melts.

If the area is inhabited, ask locals if they have any concerns about your chosen toilet site.

Washing

Don't use detergents or toothpaste in or near watercourses, even if they are biodegradable.

For personal washing, use biodegradable soap and a water container (or even a lightweight, portable basin) at least 50m (160 feet) away from the watercourse. Disperse the waste water widely to allow the soil to filter it fully before it finally makes it back to the watercourse.

Wash cooking utensils 50m (160 feet) from watercourses using a scourer, sand or snow instead of detergent.

Erosion

Deforested for centuries, Lebanon's hillsides and mountain slopes are prone to erosion, so it is important to stick to existing tracks. If you blaze a new trail straight down a slope, it will turn into a watercourse with the next heavy rainfall and eventually cause soil loss and deep scarring. Avoid removing the plant life that keeps topsoils in place.

fragile environment. Lebanese Adventure arranges different outdoor activities throughout the country each weekend. They can also tailor-make excursions for a minimum of five people. Destination Liban is a travel agency that specialises in budget and youth travel in Lebanon. They arrange trekking, rafting, paragliding and other outdoor activities. (For contact details of these companies see Organised Tours in the Getting Around chapter.)

If you decide to go it alone, remember that there is a very real danger of land mines in parts of Lebanon. Always seek local advice about the safety of your intended route.

Cycling

While Beirut's streets, with their anarchic traffic, poor surfaces and high noise levels are not most people's idea of a fun place to ride a bicycle, Lebanon's mountains and national parks are great for mountain biking. The nature reserves of Horsh Ehden and Chouf Cedar Reserve, Al-Jord (near Hermel in the Bekaa) and the Cedars are just some of the areas that are ideal for mountain biking. Several organisations run mountain-biking treks. Thermique, in Ajaltoun, just outside Beirut, runs guided bicycle tours, usually lasting one day, in Qornet as-Sawda, Lebanon's highest peak, among other destinations. Lebanese Adventure also arranges cycling trips throughout Lebanon. (See Organised Tours in the Getting Around chapter for contact information.)

If you decide to bring your own bicycle or to head off without a guide, remember that as well as being reckless, Lebanese drivers are unused to bicycles. If you're on mountain roads this means that you could find yourself perilously close to drop-offs as a car speeds into your path around a blind curve. If you must use the roads, be extremely careful and don't assume that you have been seen; mirrors are rarely used. Also keep in mind that bicycle shops are almost nonexistent outside Beirut, so you need to bring everything you are likely to need, including spare spokes, chain, cables, tubes and tyres. For further information, read *Cycling the Mediterranean* by Kameel B Nasr.

Caving

The Jeita and Afqa Grottoes may be Lebanon's most famous caverns but there are more than 400 explored cavities throughout the country, including some holes with depths of 602m – among the deepest in the Middle East. From small chambers in the rock to huge caverns, Lebanon's rugged mountains have enough crags and holes to keep most spelunkers happy for a very long time. There are four spelunking clubs in Lebanon and they organise trips throughout the country.

The Speleo-Club du Liban (SCL) was founded in 1951. The president is Hughes Badaoui (☎ cell 03-201 388). The Groupe Speleo de Wadi al-Arayech was founded in Zahlé in 1966. It is run by Walid Shoueiri (☎ cell 03-720 597). The Groupe d'Etudes et de Recherches Souterraines au Liban (Gersl) is run by Andre Azzi (☎ cell 03-293 210) and the Association Libanaise d'Etudes Speleologique (Ales) is run by Badr Gedeon (☎ cell 03-555 469, ✉ badrjg@hotmail.com). If you don't speak French, don't worry; the clubs organise events with English as well as Swiss and French spelunkers.

Paragliding

With its dramatic mountain scenery, Lebanon is prime paragliding territory and the sport is gradually being established here. The season is usually from May to October, depending on the weather, and the prime areas are the Cedars, Faraya Mzaar, Harissa and Qanat Bakiche. Thermique, the Lebanese branch of a French paragliding school, is based in Ajaltoun and offers courses ranging from one to seven days, as well as equipment rental. Current prices range from US$500 to US$700 for a week-long course, including accommodation and insurance. (See Organised Tours in the Getting Around chapter for contact details.)

Touring Wineries

Lebanon has produced wine since antiquity and over the millennia has been famous for its vintages. The wine-making tradition continues today and three vineyards, Ksara, Kefraya (both in the Bekaa Valley) and Chateau Musar (in Ghazir, Mt Lebanon) produce world-class wines, in addition to the grape-based traditional drink, arak. The vineyards are open to visitors and tasting is part of the itinerary. (For more information, see the boxed text 'Lebanese Wine' in The Bekaa Valley chapter.)

WORK

With the economy currently in recession it is not the best time to look for work. Lebanese are highly educated and most speak at least two, if not three languages fluently, so competition is stiff. If you have experience, the hotel and tourism industry is expanding rapidly and resorts may need people for seasonal work. English-language publications often need writers and copy editors. Keep in mind, though, that pay is usually very low.

If you do have a job, work permits are not difficult to get, although your employer must prove that there is no Lebanese capable of doing the job. The price varies according to nationality and profession. You need a health insurance policy that guarantees repatriation of your corpse should you die in Lebanon (presumably a war-time hangover), a letter from your employer (either here or abroad) and roughly US$667 per year for both work and residency permit.

Other options include coming in on a tourist visa and renewing it every three months, up to a maximum of four times. However, there are periodic crackdowns during which renewals are no longer issued, and customs and passport control check the number of stamps in your passport carefully upon arrival in the country.

ACCOMMODATION

With glitzy coastal resorts and glut of top-end hotels, Lebanon is not exactly a budget traveller's paradise. Nevertheless, beds can be had for as little as LL5000 a night (about US$3). Most of the budget hotels hover around the US$10 to US$25 per person level. Once you go above US$40 per person the choices widen.

Camping

Camping is starting to grow in popularity in Lebanon, although there are only two camp sites at the moment. The first is Camping Amchit, also known as Les Colombes, just north of Byblos on a beautiful promontory overlooking the sea. The other is La Reserve a tented resort in a stunning location high above the Adonis Valley, close to the Afqa Grotto. (See the Mt Lebanon chapter for more details on both.)

Hostels

There are currently no youth hostels in Lebanon, but there is talk of opening one in Beirut. Campus Travel (☎ 01-744 588) in Beirut, the agent for the International Youth Hostel Association, will have the latest news.

Pensions & Guesthouses

There are a few pensions in Lebanon; some are small family run establishments, others are simply cheap hotels that call themselves pensions. Prices start at around LL5000 per person in a dorm-style room and go up to about US$30 for a double room, including breakfast. Destination Liban arranges accommodation in pensions, monasteries and, occasionally, people's homes throughout the country. (See Organised Tours in the Getting Around chapter for contact information.)

Hotels

There is no shortage of hotels in Lebanon, especially in Beirut, and new ones seem to be springing up all the time. Most seem to be aiming at the lucrative Gulf tourist market and are marble-and-chandelier international-style expensive. There are exceptions and no matter where you stay you will find that the standards are higher than most hotels in surrounding countries.

When tourism in Lebanon does pick up, a wider selection of cheaper hotels should become available. In the meantime, there are bargains to be had, especially if you are travelling in winter when prices are slashed. And the cheap hotels that do exist are largely of a much better standard than those elsewhere in the region. If you're travelling alone, keep in mind that apart from the very cheapest places (where beds are in dorm-style rooms) the room price is often the same for singles and doubles.

The service charge is another thing to watch out for when checking into a hotel. Even mid-range hotels tend to add 15 or 16% to the basic room charge.

Mid-range hotels tend to cost about US$50 for a double room with bath. There are a number in the Hamra district of Beirut and in the regional towns. If you go for the more expensive hotels, they are comparable with three- and four-star hotels in Europe and are very comfortable. Most in this class have swimming pools and health clubs.

Homestays

If you would like to stay in an old stone house in a Lebanese mountain village, Gîtes du Levant (☎ cell 03-664 138, ✆ gitesagl@ inco.com.lb) is an organisation that acts as an intermediary between Lebanese home owners and tourists. Clustered in mountain villages between Beirut and Batroun the organisation offers houses to be rented by the week, a B&B arrangement in private houses per night, or lodging in monasteries. Destination Liban also arranges homestays for budget travellers in remote areas of the country. (See Organised Tours in the Getting Around chapter for contact details.)

Rental Accommodation

If you are planning a longer stay in Lebanon, it might be worth considering renting an apartment, although this would be an expensive option if you were travelling alone. In Beirut and most resorts, there are rental apartment buildings catering for long-term seasonal visitors (Lebanese people living abroad often visit Lebanon for the summer). These can work out much cheaper than hotels. Many of these apartment buildings have all the facilities of a hotel, but they are self-catering. Depending on the season, a small apartment will cost from US$200 to US$300 per week. If you will be staying for more than a few weeks, the price will always be negotiable.

FOOD

Lebanese cooking is one of the great cuisines of the Middle East and encompasses a wide array of dishes and cooking styles. Using fresh and flavoursome ingredients and refined spicing, the Lebanese have taken the best aspects of Turkish and Arabic cooking and given them a French spin.

The good news is that eating out need not be expensive. A traditional Lebanese meal starts with mezze, which is a selection of hot and cold starters. These can be simple or elaborate. Some are so filling that you could easily forgo a main course altogether. There are enough meatless dishes to satisfy vegetarians; there are usually aubergine or cheese dishes and sometimes pulses or beans.

Main courses are usually chicken, lamb or fish grilled with rice and salad (or the ubiquitous French fries) served with Lebanese flat bread. The national dish is *kibbeh* – a finely minced paste of lamb and bulgur wheat.

Fish and seafood in Lebanon is good, but, in common with the rest of the Mediterranean, fish restaurants are notoriously expensive and fish is priced on menus per kilogram.

Street food in Lebanon is very good indeed, and very cheap, with an abundance of snack bars selling chicken or meat *shwarma* (seasoned and spit-roasted meat) or felafels (fried chickpea balls) in delicious sandwiches. In fact, you will find almost everything stuffed into a sandwich: roast chicken, spicy sausages, cheese, you name it.

If you fancy something different, there is almost every international cuisine on offer, particularly in and around Beirut. You can find Japanese, Chinese, Indian, Italian, Mexican, French, Thai and also American burger bars.

In a good restaurant, you may find more than 40 mezze dishes on offer – some familiar, some not so – and that's just the first course!

When eating out in Lebanon, you may order as many or as few dishes as you choose. It is quite acceptable to just order a range of different mezze dishes. The more people ordering, the more variety you can experience. As a general rule, three or four mezze dishes per person should be plenty for a good lunch or dinner; two mezze dishes each is usually enough if you are ordering a main course as well.

Eating out in a Lebanese restaurant, you may come across some of the following:

Breads

khobz flat unleavened bread
manaeesh bi zaatar flat bread 'pizzas', seasoned with a mixture of thyme and sesame, drizzled with olive oil
marqouk mountain bread

Dips

hummus bi tahini puree of chickpeas and tahini with garlic and olive oil

hummus kawarmah delicious variation with grilled lamb on top

labneh thickened yogurt with garlic and olive oil

moutabbal puree of grilled aubergines with tahini, olive oil and lemon juice

tahineh creamy dip or sauce made from tahini, lemon juice and garlic

Cold Starters

bitinjaan ma'ali fried aubergine slices, usually with a minty yogurt sauce

fattoush toasted bread salad with tomatoes, onions and mint leaves

kibbeh nayye ground lamb and cracked wheat served raw like steak tartare

loubieh French bean salad with tomatoes, onions and garlic

shanklish mature goat's cheese with onions, olive oil and tomatoes

tabouleh salad of parsley and cracked wheat with onions and tomatoes

warak ainab vine leaves stuffed with rice and sometimes meat

Hot Starters

fatayer triangular pastries with minced lamb stuffing

fatayer bi sbanikh triangular pastries stuffed with spinach and (sometimes) pine nuts

felafel croquettes made with chickpeas and fava beans spiced with coriander

kibbeh maklieh ground lamb and cracked wheat croquettes stuffed with a savoury meat filling

kofta mixture of minced meat and spices that can be baked or grilled on skewers

kousa mashi courgette stuffed with minced lamb and pine nuts, served either *bi laban* (yogurt) or *bi bandoura* (tomato sauce)

makanek Lebanese lamb sausages

soujuk spicy Armenian sausages

Main Courses

daoud basha meatballs spiced with allspice and cinnamon and served with a thick sauce

kharouf mihshi lamb stuffed with rice, meat and nuts

kibbeh labaniyye kibbeh balls cooked in yogurt sauce

lahm meshwi cubes of lamb grilled on skewers

mousa'a Lebanese variation of moussaka, but without the bechamel sauce

musakhan chicken casserole spiced with sumac

ruz wi djaj chicken with rice and nuts

sayadieh fish, delicately spiced, served with rice in an onion and tahini sauce

shish tawouq pieces of chicken breast cooked on skewers

shwarma lamb or chicken grilled on a large spit and carved into slices

Desserts

kahk sweet usually almond flavoured biscuit filled with pistachios or dates

mahallabiye milk custard with pine nuts and almonds

mughly powdered rice, cumin and anise boiled with caraway and sugar. Eaten to celebrate the birth of a child and on other festive occasions.

ruz bi laban rice pudding, often with a few drops of rose-water

Snacks

Snack bars tend to specialise in one kind of food. You often come across places selling only felafels served wrapped in a flat bread roll with salad and sauce. These are very tasty and filling and cost only LL1500. *Fuul*, a paste made from fava beans, garlic and lemon and served with oil, is also a standard, filling snack at any time of the day.

Another popular and cheap snack is the manaeesh or 'pizza' which is bought at a *furn*, or oven. The crust is very thin with a small amount of topping – either meat with spices (called *lahma bi ajeen)*, cheese *(jibna)* or a mixture of thyme and sesame *(zaatar)*. These all cost from LL1000 to LL1500.

Of course the most common snacks are kebabs and shwarma, which again come wrapped in flat bread with salad and dressing. They usually cost about LL2000 and are very substantial.

Self-Catering

The shops and supermarkets in Lebanon are well stocked with Lebanese and imported food, so there is no problem if you want to buy and cook your own food. The prices are roughly the same as in Europe. The Lebanese like to buy their fruit and vegetables fresh every day and the greengrocers have a daily supply of seasonal produce. The tomatoes and salad produce are always good and there are always large, green bunches of flat-leafed parsley to make the ever-popular tabouleh.

Pickled vegetables are also very popular and these are served as appetisers or chopped

Food Glossary

Some of the following words be useful if you are buying things off the street or in markets:

Vegetables & Salad

cabbage	kharoum
carrot	jazar
cauliflower	arnabeet
cucumber	khiyaar
eggplant	toom
green beans	fasooliya
lentils	adas
lettuce	khass
okra	baamiya
onion	basal
peas	biseela
potatoes	batatas
salad	salata
tomato	banadura
turnip	lift
vegetables	khadrawat

Meats

chicken	farooj
kidney	kelaawi
lamb	lahm; kharouf
liver	kibda
meat	lahm

Fruit

apple	tufah
apricot	mish-mish
banana	moz
date	tamr
fig	teen
fruit	fawaka
grape	'inab
lime	limoon
mango	manga
olive	zeitoun
orange	burtuqaal
pomegranate	rummaan
strawberry	fraise
watermelon	batteekh

Miscellaneous

bag	kees
biscuits	biskouta
bottle	izaze
bread	khubiz
butter	zibda
cheese	jibna
eggs	beid
kilo	kilo
milk	haleeb
mineral water	maya at-ta'abiyya
pepper	filfil
salt	milh
sour yogurt drink	ayran
sugar	sukkar
water	mayy
yogurt	laban

into sandwiches. Cheeses are also very good. One of the most popular is *halloumi* – a salty, rubbery cheese which is good raw or fried. Soft, white cheese is on sale in most shops and is good in sandwiches.

If your cooking facilities are limited, you can buy delicious spit-roast chickens from many takeaway restaurants. These cost about LL9000 for a whole chicken with garlic sauce. Some butchers also sell ready-marinaded chicken pieces to grill on your barbecue or to fry in a pan.

If you are near a fish market, seafood is quite cheap to buy straight from the boat (as opposed to the fancy prices in fish restaur-ants) and is a very simple, delicious and healthy option.

Pastries

The cake shops in Lebanon look so tempting with their vast array of cookies and pastries. Most of the pastries are specialities of the region and are unfamiliar to many visitors. All of them are totally delicious and worth trying, even if you don't have a particularly sweet tooth.

To help you choose, here is a quick description, together with the Arabic name, of some of the most popular sweets and some of the lesser-known regional specialities:

asabeeh rolled filo pastry filled with pistachio, pine and cashew nuts and honey. Otherwise known as 'Lady's Fingers'.

baklava layers of flaky filo pastry with crushed pistachios or pine nuts in the centre. Cut into diamonds and soaked with syrup.

ballawryeh square slab of chopped pistachio in syrup topped with a layer of 'shredded wheat'

barazak flat, circular cookies sprinkled with sesame seeds. Very crisp and light.

borma crushed pine nuts or pistachios wrapped in a sticky coating of shredded pastry and sliced into rounds

faysalyeh triangular-shaped sweet with a filling of pistachio nuts

halawet ej-jibna soft, white pancake wrapped around a filling of cream cheese with syrup poured over. A speciality of Tripoli.

halva fruit and nuts covered with a sweet sesame paste, made into a slab and cut into squares

hriset al-fustuk green diamond-shaped pieces of sweetened pistachio paste

kol wa shkor crushed pine nuts or pistachios in syrup, wrapped in filo pastry and soaked in syrup

ktayef small half-moon shaped pastries with a nut paste filling, or sometimes cream cheese

kunafeh sort of baked cheesecake served in flat squares with syrup poured over and sometimes cream on top. This is sometimes served in a bread roll and is then called *kaake kunafeh.*

maamoul crisp, white biscuits stuffed with a paste of either pistachio or walnut

mafrouqeh sugar and butter mixture covered with rose-water and sugar syrup

malban Turkish delight

moon small squares layered in green and white with ground pistachio and almond

nammoura squares of sweet semolina cake topped with nuts

oush al-bulbul doughnut-shaped sweet of filo pastry stuffed with a sweet nut paste and topped with chopped pistachio

sanioura pale, crumbly biscuits in an oval shape. Very light and not too sweet. A speciality of Sidon.

zinoud is-sitt long, plump white pastries stuffed with cream

DRINKS
Nonalcoholic Drinks

Lebanese coffee is excellent and always popular. It is made in the Turkish way – strong and served in tiny cups. You can have it *sadah* (without sugar), *arreeha* (a little sugar), *wassat* (medium sugar) or *hilweh* (sweet). Tea is not quite as popular and is served in glasses with plenty of sugar and no milk. In spring you may find fresh almonds floating in your tea, giving the drink a delicious, softly almond aftertaste. Instant coffee is known by the generic name Nescafe, and is unfortunately the breakfast coffee of choice for most budget and medium-priced hotels. Espresso, cappuccino, lattes and other European-style coffees are available at Western-style cafes throughout Lebanon.

Fresh fruit juice is excellent and often sold by the side of the road where the vendor will squeeze it to order. Orange juice is the most popular as Lebanon is a major orange growing area, but you can also come across lemon, mango, even strawberry juice drinks. Pomegranate juice is good when in season. Juice bars sometimes also have freshly squeezed vegetable juices such as carrot, which is very refreshing in the heat of summer (not to mention healthy).

Some areas have their own specialities. In Batroun they make the best traditional *limonade* (lemonade), and in Tripoli they have a drink made out of raisins called *jellab. Ayran*, a salty yogurt drink, is sold just about everywhere and is a delicious way of taking extra salt if you are worried about dehydration.

All the usual brands of soft drinks (sodas) are widely available.

Alcoholic Drinks

All kinds of wines and spirits, both domestic and imported, are easily available throughout Lebanon. Alcohol is cheap – about US$8 for a bottle of whisky and US$5 for a bottle of mid-range domestic wine.

The national drink is *arak*, an aniseed-flavoured drink which is mixed with water and ice, much like the French Pernod or Greek ouzo. It is an acquired taste, and people either love it or loathe it. Either way it has the virtue of being quite cheap (about US$6 a bottle). Good local brands include Ksarak and Le Brun. (See also the boxed text 'Arak' in The Bekaa Valley chapter.)

Some of Lebanon's wines are very good and even the worst are drinkable. Ksara,

Kefraya and Chateau Musar are three labels that are well known internationally. Less well known labels (and many might say less tasty) are Clos St Thomas, Masaya, Faqra and Wardih.

Lebanon brews its own beer. Almaza, a lager, is the most commonly found brand. There is also Amstel, a Dutch beer brewed locally under licence.

ENTERTAINMENT
Pubs & Bars
Bars and pubs are part of Lebanon's vibrant nightlife and, at least in Beirut, range from cosy English-style pubs to sleek, glamorous and hyper-designed bars. In between you can find everything from Western-style theme bars to lounge bars and tapas joints. With the exception of Jounieh and possibly Byblos the choice drops off dramatically outside Beirut.

Discos & Clubs
Beirut is rapidly regaining its status as party capital of the Eastern Mediterranean, with a vibrant nightlife that rivals or betters many cities in Europe. The distinction between a club and a restaurant tends to blur late on weekend evenings in some establishments, when patrons push the cutlery aside and climb on tables and bars to dance. If you want to go clubbing, don't expect much until well after midnight. Outside of Beirut, the main nightlife tends to focus on Jounieh, where the (only slightly muted) partying migrated during the civil war. There are also seasonal migrations of the dance and party crowd to the ski resorts of Faraya and Faqra in the winter, and some popular summer resorts like Ehden.

Live Music
Live music and dancing shows tend to start at around 10 pm and go on until late into the night. Traditional Lebanese music and belly dancing can be seen in restaurants or big hotels, while imported cabaret acts (often from the former eastern bloc) tend to dominate the big 'super' nightclubs geared to Gulf Arabs. In Beirut a couple of bars specialise in jazz and live rock.

You don't have to eat at the nightclubs, but if you are intending only to drink, there may be a cover charge (sometimes quite hefty). Drink prices vary from the moderately expensive to the outrageous.

Cinemas
All the main towns seem to have at least one cinema and Beirut has more than a dozen. These often show the latest Western releases in their original form with Arabic subtitles. Occasionally they are dubbed into Arabic, so it is a good idea to check first. Explicit sex and frontal nudity are usually censored. Cell phone etiquette is not a high priority in many cinemas, so be prepared for annoying rings and conversation when you watch a film. Also keep in mind that audiences (particularly if predominantly young and male) can sometimes get raucous when a film contains sex or partial nudity. Apart from being annoying it can make lone female viewers uncomfortable.

Cinema tickets cost LL10,000 and only LL5000 on Mondays, although some cinemas also offer discounts on Tuesdays and Wednesdays. There are sometimes short seasons of films shown at the foreign cultural institutes. These mostly consist of art-house movies from the countries concerned and are in the language of that country. Check listings in the *Daily Star*, *L'Orient-Le Jour* or www.cyberia.net.lb, which has extensive reviews as well as listings.

Theatre
There is a lively theatre scene in Beirut. Comedy reviews and contemporary plays feature heavily, but most performances are in Arabic or French. However, many foreign performers also pass through Beirut, sponsored by cultural organisations, so you may find something in English. English plays are also shown at the American University of Beirut campus theatre. Check the theatre listings in the daily media or, if you can get it, the *Agenda Culturelle.*

Coffeehouses
The *ahweh* or coffeehouse is an institution in Lebanon, as in the rest of the Arab world.

Here is where men (and occasionally women) come to drink tea or strong, sweet coffee and smoke a nargileh (water pipe). If you don't fancy the traditional cafes, there is no shortage of European-style cafes and bars to suit all tastes and pockets.

SPECTATOR SPORTS

The Lebanese are avid football fans (is there a nationality that isn't?) and the Beirut traffic is noticeably lighter when a team from the local league is playing. Two of the more popular clubs are Beirut Nejmeh and Beirut Ansar. Basketball is also wildly popular and local teams include La Sagesse, Rosary and Antranic. Check the local media for game times.

Sunday is the day for horse racing at the Beirut Hippodrome (☎ 01-632 520), but it is not *every* Sunday. This is a very popular sport with the locals and is a great way to soak up the atmosphere. Again, check the paper for details. Admission is US$10 to the grandstand and US$3 to the 2nd-class stand. The entrance is on Ave Abdallah Yafi, not far from the National Museum.

Reflecting the Lebanese love affair with cars and reckless driving, there are currently two rallies held annually. Every spring the Rallye du Printemps takes place in Kesrouane, while in autumn the Rallye des Cédres is held up near the Cedars. Lebanon is also bidding to become the home of the first Middle East Formula One Grand Prix. The proposed route goes through Beirut, ending in the new downtown area. The first race has been tentatively set for the year 2003, to give Solidére time to complete its construction. Preparations have already been going on for three years and if the race is held it is expected to cost as much as US$40 to US$80 million to fund.

SHOPPING

You can buy almost anything in Lebanon, but with its love of imported goods and high prices, it is weak on distinctive local souvenirs. Almost all of the traditional Middle Eastern trinkets, such as inlaid boxes, kilims, scarves and silver jewellery, are made in Syria or India.

However, there are a number of shops around the country that specialise in traditional handicrafts. These include the Artisans de l'Orient shops and the Arisans du Liban. Most of their merchandise is inspired by traditional crafts, rather than being part of an ancient Lebanese tradition, but they have beautiful glass and tableware, pottery, clothing and some embroidery.

Although not strictly speaking Lebanese, another handmade product made in Lebanon is embroidery by Palestinian refugees. The beautiful traditional patterns are sold as cushion covers, scarves, traditional dresses and wallets at an outlet, Al-Badia, in Beirut. (See Shopping in the Beirut chapter for details.)

The souqs of Sidon and Tripoli are the best places to trawl in search of something handmade and original. In Tripoli, a few coppersmiths still turn out traditional work. There are large numbers of workshops in the old souqs (just follow the din) and the prices for even elaborate pieces are quite reasonable (by Lebanese standards). Tripoli is also the place to buy pure handmade soap. Made from olive oil and other natural products, the soap is reasonably priced and makes a good gift. See the Tripoli & the North chapter for more information.

Another popular souvenir is a fish fossil set in stone. These come from the mountains above Byblos and can be bought there or in other shops around the country.

When visiting the larger ancient sites (particularly Baalbek) you are likely to be approached by people selling antiquities, usually Roman coins. Most of them are (extremely good) fakes made in Syria, and be aware that even though the government is notoriously lax in enforcement, it is illegal to export antiquities.

Lebanon used to be a good source of antiques, many sold off by desperate Beirutis during the war. The Basta area of Beirut used to be *the* place for 18th and 19th-century furniture and *objets*, but much of it was snapped up by returnees after the war. Finds can still be made there, but don't expect bargains.

Lithographs from the 19th century, as well as old furniture, can also be bought at a number of shops near the American University of Beirut.

Modern Lebanese furniture and design is showcased at a shop called Artishow, in Achrafiye, Beirut. The small collections are exhibited alongside furniture and designer objects from Europe. Don't come looking for bargains.

Foodies may want to take back some dried or long-lasting cooking staples. Zaatar (thyme) and sumac (a reddish, lemony dried herb that is delicious on eggs and in salad) can both be used in cooking back home and are much fresher in Lebanon than they will be at Middle Eastern food shops outside the region. *Dibs romaan* or pomegranete syrup is hard to find outside the Middle East and can be used to sweeten meat dishes. Rose and orange blossom water are also good buys. If you're touring the vineyards, there are some vintage Lebanese wines available. They can also be bought at a couple of venues in Beirut, as well as in the airport when you leave.

Getting There & Away

Travelling to Lebanon could not be easier. There is a growing number of airlines serving Beirut from all over the world. Most visitors fly into Beirut. The exceptions are people travelling to more than one country in the region, in which case they often catch buses or taxis from nearby Syria.

AIR

Air tickets to Lebanon are more expensive from May to September and from mid-December until Christmas. At other times, you can make a saving on the price of your ticket.

Airports & Airlines

Beirut International Airport is Lebanon's only airport. Just 5km south of the city centre, the runway begins as the rooftops of the southern suburbs end, an alarming sight when you first arrive. Still sparkling and brand new, rebuilt on the site of the old airport, it is a quiet and relaxing place to arrive. The arrivals hall is well organised, with plenty of desks for passport control. Immigration procedures are reasonably straightforward and fast, though passing through customs can be slow if luggage is being checked. Facilities inside the airport are still thin on the ground, but some car rental agencies and exchange places are open. For details on getting to and from the airport, see Getting Around in the Beirut chapter.

Beirut is rapidly resuming its former standing as a transport hub for the Middle East. Connections to Europe, Africa and Asia are frequent and over 40 airlines now have routes to or via Beirut. The national carrier, Middle East Airlines (MEA), has an extensive network including direct flights to and from Australia, Europe and the Arab world. Many other major airlines service Beirut including Air France, Alitalia, British Airways, British Mediterranean Airways, Emirates, Gulf Air, KLM-Royal Dutch Airlines, Malaysia Airlines, Royal Jordanian, Scandinavian Airlines (SAS) and Turkish Airlines.

Warning

The information in this chapter is particularly vulnerable to change: Prices for international travel are volatile, routes are introduced and cancelled, schedules change, special deals come and go, and rules and visa requirements are amended. Airlines and governments seem to take a perverse pleasure in making price structures and regulations as complicated as possible. You should check directly with the airline or a travel agent to make sure you understand how a fare (and ticket you may buy) works. In addition, the travel industry is highly competitive and there are many lurks and perks.

The upshot of this is that you should get opinions, quotes and advice from as many airlines and travel agents as possible before you part with your hard-earned cash. The details given in this chapter should be regarded as pointers and are not a substitute for your own careful, up-to-date research.

Buying Tickets

An air ticket alone can gouge a great slice out of anyone's budget, but you can reduce the cost of your ticket by finding discounted fares. Stiff competition has fortunately resulted in widespread discounting – good news for travellers! The only people likely to be paying full fare these days are travellers flying in 1st or business class. Passengers flying in economy can usually manage some sort of discount. But unless you buy carefully and flexibly, it is still possible to end up paying exorbitant amounts for a journey.

For long-term travel there are plenty of discount tickets that are valid for 12 months, allowing travellers multiple stopovers with open dates. For short-term travel, cheaper fares are available by travelling mid-week, staying away at least one Saturday night or taking advantage of short-lived promotional offers.

When you're looking for bargain air fares, go to a travel agent rather than directly to the airline. From time to time, airlines do have promotional fares and special offers, but generally they only sell fares at the official listed price.

An alternative to this is booking on the Internet. Many airlines, full-service and no-frills, offer some excellent fares to Web surfers. They may sell seats by auction or simply cut prices to reflect the reduced cost of electronic selling. Many travel agents around the world have Web sites, which can make the Internet a quick and easy way to compare prices, a good start for when you're ready to start negotiating with your favourite travel agency. Online ticket sales work well if you are doing a simple one-way or return trip on specified dates. However, online superfast fare generators are no substitute for a travel agent who knows all about special deals, has strategies for avoiding layovers and can offer advice on everything from which airline has the best vegetarian food to the best travel insurance to bundle with your ticket.

The days when some travel agents would routinely fleece travellers by running off with their money are, happily, almost over. Paying by credit card generally offers protection, as most card issuers provide refunds if you can prove you didn't get what you paid for. Similar protection can be obtained by buying a ticket from a bonded agent, such as one covered by the Air Transport Operators License (ATOL) scheme in the UK. Agents who only accept cash should hand over the tickets straight away and not tell you to 'come back tomorrow'. After you've made a booking or paid your deposit, call the airline and confirm that the booking was made. It's generally not advisable to send money (even cheques) through the post unless the agent is very well established – some travellers have reported being ripped off by fly-by-night mail-order ticket agents.

You may decide to pay more than the rock-bottom fare by opting for the safety of a better-known travel agent. Firms such as STA Travel, which has offices worldwide, Council Travel in the USA and Usit Campus (formerly Campus Travel) in the UK are not going to disappear overnight and they do offer good prices to most destinations.

If you purchase a ticket and later want to make changes to your route or get a refund, you need to contact the original travel agent. Airlines only issue refunds to the purchaser of a ticket – usually the travel agent who bought the ticket on your behalf. Many travellers change their routes halfway through their trips, so think carefully before you buy a ticket that can not be easily refunded.

Student & Youth Fares Full-time students and people under 26 have access to better deals than other travellers. The better deals may not always be cheaper fares but can include more flexibility to change flights and/or routes. You have to show a document proving your date of birth or a valid International Student Identity Card (ISIC) when buying your ticket and boarding the plane. There are plenty of places around the world where nonstudents can get fake student cards, but if you get caught using a fake card you could have your ticket confiscated.

Frequent Fliers Most airlines offer frequent flier deals that can earn you a free air ticket or other goodies. To qualify, you have to accumulate sufficient mileage with the same airline or airline alliance. Many airlines have 'blackout periods', or times when you cannot fly for free on your frequent-flier points (Christmas and Chinese New Year, for example). The worst thing about frequent-flier programs is that they tend to lock you into one airline, and that airline may not always have the cheapest fares or most convenient flight schedule.

Courier Flights Courier flights are a great bargain if you're lucky enough to find one. Air-freight companies expedite delivery of urgent items by sending them with you as your baggage allowance. You are permitted to bring along a carry-on bag, but that's all. In return, you get a steeply discounted ticket.

There are other restrictions: Courier tickets are sold for a fixed date and schedule changes can be difficult to make. If you buy a return ticket, your schedule will be even more rigid. You need to clarify before you fly what restrictions apply to your ticket, and don't expect a refund once you've paid.

Booking a courier ticket takes some effort. They are not readily available and arrangements have to be made a month or more in advance. You won't find courier flights on all routes either – just on the major air routes.

Courier flights are occasionally advertised in the newspapers, or you could contact air-freight companies listed in the phone book. You may have to go to the air-freight company to get an answer – the companies aren't always keen to give out information over the phone. *Travel Unlimited* (PO Box 1058, Allston, MA 02134, USA) is a monthly travel newsletter based in the USA that publishes many courier flight deals from destinations worldwide. A 12-month subscription to the newsletter costs US$25, or US$35 for readers outside the US. Another possibility (at least for US residents) is to join the International Association of Air Travel Couriers (IAATC). The membership fee of US$45 gets members a bimonthly update of air-courier offerings, access to a fax-on-demand service with daily updates of last-minute specials and the bimonthly newsletter the *Shoestring Traveler*. For more information, contact IAATC (☎ 561-582 8320) or visit its Web site, www.courier.org. However, be aware that joining this organisation does not guarantee that you'll get a courier flight.

Second-Hand Tickets You'll occasionally see advertisements on youth hostel bulletin boards and sometimes in newspapers for 'second-hand tickets'. That is, somebody purchased a return ticket or a ticket with multiple stopovers and now wants to sell the unused portion of the ticket.

The prices offered look very attractive indeed. Unfortunately, these tickets, if used for international travel, are usually worthless, as the name on the ticket must match the name on the passport of the person checking in. Some people reason that the seller of the ticket can check you in with his or her passport, and then give you the boarding pass – wrong again! Usually the immigration people want to see your boarding pass, and if it doesn't match the name in your passport then you won't be able to board your flight.

What happens if you purchase a ticket and then change your name? It can happen – some people change their name when they get married or divorced and some people change their name because they feel like it. If the name on the ticket doesn't match the name in your passport, you could have problems. In this case, be sure you have documents such as your old passport to prove that the old you and the new you are the same person.

Ticketless Travel Ticketless travel, whereby your reservation details are contained within an airline computer, is becoming more common. On simple return trips the absence of a ticket can be a benefit – it's one less thing to worry about; however, if you are planning a complicated itinerary that you may wish to amend en route, there is no substitute for the good old paper version.

Travellers with Special Needs
Most international airlines can cater to people with special needs – travellers with disabilities, people with young children and even children travelling alone.

Travellers with special dietary preferences (vegetarian, kosher etc) can request appropriate meals with advance notice. If you are travelling in a wheelchair, most international airports can provide an escort from check-in desk to plane where needed, and ramps, lifts, toilets and phones are generally available.

Airlines usually allow babies up to two years of age to fly for 10% of the adult fare, although a few may allow them free of charge. Reputable international airlines usually provide nappies (diapers), tissues, talcum and all the other paraphernalia needed to keep babies clean, dry and half-happy. For children between the ages of two and 12, the fare on international flights is usually 50% of the regular fare or 67% of a discounted fare.

Air Travel Glossary

Cancellation Penalties If you have to cancel or change a discounted ticket, there are often heavy penalties involved; insurance can sometimes be taken out against these penalties. Some airlines impose penalties on regular tickets as well, particularly against 'no-show' passengers.

Courier Fares Businesses often need to send urgent documents or freight securely and quickly. Courier companies hire people to accompany the package through customs and, in return, offer a discount ticket which is sometimes a phenomenal bargain. However, you may have to surrender all your baggage allowance and take only carry-on luggage.

Full Fares Airlines traditionally offer 1st class (coded F), business class (coded J) and economy class (coded Y) tickets. These days there are so many promotional and discounted fares available that few passengers pay full economy fare.

Lost Tickets If you lose your airline ticket an airline will usually treat it like a travellers cheque and, after inquiries, issue you with another one. Legally, however, an airline is entitled to treat it like cash and if you lose it then it's gone forever. Take good care of your tickets.

Onward Tickets An entry requirement for many countries is that you have a ticket out of the country. If you're unsure of your next move, the easiest solution is to buy the cheapest onward ticket to a neighbouring country or a ticket from a reliable airline which can later be refunded if you do not use it.

Open-Jaw Tickets These are return tickets where you fly out to one place but return from another. If available, this can save you backtracking to your arrival point.

Overbooking Since every flight has some passengers who fail to show up, airlines often book more passengers than they have seats. Usually excess passengers make up for the no-shows, but occasionally somebody gets 'bumped' onto the next available flight. Guess who it is most likely to be? The passengers who check in late.

Promotional Fares These are officially discounted fares, available from travel agencies or direct from the airline.

Reconfirmation If you don't reconfirm your flight at least 72 hours prior to departure, the airline may delete your name from the passenger list. Ring to find out if your airline requires reconfirmation.

Restrictions Discounted tickets often have various restrictions on them – such as needing to be paid for in advance and incurring a penalty to be altered. Others are restrictions on the minimum and maximum period you must be away.

Round-the-World Tickets RTW tickets give you a limited period (usually a year) in which to circumnavigate the globe. You can go anywhere the carrying airlines go, as long as you don't backtrack. The number of stopovers or total number of separate flights is decided before you set off and they usually cost a bit more than a basic return flight.

Transferred Tickets Airline tickets cannot be transferred from one person to another. Travellers sometimes try to sell the return half of their ticket, but officials can ask you to prove that you are the person named on the ticket. On an international flight tickets are compared with passports.

Travel Periods Ticket prices vary with the time of year. There is a low (off-peak) season and a high (peak) season, and often a low-shoulder season and a high-shoulder season as well. Usually the fare depends on your outward flight – if you depart in the high season and return in the low season, you pay the high-season fare.

In Tripoli's colourful and bustling souqs, you will find herbs and spices...

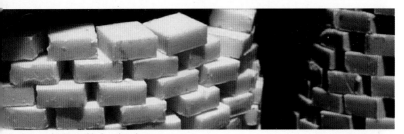

...the famous high-quality handmade soap...

...and deliciously irresistible Lebanese sweets.

A Shiite poster adorning a Beirut city wall

Beirut's Piccadilly Theatre presents mainstream comedies as well as more experimental offerings.

Departure Tax

Airline passengers must pay US$51 when departing from Beirut International Airport.

The USA

Discount travel agents in the USA are known as consolidators. San Francisco is the ticket consolidator capital of America, although some good deals can be found in Los Angeles, New York and other big cities. Consolidators can be found through the Yellow Pages or the major newspapers. The *New York Times*, the *Los Angeles Times*, the *Chicago Tribune* and the *San Francisco Examiner* all produce weekly travel sections in which you will find travel agency ads. Ticket Planet is a leading ticket consolidator in the USA and is recommended. Visit its Web site at www.ticketplanet.com.

Other Internet ticket sites with discounts are:

- www.un-travel.com – contributes 10% of its net profits to children's causes.
- www.pinotravel.com – an online bucket shop that gives good discounts to inter national destinations.
- www.travelocity.com – can give you air fares originating from anywhere in the world, not only from the US.

Council Travel, America's largest student travel organisation, has around 60 offices in the USA; its head office (☎ 800-226 8624) is at 205 E 42 St, New York, NY 10017. Call it for the office nearest you or visit its Web site at www.ciee.org. STA Travel (☎ 800-777 0112) has offices in Boston, Chicago, Miami, New York, Philadelphia, San Francisco and other major cities. Call the toll-free 800 number for office locations or visit its Web site at www.statravel.com.

The best deals on flights to Lebanon usually involve a stop either in Europe or in the Middle East. Royal Jordanian Airlines, via Amman, is one of the better deals. If you search hard you can find a fare for as little as US$700 return from New York, depending on the time of year you travel. At high season it is almost impossible to find anything under US$1500.

Canada

Canadian discount air ticket sellers are also known as consolidators and their air fares tend to be about 10% higher than those sold in the USA. The *Globe & Mail*, the *Toronto Star*, the *Montreal Gazette* and the *Vancouver Sun* carry travel agents ads and are a good place to look for cheap fares.

Travel CUTS (☎ 800-667 2887) is Canada's national student travel agency and has offices in all major cities. Its Web address is www.travelcuts.com.

Australia

There is a large expatriate Lebanese community in Australia and Emirates, Gulf Air, Malaysia Airlines, Kuwait Airways and Egypt Air all have routes linking Australia to Beirut. Both Kuwait Airways and Gulf Air offer deals from Sydney to Beirut, starting at US$1720.

Otherwise, quite a few travel offices specialise in discount air tickets. Some travel agents, particularly smaller ones, advertise cheap air fares in the travel sections of weekend newspapers, such as the *Age* in Melbourne and the *Sydney Morning Herald*.

Two well-known agents for cheap fares are STA Travel and Flight Centre. STA Travel (☎ 03-9349 2411) has its main office at 224 Faraday St, Carlton, Vic 3053, and offices in all major cities and on many university campuses. Call ☎ 131 776 Australia wide for the location of your nearest branch or visit the Web site at www.statravel.com.au. Flight Centre (☎ 131 600 Australia wide) has a central office at 82 Elizabeth St, Sydney, and there are dozens of offices throughout Australia. Its Web address is www.flightcentre.com.au.

New Zealand

The *New Zealand Herald* has a travel section in which travel agents advertise fares. Flight Centre (☎ 09-309 6171) has a large central office in Auckland at National Bank Towers (on the corner of Queen and Darby Sts) and many branches throughout the country. STA Travel (☎ 09-309 0458) has its main office at 10 High St, Auckland, and there are other offices in Auckland as well as in Hamilton,

Palmerston North, Wellington, Christchurch and Dunedin. The Web address is www.sta. travel.com.au. Malaysia Airlines and Gulf Air have flights starting from around NZ$2200.

The UK

Airline ticket discounters are known as bucket shops in the UK. Despite the somewhat disreputable name, there is nothing under-the-counter about them. Discount air travel is big business in London. Ads for many travel agents appear in the travel pages of the weekend broadsheets, such as the *Independent* on Saturday and the *Sunday Times*. Look out for the free magazines, such as *TNT*, which are widely available in London – start by looking outside the main railway and underground stations. On the Web, www.cheapflights.com consolidates information from many different airlines and is another good source of cheap fares from the UK.

For students or travellers under 26, popular travel agencies in the UK include STA Travel (☎ 020-7361 6161), which has an office at 86 Old Brompton Rd, London SW7 3LQ, and other offices in London and Manchester. Visit its Web site at www.sta-travel.co.uk. Usit Campus (☎ 0870-240 1010), 52 Grosvenor Gardens, London SW1W 0AG, has branches throughout the UK. The Web address is www.usitcampus.co.uk. Both of these agencies sell tickets to all travellers but cater especially to young people and students. Other recommended travel agencies include: Trailfinders (☎ 020-7938 3939), 194 Kensington High St, London W8 7RG; Bridge the World (☎ 020-7734 7447), 4 Regent Place, London W1R 5FB; and Flightbookers (☎ 020-7757 2000), 177–178 Tottenham Court Rd, London W1P 9LF.

Flights to Beirut start at about UK£300.

Continental Europe

Though London is the travel discount capital of Europe, there are several other cities in which you will find a range of good deals. Generally, there is not much variation in air-fare prices for departures from the main European cities. All the major airlines are usually offering some sort of deal, and travel agents generally have a number of deals on offer, so shop around. To Beirut, you'll be looking at a minimum of about US$400 for a return ticket.

Across Europe many travel agencies have ties with STA Travel, where cheap tickets can be purchased and STA-issued tickets can be altered (usually for a US$25 fee). Outlets in major cities include: Voyages Wasteels (☎ 08 03 88 70 04 – note that this number can only be dialled from within France, fax 01 43 25 46 25), 11 rue Dupuytren, 756006 Paris; STA Travel (☎ 030-311 0950, fax 313 0948), Goethestrasse 73, 10625 Berlin; Passaggi (☎ 06-474 0923, fax 482 7436), Stazione Termini FS, Galleria Di Tesla, Rome; and ISYTS (☎ 01-322 1267, fax 323 3767), 11 Nikis St, Upper Floor, Syntagma Square, Athens.

France has a network of student travel agencies which can supply discount tickets to travellers of all ages. OTU Voyages (☎ 01 44 41 38 50) has a central Paris office at 39 Ave Georges Bernanos (5e) and another 42 offices around the country. The Web address is www.otu.fr. Acceuil des Jeunes en France (☎ 01 42 77 87 80), 119 rue Saint Martin (4e), is another popular discount travel agency.

General travel agencies in Paris which offer some of the best services and deals include Nouvelles Frontières (☎ 08 03 33 33 33), 5 Ave de l'Opéra (1er), Web site www.nouvelles-frontieres.com; as well as Voyageurs du Monde (☎ 1 42 86 16 00) at 55 rue Sainte Anne (2e).

Belgium, Switzerland, the Netherlands and Greece are also good places for buying discount air tickets. In Belgium, Acotra Student Travel Agency (☎ 02-512 86 07) at rue de la Madeline, Brussels, and WATS Reizen (☎ 03-226 16 26) at de Keyserlei 44, Antwerp, are both well-known agencies. In Switzerland, SSR Voyages (☎ 01-297 11 11) specialises in student, youth and budget fares. In Zurich, there is a branch at Leonhardstrasse 10 and there are others in most major Swiss cities. The Web address is www.ssr.ch.

In the Netherlands, NBBS Reizen is the official student travel agency. You can find it in Amsterdam (☎ 020-624 09 89) at Rokin 66 and there are several other agencies around the city. Another recommended travel agent in Amsterdam is Malibu Travel (☎ 020-626 32 30) at Prinsengracht 230.

In Athens, check the many travel agencies in the backstreets between Syntagma and Omonia Squares. For student and non-concessionary fares, try Magic Bus (☎ 01-323 7471, fax 322 0219).

Africa

Nairobi and Johannesburg are probably the best places in East and South Africa to buy tickets. Some major airlines have offices in Nairobi, which is a good place to determine the standard fare before you make the rounds of the travel agencies. Getting several quotes is a good idea as prices are always changing. Flight Centres (☎ 02-210 024) in Lakhamshi House, Biashara St, has been in business for many years.

In Johannesburg the South African Student's Travel Services (☎ 011-716 3045) has an office at the University of the Witwatersrand. STA Travel (☎ 011-447 5551) has an office in Johannesburg on Tyrwhitt Ave in Rosebank.

The main international airports in West Africa are Abidjan, Accra, Bamako, Dakar and Lagos. There are also some regular charter flights from some European countries to Banjul (Gambia). It is usually better to buy tickets in West Africa through a travel agency rather than from the airline. Travel agents' fares are generally the same as the fares offered by the airlines, but agents may be more helpful if anything goes wrong.

In Abidjan, you will find Saga Voyages (☎ 32 98 70), opposite Air Afrique in Le Plateau. Haury Tours (☎ 22 16 54, fax 22 17 68, ✉ haury@africaonline.co.ci), 2nd floor, Chardy Bldg in Le Plateau, is an affiliate of the French-based travel group Nouvelles Frontières.

In Accra, try Expert Travel & Tours (☎ 021-775 498) on Ring Rd East near the US embassy.

There are several agencies dealing in international and regional flights in Bamako.

Two of the best are ATS Voyages (☎ 22 44 35) on Ave Kassa Keita and TAM (☎ 23 92 00, ✉ tvoyage@sotelma.net) on Square Lumumba, which is open until midnight Monday to Saturday and on Sunday morning.

Agencies in Dakar include Senegal Tours (☎ 823 31 81), 5 Place de l'Indépendance, and SDV Voyages (☎ 839 00 81), 51 Ave Albert Sarraut.

In Lagos there are many travel agencies in the Race Course Rd complex on the southern side of Tafawa Balewa Square on Lagos Island. Most of the airline offices are in this area too. Try L'Aristocrate Travels & Tours (☎ 01-266 7322), corner Davies and Broad Sts, or Mandilas Travel (☎ 01-266 3339) on Broad St.

Middle East

Beirut is well connected to other Middle Eastern cities but you are unlikely to find good deals if you're originating anywhere in the region. Although Cairo, Istanbul, Tel Aviv and Dubai are the main cities visited by travellers in the Middle East, they are not the best places to look for good travel deals. Usually the best travel deal you will manage in the Middle East is an airline's official excursion fare. Some travel agencies will knock down the price by up to 10% if you're persistent, but they may then tie you into fixed dates or flying with a less-popular airline.

The nearest thing you will find to a discount travel ticket market in the Middle East is offered by some travel agencies in Istanbul, especially around Taksim Square and in Sultanahmet.

Beirut is well connected to other Middle Eastern cities. Syrian Arab Airlines and MEA both have one service a week from Damascus to Beirut with a return ticket costing from US$65. Both Royal Jordanian Airlines and MEA fly daily from Amman with return fares from US$162. EgyptAir and MEA both have six flights per week from Cairo with fares from US$280 return. If you are coming from the Gulf, Emirates, Gulf Air and MEA fly daily from Dubai or Abu Dhabi and fares are US$620 one way and US$675 return.

LAND
Border Crossings

The only land borders open to Lebanon at the moment are those with Syria. Despite the Israeli withdrawal, the southern border will remain closed until a peace accord is signed – still a distant prospect. You cannot get a Syrian visa in Lebanon, but you can now get a Lebanese visa at the border when entering from Syria. For more details, see Visas in the Facts for the Visitor chapter.

There are four different crossing points from Lebanon into Syria: Masnaa, on the Beirut-Damascus Hwy, Al-Qaa, at the northern end of the Bekaa Valley, Aarida on the coastal road from Tripoli to Lattakia and Aabboudiye on the Tripoli to Homs route.

Syria

Bus Buses to Syria from Beirut leave from Charles Helou bus station, just east of the restored downtown area. You must go in person to buy your ticket and, if possible, it's best to book a seat the day before you travel. The first bus to Damascus leaves at 5.30 am, and they run every half-hour until 7 am, after which they leave hourly. Buses to Aleppo (ask for Halab) start at 7.30 am and leave at half-hourly intervals until midday. There are also three buses a day (10.30 am, 2 pm and 5.30 pm) to Lattakia, six to Homs (7.30 and 9.30 am and 1.30, 5, 7 and 9.30 pm) and four to Hama (9.30 am, 5, 7 and 9.30 pm).

Tripoli also has extensive bus services to Syria. A number of bus companies cluster around Jamal Abdel Nasser Square in the city centre, many offering air-con and, unfortunately, on-board videos. There are frequent departures to Homs, Hama and Aleppo in the morning, starting at around 9 am until midday; there are not as many buses in the afternoon. Buses travelling to Lattakia and Damascus are fewer in number and tend to depart in the afternoon. For average prices and travel times, see the boxed text 'Fares to Syria'.

In Damascus, private and Karnak (government-run) buses travel to Lebanon. Both types of buses leave from the Baramke ter-

---

Fares to Syria

Bus

route	cost	duration
Beirut – Aleppo	LL10,500	6 hrs
Beirut – Damascus	LL7000	3 hrs
Beirut – Hama	LL9000	6 hrs
Beirut – Homs	LL8500	4 hrs
Beirut – Lattakia	LL9000	4 hrs
Tripoli – Aleppo	LL8000	4 hrs
Tripoli – Hama	LL6500	2 hrs
Tripoli – Homs	LL5000	1½ hrs
Tripoli – Lattakia	LL6000	2 hrs

Service Taxi

route	cost	duration
Beirut – Aleppo	LL21,000	5 hrs
Beirut – Damascus	LL15,000	3 hrs
Beirut – Hama	LL15,000	4 hrs
Beirut – Homs	LL15,000	3 hrs
Beirut – Lattakia	LL15,000	3 hrs
Beirut – Tartus	LL12,000	2 hrs
Baalbek – Damascus	LL9000	1½ hrs
Baalbek – Homs	LL9000	1½ hrs
Tripoli – Hama	LL9000	2 hrs
Tripoli – Homs	LL7000	1½ hrs
Tripoli – Lattakia	LL9000	2 hrs

Note Travel times do not include the border crossings, which depend on the traffic. If traffic is light, border formalities shouldn't take more than half an hour.

---

minal, which is about a 15-minute walk to the west of Martyrs Square. The prices quoted in the table are for the privately operated buses; Karnak bus fares tend to be a bit cheaper.

From Aleppo, the buses leave from the bus station tucked away just behind Baron St, not two minutes from the Baron Hotel. Again the services to Beirut are mainly privately operated buses.

Taxi If you prefer to take a taxi, either service or private, in Beirut they leave from the Cola bus station and taxi stand or from Charles Helou bus station. In Tripoli they leave from Jamal Abdel Nasser Square.

The service taxis leave when they are full but there is seldom a wait of more than 20 minutes. Private and service taxis go to and from Damascus, where you can change to go on to Jordan. A private taxi from Beirut to Damascus costs about US$50.

Car & Motorcycle If you are bringing a foreign-registered vehicle into Lebanon, there is a hefty charge levied at the border (refundable when you leave). This is calculated on a sliding scale depending on the value of the vehicle. Unless you have large amounts of cash to leave as a deposit, this ruling effectively makes it unfeasible to bring your own car into Lebanon. A better plan would be to arrive by bus or service taxi and then rent a car locally.

If you do decide to drive into Lebanon, you will need an International Driving Permit (IDP), the vehicle's registration papers and liability insurance. It is possible to service most common makes of vehicle in Lebanon. Petrol, available in the usual range of octanes and lead-free, is sold at most petrol stations. (See the Car & Motorcycle section in the Getting Around chapter for details of driving in Lebanon.)

Elsewhere in the Middle East

There are a few buses that originate in Beirut and pass through Syria to other Middle Eastern destinations. The Mirr Company (☎ cell 03-899 399) at Beirut's Charles Helou bus station operates daily services to Amman and Istanbul. Currently, the Amman service leaves at 9 am and costs LL25,000. The bus to Istanbul leaves at 9 pm and costs US$40. From Amman you can change for buses to Egypt, Israel or the Gulf; those with stamina can change at Istanbul for buses to Europe.

SEA

From May to October the Louis Tourist Company in Cyprus operates a two-day cruise between Limassol and Beirut. The boat leaves Limassol on Friday at 8 pm and arrives in Beirut at 7 am on Saturday. It leaves Beirut at 1.30 am on Sunday and arrives Limassol at 11 am Monday. The fare is US$125 one way, including taxes and the cost of an organised excursion. For more information, call Louis Tours in Nicosia (☎ 357-2 678 000).

ORGANISED TOURS

Lebanon is becoming an increasingly popular package-tour destination and a number of tour operators now run either combined Syria and Lebanon or Lebanon-only tours. These tend to be at the upper end of the price range and concentrate on the cultural aspects of the country. Generally speaking the itineraries are rushed, not allowing much time in each place, but if your time is short and your purse long, then they may be what you're looking for. They all take in the main attractions of Baalbek and Byblos, and tend to be based at hotels in Beirut. The following British tour operators run tours to Lebanon:

Cox & Kings (☎ 020-7873 5003) St James Court, 45 Buckingham Gate, London SW1E 6AF. At the upper end of the market, it offers a 15-day 'Grand Tour of the Middle East', which includes Jordan, Syria and Lebanon. Prices start at UK£1735. It also runs a five-day tour of Lebanon from UK£750.

Jasmin Tours (☎ 01628-531121), High St, Cookham, Maidenhead, Berks SL6 9SQ. A long-time Middle East specialist, it has a combined 10-day Lebanon/Syria tour for UK£1200 and a nine-day Lebanon Express tour starting at UK£799.

Prospect Art & Music Tours (☎ 020-8995 2151), 454–458 Chiswick High Rd, London W4 5TT. Does a five-day tour of Lebanon from UK£850 and an eight-day tour for UK£1300.

Voyages Jules Verne (☎ 020-7723 5066), 21 Dorset Square, London NW1 6QG. A top-class (and top-price) tour operator. Offers a five-day tour called 'From Baalbek to Byblos', which is based in Beirut and costs from UK£700.

Other tour operators who go to Lebanon include: Bales Tours (☎ 01306-885923) at Bales House, Junction Rd, Dorking, Surrey RH4 3HL; Swan Hellenic Tours (☎ 020-7800 2300) at 77 New Oxford St, London WC1A 1PP; and British Museum Tours (☎ 020-7323 8895) at 46 Bloomsbury St, London WC1.

The following French tour operators run tours to Lebanon:

Clio (☎ 01 53 68 82 82) 34 Rue du Hameau, 75015 Paris. Runs specialised cultural tours of Lebanon for groups of 15 and 23 people. It offers a seven-day tour of Lebanon's major cities and sights for 8450FF.

Djos'Air Voyages (☎ 0800 48 19 71, 01 48 67 15 60), Le Bonaparte 20, CAPN, 93153 Le Blanc Mesnil Cedex. Has an eight-day tour to northern Lebanon for 8350FF.

Intermèdes Art et Voyages (☎ 01 45 61 90 90) 60 Rue La Boétie, 75008 Paris. Offers combined tours to Lebanon, Syria and Jordan. A 14-day tour, with four days in Lebanon, costs from 15,800FF.

Voyageurs au Proche-Orient (☎ 01 42 86 17 90) 55 Rue Sainte-Anne, 75002 Paris. Runs private tours to Lebanon for between 7800FF and 9270FF for seven days. The price includes a private car with driver (no guide) and breakfast only.

Clio also has offices in Lyon (☎ 04 78 52 61 42) 128 Rue Bossuet, 69009; Marseille (☎ 04 91 54 02 13) 45 Rue de la Paix, 13001; and in Geneva (☎ 022-731 70 26) at 11 Rue du Mont-Blanc, 1201.

There are no tour operators in Australia and New Zealand that offer tours to Lebanon. Some specialised travel agents can organise tours with Lebanese-based operators out of Beirut. If you want to book a tour when you arrive in Lebanon, there are a number of good local tour operators in Beirut who can arrange a variety of itineraries. See Organised Tours in the Getting Around chapter for further details.

Getting Around

Lebanon is a tiny country, and although there are no internal air services, you don't really need them. You can drive from one end of the country to the other in about three hours, depending on traffic congestion. Most visitors use the ever-useful service taxis *(servees)* to get around. A huge number run on set routes around the country, although you may have to use more than one to get to where you want to go. There are also many 'pirate taxis' cruising for fares. If you're going to less-travelled areas, taxis can add up and it could be worth your while to rent a car, which can be done very reasonably in Beirut.

Buses and minibuses also link the larger Lebanese towns, and there are two bus companies with extensive routes throughout Beirut and the outlying areas.

BUS

Buses travel between Beirut and Lebanon's major towns. There are three main bus pick-up and drop-off points in Beirut:

Charles Helou bus station Just east of downtown, for destinations north of Beirut (including Syria).
Cola bus station & taxi stand This is in fact a confused intersection that is sometimes called Mazraa. It is for destinations south of Beirut.
Dawra East of Beirut, and covering the same destinations as Charles Helou, it is usually a port of call on the way in and out of the city.

Charles Helou is the only formal station and is systematically divided into three sign-posted zones:

Zone A For buses to Syria
Zone B For buses servicing Beirut (where the route starts or finishes at Charles Helou)
Zone C For express buses to Jounieh, Byblos and Tripoli

Zones A and C have ticket offices where you can buy tickets for your journey.

Cola is not as well organised as Charles Helou but if someone doesn't find you first (which is what usually happens) ask any driver where the next bus to your destination is leaving from. They usually have the destination displayed on the front window or above it in Arabic only. There is also a growing number of microbuses covering the same routes, which are slightly more expensive than regular buses, but a lot cheaper than service taxis. Microbuses are operated by individuals. The beauty of them is that they are small, comfortable and frequent, but you take your chances regarding the driver's ability. You pay for your ticket on the microbus, at either the start or the end of your journey.

TAXI & SERVICE TAXI

Taxis are recognisable by their red number plates and, on some cars, a white sign with 'TAXI' written on it in red letters. It is unusual to wait more than two minutes before a

Bus Fares

The price, operational hours and duration for regular (reg) and express (exp) buses from Beirut (they all run every 15 minutes) to the following destinations are:

destination	cost (LL)	operational hours	duration (hrs)
Byblos	500	from 7 am to 8 pm	½
Sidon	750 (reg) 1500 (exp)	from 5.45 am to 8.30 pm	1
Tripoli	1500	from 7 am to 8 pm	1
Tyre (change at Sidon)	1500 (reg) 3000 (exp)	from 5.45 am to 8.30 pm	1½

Service Taxi Fares

route	cost (LL)
Around Beirut	1000
Beirut – Aanjar	6000
Beirut – Baalbek	8000
Beirut – Beiteddine	4000
Beirut – Byblos	4000
Beirut – Deir al-Qamar	4000
Beirut – Hermel	10,000
Beirut – Jounieh	4000
Beirut – Qana	8000
Beirut – Sidon	2500
Beirut – Tripoli	5000
Beirut – Tyre	6000
Sidon – Tyre	3000
Tripoli – Bcharré	6000
Tripoli – The Cedars	10,000

taxi turns up. There are two systems: private taxis and service taxis. Private taxis go wherever you want to go for a negotiated fare; service taxis follow a specific route and take more than one passenger for a set price. Within Beirut, the service taxi fare is usually LL1000; the taxi fare is LL5000, more to outlying areas. You may sometimes have to take more than one service taxi if your destination is not straightforward, ie, if it includes more than one of the service taxi's routes.

Outside of Beirut, service-taxi fares range from LL2000 to LL8000, depending on the destination. Although the fares are not listed anywhere the driver will usually ask for the correct fare. When a taxi slows down, say your destination and the driver will either nod or shake his head. However, always inquire '*servEES*?' before getting into the car, especially if there are no other passengers, to avoid being charged a full taxi fare. If the driver responds 'taxi' it means he'll only take you as a private taxi.

You can stop or be let out at any point on a service taxi's preset route. Just say '*anzil huun*' (I get out here) to the driver. The same service taxi can become a taxi if you pay for the fare of the four other seats in the car. This avoids the delay of stopping to let other passengers in or out and the driver will deposit you right outside your destination.

Beware of taxi drivers who try to bump up the prices – some are honest, but others will charge whatever they think they'll get away with. Private taxis within Beirut should cost anywhere from LL5000 to LL8000, depending on the length of the trip. However, taxis from the airport are a notorious rip-off, often costing US$25 or US$30 (about LL40,000) for the 20-minute ride into town.

If you have a lot of sightseeing to do in out-of-the-way places, you can hire a taxi and driver by the day. Haggling skills come to the fore here, but expect to pay at least US$50 per day plus tip.

You can order taxis by telephone from a number of private companies; they will take you anywhere in Lebanon and some also have services to Syria and Jordan. See the Taxi section under Getting Around in the Beirut chapter for contact numbers.

CAR & MOTORCYCLE

If your budget can cover renting a car, it is the best way to see the most beautiful areas of Lebanon. Petrol, including unleaded, and diesel fuel are easily available and reasonably priced (about LL1450 per litre for unleaded). You will need an International Driving Permit (IDP) and insurance can be arranged by the rental company. For information about bringing a vehicle into Lebanon see the Land section in the Getting There & Away chapter.

Road Rules

The first rule of driving in Lebanon is: forget rules. Driving is on the right side of the road, unless the vehicles in front are not fast enough, in which case one drives on the left. The horn is used liberally because nobody uses their mirrors. There is no speed limit and moving violations do not exist. In other words, anarchy is the name of the game and if you like aggressive driving, you'll do just fine. If you're a nervous driver, you might be too intimidated to nose your way out of the car-rental garage. If you do take the plunge (and it's surprisingly easy to unlearn the rules of the road), stay extremely alert, particularly on mountain roads, where cars hurtle around hairpin bends without a thought to oncoming traffic. The only other thing to remember is that you must stop at ALL military checkpoints. See boxed aside 'Checkpoint Etiquette' for tips on getting through them with your dignity intact.

Rental

Cars can easily be rented in Lebanon and, if you shop around, for surprisingly reasonable prices. If there are three or four of you, it becomes a very feasible way to travel, even if you're on a tight budget. Most of the big rental agencies are in Beirut, although a few can be found in other cities. If you shop around, you can find a small two- or three-door car for as little as US$20 per day with unlimited kilometres. A more luxurious model (Mercedes, for example) will be more like US$250 per day. If you want a local driver, it will set you back an additional US$20 to US$50 per day.

The following is a list of rental companies and a sample of their prices.

Budget (☎ 01-740 740/1, @ budget.rentcar@ Lebanon.com) Wide range of vehicles starting at US$30 for a Hyundai.

City Car (☎ 01-803 308, @ citycar@citycar .com.lb) Very reasonably priced vehicles, starting with Kias for US$20 per day and medium-sized sedans at around US$70 per day.

Hala Rent A Car (☎ 01-393 904, cell 03-272 837 @ hala.car@lebanon.com) One of the best deals in town with small Kias for US$20 per day, unlimited mileage. Larger cars have higher tariffs.

Hertz (☎ 01-423 244, 427 283) The cheapest car is an Opel Corsa for US$40 per day. The price includes unlimited mileage after one day's rental.

Lenacar-Europcar (☎ 01-480 480, 363 636, @ lenacar@cyberia.net.lb) The cheapest car is a Hyundai, which costs US$30 per day. After three days or 150km the price includes unlimited mileage.

Leo Car (☎ 01-374 737, cell 03-880 070, @ leo car@cyberia.net.lb) Prices range from US$30 a day for a Hyundai to over US$400 for a top-of-the-line Mercedes. Can provide drivers for US$20 per day.

Prestige (☎ 01-866 328, 866 222) It charges US$19 per day for a Tico, US$25 for a Kia, US$35 for a Hyundai and US$45 for a Nissan Maxima. All prices include unlimited mileage.

All companies require a refundable deposit from all except credit-card holders, and offer

---

Checkpoint Etiquette

Israeli soldiers may finally have left the south, but that doesn't mean that Lebanon's ubiquitous checkpoints have disappeared. If you find the guns and tanks a little intimidating, remember that the days of kidnapping foreigners are long gone and Lebanon's crime rate is now negligible, so unless you're an undercover agent for Mossad, you aren't the person they're looking for. Following are a few tips to help you negotiate the unfamiliar with humour.

Know Your Checkpoints

Syrian checkpoints are distinguishable by their general shabbiness, the iconic pictures of late Syrian President Assad and his son Bashar, and, of course, the Syrian flag. Lebanese checkpoints are neater, the soldiers wear cool sunglasses and natty uniforms, and there's a strong chance that at least one will be talking on a mobile phone. If you still can't tell, look for the cedar emblem.

Driving Through

Knowing how to get through a checkpoint with your cool intact will distinguish you from other tourists and help you blend in with locals. Keep in mind the following:

• Try not to stare in horror at the automatic weaponry.
• Do not look nervous; an alert nonchalance is advisable.
• Under no circumstances take photographs in the vicinity of a checkpoint.
• Switch on the car's interior light at night, particularly if there are no street lights.
• Slow down to a gentle roll and act as if you're going to stop, but don't actually stop unless you're told to or you will annoy the soldier and set off a cacophony of horns from those waiting behind you. However:
• Do not accelerate until you have received a signal that you may pass. This could be a wave, a raised eyebrow, an almost imperceptible movement of the head or a slight twitch, depending on the mood of the soldier. Watch him carefully.

Road Distances (km)

	Amioun	Baalbek	Batroun	Bcharré	Beirut	Beiteddine	Byblos	Hermel	Jezzine	Jounieh	Marjeyun	Sidon	Tripoli	Tyre	Zahlé
Amioun	---														
Baalbek	97	---													
Batroun	24	113	---												
Bcharré	37	60	53	---											
Beirut	82	83	58	111	---										
Beiteddine	125	88	97	154	43	---									
Byblos	47	119	223	75	36	78	---								
Hermel	117	62	133	80	146	150	155	---							
Jezzine	153	109	129	182	71	29	107	179	---						
Jounieh	61	101	37	90	214	64	14	167	92	---					
Marjeyun	185	115	160	175	102	85	138	185	56	124	---				
Sidon	123	124	99	152	41	42	77	187	30	62	61	---			
Tripoli	222	109	33	49	91	134	55	102	162	70	193	132	---		
Tyre	161	163	137	190	79	80	115	225	48	101	79	38	170	---	
Zahlé	133	36	105	96	47	52	79	99	73	65	78	88	138	126	---

free delivery and collection during working hours. The minimum age for drivers is 21 years. You cannot take hire cars over the border into Syria.

BICYCLE

If you are bringing a bicycle to Lebanon, make sure it is suitable for the road conditions – and that you are fit enough to ride it! The terrain is extremely steep once you leave the coastal strip and really only a mountain bike would be feasible. The state of some of the urban roads also demand a rugged all-terrain type bike. Keep in mind that the traffic problems described earlier under Road Rules will also present a hazard to the cyclist and extreme care should be taken when riding anywhere in Lebanon. Having said that, the scenery is beautiful and the air in the mountains clear, although it would be best to avoid the summer months when heat exhaustion can be a real hazard. (See Cycling in the Facts for the Visitor chapter for more information.)

HITCHING

Hitching is never entirely safe anywhere, and we don't recommend it. Travellers who decide to hitch should understand that they are taking a small but potentially serious risk. People who do choose to hitch will be safer if they travel in pairs and let someone know where they are planning to go.

Hitching is not very common in Lebanon – the tourists who venture off the service-taxi routes tend to either rent cars or private taxis. This may be to your advantage if you decide to try hitching a lift. The novelty of foreigners increases your chances of a lift – it helps if you *look* foreign. The usual precautions apply, though: *never* hitch alone if you are a woman, and even two women travelling together are vulnerable.

With the habit of private cars turning into taxis at will, there is a chance that the driver will expect payment. There does not seem to be a very polite way out of this situation, except to ask first if the driver is going to charge you for the ride.

LOCAL TRANSPORT
Bus

Beirut and its environs now have two bus services, one operated by the privately owned Lebanese Commuting Company (LCC), the other by the state-owned OCFTC. They both operate a hail and ride system and have a fare of LL500 for all except the most distant destinations (such as Byblos and far-off suburbs). For route details, see the Getting Around section in the Beirut chapter.

Taxi

Apart from hailing a taxi on the street, you can telephone one of several private hire firms (see the Beirut chapter). It is a good idea to establish the price on the telephone beforehand. See Taxi & Service Taxi earlier this chapter for more information.

ORGANISED TOURS

Local tour operators offer a variety of tours – most (with a couple of exceptions) offer one-day excursions starting and ending in Beirut. There are some longer tours available which include Syria and/or Jordan.

Campus Travel (☎ 01-744 588) Maktabi Bldg, Rue Makhoul, Hamra, Beirut. Travel agency focusing on student travel. Arranges skiing trips, tours in Lebanon and to neighbouring countries such as Syria and Jordan. For more information check their Web site at www.campus-travel.net.

Destination Liban (☎ 01-293 066, cell 03-497 762, @ lucien@intracom.net.lb) Sawaya Supermarket Bldg, Rue Habib Lteif, Ain al-Remmaneh, Beirut. Specialising in youth and budget travel, Destination Liban arranges cheap accommodation, gives information on places to eat and offers small tours of archaeological sites (usually guided by archaeology students) for about US$30 to US$45 per day, all inclusive. Also arranges outdoor activities such as rafting and hiking. They also have an office in France: (☎ 06-61 95 47 71).

Greenline (☎/fax 01-746 215 @ grline@sodetel .net.lb) One of Lebanon's most active environmental organisations, it arranges treks and day trips into the mountains and countryside of Lebanon. They take place on Sundays and usually cost LL10,000 or LL15,000 per person. Check out their Web site at www.greenline .org.lb.

Lebanese Adventure (☎ 01-398 982, @ infos@ Lebanese-adventure.com,) 39 Rue Antoine Salhani [72], Secteur 67 Sioufi, Beirut. Different outdoor activities throughout the country are arranged each weekend. They can also tailormake excursions for a minimum of five people. Check out their Web site at www.lebanese-adventure.com.

Liban Trek (☎ 01-390 790, @ trek@dm.net.lb) A well-established trekking club that arranges weekend treks throughout Lebanon. It also organises other mountain sports.

Nakhal & Co (☎ 01-389 389, fax 389 282, @ tours @nakhal.com.lb) Ghorayeb Bldg, Rue Sami al-Solh. Their local tours cover Aanjar, Baalbek, Beiteddine, Byblos, The Cedars, Sidon, Tripoli and Tyre. They also organise tours from Lebanon to Syria.

Rida Travel (☎ 01-643 341, 648 101, fax 348 097, @ ridaint@ridaint.com.lb) Amoudi Bldg, Barbir Centre, Corniche al-Mazraa, Beirut. Rida organises one-day tours to the Casino du Liban, the Chouf Mountains, Ksara Winery, Baalbek, The Cedars and Faraya ski resorts, Nahr al-Kalb, Jeita Grotto, Harissa, Byblos, Bcharré and Tripoli. Prices range from US$20 to US$60 per person. Meals and drinks are not included in the price.

Tania Travel (☎ 01-803 547, 739 682/3/4, fax 340473 @ taniatv@dm.net.lb) Rue Sidani. Opposite Jeanne d'Arc theatre. They have tours to Aanjar, Baalbek, Bcharré, Beiteddine, Byblos, The Cedars, Deir al-Qamar, Sidon, Tyre and one-day trips to Damascus. Check out their Web site at members.aol.com/TaniaTravl/main.html.

Thermique (☎ 09-953 756, cell 03-288 193, fax 09-953 756) In Ajaltoun, just outside Beirut, runs day-long guided bike tours in Qornet as-Sawda, Lebanon's highest peak, among other destinations. They also arrange paragliding expeditions.

Tour Vacances (☎ 01-424 509, 426 672) A consortium of four tour operators that, in addition to the local sightseeing trips and tours to Syria and Jordan, offers three-day package deals starting from US$125/180 in singles/doubles. The price includes transfer to and from the airport, two nights in a Beirut hotel with breakfast, transfer to and from the Faraya ski resort and one night in a Faraya hotel with breakfast. Additional nights are available for a longer stay.

Beirut

بيروت

☎ 01 • pop 1.2 million

Beirut is the vibrant, still-slightly battered capital of Lebanon. Split down the middle and pounded by bombs and mortars for 15 years, it has picked itself up, shaken off the cement dust and undergone an astonishing renaissance.

Visitors to Beirut can see this Phoenix-like transformation in progress. Traces of the notorious Green Line that divided the city between the Christian east and the Muslim west are still there, although the most damaged buildings have been bulldozed. Many of those that remain are busily being renovated and turned into restaurants and bars. The historic downtown area, which was almost perversely obliterated by warring militias, is slowly coming to life with restored and recreated buildings, shops and sidewalk cafes.

About half of Lebanon's population lives in Beirut so perhaps it's not surprising that the city is a concentrated reflection of the country's contradictions. Glittering high-rises with multimillion dollar apartments stand next to pockmarked buildings where homeless squatters anxiously await eviction in appalling conditions. Late-model Mercedes pass through squalid refugee camps. A nightclub sits on the site of a wartime torture centre.

Visitors arriving here with expectations of souqs and archaeological sites will be disappointed – there is little left of Beirut's long history. Much of it was obliterated before the war and the fighting destroyed most of what was left. True to their reputation, the city's inhabitants are doing their best to forget their troubled past by eating well, dancing and enjoying life, imbuing the place with a buzz that is absent from almost every other city in the region.

HISTORY

The earliest traces of habitation in Beirut date from the Stone Age when the area now occupied by the city was in fact two islands

Highlights

- Be part of Beirut's social mosaic on an evening stroll along the Corniche.
- Experience 6000 years of history at the National Museum.
- Watch a city being reborn in the partially reconstructed Beirut Central District.
- Laze away the hours at one of the city's seafront cafes.
- Explore the shattered remains of the civil war along the city's former Green Line.
- Dance the night away at one of the city's many bars and clubs.

in the delta of the Beirut River. Later, when the river silted up, the area became one land mass. It seems likely that the area has been continuously occupied throughout prehistory. Its location is favourable with fresh water and abundant fish from the sea.

Excavations between Place des Martyrs and the port have revealed a Canaanite site dating from 1900 BC. This Bronze Age city has an entrance gate of dressed stone. Nearby are the remains of Phoenician canals with sloping sides. The Phoenicians reused the Canaanite stones as well as smooth, round stones brought from the Beirut River.

New light on the obscure origins of this city may be shed by the excavations that have been carried out in the downtown district – the site of the original city. Large areas have had to be bulldozed in order to redevelop the centre of the city, giving archaeologists a unique opportunity to dig beneath the accumulated strata. From finds already uncovered, it is clear that the city was larger and more significant than had been previously thought. However, disagreements between developers and archaeologists over the timing and funding of excavation and publication of results mean that there is still a huge amount of research to be done before the past is revealed.

The first historical reference to Beirut dates from the 14th century BC, when it is mentioned in tablets with cuneiform script discovered at Tell al-Amarna in Egypt. The tablets were letters from the Canaanite king of Beirut asking the pharaoh Akhenaten for military assistance.

The original name of the city seems to have been variously Birut, Birrayyuna or Birrayat, which suggests that it was named after a well or wells (modern Arabic still uses the word *bir* for well). On the other hand, according to Philo in his *History*, Birut was the first queen of the city.

In Phoenician times, Beirut appears to have been overshadowed by Sidon, Tyre and Byblos, although after Alexander the Great's conquest, it is mentioned in Hellenistic sources and excavations carried out in the downtown area have revealed an extensive Hellenistic city upon which the later Roman grid was based.

It was during the Roman period that the city came into its own. It was conquered by Emperor Pompey in 64 BC and his successor, Augustus, renamed the city in honour of his daughter, Julia – its full name became Colonia Julia Augusta Felix Berytus. He then installed his son-in-law Vespasianus Agrippa as its governor. The veterans of the 5th Macedonian and 3rd Gallic legions were established in the city and it quickly became 'Romanised'; large public buildings and monuments were erected and Berytus enjoyed full status as a part of the empire.

In the 3rd century AD the city found fame and prestige through its School of Law, which rivalled those in Athens, Alexandria and Caesarea. The basis of the famous Justinian Code, upon which the Western legal system drew inspiration, was established. The city's importance as a centre of learning and commercial hub continued as the Roman Empire gave way to the Byzantine, and Beirut became the seat of a bishopric.

In the middle of the 5th century, a series of devastating earthquakes and tidal waves almost destroyed the city. The death toll was high: 30,000 were killed in Berytus alone and, along the Phoenician coast, total casualties were close to 250,000. The School of Law was evacuated and moved to Sidon in the south. This calamity marked the decline of the city for centuries to come.

When the Arabs came in AD 635, they took the city without much of a struggle. Their rule was uninterrupted until AD 1110 when, after a long siege, the city fell into the hands of Baldwin I of Boulogne and a Latin bishopric was established.

Beirut remained in Crusader hands for 77 years, during which time the Crusaders built the Church of St John the Baptist of the Knights Hospitallers on the site of an ancient temple (now the Omari Mosque). In 1187 Saladin (Salah ad-Din) managed to wrest the city back into Muslim hands. But was only able to hold on to it for six years before Amoury, King of Cyprus, besieged the city once again and the Muslim forces fled. Under the rule of Jean I of Ibelin, the city's influence grew and spread throughout the Latin East, but the Crusaders lost the city again, this time for good, in July 1291 when the Muslim Mamluks took possession.

There were periodic attempts to invade the city during the following centuries. In the 14th century, the Franks made a number of unsuccessful assaults, and in the 15th century they returned again, but this time peacefully, as traders.

The Mamluks remained in control of Beirut until they were ousted from the city by the Ottoman army in 1516. Once part of the powerful Ottoman Empire, the city was granted semi-autonomy in return for taxes paid to the sultan. The local emirs had free rein as long as the money flowed into the coffers of the Sublime Porte. One of the emirs, Fakhreddine (Fakhr ad-Din al-Maan II), established what was in effect an independent kingdom for himself and made Beirut his favourite residence (for more information, see the boxed text 'Fakhreddine' in The Chouf Mountains chapter).

Fakhreddine's keen business sense led him to trade with the European powers, most notably the Venetians, and Beirut began to recover economically and regain some of its former prestige, although it remained a tiny

[Continued on page 113]

BEIRUT

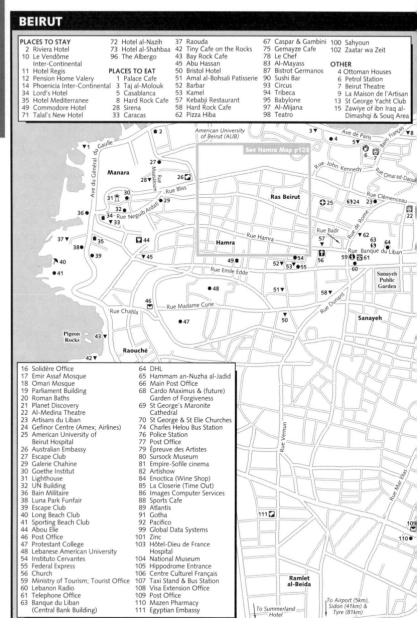

PLACES TO STAY
2 Riviera Hotel
10 Le Vendôme Inter-Continental
11 Hotel Regis
12 Pension Home Valery
14 Phoenicia Inter-Continental
34 Lord's Hotel
35 Hotel Mediterranee
49 Commodore Hotel
71 Talal's New Hotel
72 Hotel al-Nazih
73 Hotel al-Shahbaa
96 The Albergo

PLACES TO EAT
1 Palace Cafe
3 Taj al-Molouk
5 Casablanca
8 Hard Rock Cafe
28 Sirena
33 Caracas
37 Raouda
42 Tiny Cafe on the Rocks
43 Bay Rock Cafe
45 Abu Hassan
50 Bristol Hotel
51 Amal al-Bohsali Patisserie
52 Barbar
53 Kamel
57 Kebabji Restaurant
58 Hard Rock Cafe
62 Pizza Hiba
67 Caspar & Gambini
75 Gemayze Cafe
78 Le Chef
83 Al-Mayass
87 Bistrot Germanos
90 Sushi Bar
93 Circus
94 Tribeca
95 Babylone
97 Al-Mijana
98 Teatro
100 Sahyoun
102 Zaatar wa Zeit

OTHER
4 Ottoman Houses
6 Petrol Station
7 Beirut Theatre
9 La Maison de l'Artisan
13 St George Yacht Club
15 Zawiye of ibn Iraq al-Dimashqi & Souq Area

American University of Beirut (AUB)

See Hamra Map p123

Ave de Paris

Bains Français

Ave du Général du Gaulle

Manara

Rue Maxaillum

Rue John Kennedy

Rue Omar ad-Daou

Rue Bliss

Ras Beirut

Rue Clémenceau

Rue Neguib Ardati

Rue de Rome

Hamra

Rue Hamra

Rue Badr

Rue Banque du Liban

Rue Emile Edde

Sanayeh Public Garden

Rue Madame Curie

Sanayeh

Rue Chatila

Rue Dunant

Pigeon Rocks

Raouché

16 Solidére Office
17 Emir Assaf Mosque
18 Omari Mosque
19 Parliament Building
20 Roman Baths
21 Planet Discovery
22 Al-Medina Theatre
23 Artisans du Liban
24 Gefinor Centre (Amex; Airlines)
25 American University of Beirut Hospital
26 Australian Embassy
27 Escape Club
29 Galerie Chahine
30 Goethe Institut
31 Lighthouse
32 UN Building
36 Bain Militaire
38 Luna Park Funfair
39 Escape Club
40 Long Beach Club
41 Sporting Beach Club
44 Abou Elie
46 Post Office
47 Protestant College
48 Lebanese American University
54 Instituto Cervantes
55 Federal Express
56 Church
59 Ministry of Tourism; Tourist Office
60 Lebanon Radio
61 Telephone Office
63 Banque du Liban (Central Bank Building)
64 DHL
65 Hammam an-Nuzha al-Jadid
66 Main Post Office
68 Cardo Maximus & (future) Garden of Forgiveness
69 St George's Maronite Cathedral
70 St George & St Elie Churches
74 Charles Helou Bus Station
76 Police Station
77 Post Office
79 Épreuve des Artistes
80 Sursock Museum
81 Empire-Sofile cinema
82 Artishow
84 Enoctica (Wine Shop)
85 La Closerie (Time Out)
86 Images Computer Services
88 Sports Cafe
89 Atlantis
91 Gotha
92 Pacifico
99 Global Data Systems
101 Zinc
103 Hôtel-Dieu de France Hospital
104 National Museum
105 Hippodrome Entrance
106 Centre Culturel Français
107 Taxi Stand & Bus Station
108 Visa Extension Office
109 Post Office
110 Mazen Pharmacy
111 Egyptian Embassy

Rue Vernun

Rue Mar Elias

Ramlet al-Beida

To Summerland Hotel

To Airport (5km), Sidon (41km) & Tyre (81km)

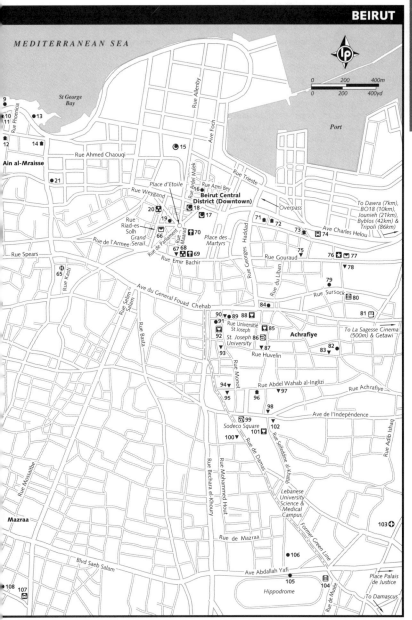

MEDITERRANEAN SEA

St George Bay

Port

Rue Phoenicia

Ain al-Mraisse

Rue Ahmed Chaouqi

Rue Allenby

Ave Foch

Rue Trieste

Place d'Etoile

Rue Azmi Bey

Rue Weygand

Beirut Central District (Downtown)

Rue Abdel Malek

Overpass

To Dawra (7km), BO18 (10km), Jounieh (21km), Byblos (42km) & Tripoli (86km)

Rue Riad-es-Solh

Grand Serail

Rue de Parlement

Rue Maarad

Place des Martyrs

Rue de l'Armee

Rue Georges Haddad

Ave Charles Helou

Rue Emir Bachir

Rue Gouraud

Rue du Liban

Rue Spears

Rue Kasti

Ave du General Fouad Chehab

Rue Sursock

Rue Selim Salam

Rue Basta

Rue Université St Joseph

St Joseph University

Achrafiye

To La Sagesse Cinema (500m) & Getawi

Rue Huvelin

Rue Monot

Rue Abdel Wahab al-Inglizi

Rue Achrafiye

Ave de l'Indépendance

Rue Adib Ishaq

Sodeco Square

Rue de Damas

Rue Mohammed Hout

Rue Bechara el-Khoury

Rue Selfedine al-Khatib

Lebanese University Science & Medical Campus

Mazraa

Rue Mossaitbe

Former Green Line

Rue de Mazraa

Blvd Saeb Salam

Ave Abdallah Yafi

Hippodrome

Rue de Mulek

Place Palais de Justice

To Damascus

THE REBUILDING OF BEIRUT

Trying to repair the catastrophic damage to Beirut's Central District (BCD) was one of the greatest challenges facing the government in the aftermath of the war. Redevelopment had a symbolic as well as a practical purpose: by recreating the area associated with Lebanon's past prosperity the country was signalling that it was once again open for business.

In 1992 the Lebanese parliament, headed by Prime Minister Rafiq Hariri, formed the Lebanese Company for the Development and Reconstruction of Beirut Central District, known by its French acronym Solidére, a joint stock company in which pre-existing property owners were majority shareholders.

While this sounds relatively straightforward, it was in fact plagued with legal problems. Just sorting through the claimants involved untangling complicated legal knots. In the most extreme case there were 4700 claimants to a single plot of land in the souq area.

The solution was to give everyone with some sort of legal claim shares in Soldidére equal to the value of their property holding. Altogether the value of the claimants' shares was some US$1.7 billion.

Solidére was to carry out all infrastructure projects and restore more than 200 Ottoman and French mandate-period buildings. They were also to cooperate with archaeologists, who were given a unique, but double-edged, opportunity to excavate to the very earliest periods of Beirut's history before the whole lot was destroyed or once again buried under new buildings. In return for all this, Solidére itself would get some 1650 real estate lots, worth around US$1.17 billion, in addition to investment from the state and private investors.

Phase one of the project lasted from 1994 to 1999 and concentrated on completing basic infrastructure and restoring all retained buildings. Although a slowdown in the economy in 1997 hindered progress, most of the infrastructure was completed on time.

Nevertheless, the controversy that has dogged the project since its inception continues. Many say that Solidére grossly underestimated land values when distributing shares to property owners, pulling off a massive land-grab at their expense. Archaeologists complain that they arrived at sites only to find that bulldozers had come in beforehand and destroyed all historical traces. And that Solidére is not living up to its commitments to fund the publishing of the archaeological findings. Finally, many charge that the company is creating a Disney-style version of a neighbourhood that is nothing more than a ghetto of offices for multinational companies.

But even the staunchest critics have to concede that the first real city planning in Beirut for decades is a positive step. And only the most churlish could deny that in only six years the BCD has undergone an immense change for the better.

Top: The clock tower in Beirut's Place d'Etoile (Photo: Bethune Carmichael)

Top: Postcard of the bustling Place des Martyrs in 1973, on the eve of the civil war

Second from Top: The same place, three years later

Third from Top: In 1994, almost 20 years on, the area had been cleared by Solidére and the Martyrs Statue was the only recognisable feature left from prewar days.

Bottom: Contemporary view of the reconstructed downtown area

COURTESY OF SOLIDÈRE

BETHUNE CARMICHAEL

Top: An aerial view of Beirut showing the reconstruction under wa

Bottom: Roman baths featuring a hypocaust floor have been uncovered during recent excavations in Beirut.

[Continued from page 109]

city. The sultan, meanwhile, became alarmed over Beirut's growing power and confronted Fakhreddine's army, defeating him at Safed. Fakhreddine was captured and taken to Constantinople, where he was executed in 1635.

The 18th century presented mixed fortunes for the city, depending on the whims and preferences of the local rulers. One, Bashir Shihab II (1788–1840), injected new vigour into the city, renewing its prosperity and stability once again. However, in 1832, he entered into an alliance with Ibrahim Pasha, son of the rebellious Mohammed Ali of Egypt. Mohammed Ali's threat to the Ottoman Empire, and by extension the balance of power with Europe, alarmed the British and in 1840 the city was bombarded and subsequently recaptured for the Ottomans by the combined Anglo-Austro-Turkish fleet.

The population of Beirut at that time was only 45,000, but the booming silk trade and influx of Maronites fleeing from massacres in the Chouf Mountains and Damascus meant that the numbers doubled during the following 20 years. This was the start of the commercial boom which resulted in Beirut being transformed from a backwater into a commercial powerhouse. It was also the beginning of European meddling in Lebanon. The massacres of the Maronites resulted in French troops landing in Beirut and ties with Europe grew in the coming decades. In 1866 Syrian and American missionaries founded the Syrian Protestant College, now known as the American University of Beirut (AUB), which became one of the most prestigious universities in the Middle East, adding to the importance of the city.

During WWI, Beirut suffered a blockade by the Allies, which was intended to starve out the Turks. This, combined with a series of natural disasters, resulted in widespread famine, followed by plague, which killed more than 25% of the population. A revolt broke out against the Turks and resulted in the mass hanging of the rebel leaders in what became known as the Place des Martyrs.

WWI brought Turkish rule to an end and on 8 October 1918, the British army (including a French detachment) arrived in Beirut. On 25 April 1920 the League of Nations granted a French mandate over Syria and Lebanon, and Beirut became the headquarters of the French High Commissioner as well as the capital of the state of Greater Lebanon.

During WWII the city was occupied by the Allies and, thanks to its port, became an important supply centre. In 1946 the French left the city, and subsequently Beirut became one of the main commercial and banking centres of the Middle East. The 1948 Arab-Israeli War resulted in huge numbers of Palestinian refugees settling in refugee camps in the south of Beirut, where, despite massacres and great poverty, they still live today.

Beirut was the epicentre of anarchy during the civil war. The city was ruled, area by area, by militias loyal to one or other factions and the infamous Green Line tore the city into Christian and Muslim halves. Continual intercommunal fighting between militias, combined with shelling from Israeli fighter planes, devastated the city. The human casualties were enormous and the affect on the economy was catastrophic. By 1991 the Green Line was dismantled but it remains a physical and psychological scar on the city.

The postwar government faced an enormous task in repairing the country's destroyed infrastructure. After his election in 1992, Prime Minister Rafiq Hariri launched his US$14 billion plan for the reconstruction of the country, Horizon 2000. This concentrated on rebuilding Beirut in a bid to reestablish the city as the financial capital of the Middle East. Although the reconstruction is ongoing, the bulk of the city's infrastructure was up and running again by 1998.

The subsequent government of President Emile Lahoud changed the emphasis of the reconstruction effort, moving the primary focus away from Beirut to other areas of Lebanon. This, coupled with a recession, has left many buildings in the Beirut Central District unfinished.

ORIENTATION

Beirut is a promontory bound by the Mediterranean Sea on the north and west coast. The headland of the promontory has dramatic cliffs falling away into the sea, while to the south, the coast gives way to a sandy beach. In the west of the city, the land is very hilly, flattening out as you travel east.

The Hamra district in West Beirut is one of the city's hubs. This is where you'll find the Ministry of Tourism, major banks, hotels, travel agents, airline offices and restaurants – all within walking distance of each other.

North of Hamra is Ras Beirut and the large American University of Beirut (AUB) campus with lots of coffee bars and cheap restaurants catering for the students. Prior to the war, this was home to the liberal-thinking intelligentsia and artistic community and it remains one area of the city where Christians and Muslims still live side by side.

The Corniche (Ave de Paris and Ave Général de Gaulle) runs around the coast from Raouché in the south-west to the St George Yacht Club in Ain al-Mraisse (also called Minet al-Hosn), just before the downtown district. This is the area where Beirutis come to promenade, jog, fish and generally hang out. There are many restaurants, cafes and snack stalls lining the Corniche, with some of the most popular overlooking the famous Pigeon Rocks.

Heading east from the St George Yacht Club, you come to the downtown district, which is still under restoration but has a growing number of cafes and shops. Further on are the port and the Beirut River, which is little more than a concrete canal surrounded by highways. On the east side of the river is the working class suburb of Burj Hammoud, a predominantly Armenian area with pockets of industry.

On a hill to the south-east of the port is Achrafiye. This prosperous quarter is where much of Beirut's famed restaurants and nightlife are concentrated. Because it suffered less damage than other areas of the city during the war, many older buildings are still intact and it is a pleasant place to wander.

Heading into the south from Hamra you pass through Verdun, a bland area of high-rise apartments and upmarket shopping malls. Further south from here you abruptly pass into the third world. The southern suburbs (once famous for being first port of call

> ## Verdun
>
> A certain segment of Beirut is very proud that Rue Verdun has been rated as the 33rd most expensive shopping street in the world, sharing honours with New York's Madison Ave, Hong Kong's Causeway and London's Oxford St. Average rental prices here hover at around US$800 per square metre.

for kidnap victims) are a world apart from the glossy chic of Achrafiye and Hamra and are predominantly Shiite. They are also where the infamous Palestinian camps of Sabra-Chatila and Burj al-Barajnah can be found. Beyond here is the airport.

Navigating your way around town can initially seem tricky because there are no numbers on buildings and often the street names written on signs (when there are signs) are different from the name they're known under locally. When giving directions, Beirutis launch into complicated explanations involving local landmarks. Buildings are often known either by the name of their owner or by their function (eg, the British Bank building). This sounds more confusing than it actually is and, luckily, Beirut is small so you cannot go too far off track.

Maps
The best map of Beirut is on the reverse of the GEOprojects map of Lebanon, available from the major bookshops in Beirut. There is also a commercial map, published by All Prints of Beirut, which has a good city map of Beirut on the reverse. English and French versions are available. It is also stocked by Stanfords in London.

INFORMATION
Tourist Office
Beirut's tourist information office (☎ 343 073, fax 340 945, 343 279) is on the ground floor of the same building as the Ministry of Tourism, on Rue Banque du Liban (an extension of Rue Hamra and Rue de Rome). The entrance is through a covered arcade, which runs underneath the block. This office has a series of up-to-date brochures on the

main archaeological and tourist sites of Lebanon. It also has some country and city maps. The staff are helpful and friendly, and speak English and French. They have a comprehensive list of hotels and apartments and can advise you about accommodation options. The office is officially open from 8 am to 2 pm daily except Sunday, although often there is no one there until after 9.30 am.

Money

There seems to be a bank and ATM every 50m in the centre of Beirut, so finding a place to change or get money is never a problem. There are also numerous moneychangers, but not all of them will deal with travellers cheques. The Beirut Finance & Exchange Company (☎ 864 280), in the Abdel Baki building on Rue Hamra, changes both cash and travellers cheques. Failing that, you can usually change money or travellers cheques at many of the larger hotels, although commission charges are often higher. The banks are open from 8.30 am to 12.30 pm daily except Sunday. The private moneychangers have more liberal business hours and often stay open until the early evening.

The American Express Bank (☎ 360 390) is on the 1st floor in the Gefinor Centre on Rue Maamari, Hamra. It is open from 8.30 am to 12.30 pm except Saturday and Sunday. This is the place to come if you lose your travellers cheques. There is also an American Express (AmEx) cards office on the same floor where you can draw cash on your AmEx card or pick up a replacement card. The office is open from 8 am to 6 pm weekdays and to 1.30 pm Saturday.

Post

The postal system is reviving after the war and a full range of services is more or less available. Deliveries have become more reliable but there is no poste restante service available.

The main post office is on Rue Riad es-Solh in the downtown district, but it's a bit out of the way. In Hamra the most convenient post office is on Rue Makdissi, almost opposite the Embassy Hotel. It is on the 1st floor above Star Stationers, but the entrance is not clearly signposted at all – it is the door to the left of the shop as you face it. The opening hours are from 8 am to 2 pm daily, except Sunday and public holidays.

Also nearby is the AUB's on-campus post office, which can be used by visitors. If you use the main entrance to the campus on Rue Bliss, turn left and it is down a flight of stairs. It is also open from 8 am to 2 pm daily, except Sunday. It does not sell stamps so you have to leave your letters to be stamped.

Telephone

There is a government-run telephone office in Hamra near the Ministry of Tourism building on the corner of Rue Banque du Liban and Rue de Rome. It is open from 8 am to 2 pm Monday to Saturday (to 11 am Friday). The other office is on Blvd Saeb Salam, not far from the Cola bus station, and has the same opening hours. To make a call, you go to the counter and fill in a slip of paper with the country and number you want and wait to be directed to a booth. You pay when you have finished your call.

The private offices are often located in shops and operate on a similar system, although their rates are a bit more than the government places. Their opening hours are usually longer, and because there are more of them, the extra expense is probably worth it. One convenient office is the Hamra Telecom Centre on the corner of Neame Yafet and Jabre Doumit in Hamra. If you are stuck in the evening and need to make a call, your best bet is to use one of the larger hotels.

Fax

There are many private fax bureaus in Beirut (most double up as telephone offices as well). Many of these are on Rue Bliss, near the AUB campus. An alternative is to use the larger hotels. Most have a business centre which you can use whether you are a guest or not. These tend to be more expensive than the private bureaus.

Email & Internet Access

Beirut is blessed with a number of Internet cafes, many clustered around the AUB campus. Here are a few:

Global Data Systems (☎ 615 578) Sodeco Square, Saydeh St. This is the most expensive Internet cafe (LL7,000 per hour), but it is one of the few in Achrafiye to stay open on Sunday (from 5 to 11 pm). Open from 11 am to 11 pm Monday to Saturday.

Images Computer Services (☎ 338 933) Rue Lebanon, Achrafiye. Open from 8.30 am to 10 pm weekdays (8 pm Saturday), closed Sunday. Rates are a competitive LL2000 per hour.

MagNet (☎ 748 223) Rue Makhoul, Ras Beirut. A pleasant place to sit. Open from 10 am to 2 am. Access is LL5000 per hour.

PC Club (☎ 740 382) Rue Mahatma Ghandhi, Hamra. A student hang-out. Open 24 hours. LL3000 per hour.

The Net (☎ 740 157) Rue Mahatma Ghandi, Hamra. Open from 9 am to 1 am, it costs LL4000 per hour but often discounts to LL3000 after 9 pm.

Web Cafe (☎ 348 880) Rue Khalidi, Ras Beirut. One of the best, with plenty of terminals and a real cafe ambience. Open from 9 am to midnight daily. Net use costs LL5000 per hour.

Internet Resources

Because Lebanon is so small, most Lebanese Web sites are Beirut focused. See 'Internet Resources' in the Facts for the Visitor chapter for more information.

Travel Agencies

There are dozens of travel agencies all over Beirut. For some addresses and information, see Organised Tours in the Getting Around chapter.

Bookshops

Both East and West Beirut are well supplied with bookshops. The best concentration, though, is in Hamra and around the AUB (not surprisingly). As well as academic and specialist books, you can buy novels, general interest books and books about Lebanon.

The best-stocked bookshop is the Librairie Antoine on Rue Hamra. It has a good selection of books and international newspapers and an array of imported magazines in French, English and Arabic. Librairie Antoine also has a smaller branch in Achrafiye and four branches around the country.

Other recommended bookshops are Four Steps Down and Way In on Rue Hamra,

both of which mainly stock English-language books. Another good bookshop is Librairie du Liban on Rue Bliss.

Libraries

Unless you have an academic connection that can get you into the AUB library, there is not much on offer in Beirut. There is a small library at the British Council, which stocks a variety of British newspapers and magazines. For details, see the Cultural Centres section.

Universities

The main campus in Beirut is the AUB. Nonstudents can visit the campus and use the post office, visit the museum, and find out about upcoming events. There is a free English-language weekly newspaper, *Campus*, which lists various events at AUB and other campuses in Lebanon.

The Lebanese University (☎ 423 137/8) is the the only state-funded university in Lebanon and has campuses throughout the city, with its main administration located close to the museum.

Université St Joseph (☎ 200 625) is primarily a French-language institution and has campuses in Achrafiye and East Beirut.

The Lebanese American University (☎ 786 456) has a campus in Ras Beirut, not too far from its more famous cousin, the AUB.

The Beirut Arab University (☎ 300 110) was founded in 1960 and is a regional university affiliated with Alexandria University in Egypt.

Cultural Centres

There are several cultural centres in Beirut and they often have art exhibitions and film festivals, showing work from their respective countries. They are also a good place to drop by and catch up on the newspapers from home – most of them have a small library which you can use for a quiet read. You can check for details in the press or by calling them to see what's on.

British Council (☎ 740 123/4/5) Azzar Bldg, Rue Yamout (off Rue Sidani), Ras Beirut

Centre Culturel Français (☎ 615 859) Cité Bounnour, Rue de Damas

Goethe Institut (☎ 740 524, 745 158) Gideon Bldg, Rue Bliss, Manara

Instituto Cervantes (☎ 347 755) Assaf Bldg, Rue Baalbek, Hamra

Italian Cultural Centre (☎ 749 801) Najjar Bldg, Rue de Rome

Russian Cultural Centre (☎ 864 534) Rue Verdun

Unesco (☎ 830 013, 824, 854) Downtown

Laundry

There are no laundrettes in Beirut so if you want to do laundry you must take your washing to a dry-cleaners or, if you're staying in a mid-range to top-end hotel, use the hotel laundry. Most neighbourhoods have at least one dry-cleaner and they offer a choice of one- or two-day service.

Medical Services

All medical services, including ambulances, have to be paid for. If you need an ambulance, call either the Red Cross or Civil Defence. If you have any sort of nonserious accident and you do not need an ambulance, it is better to get a taxi to take you to one of the hospitals. The general consensus is that the American University of Beirut Hospital (☎ 350 000, 340 460) on Rue du Caire is the best choice. The AUB also has a separate private clinic (☎ 341 898) on Rue Ahmed Abdul Aziz. Other hospitals include:

Hôtel-Dieu de France (☎ 422 970) Rue Hôtel-Dieu, Achrafiye

Makassed (☎ 646 590/12) Rue Tariq al-Jedide, Ouzai (near Hippodrome)

Abou Jaoude Hospital (☎ 404 400-2) Jal ad-Dib

There is a 24-hour/seven-day pharmacy, Mazen Pharmacy (☎ 343 779), on Blvd Saeb Salam, almost opposite the large post office. It offers a delivery service to 8 pm. You simply telephone your order through and pay on delivery. The pharmacist speaks English and French and can advise you on what drugs you may need. Another late-night pharmacy is Berty (☎ 330 033) in Achrafiye.

Emergency

The following telephone numbers may be useful in case of emergency (see also Emergencies in the Facts for the Visitor chapter):

Ambulance	☎ 865 561, 863 295
Fire Brigade	☎ 310 105
Police	☎ 425 250, 392 750
Red Cross	☎ 323 345
Tourist Police	☎ 343 209

Dangers & Annoyances

The most obvious hazard in Beirut is the traffic, especially when you are travelling on foot. Waiting for a gap in the flow as you cross busy roads seems to take forever. Locals seem to take the fatalistic approach and saunter across, trusting that cars will slow down, which they usually do.

Another thing to watch out for when walking, particularly at night, is potholes and uneven stones. It is easy to twist your ankle or fall if you are not paying attention.

Theft is not a great problem, so don't be unduly paranoid, but it pays to be vigilant with your bags especially at busy places such as taxi stations. Keep your wallet or purse on your body. Remember also to keep your passport handy in case you come across a checkpoint.

WALKING TOUR

The logical place to start any walking tour of Beirut is the Corniche. This is where Beirutis of all social classes and religious persuasions come to stroll, jog or rollerblade, weather permitting. If you don't mind a long walk, start off by the **Pigeon Rocks** at Raouché and make your way down the hill, maybe stopping at one of the **seafront cafes** along the way.

Follow the Corniche around the corner and you'll see the campus of the AUB to your right. When you're almost at the end of the Corniche, look out for the last remaining **Ottoman houses** with their red-tiled roofs, to the right. Just below them is a tiny **fishing port** that has been all-but buried underneath the Corniche.

Coming to the end of the Corniche, at Rue Minet al-Hosn, you will pass some of the city's five-star seafront hotels. Walk around by the Phoenicia Inter-Continental and then cross over to Rue Weygand, which will take you to downtown. On your left, just before Rue Weygand, you can see the

Zawiye of ibn Iraq al-Dimashqi and the now obliterated site of the ancient **souqs**. At Rue Riad es-Solh, turn right and look out for the remains of the **Roman baths** down the hill from the Ottoman-era **Grand Serail**. From here, take your next left into **Place d'Étoile** and go left again to the **Omari Mosque**, a former Crusader church.

Heading back up through Place d'Étoile to Rue Emir Bachir, turn left and look over the remains of Roman Beirut's **cardo maximus**, site of the future Garden of Forgiveness. Next to this you'll find the **St George's Maronite Cathedral**. Carrying on along Emir Bachir you will come to the vast open space of the **Place des Martyrs**.

Cross over to Rue Gouraud and then turn right up to Rue Sursock. Check out the fabulous high-Ottoman architecture of the **Sursock Museum** and then walk up to Ave du General Fouad Chehab. Cross over into the narrow, shady streets of Achrafiye, turning right on **Rue Abdel Wahab al-Inglizi**, and wander past the gracious old buildings until you arrive at Rue de Damas, which demarcated the **Green Line** during the war. From here, if you're really energetic, you can turn left and take a detour to the **National Museum**. If not, head left again and walk alongside the bombed-out buildings until you reach Ave de l'Indépendence. Cross over Rue de Damas and follow the avenue until you reach Rue Basta, site of secondhand and antique furniture stalls.

Keep walking heading north back towards downtown and then bear left along Rue Spears. Take a rest in **Sanayeh**, Beirut's only public green space, and then head left again to Rue de Rome. Turn right here and walk along **Rue Hamra** with its cafes and shops, and then turn right down Rue Jeanne d'Arc and then take a left on Rue Bliss, where you will find the entrance to the **American University of Beirut**. You can either go and visit the AUB museum, with its impressive collection of ancient artefacts, or simply sit among the trees and enjoy the views.

To finish up, head on foot or by taxi to one of Beirut's famous bars or restaurants for well-deserved refreshment.

NATIONAL MUSEUM المتحف الوطني

Lebanon's main museum (☎ 380 810) couldn't have been in a worse position during the war – right on the Green Line, and on one of the main crossing points from east to west. There were times when the crossing was closed for days at a time due to heavy shelling and gunfire. The building was closed for the duration of the war and the exhibits bricked up to avoid damage, but that didn't prevent many artefacts from being destroyed. Following the cease-fire, work began in earnest to restore the building.

The museum building dates from 1937 and has a rather surprising neo-Pharaonic style that brings to mind Egypt rather than Lebanon. Extensive restoration and rehabilitation was carried out after the war and it opened its doors again in 1999. Opening hours are from 9 am to 5 pm daily except Monday. Entry is LL5000 for adults and LL1000 for under 18s. On the left of the foyer is a small museum shop, to the right is a screening room where you can watch a video documenting the fate of the museum during the war and its restoration.

Inside, the museum is more or less open plan and organised in roughly chronological order, following a clockwise rotation on both floors. All exhibits are labelled in English, Arabic and French. Unfortunately, given the amount of money spent on the museum's restoration, while the display cases and lighting are excellent, the labels do not give much background or context to the exhibits. At the time of writing written guides to the museum were not available.

Ground Floor

This floor contains the museum's largest artefacts, including colossi, sarcophagi and mosaics from the 1st and 2nd millenium BC up to the Roman and Byzantine periods.

2nd Millenium BC To the left of the entrance are artefacts from the 2nd millenium BC, most of which show evidence of Lebanon's close relations with Egypt. A number of faded hieroglyphic reliefs, mostly from Byblos and Tyre, sit against the left wall.

War & Pillage

Amid the chaos of Lebanon's civil war, the country's archaeological treasures were subject to a degree of pillage not seen since European colonists descended on the Middle East in the 18th and 19th centuries and hauled off the region's treasures to stock their museums.

Militias stole from Department of Antiquities storerooms, ransacked archaeological sites and bulldozed entire cemeteries and ancient settlements in their search for treasure. Even sarcophagi at the National Museum were smashed in the hope of finding treasure inside. The thieves were aided and abetted by unscrupulous middle men and Western art dealers who turned a blind eye to the provenance of the artefacts. According to Robert Fisk (in an excellent article 'The Biggest Supermarket in Lebanon', in *Berytus*, vol. XXXIX), an astounding 11 tons of stolen Lebanese Graeco-Roman and Byzantine-era artefacts arrived at an English port in February 1991. After determining whether or not taxes were due on the shipment, British customs let them into the country and they were later sold by a British dealer.

The only thing worse than the haemorrhage of national treasure was the accompanying destruction of the ancient sites. By bulldozing through layers of history, any information that the sites may have been able to tell us about the past was lost.

1st Millenium BC Following the clockwise rotation, you then enter into a chamber, which covers the period from the 1st millenium BC. One of the highlights of the room are beautifully preserved 5th century BC marble sarcophagi from Ain al-Helwa, which clearly show the coming together of Egyptian, Persian and Hellenistic influences. More evidence of Egypt is seen in a pair of Sphinxes and statues with Egyptian-style loincloths and frontality.

Returning to the main room, immediately to your left, are a series of Hellenistic funerary stelae. Next to these, on the back wall to the left of entrance, are a series of Thrones of Astarte, which were characteristic of the Phoenician mainland. Most are from the Hellenistic period and are made of limestone.

Roman & Byzantine On the other side of the main hall, is the much better Roman and Byzantine section. At the back of the room are a series of beautifully rendered white marble baby boys from Echmoun, one of which has Phoenician inscriptions. The rounded bodies and dimples give an amazingly realistic sense of chubby toddlers. The boys were sons of Sidonian aristocrats and the statues were offered to the gods in thanks for healing the child. Dating back to the 5th century BC, the statues are also significant because they are executed in Hellenistic style but were made some 150 years before Alexander the Great arrived in Phoenicia.

Next to the statues is a 3rd-century mosaic from Byblos depicting the abduction of Europa. Beside it is another, particularly beautiful, 4th-century mosaic, depicting the birth of Alexander.

Immediately to the right of the entrance is a stunning Roman torso in white marble. Beside this is an enormous white marble sarcophagus from Tyre. Beautifully preserved, and topped with an imposing reclining figure of a man and a woman, a frieze around its sides tells the legend of Achilles.

Just before heading up the stairs, look out for the 2nd century AD architectural models of theatres and temples from Baalbek.

1st Floor

Perhaps because of weight considerations, the first floor has smaller artefacts than the ground floor, almost all of which are in glass cases and date from prehistoric time until the Islamic era.

Prehistory & Bronze Age You jump back in time again as you turn left at the top of the staircase. The first half of the room shows an impressive array of prehistoric and bronze age artefacts. Immediately upon entering the room, a series of cases show some fascinating prehistoric implements, some dating back as far as 3200 BC. Sliding magnifying glasses let you take a close-up look at the flint arrow heads and daily implements. Case 3 has a number of small statues from this era, many betraying the Egyptian influence. Case 5 has some fine examples of jewellery, including a necklace with a gold medallion inlaid with carnelian and semiprecious stones. This, along with other objects in the case, was an offering found at Byblos and dating from between 3200 and 2000 BC.

Moving around the room, in case 9 there are some fine examples of late bronze age amphorae in white alabaster and granite. Case 10, overlooking the ground floor, has a delicately made obsidian-handled scimitar and mirror, both funerary objects dating to between 2000 and 1500 BC and found at Byblos. On the other side of the room, case 11 showcases a stunning collection of jewellery dating from 1500–600 BC. Again the Egyptian influence is present. One vase in gold and obsidian has hieroglyphic inscriptions with the name of the pharaoh Amenemhet IV (1798–1786 BC). In the middle of this section, in cases 13 and 17, are a series of tiny army figures armed with spears and swords. Cases 19 and 20 contain some beautiful weaponry found at Byblos and dating back to between 2000 and 1500 BC. Particularly fine is a dagger and sheath in gold, silver and ivory. So, too, are the axe heads devoted to the war gods at Byblos.

Turning the corner, a series of cases contain more funerary jewellery and figurines, most from Byblos. Case 25 has some fascinating cuneiform tablets, one of which contains a letter that has been translated:

To Zalaya, the Man of Damascus.
So speaks the King: I am sending you this tablet, my message to you. In addition, send me Hapiru...about whom I have already written in those words: 'I will give them to the cities of Kasa land where they can live instead of those I have deported.' Also know that the king is in good health as the sun in the heavens. His troops and his chariots are numerous...from the Upper country until the Lower country, from the Levant till the sunset, all is for the best.

Iron Age This period, from 1200–333 BC, was the apogee of Phoenician civilisation, despite domination by the Assyrians, followed by the Babylonians and Persians. The influence of the conquerors can be seen in some of the artefacts on display. Highlights include black, glazed Greek pottery in case 32 that was traded between the 4th and 6th centuries BC; funerary offerings from Tyre in case 33 and, in case 38, some gold jewellery with semiprecious stones that came from the tomb of a woman near Sidon.

Hellenistic Period Lasting from only 333–64 BC the Hellenistic period is represented with only a brief display, which includes a collection of funerary objects and coins as well as, in case 43, some terracotta figurines. Note that some of the cases in this section do not have English descriptions.

Roman Period The Roman period is well represented with some beautiful 3rd and 4th century jewellery in case 45. Case 48 also has a number of glittering, gold-leaf funerary ornaments. Case 49 shows the high quality of Phoenician glassware, with tiny amphorae and glass and alabaster flasks. In case 53 there are a number of masks with comic and tragic expressions and in case 51, daily objects that answer the question of what a Roman frying pan actually looked like (rather similar to a modern one). Case 56 contains a group of bronze objects that include a Greek votive ship transformed into a lamp. An inscription says that it was dedicated to the god Zeus Beithmares in AD 232. Moving around the room, cases 61 and 62 contain beautiful examples of Roman/Phoenician glass.

Byzantine to Mamluk The continuation of early Christian to Islamic civilisation can be seen in this last part of the exhibit. Case 62 contains fine glassware from the Byzantine to Ottoman periods. In case 64 there is some very beautiful Byzantine jewellery made of gold inlaid with precious stones. The Byzantine technique of granulation, in which tiny balls of gold formed part of the decoration, is carried over into the Mamluk-era jewellery in case 65. Other exhibits in this section include coins in cases 63 and 67, and some examples of Mamluk pottery in cases 68 and 69.

Just before you reach the stairs there is a small display case showing lumps of melted objects, a twisted mess of metal, ivory, glass and stone. These are some of the museum's war casualties and show just how high the temperatures rose when a shell hit the storage area and set it on fire.

AMERICAN UNIVERSITY OF BEIRUT MUSEUM

The museum on the AUB campus is small but charmingly old-fashioned and well worth a look, especially as it is the only other archaeological museum in the city apart from the National Museum. It is housed in an attractive 19th-century building near the Main Gate on Rue Bliss. If you tell the guard on the gate that you want to visit the museum he will direct you to the visitors desk. Once inside the campus, turn right and the museum is a large castellated building on your right past the church. The museum has a guidebook available to borrow while you walk around – ask at the desk as you go in. There are versions in English and French.

The museum has a collection of some 12,000 objects dating predominantly from prehistory but going up to the Islamic era. Unfortunately, the AUB did not escape looting and damage during the war. A number of figurines and seals were stolen and mosaics were damaged. Nevertheless, there is a good collection of Phoenician glassware and ceramics and some earlier artefacts, including some particularly interesting figurines.

There is no photography allowed inside the museum, but you can buy some overpriced postcards of the star exhibits at the desk. Entry is free and the museum's opening hours are from 10 am to noon and 2 to 4 pm weekdays.

SURSOCK MUSEUM

Just about the best thing to visit in East Beirut is the Sursock Museum (☎ 334 133) in Achrafiye. It is in a part of the city that still retains a fair amount of traditional architecture in the form of large 19th-century mansions. The Sursock Museum is the former home of the Sursock family and is a splendid example of 19th-century Italianate architecture – white, lacy stucco and sweeping staircases inspired by Italian villas.

The interior is suitably grand in style with heavy, wood panelling and marble floors. Some of the rooms are decorated in oriental style and the main hall has a collection of 19th-century Turkish silver. In the centre of the room is a gigantic 7th-century Abbasid jar. On the same floor is a small but interesting library, which is open by arrangement if you fancy doing some research. The former study of Nicholas Ibrahim Sursock features his portrait by Van Dongen. The room also houses a small collection of icons.

The museum's main function these days is to provide a venue for contemporary Lebanese artists. These exhibitions change periodically, but there is a permanent exhibition of Japanese prints and Islamic art.

The official name of the museum is Musée Nicholas Ibrahim Sursock and it at is Rue de l'Archevêché Grec-Orthodoxe, Achrafiye. The museum is open only during exhibitions. It is a good idea to telephone before you visit as it is sometimes closed while new exhibitions are being installed.

PLANET DISCOVERY

Planet Discovery (☎ 980 650) on Rue Omar al-Daouk is a children's science museum built by the downtown developer Solidére. Interactive exhibits related to building, physical phenomena, unfinished houses, the human body and communication techniques target children between the ages of three and 15. It is open from 9 am to 6 pm weekdays and 10 am to 8 pm weekends and holidays. For more information, see Travel with Children in the Facts for the Visitor chapter.

GALLERIES

Beirut's vibrant art scene means that there is a huge number of galleries. For more on the art scene, see the Facts about Lebanon chapter. Check local listings to see what's showing where (see Newspapers & Magazines in the Facts for the Visitor chapter).

Agial Art Gallery (☎ 345 213, cell 03-634 244) 63 Abdel Aziz St, Hamra. A shopfront gallery close to the AUB that specialises in local artists.

Epreuve d'Artiste (☎ 563 911) 16 Sursock St, Tabaris, Achrafiye. Well-known gallery specialising in modern art and sculpture.

Galerie Alice Mogabgab (☎ 336 525) 207 Ave Charles Malek, Achrafiye. Specialises in modern art, including artists from abroad.

Galerie Chahine (☎ 346 522) Hamra, near Concorde Square. Small gallery exhibiting nineteenth and early twentieth century art by Lebanese and foreign artists.

Galerie Janine Rubeiz (☎ 868 290) 2nd floor, Majdalani Bldg, Raouché. Run by one of the leading members of the Lebanese art scene since the 1960s, this is one of Lebanon's most renowned galleries.

PIGEON ROCKS

This is the most famous (in fact the only) natural feature of Beirut. The offshore natural rock arches of the Pigeon Rocks are fairly spectacular and a natural magnet for city dwellers who are craving something beautiful to look at, particularly at sunset. The stretch of the Corniche directly in front of the rocks is a vey good vantage point. Far more interesting is to take one of the tracks down to the lower cliffs. One track starts from the southern side of the rocks and, after a steep 100m, you find yourself down on the lower level of chalk cliffs. Almost immediately, you can completely forget you are in the city.

The way across the rocks is quite rugged and sensible shoes are a good idea, although you see local women teetering precariously across the cliffs in high heels. Down on the lower levels, you get a good side view of the Pigeon Rocks with the city behind. If you fancy sitting for a while to watch the waves crash through the rocks, there is probably the smallest cafe in the world (two chairs) overlooking the scene. Further down towards the open sea there is a larger cafe (four chairs), where you can sit and watch the sunset.

There are a number of inlets and caves in the cliffs. During summer, small boats take people around the rocks and to the caves for a small fee.

Monument to Peace

If your idea of public art is 10 storeys of military weaponry squashed between layers of concrete and sandbags, then the new Lebanese monument to peace is the place to visit. Unveiled in 1996 outside the Ministry of Defence building on the outskirts of Beirut, this permanent sculpture was created by French artist Armand Fernandez. Many of Fernandez's earlier works of art were assemblages of everyday articles, including a rubbish sculpture made up of the contents of unsuspecting consumers' rubbish bins.

This 5000-ton structure contains real Soviet T-55 tanks, armoured vehicles and artillery. Fernandez believes the monument will become the symbol of continued peace in Lebanon by ensuring a constant reminder of the recent civil war's death and destruction.

There is no direct service taxi to visit the monument. Take a service taxi to the museum area and change to one heading to the Ministry of Defence. The trip will cost LL2000 one way.

Katrina Browning

HAMRA

While rival militias pulverised Beirut's downtown during the war, the businesses and shops that were once clustered there moved to the Hamra district. Close to the university campus and many of Beirut's hotels, it has lost some of its gloss with the re-emergence of the original downtown area and the growing popularity of Achrafiye to the east. Nevertheless, it is still one of the city's main hubs, with a varied streetlife and a good selection of restaurants, fast-food joints, cafes, street vendors, bookshops, cinemas and so on.

Just off the eastern end of Rue Hamra is the **University of Lebanon** campus, with its 19th-century buildings and very attractive grounds. This is also where the **Sanayeh Public Garden**, one of the city's few public parks, is located.

Although most of the buildings here are bland modernist, there are some exceptions tucked away in the side streets. The nearby areas of **Ain al-Mraisse**, close to the little fishing port inside the Corniche, and **Minet al-Hosn**, slightly to the east, both have some older buildings that have been restored.

AMERICAN UNIVERSITY OF BEIRUT

Established in 1866 by an American Protestant missionary, Daniel Bliss, the AUB is one of the Middle East's most prestigious educational institutions. Most of the campus survived the war, with the exception of the central College Hall building, which was destroyed by a car bomb in 1991. Unfortu-

nately, the staff did not fare so well. AUB President Malcolm Kerr was assassinated in his office in 1984 and a number of staff were kidnapped and murdered. Nowadays it is a calm oasis of green in the centre of Beirut.

BEIRUT CENTRAL DISTRICT (DOWNTOWN)

Prior to the war, the downtown area, now known as the Beirut Central District (BCD), was Beirut's pulsating centre. This was the financial and commercial centre of the city, and home to a varied community of some 40,000 people. The old souqs were here, as

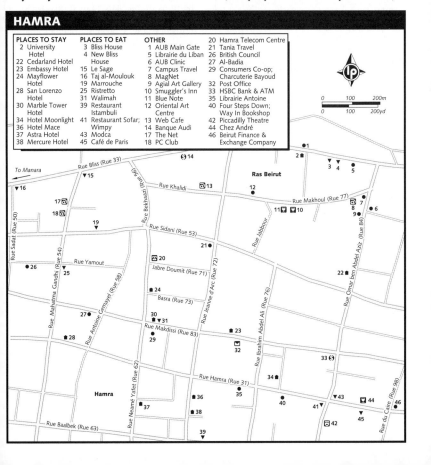

HAMRA

PLACES TO STAY	PLACES TO EAT	OTHER	
2 University Hotel	3 Bliss House	1 AUB Main Gate	20 Hamra Telecom Centre
22 Cedarland Hotel	4 New Bliss House	5 Librairie du Liban	21 Tania Travel
23 Embassy Hotel	15 Le Sage	6 AUB Clinic	26 British Council
24 Mayflower Hotel	16 Taj al-Moulouk	7 Campus Travel	27 Al-Badia
28 San Lorenzo Hotel	19 Marrouche	8 MagNet	29 Consumers Co-op; Charcuterie Bayoud
30 Marble Tower Hotel	25 Ristretto	9 Agial Art Gallery	32 Post Office
34 Hotel Moonlight	31 Walimah	10 Smuggler's Inn	33 HSBC Bank & ATM
36 Hotel Mace	39 Restaurant Istambuli	11 Blue Note	35 Librairie Antoine
37 Astra Hotel	41 Restaurant Sofar;	12 Oriental Art Centre	40 Four Steps Down; Way In Bookshop
38 Mercure Hotel	Wimpy	13 Web Cafe	42 Piccadilly Theatre
	43 Modca	14 Banque Audi	44 Chez André
	45 Café de Paris	17 The Net	46 Beirut Finance &
		18 PC Club	Exchange Company

Coffee Craze

In 1526 Ali, son of pious mystic Mohammed ibn Iraq al-Dimashqi, learned that his father had died in Mecca. The distraught son departed for Arabia immediately and spent almost 15 years in the holy city. During his time there he adopted some of the local customs, including the drinking of coffee, then unheard of in Beirut.

Unable to kick the habit, he returned to his home town with sacks of beans and is credited with single-handedly creating generations of caffeine addicts. In Ali's time, those who could afford it drank their brew out of imported Chinese porcelain cups. For the rest, local potters turned out pretty good imitations. During the excavations of the souq area hundreds of coffee cup shards were unearthed.

were the glittering hotels and restaurants. Even the red light district had its place.

By the end of the civil war all this was gone. The government gave the enormous task of rebuilding to a specially formed private company, **Solidére**, which embarked on an ambitious plan to save the city (see the special section 'The Rebuilding of Beirut' earlier in this chapter).

The heart of the downtown district was the **Place des Martyrs** (also known as the Place des Canons, but always called al-Burj by locals because of a medieval watchtower that once stood on the site). This huge, open space was named after the rebels who were executed here by the Turks in 1915. By the end of the war, the only feature that remained in the famous square was the bronze statue in the centre, known as the **Martyrs Statue**. Riddled with bullet holes, the statue became a symbol of all that was destroyed during the fighting and the holes were filled with flowers. Nowadays, perhaps also symbolically, the statue is being cleaned up while developers create an underground car park beneath the soon-to-be redeveloped square.

Heading west from here, along Rue Emir Bachir, you come to **St George Cathedral**, a Maronite church, which dates back to the Crusades and lays claim to being the site where St George killed the dragon (although there is another place in Beirut that makes the same claim move convincingly – see the following East Beirut section).

Beside the church are the remains of Roman Beirut's **cardo maximus**. This was part of the Roman market area and the remains of a number important buildings have been uncovered. For the moment they languish as the archaeologists left them, a jumbled mess of layers and stones, with a clearly visible road or footpath cutting through the middle. There are plans to turn the ruins into a 'garden of forgiveness', an archaeological park in which Beirut's layers of history will be brought together to allow people to reflect on the past. An international competition has been launched to choose an appropriate design.

Turning from here down Rue Maarad, you arrive at the **Place d'Étoile** (also known by its Arabic name, Nejemeh Square). This area follows the plan drawn up by the French, who cleared a swathe of the medieval city and organised the new grid in the shape of a star, with boulevards reminiscent of Hausseman's Paris. This is where the life of the downtown area is concentrated for now. The newly renovated Lebanese **parliament** sits on the square, and a number of cafes and shops are springing up in the surrounding streets.

On the corner of Rue Maarad and Rue Weygand stands the **Omari Mosque**, sometimes called the Grand Mosque, which was quite badly damaged during the war. The mosque was originally built in the mid-12th century as the Church of John the Baptist of the Knights Hospitallers over a site previously occupied by a Roman Temple of Jupiter. Some parts of the original temple were re-used in the construction of the church. The conversion to a mosque took place in AD 1291 when Saladin retook Beirut. The building still contains traces of its former pagan and Christian origins, despite some drastic alterations.

Just north of the mosque is a huge empty area with a single domed building. These were the city's souqs and the building is the Zawiye of Ibn Iraq (see the boxed text 'Spir-

Spirits Against Bulldozers

In 1992 the rubble of Beirut's souqs was being cleared as archaeologists, working against the clock, tried to investigate the site before it was built over by developers. A bulldozer clearing an area in what had been Souq Tawile was scooping up debris and came up against small, domed building. The machine suddenly stopped. The driver, wanting to finish his job, started the machine up again but when he tried to move the controls, his hand was suddenly paralysed. Later, when he was away from the site, the paralysis disappeared.

News quickly spread of the 'miracle' that saved the building, which turned out to be part of a *zawiye*, or hospice and religious school, built by 16th-century mystic and scholar, Mohammed ibn Iraq al-Dimashqi. Crowds visited the shrine and reports began to circulate of miraculous healing among the ill who had prayed there.

Muslim religious authorities erected a protective wall around the zawiye and announced that it would not be demolished. It is now the only Mamluk building left in Beirut and stands alone waiting to be incorporated into the new downtown development.

its Against Bulldozers'). Excavations revealed that markets and workshops existed here before Alexander the Great arrived in Lebanon. Even the present-day Rue Weygand follows the line of a Roman street. Redevelopment of the area appears to be on hold, but according to Solidére's plans, this will be a shopping and entertainment area with residential buildings and offices. Traditional vaulted souqs will be re-created to stand beside modern buildings.

On a hill to the south-west is the Ottoman-era **Grand Serail**, which was built in 1890 and served as both a barracks and the seat of government. The newly restored serail opened its doors again in August 1998 after a four-year, US$27 million renovation.

At the bottom of the steps just before Rue Riad es-Solha and below the serail are the archaeological remains of **Roman Baths**. In Roman times this was one of Beirut's premier bath houses and you can still see the pipes that carried water between the chambers.

EAST BEIRUT

East Beirut suffered relatively light damage during the war and much of the area's Ottoman and French colonial period architecture remains intact. Achrafiye, up from the port and to the east of the Damascus road, has some beautiful buildings tucked away in its shady streets. The lavish Sursock Museum is one of the most outstanding, but Rue Sursock has some lovely old apartment buildings and villas. As the area's popularity grows, early 20th-century buildings are being renovated and provide some idea of how parts of the city might have looked before the ravages of developers and war.

Few buildings have any historical interest. One exception is **St George's Church** (now the Al-Khader Mosque) in the Khodr district. This is supposed to be the site of

St George & the Dragon

The legend of St George slaying the dragon is known the world over but where it actually took place has been disputed for centuries. Libya, Cappadocia (modern Turkey) and Beirut all lay claim to the drama.

St George was born in Palestine and served in England with the Romans. He converted to Christianity and was martyred in AD 203.

According to Beirut lore, a monster terrorised the city and in an effort to appease it the town's king offered to sacrifice his daughter. St George appeared on a horse, rescued the princess and killed the dragon at a spot close to the old city walls.

The dragon is seen as the symbol of evil, in particular, of paganism. In the time of the Crusades, the Christians believed that a country could be converted to Christianity by the saint's killing of the evil – the dragon. The princess symbolises where this took place. So by killing the dragon, St George saved Beirut from the evil of pagan religion.

The site of the battle with the dragon became sacred ground and in Crusader times a chapel was built here.

where St George killed the dragon. The building itself is very small and tucked away near the junction of Ave Charles Helou and Rue al-Khodr, just south of the highway. There is supposed to be healing power in the water from the nearby well, called the **Dragon's Well**.

ACTIVITIES
Swimming

Swimming is one of the most popular activities in summer. The only free place to swim in Beirut is the public beach, Ramlet al-Bayda, south of Raouché. However, given the polluted waters off Beirut, this is not recommended. If you cannot get out of the city, private beach clubs are a far better option. These have no sand, but are seaside clubs, many with pools and a load of other extras. If you decide to go, be warned: cell phones, unnaturally sculpted bodies and designer bathing suits are the norm and the experience is as much about seeing and being seen as it is about having a swim. Here is a list of clubs:

AUB Beach Accessible only via a tunnel from the university this is smack in the middle of the Corniche. Canvas awnings keep things relatively private. Open to AUB students and their friends.

Bain Français Ain al-Mraisse. Not one of the better places, but easier to access than some of the more exclusive clubs. Entry is LL10,000 and there is a pool, concrete sunbathing area and cafeteria/restaurant.

Long Beach Club This is members only, but if you know someone who belongs, you can go as a guest for LL20,000. There is a large concrete bathing area, two pools, jet skis, restaurants and snack bars.

Riviera Beach Club (☎ 373 210-9) Manara. Belonging to the upmarket Riviera Hotel and therefore free to guests, otherwise by membership only. Facilities include a marina (you too can tie up your yacht for LL1,000,000!) and the usual pools and restaurants. If you find someone to take you, entrance fee is LL20,000.

St George Yacht Club (☎ 356 350) Ain al-Mraisse. A newly renovated version of what was *the* club of the 1960s. Has a marina, nice swimming pool, jet skis, restaurants and grass on which to stretch out. Entry is LL20,000 Tuesday to Sunday, LL15,000 on Monday.

Waste Not, Want Not

When the civil war drew to a close the seafront on the northern side of the once-glamorous St George Hotel was hidden by a 12m-high pile of waste, stretching over 25 hectares. This included everything from domestic rubbish and rubble to hospital waste and unexploded ordinance.

How to dispose of this enormous and dangerous heap was a huge problem. In the end, Solidére hired foreign firms to help with the clean up and is using the waste to create a large swath of reclaimed land, beside which the new St George Marina has been built.

Sporting Beach Club (☎ 742 481) Manara. Open all year to members and guests of the Hotel Mediterranee, the club has two pools, scuba club, basketball courts, restaurants and steps down to the sea. Guest entry is LL20,000.

Hammam

You can indulge yourself with a massage, sauna and bath at the **Hammam an-Nuzha al-Jadid** (☎ 641 298) on Rue Kasti, off Ave du General Fouad Chehab. It is open 24 hours daily, but women can only visit between 9 am to 2 pm on Monday. The hammam provides soap and towels. Be warned, letters from women readers have complained of overtures from the staff and most locals assume that the place is a brothel.

Health Clubs

A burgeoning number of sports clubs are helping Beirutis keep those well-maintained bodies trim. Escape (☎ 740 944/55) in Manara offers aerobics, squash and tennis. Monthly membership is possible, and guests must pay US$7 per day; the Summerland Health Club belongs to the Summerland Hotel (see Places to Stay – Top End) and has a weight room, aerobics classes, tennis, steam bath and can put you on a weight-loss plan if you've over indulged in mezze (a selection of hot and cold starters). Entry costs US$13. Complete club listings can be found in *The Guide*. See Newspapers & Magazines in the Facts for the Visitor chapter for details.

Golf

Beirut Golf Club (☎ 822 474) in Bir Hassan has been open since the 1960s and has an 18-hole course, tennis and squash courts, swimming pool, and billiard tables. Although you are supposed to be a member to play here, they sometimes allow nonmembers in.

ORGANISED TOURS

Because Beirut is so small and has few archaeological sites, there is little need to go on an organised tour of the city. However, Destination Liban and Campus Travel are both highly recommended for budget travellers who want some help getting about, or for independent travellers who don't want to share their experiences with an enormous coach load of strangers. See Organised Tours in the Getting Around chapter for more details.

PLACES TO STAY – BUDGET
Hostels

There are no hostels per se in Lebanon but Destination Liban (☎ 293 066, cell 03-497 762) has five apartments in Achrafiye that are based on the hostel idea. The very clean rooms with shared bathroom and kitchen facilities are highly recommended and cost US$16/28/36/40 a single/double/triple/quad.

Hotels

There is a small but growing number of cheap hotels in Beirut, although if you've come from elsewhere in the region they won't seem like such a bargain. *Hotel al-Shahbaa (☎ 564 287)* is beside the bus station (climb up the stairs out of the station and up to Ave Charles Helou) and has friendly management, which has recently painted some of the rooms. A bed in a reasonably clean dorm-style room with four or five beds goes for LL5000. All rooms have fans and there are kitchen facilities.

Hotel al-Nazih (☎ 534 868) is just off Ave Charles Helou, very close to Place des Martyrs. It has reasonably clean rooms with beds ranging from LL5000 to LL10,000, depending on the size of the room and the number of people in it. Showers are shared and relatively clean. There are also kitchen facilities.

Talal's New Hotel (☎ 562 567) is just across the street and has larger rooms costing LL15,000/18,000/20,000 for a double/triple/quad. Prices can be negotiated. Most of the people staying here are Syrian men; women should steer clear.

Pension Home Valery (☎ 362 169, 2nd floor, Saab Bldg, Rue Phoenicia, Ain al-Mraisse) is Beirut's main backpacker haunt. Walk through a dingy hallway, next to the Wash Me car wash, until you reach the lift. There are no less than three places calling themselves Pension Home Valery in the building, but the 2nd-floor pension is the best, with spotless bathrooms, sandwiches and soft drinks on sale and Internet access for LL5000 per hour. Beds in the dorm rooms cost US$5 per person (and US$1 extra for a shower). The 3rd-floor version is not quite as polished, but the management is also friendly and prices are the same. The 4th floor is to be avoided.

Hotel Regis (☎ 361 845, Rue Razi, Ain al-Mraisse) is down a side street close to the end of the Corniche. All rooms here have private baths, making it a little more comfortable than the dorm option, and it's a bargain at US$10 for a double with fan (US$20 for the same with air-con). However, it is rundown, with peeling wallpaper and a sad air.

University Hotel (☎ 361 845, Rue Bliss, Ras Beirut) is one of the better options. Although it operates as a hotel for AUB students, travellers can stay here, although it is pricey at US$10 in a four-bed dorm. There are rooms with private baths starting at US$15/20 for singles/doubles. Special rates can be negotiated for longer stays.

San Lorenzo Hotel (☎ 348 604/5, Rue Hamra) is above the Taverne Swiss restaurant, near the junction with Rue Mahatma Gandhi. Recently painted, the rooms have fans and balconies but can be noisy because of their location. Singles/doubles without bath go for US$15/20 and US$20/25 with bath.

Hotel Moonlight (☎ 352 308) is tucked away on a side street off Rue Hamra. One of the increasingly down-at-heel rooms here cost US$20/25/30 for a single/double/triple. Hot water is available in the evenings only.

BEIRUT

Astra Hotel (☎ 346 600, Rue Neamé Yafet, Hamra) is a modernist low rise building with large, if somewhat gloomy, air-con rooms for US$25/30. All rooms have fridges, air-con and their own bathrooms. Prices are reduced for longer stays.

PLACES TO STAY – MID-RANGE

Most mid-range places are located in the Hamra area and range from the slightly run-down to the extremely smart.

Embassy Hotel (☎ 340 814, fax 340 815, Rue Makdissi, Hamra) is a comfortable, family-run place with singles/doubles/triples for US$40/50/65, including a 16% service charge. You may also be able to negotiate a discount.

Mayflower Hotel (☎ 340 580, Rue Neamé Yafet, Hamra) is something of an institution and was a favourite press hang-out in the postwar period. Its bar, the Duke of Wellington, remains popular with expats and the management is very friendly. It has a wing of 'economy' single/double rooms that go for US$35/40. For this you get to use the hotel pool and other facilities. Regular rooms cost US$50/60, including breakfast. All have air-con, TV and phone.

Mace Hotel (☎/fax 344 626/7, 340 720) is on Rue Jeanne d'Arc and is very friendly. The rooms, all with bathrooms, TV and air-con are clean, if somewhat tacky, and a good deal at US$30/40, with breakfast.

Mercure Hotel (☎ 340 600, Rue Jeanne d'Arc, Hamra) is pushing the limit of the mid-range but is a reliable, if bland, almost-top-ender run by the Accor chain. It has all the five-star features such as air-con, satellite TV and minibar for US$65/75, including breakfast and taxes.

Cedarland Hotel (☎ 340 233/4, Rue Omar Ben Abdel Aziz) is just off Rue Hamra and has clean rooms with private bath, air-con and TV. Rooms cost US$35/45 and twin beds cost US$40. Breakfast is an extra US$5.

Marble Tower Hotel (☎ 346 260, fax 346 262, Rue Makdissi) is a very comfortable 60-room hotel that gives top-end service at more or less mid-range prices. Rooms cost US$50/60, including breakfast and service. There is a rooftop lounge and restaurant.

Embassy Hotel (☎ 340 814/5, Rue Makdissi) is right in the heart of Hamra, almost opposite the post office. It charges US$40/50, including service, for slightly gloomy singles/doubles with air-con. The Embassy claims to be the only hotel in Hamra with a garden.

Lord's Hotel (☎ 740 382/3, Rue Neguib Ardati, Manara) is opposite the Bain Militaire (Military Beach) and has flexible prices for its rooms: US$35/45 with a 'student' discount or US$70/85 without. The rooms are musty but some have good sea views. Try to negotiate.

PLACES TO STAY – TOP END

There is a glut of expensive hotels in Beirut, and more are being built all the time. If you can afford it, you are spoilt for choice – so this is just an edited highlight of the best of the best.

The Albergo (☎ 339 797, Rue Abdel Wahhab al-Inglizi, Achrafiye) is in a restored building, very close to Achrafiye's ever-expanding restaurant and bar enclave. Smaller and more exclusive than Beirut's high-rise five-star hotels, it consists of 33 suites, each with its own distinctive style. There is also a rooftop pool and two very good restaurants. None of this comes cheap: rooms range from US$215 to US$325.

Bristol Hotel (☎ 351 400, fax 602 451, Rue Madame Curie, Hamra) is one Beirut's most established five-star hotels, with chandeliers and fine silver service. A basic single/double room costs US$110/115 plus a 16% service charge.

Commodore Hotel (☎ 350 400, fax 602 250, Rue Commodore, Hamra) is one of the few five-star establishments in the centre of town and was a home away from home for foreign journalists during the civil war. It is now a rather bland Meridien, but some of the old staff remain. Rooms here cost US$120/135, plus service and taxes.

Hotel Mediterranée (☎ 741 824/5/6, Ave du Général de Gaulle, Manara) is on the Corniche near the Bain Militaire and has rooms with a sea view for US$105/130, including breakfast and 16% service charge.

Phoenicia Inter-Continental (☎ 369 100, fax 369 101, @ phoenicia@inter conti.com) reopened in 2000 to a rapturous reception from Beirut's middle-aged beau monde. The original Phoenicia was one of prewar Beirut's legendary locales and its renaissance is seen as a symbol of the city's return to normality. Unfortunately its emphasis on glitz makes it less than interesting from an architectural point of view. But it is very comfortable and has everything you'd expect from a top-end hotel. Singles/doubles with sea views cost US$155/175 per night, plus service and taxes. Garden-view rooms are slightly cheaper.

Riviera Hotel (☎ 373 210/9, fax 602 272, Ave de Paris, Manara) sits on the Corniche and has 125 rooms and all the luxuries you'd expect, plus its own swimming pool and health club. Sea-view rooms cost US$155/175 plus 16% service. Garden rooms are about US$25 less.

Summerland Hotel (☎ 858 000, fax 856 666) deserves a mention simply because it was built during the war and served as an escape from the carnage for Lebanon's wealthy elite. To protect its guests it had its own militia and enough infrastructure and supplies to keep going for about a month if placed under siege. Now it's just a five-star hotel/resort on the seafront that charges US$200/225, including service.

Le Vendôme Inter-Continental (☎ 369 280, fax 360 169, Rue Minet al-Hosn) the favoured hang-out of the designer-clad Beiruti until the Phoenicia reopened. Beside the seafront, near the Hard Rock Cafe, it has great views and a continental restaurant. City-view rooms cost US$190/210 and US$230/250 with a sea view.

PLACES TO EAT
Restaurants
Beirut is a culinary paradise, with a vast array of restaurants and cafes offering everything from traditional mezze to Thai curry. At the lower end of the price scale, there's a large selection of Lebanese restaurants on offer. If money's no problem you're spoiled for choice in Beirut. There are surprisingly few top-notch Lebanese restaurants in town

(Beirutis insist the best are outside the city) but there are one or two very good ones and there is a huge selection of other cuisines. For more listings, see Pubs & Bars in the Entertainment section later; many of the bars listed there double as restaurants.

Abu Hassan (Rue Salaheddine al-Ayoubi, Manara) is a small, unpretentious neighbourhood restaurant with good Lebanese food served in no-nonsense surroundings. A meal of mezze and grills will cost you about LL20,000.

Marrouche (☎ 743 185, Rue Sidani, Hamra) is a local chain with good, reasonably priced Lebanese food. Mezzes start at LL2500. No alcohol is served.

Restaurant Sofar (☎ 345 606, Rue Hamra) is a quirky old place sitting above Wimpy and serving a mixture of Lebanese and international cuisine at reasonable prices. There is a daily set-lunch menu that is a bargain at LL9000 for a salad, plat du jour and dessert.

Restaurant Istambuli (☎ 352 049, Rue Baalbek, Hamra) serves reasonably priced Lebanese and Turkish food and is popular with local families. Meals are excellent value, with mezzes starting at LL3000 and grills at about LL8000.

Walimah (☎ 745 933, Rue Makdissi, Hamra) is owned by two women who recreate delicious Lebanese home cooking in a charming old house. Meals range from LL8000 to LL15,000, or you can stick to mezzes and soups, which start at LL3000.

Casablanca (☎ 369 354, Rue Ain al-Mraisse) is possibly the most original restaurant in the city. Set in one of the few intact Ottoman houses left on the Corniche it serves a delicious fusion of Eastern and Western cuisines in cool, tasteful surroundings. Its Sunday brunch is famous and is popular with professors from the nearby AUB. Expect to pay at least US$25 per person for dinner, not including drinks.

Sirena (☎ 374 840, Rue Maasaloum, Ras Beirut) is an Indian restaurant specialising in tandoori dishes. It has smart decor and the food is good and not too expensive at US$20 to US$25 for a main course and a few side dishes with drinks.

Babylone (☎ 219 539, Rue Abdel Wahab al-Inglizi) is a perennially popular restaurant and bar in an old house in Achrafiye. The food is French/international/fusion, the music is eclectic and the clients an interesting mixture of 20- to 50-somethings. On weekends the bar takes over from the restaurant. Main dishes are about US$10 to US$15.

Sushi Bar (☎ 338 555, Rue Monot, Achrafiye) is very busy and very trendy but also very good. Like everywhere, good sushi doesn't come cheap; a platter will cost you LL35,000.

Al-Mijana (☎ 328 082, Rue Abdel Wahab al-Inglizi, Achrafiye) serves some of the city's best Lebanese food in a beautifully restored Ottoman villa. In summer you can sit in a garden complete with fig trees and an ancient well. One of the specialities here is *kibbeh nayye* (raw kibbe) and there are also a number of less-common mezze dishes. The combination of the food and the surroundings make for a special evening. A meal with drinks will cost about US$40 per person.

Al-Mayass (☎ 215 046, Rue Trabaud, Achrafiye) serves extremely good Armenian and Lebanese specialities in cosy surroundings and at reasonable prices. Lunch here will cost about LL10,000 per person.

Le Chef (☎ 445 373, Rue Gouraud, Gemayze) has something of a cult following and is a slightly cleaned up, funky version of a truckers' caff. It's open from 8 am to 6 pm daily and is always packed at lunch time. The mostly simple but good meals cost from US$4 to US$7.

Cafes

There are many cafes dotted around Beirut and range from traditional Arabic to trendy European. In traditional cafes, coffee costs between LL1000 and LL2000.

Café de Paris (☎ 341 115, Rue Hamra) is one of a strip of landmark cafes on Rue Hamra and is known as an intellectual's haunt. Breakfast here costs US$8. The nearby *Modca* (☎ 345 501, Rue Hamra) offers three cups of coffee for the price of one and has traditional Lebanese food. *Wimpy* (☎ 345 440) has nothing to do with the fast-food restaurant of the same name and has

some fabulous 1960s-style furniture in addition to tea and coffee.

Ristretto (☎ 739 475, Rue Mahatma Gandhi, Hamra) is a very good place for an American-style breakfast or simply for an espresso. Newspapers are on hand and breakfast comes with vitamin C pills for those who overindulged the night before. Pancakes with maple syrup will set you back LL5000.

Raouda (☎ 743 348, Ras Beirut near Bain Militaire) is a Beirut institution where you can sit beside the sea and drink a freshly squeezed juice (about LL2000) or smoke a nargileh (water pipe). A favourite hang-out for artists and intellectuals and their families, it is an extremely pleasant place to spend an afternoon. A similar place, but without the intellectual pretensions, is the *Palace Cafe*, beside the water just where Ave du Paris turns into Ave du Général de Gaulle. Here you can see fishermen sitting atop poles and feel the spray in your face as you puff your nargileh. Back round at the Pigeon Rocks is the *Bay Rock Cafe*, which has a fantastic view over the famous rocks and serves a selection of salads, sandwiches and crepes for between LL4000 and LL9000.

Casper & Gambini (☎ 983 666, Rue Riad al-Solh) has a terrace overlooking the cardo maximus in downtown and serves a large selection of sandwiches for between LL7000 and LL10,000.

Bistrot Germanos (☎ 329 008, Rue Huvelin, Achrafiye) is a French-style cafe that is a hang-out for students from nearby Université St Joseph. Daily lunch specials, with a large main course, salad, soft drink and coffee cost around LL20,000. A selection of herbal teas and good espressos are on offer.

Tribeca (☎ 336 338, Rue Monot, Achrafiye) is a New York-style deli that specialises in bagels, which it makes surprisingly well. It has good coffee, background jazz music and a relaxed, if slightly trendy, atmosphere. Bagels with salads cost about LL8000.

Gemayze Cafe (Rue Gouraud, Gemayze) is one of the city's most famous traditional cafes, with high ceilings and the clack of backgammon pieces being moved about by the old Beirutis who pass their time here.

The cafe was used as a set in the film *West Beirut*. Coffee and tea costs about LL1500.

Fast Food

Most of the main Western fast-food chains have branches in Beirut, but for something different, Lebanese fast food is delicious, cheap and available on almost every street in the city. For a detailed explanation on Lebanese food and definitions of all the names and terms used here, see under Food in the Facts for the Visitor chapter.

Kamel *(☎ 351 586, Rue Baalbek)* is a tiny little hole-in-the-wall that sells only fuul and hummus. A plate of fuul with bread costs about LL2000.

Barbar is a series of restaurants that take up most of a city block on Rue Abdel Aziz just above Rue Baalbek in Hamra. They do all the usual Lebanese staples, with shwarma for LL2000 or a plat du jour for LL7000.

Kebabji *(Rue Hamra)* is known for its excellent shwarma and shish tawouq for LL2000. A selection of other Lebanese fast-food staples, such as lahma bi ajeen and hummus, is also on offer.

Sahyoun *(Rue de Damas)* is on the former Green Line and may be out of the way but is known for its felafel, which costs LL1500.

Zaatar wa Zeit *(☎ 614 302, Rue Nasra, Sodeco, Achrafiye)* serves a bewildering array of *manaeesh* (flat-bread pizzas) and Lebanese-style sandwiches. A plain manaeesh costs LL1000; *lahma bi ajeen* (spicy meat pizza) costs LL1500.

Le Sage *(Rue Bliss, Ras Beirut)* is a Lebanese sandwich place popular with AUB students. You can have zaatar, *halloumi* cheese or even chocolate and banana melted into Lebanese bread for LL1500. Further along Rue Bliss is **New Bliss House**, one of the most popular takeaways in West Beirut. Shwarma and kebab go for LL2500 and LL3500 respectively, and dessert is taken care of next door at **Bliss House** which serves ice cream and fresh juices (around LL1800 for a small glass).

Hard Rock Cafe *(☎ 371 247, Rue Minet al-Hosn)* had to be included here because it is such a landmark and surprisingly popular with young middle-class Beirutis. Burgers are expensive at LL12,000 to LL15,000. This being Beirut, one such venue was insufficient, so a competing Hard Rock Cafe exists up the hill on Rue Verdun.

Self-Catering

Beirut, particularly the Hamra area, is packed with small neighbourhood grocery shops selling such basics as bread, dairy products and, usually, a selection of fruit and vegetables. There are also a number of small supermarkets. One of the best is the **Consumer's Co-op** on Rue Makdissi. Apart from a reasonable selection of the usual supermarket fare there is a takeaway section with prepared chicken and pies. For larger supermarkets, you must drive to the suburbs.

Beside the Co-op there is a small deli called **Charcuterie Bayoud** which sells local and imported meats and cheeses plus a good selection of Lebanese wine, in addition to imported spirits. Special vintages of Lebanese wine can also be bought at **Enoctica**, a wine shop near the SNA building on Ave General Fouad Chehab in Achrafiye.

If you want to sample some of Lebanon's famous pastries, head over to **Amal al-Bohsali** *(Rue Omar ben Abdel Aziz)*, Beirut's most famous pastry shop for decades. This is the place to try melt-in your mouth *kahk* (sweet usually almond flavoured biscuit filled with pistachios or dates) and baklava.

If you want a place to sit down and try your goodies immediately, head to either branch of **Taj al-Molouk** *(Corniche, Ain al-Mraisse or Rue Bliss, Ras Beirut)*. Although both are pastry shops, they also have a cafe area.

ENTERTAINMENT

Thanks to its bewildering away of venues, Beirut is fast regaining its legendary status of party capital of the eastern Mediterranean. Thursday, Friday and Saturday are the busiest nights and because many of the clubs double as restaurants you will need reservations at some of the trendier places. Generally speaking, the evening starts late; most people do not eat before 9 pm and the clubs do not get in gear until about 1 am. There are a number of bars and clubs in Hamra but the place of the moment is Achrafiye, where a new bar or restaurant seems to open each week. The following is just a selection.

Pubs & Bars

Beirut has a huge variety of bars, from the laid-back student hang-out to the sleek designer cool. Most bars are also restaurants, and many become discos thanks to the exuberance of the clientele.

Abou Elie (☎ 741 645, Yaacoubian Building, Caracas, Manara), also known as Che Guevara's, is a tiny pub in a nondescript high-rise with red plywood in place of windows. It used to be a hang-out for communists, and Che posters share the walls with pictures of Fidel and, for local content, Kamal Jumblatt. It is also infamous for its gun-toting barman, who likes to reminisce about the good old days of the Soviets.

Chez André (☎ 345 662, Rue Hamra) is a tiny bar/restaurant that predates the war and eschews the pretensions of Beirut's trendier places. This was a meeting place for intellectuals and, disconcertingly, politicians and still has an avant-garde feel. Armenian food is served for about US$5 to U$10 per person.

Blue Note (☎ 344 362, Rue Makhoul, Hamra) is an established favourite, with live jazz on Friday and Saturday and a cover charge of LL6000. Drinks are reasonable (LL4500 for beer) and food is available.

Caracas (☎ 741 634, Rue Caracas, Ras Beirut) is a bar/restaurant but is famous for its staff and customers dancing on tables. It's not cheap, but it's smart and good fun. Drinks cost about US$8 and dinner is about US$25.

Smugglers Inn (☎ 388 656, Rue Makhoul, Hamra) is a student hang-out that is invaded by nonstudents thanks to the low prices (LL1000 for a shot; meals for US$5). Friendly and casual, it is one of the many places in the city where the tabletops become impromptu dancefloors in the wee hours.

Pacifico (☎ 204 446, Rue Monot, Achrafiye) has the best cocktails in Lebanon served in a Cuban-themed bar. It's a small place that is immensely popular with bright young things, it has a great atmosphere and a happy hour between 7 and 8 pm.

Circus (☎ 332 523, Rue Monot, Achrafiye) is a large bar/restaurant that frequently has live music. Alternatively there's a DJ keeping the crowd hopping. It is often full, so reservations are needed. The food here is a blend of Far-Eastern and French and there is a set dinner menu for US$17.

La Closerie (Time Out) (☎ 331 983, Rue du Liban, Achrafiye) is a laid-back lounge bar in a lovely old house. The stone-vaulted basement is beautiful and the place has the feel of a hip but tranquil private club. A variety of food is on offer, too, encompassing everything from sushi to halloumi cheese and costing between LL8000 and LL16,000.

Sports Cafe (☎ 335 600, Ave Fouad Chehab, Achrafiye) is a Canadian chain that has something like 100 TV screens for those who don't want to miss a moment of their favourite game. A good way to bond with local sports fans; it also has a happy hour starting at 5 pm.

Teatro (☎ 616 617, Ave de l'Independence, Achrafiye) is a bar/restaurant in a beautiful old house. It's dimly lit and gothic, with an amazing chandelier and a theatrical feel (hence the name). Favoured by 20- to 40-somethings, there may be no tabletop dancing here but there is still an upbeat atmosphere, particularly after 11 pm. Food is French/international with some oriental dishes thrown in and costs about US$20 per person.

Zinc (☎ 612 612, Rue Seifeddine al-Khatib, Achrafiye) is in a tastefully decorated old Achrafiye house and another restaurant (serving international food) that doubles as a bar. Trendy and young, live jazz and blues can be heard here too.

Discos & Clubs

The boundary between restaurants and discos is blurred in many of Beirut's establishments, with restaurants often becoming impromptu discos after dinner. The following are officially designated as clubs, and don't expect to see much happening until after midnight. Unfortunately, all are expensive, so if you're on a budget you'll need to stick with the bars (which are often more fun) or nurse your pricey drink.

Atlantis (☎ 203 344, Rue Université St Joseph, Achrafiye), true to its watery name, has a marine theme. Fish swim underneath the bar and in plexiglass channels around the floor. In the centre of the dancefloor a round fish tank filled with piranhas rises up (inevitably with one or two people gyrating on top) as the crowd gets going. Entry is through an air-lock type door. Food is also served, for about US$30 per person. The crowd is hip and a mixture of 25 and up. Reservations are advisable at weekends.

BO18 (☎ 580 018, cell 03-800 018, Forum de Beyrouth, Qarantina) is quite simply *the* place to experience Beirut's cutting-edge decadence. Sunk below ground in a bunker-like structure rumoured to have once been a torture centre during the war, it is a mixture of ingenious design and high gothic funerary imagery. As the place heats up, the roof slides open to let in the air. Packed to the rafters with a trendy crowd dancing to a mixture of music, this is a place where anything goes. It's not for the fainthearted, nor the broke: beers go for about LL10,000. It's about 3km west from downtown.

Gotha (☎ 336 533 Rue Université St Joseph, Achrafiye) is just off Rue Monot and is filled with well-dressed people watching each other amid plush decor. Reservations are essential at weekends.

Kookoo Club (☎ 425 886, Rue Elias Saab, Achrafiye) is a kitsch-lover's dream with an interior modelled on an Amazon rainforest, complete with waterfalls. The proprietor, Elie, is a Barry White lookalike who tends to grab the microphone during the evening. An eclectic crowd of all ages adds to the potent mix. Beers go for LL10,000 and meals can be had for about US$30 per person.

Cinemas

The best way to check what's on is to look in the *Daily Star*, *L'Orient-le Jour* or *The Guide*. If you have a computer handy, www.cyberia.net.lb also has up-to-date listings of film showings. Failing that here is a list of the most convenient cinemas. Cinema tickets cost LL10,000, except on Monday, when they cost LL5000. Note: all the cinemas listed show Western films, usually the latest Hollywood offerings with subtitles. For art films or classic movies, check

with the foreign cultural centres (see Cultural Centres earlier this chapter).

Broadway (☎ 345 294) Rue Hamra
Clémenceau (☎ 366 540) Rue Hamra
Colisée (☎ 342 962) Rue du Caire, Hamra
Concorde (☎ 347 144) Rue Dunant, Hamra
Eldorado (☎ 341 723) Rue Hamra
Empire-Dunes (☎ 792 123/4) Rue Verdun
Empire-Sodeco Square (☎ 616 707) Achrafiye
Empire-Sofil (☎ 204 080) Achrafiye
Étoile (☎ 342 616) Rue Hamra
Hamra (☎ 342 044) Rue Hamra
Monte Carlo (☎ 340 520) Rue Omar ben Abdel-Aziz, Hamra
Planéte Concorde (☎ 738 439) Rue Verdun
Planéte La Sagesse (☎ 201 494) Rue Sagesse, Achrafiye

Theatres

Although there are several theatres in Beirut, the following are the most likely to have non-Arabic productions and have reputations for showing high-quality plays and performances. Listings for what's on at individual theatres can be found in the publications listed under Cinemas.

Al-Medina Theatre (☎ 371 962) Clemenceau. Long-standing theatre that shows modern Lebanese plays in Arabic, French and occasionally English. Sometimes hosts a children's puppet theatre. Also used as a venue for traditional Lebanese music.
Beirut Theatre (☎ 343 988) Ain al-Mraisse. Small theatre that shows modern and avant-garde productions from Lebanon and abroad in Arabic, English and French.
Monot Theatre (☎ 202 422) just off Rue Monot, Achrafiye. French-language theatre attached to the St Joseph university campus.
Piccadilly Theatre (☎ 340 078) Rue Hamra. Shows Arabic productions, usually mainstream comedies, but also more experimental offerings.

SPECTATOR SPORTS
Horse Racing

Just behind the National Museum, the racecourse or Hippodrome (☎ 632 515) is one of the only places in the Middle East where you can legally place a bet.

The racecourse was built by the Sursock family just after WWI. It, and the large Ottoman-era building to its west, which was going to be a private club and casino, were to be part of what would today be called a leisure complex. However, the Ottoman building, called the Residence des Pins became the French ambassador's residence, which it will be once again when its war damage has been repaired.

Horse racing has always been wildly popular with the Lebanese; in the old days the Hippodrome was *the* place to go at weekends. It is no longer chic but is a fun way to spend a Sunday.

Races are held at 1 pm April to September and 11 am October to March on most Sundays. Entry varies from LL5000 to LL15,000, depending on seating.

Football
Beirut's most popular teams are Beirut Nejmeh and Beirut Ansar. Football is held at the Sports City Complex in the southern suburbs. See the *Daily Star* or www.cyberia.net.lb for listings.

SHOPPING
There are few things to buy which are exclusive to Beirut, but there are a number of shops that sell handicrafts that are either traditional or inspired by tradition. The best places for local crafts in Beirut include the Artisans du Liban shop on Rue Clémenceau in Hamra, La Maison de l'Artisan on Rue Minet al-Hosn in Ain al-Mraisse and L'Artisanale near the Bristol Hotel.

Traditional Palestinian embroidery is sold at Al-Badia (☎ 746 430), 78 Rue Makdissi. The shop has a selection of colourful Palestinian dresses, cushion covers and shawls, all handmade by refugee women. The proceeds go to Palestinian refugees in Lebanon.

Although the Basta area is famed for old furniture, smart Beirutis have cleaned out the best stuff and now much of the area resembles a garage sale. Occasional treasures can be found but don't expect to find anything cheap. A better bet for antiques could be Oriental Art Centre (☎ 349 942) on Rue Makhoul. It has a selection of 19th-century lithographs and some old furniture.

Modern Lebanese furniture and design is showcased at Artishow (☎ 323 531) on Rue

Baroudy in Achrafiye. Exhibitions are held from time to time and the small collections are exhibited alongside furniture and designer objects from Lebanon and Europe. Don't come looking for bargains.

GETTING THERE & AWAY
Air
Beirut international airport is served by the local carrier, Middle East Airlines (MEA), and several Arab, Asian and European airlines. For details of airlines and routes, see the Getting There & Away chapter.

Several airlines have offices in the Gefinor Centre in Hamra, including Aeroflot (☎ 739 596), British Airways (☎ 747 777), Cathay Pacific Airways (☎ 741 391), KLM-Royal Dutch Airlines (☎ 746 559), Malaysia Airlines (☎ 741 344/6) and MEA (☎ 737 000). Elsewhere are the following:

Air Canada (☎ 811 690/4) Rue Verdun
Air France (☎ 740 300/1/2/3/4) Rue Bliss
Alitalia (☎ 340 280) Rue Hamra
Austrian Airlines (☎ 343 620) Rue Hamra
Cyprus Airways (☎ 200 886) Rue Sursock
EgyptAir (☎ 980 165) Rue Riyad al-Solh
Emirates (☎ 739 040/2/3) Rue Hamra
Gulf Air (☎ 323 332) Al-Ghazal Tower, Tabaris
Lufthansa Airlines (☎ 349 001/2) Rue Hamra
Royal Jordanian (☎ 379 990) Rue Bliss
Swissair (☎ 376 276) Rue Lyon, Hamra

Bus
Buses to Syria from Beirut leave from Charles Helou bus station. For details, see Bus under Syria in the Getting There & Away chapter.

Taxi & Service Taxi
Taxis to Syria depart from the Charles Helou and Cola bus stations and operate on the usual system of waiting until the vehicle fills up before leaving. They have an advantage over the buses in that you don't have to wait around too long to depart, but the disadvantages are that they can be a bit of a squash, especially on a long journey. If you want the taxi to yourself, you will have to pay for all five passenger seats. See under Land in the Getting There & Away chapter for more details.

Car & Motorcycle

For information about bringing a private vehicle into Lebanon and a list of car rental agencies, see under Land in the Getting There & Away chapter and under Car & Motorcycle in the Getting Around chapter.

GETTING AROUND
To/From the Airport

Getting to and from the airport is one of Beirut's great scams. Only 5km south of the city, taxis charge US$10 to take you from the city and as much as US$25 to take you from the airport into town. For some reason buses do not go to the terminal; the LCC bus Nos 1 and 5 (see table) drop passengers at a roundabout 1km away. OCFTC also has buses (Nos 5, 7 and 10) that drop off at the same place. (OCFTC No 7 is supposed to go to the airport terminal but drivers say the route has changed. Check with the tourist office for the latest information.) If you don't mind a hike, this remains the cheapest option, at LL500. The services run from 5.30 am to 6 pm.

If you know where you're staying before you arrive, a solution is to see if your hotel can arrange someone to pick you up. Another is to walk about 1km to the highway and hail a service taxi heading north into Beirut. Microbuses sometimes drop people at the airport so you can wait.

Bus

There is an extensive bus network covered by two companies, the private red-and-white LCC and the blue-and-white, state-run OCFTC. Both operate on a 'hail and ride' system. Short hops cost LL500 and longer journeys are LL1000. Most LCC buses run from 5.30 am to 9.30 pm and route maps are available on buses at the tourist office or at www.cyberia.net.lb. OCFTC routes operate from 6 am to 7 pm. Copies of the route map can be found at the tourist office. There are no timetables for either company but buses run every five to 10 minutes.

Bus Routes – Lebanese Commuting Company
1 **Hamra (Rue Sadat) – Khalde** Rue Emile Eddé, Bristol, Verdun, Cola, airport roundabout, Mucharafieh, Lebanese University, Kahalde

2 **Hamra (Rue Sadat) – Antelias** Rue Emile Edde, Basta, Sassine Square, Dawra, Jdaide, Jal al-Dib, Antelias
3 **Ain al-Mraisse – Dawra** Ain al-Mraisse, AUB Beach, Bain Militaire, Raouche, Verdun, Museum, Corniche al-Nahr, Qarantina, Burj Hammoud, Dawra
4 **Wardieh – Sfeir** Wardieh, Radio Lebanon, Sanayeh, Place des Martyrs, Barbir, Chiyah, Sfeir
5 **Charles Helou – Hay es-Seloum** Charles Helou, Place des Martyrs, Bechara al-Khoury, Barbir, Chatila roundabout, airport roundabout, Cocool, Hay es-Seloum
6 **Dawra – Jbeil (Byblos)** Dawra roundabout, Jal al-Dib, Jounieh, Maamaltein, Nahr Ibrahim, Jbeil (Byblos)
7 **Museum – Baabda** Museum, Hayek roundabout, Mansourieh, Ain Saade, Beit Meri roundabout, Broummana, Baabda
8 **Wardieh – Fanar** Wardieh Rue Emile Eddé, Radio Lebanon, Basta Tahta, Sassine Square, Burj Hammoud, Jdaide, Fanar
9 **Barbir – Nahr al-Mott** Barbir Museum, Furn al-Shebbak, Sin al-fil roundabout, Hayek roundabout, Fanar, Nahr al-Mott
12 **Wardieh – Burj al-Barajneh** Radio Lebanon, Mar Elias, Cola, Shatila roundabout, Burj al-Barajneh
13 **Charles Helou – Cola** Charles Helou, Marfa, Place des Martyrs, Riad al-Solh Square, Basta Tahta, Selim Salam, Cola
15 **Cola – Qmatiye** Cola, Bir Hassan, Ghobeire, Galerie Semaan, Fayadiye, Jamhour, Kahhale, Aley, Qmatiye

Bus Routes – OCFTC
1 **Bain Militaire – Khaldé** Bain Militaire, Bristol, Unesco, Summerland, Ouzai, Khaldé
2 **Charles Helou – Lebanese University** Charles Helou, Forum, Justice, Chevrolet, Gal Semaan, Hadeth, Lebanese University
3 **Bain Militaire – Hay es-Saloum** Bain Militaire, Ministry of Information, Verdune, Mar Elias Church, Cola, Arab University, Shatila, Burj al-Barajneh, Hay as-Salloum
4 **Dawra – Jounieh** Dawra, Jal al-Dib, Antelias, Dbayé, Kaslik, Jounieh
5 **Ministry of Information – Jdeideh Palace** Ministry of Information, Rachid Karamé Square, Rue Independance, Sodeco Square, Sassine Square, Burj Hammoud Stadium, Jdeideh Palace
6 **Kuwaiti embassy – Jdeideh** Palace Kuwaiti embassy, Hazmieh, Mekalles roundabout, Cité Industrielle, Jdeideh Palace
7 **Bain Militaire – Airport** Bain Militaire, Raouché, Ramlet al-Bayda, Summerland, Kuwaiti embassy, airport roundabout, Burj al-Barajneh, Cocodile roundabout, airport

8 **Ain al-Mraisse – Jdeideh Palace** Ain al-Mraisse, Charles Helou, Beirut Bridge, Burj Hammoud, Dawra, Almaza, Jdeideh Palace
9 **Bain Militaire – Jdeideh Palace** Bain Militaire, Rue Bliss, Rue Abdel Aziz, Rue Clemenceau, Rue Weygand, Tabaris Square, Sassine Square, Justice Square, Hayek roundabout, Jdeideh Palace
10 **Charles Helou – Airport** Charles Helou, Rue Bechara al-Khoury, Rue 22 November, Shatila roundabout, airport roundabout, Cocodile roundabout, airport
11 **Charles Helou – Lebanese University** Charles Helou, Place des Canons, Shatila roundabout, Sidon Road, St Thérése, Lebanese University
12 **Museum – Aley** Museum, Chevrolet, Jamhour, Araya, Dhour Abadieh, Aley
13 **Charles Helou – Yarzé** Charles Helou, Rue Bechara al-Khoury, Damascus road, Museum, Hazmieh, Ministry of Defence, Yarzé
14 **Jdeideh Palace – Dbayé** Jdeideh Palace, Zalka, Jal al-Dib, Antelias, Awkar, Dbayé
15 **Ain al-Mraisse – Nahr al-Mott** Ain al-Mraisse, Raouché, Ave Charles de Gaulle, Museum Square, Place de Justice, Sin al-Fil Blvd, Nahr al-Mott
16 **Charles Helou – Cola** Charles Helou, downtown, Msaitbé, Selim Salam, Corniche al-Mazraa, Cola
17 **Chevrolet – Mountazah** Chevrolet, Futuroscope, Mekalles, Mansourieh, Mountazah
18 **Cola – Wadi Zeine** Cola, Cité Sportive, Kuwaiti embassy, Beach Club, Mar Takla, Damour, Wadi Zeine
19 **Khaldeh – Sahet al-Ain** Bif Aramoun, Haret Qobbeh, Lebanese University, Hadeth, Haret al- Botom, Hadeth Sahet al-Ain
20 **Charles Helou – Shatila** Charles Helou, Rue Weygand, Rue Basta, Cola, Arab University, Makassed Hospital, Ouzai, Shatila roundabout
21 **Ain al-Mraisse – Shatila** Ain al-Mraisse, Rue Mar Elias, Cola, Arab University, Shatila roundabout
22 **Burj Hammoud – Baabda** Burj Hammoud, Nabaa, Futuroscope, Chevrolet, Hazmieh, Haret al-Btom, Baabda Serail
23 **Bain Militaire – Dawra** Bain Militaire, Ain al-Mraisse, Rue du Port, Charles Helou, Ave Charles Helou, Forum, Dawra
24 **Museum – Ministry of Information** Museum Square, Barbir, Ave Saeb Salam, Arts et Metiers, Ministry of Information
25 **Jdeideh – Beit Chaar** Jdeideh Palace, Zalka, Jal al-Dib, Antelias, Kornet Shehwan, Bharsaf, Sakiet al-Misk, Beit Chaar
26 **Museum – Houmel** Museum, Chevrolet, Baabda, Hadeth, Sebnai, Blaibel, Houmel
27 **Museum – Shoueifat** Museum, Chevrolet, Hadeth, Regie, Kfarchima, Shoueifat

Service Taxi

Service taxis are plentiful and cheap in Beirut. Most routes around the capital are covered and you can hail one at any point on the route. The only way to find out if the driver is going where you want is to hail him and ask. They will drop you off at any point along their route. Occasionally when the drivers have an empty car they will try and charge you a private taxi fare. To make sure, ask '*servees?*'. Taxis are usually Mercedes and have red licence plates and (usually) a taxi sign on the roof. The fixed fare for all routes in central Beirut is LL1000. You can pay the driver at any point in the journey. The fare to outlying suburbs is LL2000.

Taxi

Taxis are not metered and it is a good idea to agree on the fare with the driver before you set off. Official taxis have red licence plates, but there some pirate taxis touting for trade. These just have the regular black plates and can be anything from a full-time driver who hasn't got a licence, to individuals on their way somewhere and looking for a paying fare. Women should avoid using unlicensed taxis, especially at night and if there are no other passengers.

The fares within Beirut should be between LL5000 and LL10,000 to the outlying suburbs, which is basically five times the service taxi rate. If you think the taxi driver is asking too much, wave him on and wait for another taxi.

You can also telephone for a taxi from a number of private hire firms. They charge a bit more, but are safer at night. Remember to ask the fare over the phone. Some of the better-known companies include:

Allo Taxi (☎ 366 661)
Auto Tour (☎ 888 222)
Beirut Taxi (☎ 805 418)
City Taxi (☎ 397 903)
Dabour Taxi (☎ 346 690/1)
Lebanon Taxi (☎ 353 152/3)
Radio Taxi (☎ 804 026, 352 250)
TV Taxi (☎ 862 489, 862 490)

Mt Lebanon

Mt Lebanon is the heartland of modern Lebanon. In medieval times the name referred to the mountain range between Byblos and Tripoli, the traditional stronghold of the Maronites. Today, however, Mt Lebanon is an administrative district that incorporates the coast from Beirut almost as far north as the town of Batroun (which we have included in this chapter for simplicity's sake), as well as the steep mountains around the city. (Administratively the Chouf Mountains are also part of the area, but as they have a separate character we have given them their own chapter.)

The proximity of Mt Lebanon's steep coastal mountains to Beirut means that many of the mountains have become urbanised, with the same high-rise blocks that crowd central Beirut precariously perched on their sides. Amid this quasi-urban sprawl are the resort towns where Lebanese families spend the summer months in an effort to escape the heat and humidity of the coast. Things get more interesting as you move away from these towns. Higher up are Lebanon's most famous ski resorts, and even further afield is the surprisingly wild and beautiful Adonis Valley.

The coast is also built up but contains Byblos, one of Lebanon's most important historical sites, as well as beaches and nightlife. Amazingly, all this diversity is within easy reach of Beirut.

The Metn & Kesrouane المتن كسروان

The **Metn** is the mountainous area east of Beirut and was the frontline between the Christians and the Druze during the civil war. Now it is where middle-class Beirut decamp in the summer months; glitzy restaurants and discos proliferate, but there are still pleasant stretches where you can savour the views.

> ## Highlights
>
> - Explore 7000 years of history in the fascinating Phoenician, Greek, Roman and Crusader ruins at Byblos.
> - Imagine yourself as a 1960s jet-setter in the bar of the Byblos Fishing Club.
> - Wander through one of the world's largest natural caverns at the Jeita Grotto.
> - See where Adonis and Aphrodite first kissed at the Afqa Grotto.
> - Picnic amid the ruins of a forgotten hilltop temple at Mashnaqa.
> - Discover the secret of perfect lemonade in the old port town of Batroun.
> - Experience the Lebanese art of apres-ski at Faraya Mzaar.

The **Kesrouane** is the *caza* (or district) adjoining the Metn and lies above Jounieh. Historically the Kesrouane was inhabited by Shiites but in the 13th and 14th centuries the area's Mamluk overlords settled Sunni Muslim Turkoman clans to police the territory. It was from these Turkomans that the dominant Assaf dynasty emerged, and under the Ottomans the Assafs in turn encouraged Maronite emigration to the Kesrouane to keep the Shiites under control. This they did with such efficiency that by the 18th century most of the original Shiites had been driven out of the area and it became primarily Maronite. Nowadays, it is famed for its spectacular vistas and its ski resorts.

BEIT MARY بيت مري
☎ 04

This popular resort is 17km from Beirut centre and 800m above sea level. The views from the town are very good in both directions: on one side, you see Ras Beirut jutting out into the sea and on the other, the deep valley of Nahr al-Jamani blocked to the east by the Sannine massif. The original village has grown into a small town, with many villas built in strategic positions to take advantage of the views. To cater for summer visitors there are also a few hotels, including the Hotel al-Bustan (one of the most luxurious in Lebanon), but most cater to long-term guests only.

Beit Mary has been occupied since Phoenician times and is currently occupied by Syrian troops who don't mind you wandering about – but watch where you point your camera.

Things to See

The **ruins** that remain here date from the Roman and Byzantine periods. They can be found at the end of the road leading to the right from the town's main roundabout junction, about 1km in the direction of the Hotel al-Bustan. Worth seeing in particular are the fine **mosaics** on the floor of the Byzantine church dating from the 5th century AD. The remains of a number of small **temples** surround the mosaics, including one dedicated to Juno which was built in the reign of Trajan (AD 98–117). There is also a fairly well preserved public bath, where you can see the original hypocaust tiles that acted as the heating system.

Nearby is the Maronite monastery of **Deir al-Qalaa**, which was built in the 17th century on the remains of a Roman temple, which in turn was probably built on an earlier Phoenician temple. As at Baalbek, the Roman temple was dedicated to Baal, known here as Baal Marqod. Although the site was heavily damaged in the war, you can still see a Roman column built into one of the monastery walls.

On this same road there is an old church, the **Marsassine Church**, which is worth seeing. It is unlocked and there is an unusual internal staircase leading up to the bell tower.

Other than visit these sites, there is little to do in Beit Mary except walk around and enjoy the views, which is a pleasant enough way to pass a few hours. Every year, in February and March, there is an **international music festival** at the Hotel al-Bustan. For more details, see the boxed text 'Lebanon's Festivals' in the Facts for the Visitor chapter.

Places to Stay & Eat

The only hotel, apart from some long-stay apartments, is the ultraposh *Hotel al-Bustan* (☎ 972 980/1/2). It is the last word in luxury and has stunning views over Beirut. The rooms, service and food are first rate, but the place is as expensive as it looks. Singles/doubles start at US$225/250 per night and that doesn't include breakfast or the 16% service charge. Still, it's worth dropping into the Scottish bar for a drink; it has a rather British, clubby feel to it and a beer will set you back US$3. There are also two restaurants: *Il Giardino* (Italian, US$25 to US$30 per person) and *Les Glycines* (French, at least US$50 per person).

If you want something more simple, there is a good snack bar-cum-restaurant on the main roundabout called *Hakim's Fast Food* (☎ 971 278). It has a wide range of drinks and simple meals which are fairly cheap.

Getting There & Away

From Beirut you can catch a service taxi to Beit Mary at Dawra bus station or at the National Museum for LL2000. The taxis stop on the main roundabout in the town and you can easily walk around the whole town from there. Two buses, the No 17 OCFTC bus or the No 7 LLC bus, also head up here from near the National Museum.

BROUMMANA   برمانا
☎ 04

The 6km walk north-east from Beit Mary to the resort town of Broummana is quite interesting, although slightly uphill. The road runs along the crest overlooking the Nahr al-Jamani. Whereas Beit Mary is sedate and quiet, Broummana is a bustling little town heaving with hotels, cafes, shops and nightlife. As a consequence, the place can be crowded to bursting point at weekends and the traffic congestion horrendous.

The views down to Beirut and the Mediterranean are even better than at Beit Mary, and there are pleasant **walks** you can take down the pine-studded hillside. Broummana is situated perfectly to catch the breeze and has a pleasant climate, even during the height of summer. The town has nothing as serious as

MT LEBANON

To Tripoli (30km)
Qubba
Moussalayha Castle
Qadisha Valley
Batroun
Hadet al-Jabbeh
Rachana
Chabtine
Assia
Nahr al-Jaouz
Douma
Maad
Tartij
Tannourine al-Faouqa
Hsarat
Mechmech
Laklouk
Jebel Tannourine
Amchit
Bentaael
Aaqoura
Byblos (Jbail)
Ehmej
Mashnaqa
Qartaba
MEDITERRANEAN SEA
A d o n i s   V a l l e y
Nahr Ibrahim
Afqa Grotto
Mchati
Safra
Hrajel
Ghazir
Faraya
Raachine
Mayrouba
Ghosta
Raifoun
Faqra
Faraya Mzaar
Jounieh
Mazraat Kfardibiane
K e s r o u a n e
Harissa
Faytroun
Aintoura
Jeita
Ajaltoun
Qanat Bakiche (2250m)
Jebel Sannine (2628m)
Nahr al-Kalb
Jeita Grotto
Baskinta
Nebaa Sannine
Antelias
Bikfaya
Bteghrine
Zaarour (2000m)
BEIRUT
Nahr Antelias
Dour Ech-Choueir
Nabay
Jdaidé
Baabdat
Qaa er Rim
Beit Mary
Broumana
M e t n
Ras al-Metn
Nahr al-Metten
Jebel Keniseh (880m)
Hemoul
Aabadiyé
Zahlé

MT LEBANON

ancient monuments to distract you from the pleasures of eating, drinking and all-round partying, which are the main attractions.

At night the revelries continue at several discos, all strung out along the main road which loops around like a horseshoe. There is also a cinema if you prefer. If you visit Broummana out of season things are a lot quieter – and cheaper – but most of the fun has gone out of the place, unless scenic walks are really your thing.

One special event is worth noting: in August, Broummana hosts a **national tennis tournament**.

Places to Stay

As with any of the Mt Lebanon resorts, the problem at Broummana is the shortage of cheap, or even mid-range, accommodation. The whole place is geared towards well-off middle-class tourists. If you are prepared to visit during the low season, the prices drop dramatically – often by half or more, which is why the cheaper places tend to shut up shop altogether, opening only in high season.

One of the nicest hotels which is open all year is the 17-room *Kanaan Hotel* (☎ 960 025, fax 961 213), an old family-run place with friendly owners. Rooms are simple but all have attached bathrooms and balconies. The hotel is right on the main road with views overlooking the Mediterranean. The lounge is decorated with old Lebanese *objets d'art*, oil paintings and chandeliers. A large terrace, where you can sit and watch the world go by, overlooks the road. Singles/doubles cost US$40/60 for B&B in the high season and US$35/40 in the low season.

The *Grace Hotel* (☎ 961 065, 960 751) is further along the main road away from Beirut. The entrance is around the hairpin corner. It has 24 clean and comfortable double suites. It is only open from June to November, but after September prices drop dramatically. In summer, suites go for US$125 per night, while in low season they go for US$50 per night or US$400 per month.

Further up the hill, past the Grace Hotel, is the *Belvedere* (☎ 961 103), a moderately priced two-star place with 55 rooms. Singles/doubles cost US$30/50. The four-star, 16-room *Primotel* (☎ 963 700, fax 963 021), just beyond the Belvedere, is more upmarket with rooms from US$125 to US$275 plus 16% service charge.

The most luxurious hotel in Broummana, *The Printania Palace* (☎ 960 416/7/8/9, fax 960 415), is at the opposite end of town. Well situated, with gardens, a swimming pool and all the accoutrements of a top-end hotel, it is predictably expensive. Singles/doubles start at US$160/190 plus 16% service. The price varies according to the season.

Places to Eat

If you are looking for a restaurant, there are dozens to choose from in all price brackets. Apart from the usual shwarma restaurants, which are scattered about the main road, there is *Pizza Place* (☎ 960 591) near the Printania Palace Cinema, where you can eat for between US$5 and US$10. If you want a burger, *Juicy Burger* (☎ 963 319) is also near the main road.

If you are looking for a cheap snack, *Crepaway* (☎ 964 347) is a fast-food restaurant that serves savoury French-style crepes that start at LL3000.

Along the same stretch there is the *Safari Restaurant* (☎ 961 270), which has a variety of snacks and drinks starting at LL1500.

The Fox (☎ 04-960 267, cell 03-860 267) is a pub in the Batrouni Building on the main road that has good atmosphere and occasionally has British DJs in the summer. Beer starts at US$3.50 and cocktails at US$7.

Mounir (☎ 873 900) is reckoned by many to serve the best traditional Lebanese food in the country. As well as the usual mezze (starters) staples it serves some less common items such as fried *haliwat* (sweetbreads) and *kibbeh nayye* (raw kibbeh). Grills are perfectly cooked and there is a good selection of Lebanese wine. There are fabulous views to complement the food. Expect to pay at least US$25 per person. A booking is essential in summer.

Getting There & Away

The same service taxis which serve Beit Mary often go on to Broummana; they will drop you anywhere along the main road through the town. It is a good idea to take the taxi to the far end of town and then stroll back down to the lower end if you are just making a day trip. That way you can flag a taxi quite easily on the road back to Beit Mary. The fare to and from Beirut is LL5000.

BIKFAYA بِكْفَيَّا

The road from Broummana to Bikfaya runs along the valley of Nahr Antelias and passes through the village of Baabdat, from where there is a good view of **Jebel Keniseh** (880m), part of the Mt Lebanon Range.

Bikfaya is a village which has grown into a summer resort. The area is famous for its fruit and its hot springs, which are reputed to be good for liver ailments – just the thing if you have been partying too much. Historically, the village made its money from the silk trade, but these days Bikfaya relies on the beauty of its surroundings to attract visitors and also, to an extent, on agriculture. Every August there is a popular **flower festival**.

The town is most famous, however, for being the Gemayel family HQ. Pierre Gemayel founded the Phalangist party in 1936. His grandson Bashir was president for three weeks in 1982 before he was assassinated. His brother Amin replaced him and survived in office until the end of his term in 1988. Not surprisingly, the town got caught up in the fighting between the Phalange and rival Maronite militias in 1987 and 1988 and was heavily damaged. The Ottoman-era Gemayel mansion is north of the main road, but steer clear unless you have an invitation.

Getting There & Away

You should have no trouble getting a service taxi from either Beit Mary or Broummana, which is about 15km away. If you are coming directly from Beirut, you can get a service taxi to Antelias (which is on the coast road on the way to Jounieh) and then pick up another service taxi to Bikfaya at the turn-off. It should cost about LL3000.

JEBEL SANNINE   جبل صنّين

This impressive mountain (2628m) is worth climbing in the summer for the unparalleled views of Lebanon from its summit. Actually it has two summits: the higher one is less interesting and it is the slightly lower peak which affords the spectacular views. To make the climb, head for the village of **Baskinta**, which is east of Bikfaya. From there, continue 6km to the hamlet of **Nebaa Sannine**, where there is a *nebaa* (spring) that feeds the **Wadi Sellet ash-Shakroub**, the starting point for the climb. It is best to make the climb from the most southerly slopes rather than tackling the slopes that overlook the hamlet. It is a moderately steep climb and should not take more than three hours. The last part of the climb is easier; there is a path which runs like a ledge around the mountain top.

From the top, you can see Qornet as-Sawda, Lebanon's highest peak at 3090m, to the north and Jebel ash-Sheikh (2814m) to the south. The Bekaa Valley and the Anti-Lebanon Range are clearly visible to the east and in the foreground is Jebel Keniseh and Jebel Barouk (1980m). To the west you can see the foothills of the Mt Lebanon Range slope all the way down to Beirut. Choose a clear, fine day to make this ascent; you will also need to be well shod and reasonably fit.

Getting There & Away

If you do not have your own transport, the only practical solution would be to take a taxi to the hamlet of Nebaa Sannine and arrange to be picked up at a specific time and place. Failing that, you would have to make the walk back to Baskinta, about 6km, and pick up a service taxi from there. It would be a wise idea to inform someone (your hotel or friends) of your plans and what time you expect to return.

QANAT BAKICHE & ZAAROUR

Qanat Bakiche and Zaarour sit on the slopes of Jebel Sannine and are Lebanon's two smallest ski resorts (although both are developing their facilities). Both have spectacular views but were heavily damaged during the war. Zaarour is supposed to be private but is willing to accept visitors. You can rent equipment and there are instructors on hand for weekends. For more details, see the boxed text below.

The ski resorts are difficult to find. When leaving Bikfaya head towards the village of Dour Ech-Choueir and then to Baskinta; turn right to Zaarour and left to Qanat Bakiche. There are no service taxis beyond Baskinta, so you'll have to arrange a car or a taxi from here. Expect to pay about LL20,000 one way.

Ski Facts: Qanat Bakiche & Zaarour

Altitude: 1904m to 2250m (Bakiche); 1651m to 2000m (Zaarour)
Number of Lifts: Each has two, with seven slopes (Bakiche) and nine (Zaarour)
Opening Hours: 8 am to 4 pm
Phone Numbers: Bakiche ☎ cell 03-340 300; Zaarour ☎ 04-310 010
Adult Day Pass (Weekends): Bakiche US$18; Zaarour (private) US$25

Both resorts suffered during the war and are being rebuilt. They have a disproportionate number of advanced slopes (currently four each) but are good if you want to avoid the crowds at some of Mt Lebanon's other resorts.

FARAYA

فاريا

☎ 09

There are two routes up to the ski resorts of Faraya Mzaar (which lies about 6km above the village of Faraya) and nearby Faqra: one from Jounieh via Harissa and the other via the road to Jeita Grotto. The latter is the most scenic route. The first few kilometres along this route are solidly developed with shops, restaurants and apartments. Past that there is a small place called **Aintoura** which has a large college run by the Lazarist fathers (the first French establishment to be founded in Lebanon). Unfortunately, the old building was destroyed by the Turks who occupied it between 1914 and 1918 and the buildings are now modern.

Further on, at **Ajaltoun**, the views of the coast and Beirut in the distance are lovely. Unfortunately, Ajaltoun itself is not. When you reach **Raifoun**, you come to a roundabout; take the left exit which leads up to **Faytroun**. There is nothing much of interest in the village, but there are some ski shops where you can buy or hire equipment. Past Faytroun there are some dramatic rock formations in the dolomite limestone. Known by the locals as the 'House of Ghosts', these are actually **rock tombs** which seem to be cut in the side of these hills and are visible from the road.

Faraya Mzaar is the Achrafiye of the slopes and half the people hanging about in the cafes, restaurants and clubs are too busy partying to actually strap on skis. Even those who do are likely to talk into their mobile phones as they slalom their way down the mountain. Still, with six advanced slopes, Faraya Mzaar offers more choice for serious skiers than anywhere else in Lebanon. There are also a few cross-country skiing trails. In the summer, most of the larger hotels stay open and offer mountain biking and hiking. See the boxed text 'Ski Facts: Faraya Mzaar' for lift information.

Away from the piste, Faraya village is pretty in a Swiss-alpine kind of way. The **Christian cemetery** is atmospheric and worth a look. The main attraction of the area is its natural beauty. If you're not there for the skiing, then there are some beautiful **walks**; you

Ski Facts: Faraya Mzaar

Altitude: 1850m to 2465m
Number of Lifts: 16 lifts and 17 slopes
Opening Hours: 8 am to 4 pm
Phone Numbers: ☎ 09-341 034/5
Adult Day Pass: US$15 to US$41 (weekends); US$13 to US$26 (weekdays)

This is where *le tout* Beirut goes on weekends throughout the winter and, even though this is Lebanon's largest ski resort, the slopes can get crowded. Serious skiers complain that the Lebanese ski like they drive (ie, recklessly) and with the weekend crowds in Faraya this can be dangerous. On weekdays, though, you'll have the place to yourself. And if you're into the Beirut party scene, this is the place to come: apres-ski is almost – if not more – important than the conditions of the piste. If you do want to ski, equipment can be rented from a number of places for between US$10 and US20 per day, and there are rescue and red cross teams on hand.

could walk to Faqra (6km) and back in a couple of hours. The ski station, Faraya Mzaar (also called Ouyoun al-Simaan), is 7km up the mountain road which is above the village. One of the most famous natural features of the area is the **Faraya Natural Bridge** (Jisr al-Hajar) just off the road between Faraya and Faqra. It is easy to spot from the road if you look to the right. There is a parking place just off the road. It is an interesting but steep walk down to the bridge itself. Centuries ago the bridge was thought to be a work of human construction, but it is in fact entirely a freak of nature.

Places to Stay

The **Coin Vert Hotel** (☎ 321 260/1, fax 720 812) is right on the main road in the village. It is a simple but clean and cosy one-star hotel that is open all year. It has only 24 rooms and singles/doubles/triples cost US$30/35/45, including breakfast. As well as a restaurant which serves European and Lebanese dishes (with an average cost of US$10 for lunch or dinner) it also has a lively disco, La Kayak. For those here to ski as well as party, there is a ski shop where you can rent equipment.

The family-run *Tamer Land Hotel (☎ cell 03-818 981)* is in the centre of the village and is friendly and informal with a choice of regular rooms or suites. The regular rooms, with private bathroom and satellite TV, cost between US$30 and US$50 per night, including breakfast. Its restaurant specialises in fresh fish (straight from the tank), but you can have a more simple meal of steak, fries and salad for US$6.

Above the village, about 5km along the road to the ski station, is the excellent *Chateau d'Eau (☎ cell 03-605 790)*. It is very comfortable with a nice clubby atmosphere and, like most places in Faraya, a lively apres-ski scene with plenty of partying. The hotel gets its name from the crashing cascade nearby which adds an interesting sound effect. Singles/doubles/triples, including breakfast, cost US$35/45/65 in the low season and US$45/50/70 in the high season. There is a restaurant serving French and Lebanese food at mid-range prices.

Mzaar 2000 (☎ 340 100) is a 93-room Inter-Continental resort that opened in the winter of 2000 and is the most expensive place in Faraya. It has all the usual five-star amenities, including equipment rental. Rooms start at US$150 per night.

Places to Eat

With so many people crowding into Faraya on weekends, there is certainly plenty of choice when it comes to restaurants. *Chez Mansour (☎ 341 000, cell 03-671 737)* is a shopping and restaurant complex at the heart of the resort. Less glitzy than many of the other offerings around here, it has reasonably priced, unpretentious food that matches its atmosphere. Expect to pay about LL7000 for a cheeseburger, fries and a salad.

Soulouge (☎ cell 03-376 969) is a chalet complex that sits between Faraya and Faraya Mzaar. On its ground floor it has a good pizzeria that's open to all. Pizzas and snacks are eaten in front of a huge log fire.

Jisr al-Qamar (☎ cell 03-877 993) means 'Bridge of the Moon' and is the name of a good Lebanese restaurant near the Coin Vert Hotel. If you go in for grills as well as mezze, expect to spend between US$25 and US$30 per person.

During 'the season' Faraya's nightlife rivals Beirut's. *Igloo (☎ 720 015)* is currently one of *the* spots. A restaurant/bar in a white, conical-shaped building, it has been called 'Monot-on-Ice' by one magazine, referring to the nightclub area of Achrafiye in Beirut. A pasta dish here will set you back about LL15,000. Later in the evening, the food is cleared away and the dancing starts, often continuing through the night. There's even a laser show.

L'Interdit (☎ cell 03-822 283) is another popular restaurant/nightclub with a dance floor surrounded by tables. The food, mostly French, is predictably expensive, and a drink will set you back US$10, but if you want to dance there's everything from techno to funk and soul.

Getting There & Away

You may be able to pick up a service taxi all the way to Faraya from East Beirut's Dawra bus station, but only in the busy winter season when there are plenty of people coming and going. Unfortunately Faraya is not on the main route to anywhere else. More likely you will have to go by service taxi to Jounieh and get a taxi from there. If you haggle, you will probably get a taxi to take you for US$15 for the 30-minute ride from Jounieh. When you leave, you will either need to get the hotel to call a taxi for you or, if you are lucky, find one in the main street in the Faraya village on its way back to Jounieh or Beirut.

FAQRA   فقرا

Faqra, 6km beyond Faraya, is another resort. However, it is a private club and you can only ski here if you stay at the (expensive) hotel or are invited by a member who has one of the 250 chalets in the vicinity. If you do manage to get invited, the ski slopes are well run, with a total of seven slopes and three lifts, plus medical facilities.

The main reason to come here, apart from skiing, is to see the **ruins**. These date from the Greek era, look dramatic when covered

MT LEBANON

with snow and lie very picturesquely on the side of a hill overlooking the valley below.

There is a heavily restored large temple with six Corinthian columns that feature heavily on postcards of Lebanon. The temple is dedicated to Adonis, the 'very great god', and sits in the middle of a labyrinth of rocks. It is preceded by a rectangular court cut out of the rock. Nearby are a couple of altars, one dedicated to Astarte, the other to Baal Qalach.

Just down the hill from here is another smaller temple that was originally a dedicated to the Syrian goddess Atargatis and later to Astarte. In the 4th century AD it was transformed into a church and a Byzantine style cross can still be seen on one of fallen stones in what was the nave.

Surrounding the larger temple are some rock-cut tombs and to the north is a ruined cube-shaped base known as the **Claudius Tower**. According to an inscription above the entrance it was rebuilt by the Emporer Claudius in AD 43–44, but is likely to date back even further. It is thought to have been dedicated to Adonis. The base was originally covered with a step pyramid, perhaps like the one at Amor, near Hermel. Inside there are steps that lead up on to the roof. Beside the base there are two altars. One has been restored and has 12 tiny columns supporting its table-top.

Places to Stay & Eat

The only place to stay in Faqra is the ultra-smart *L'Auberge de Faqra* (☎ 01-885 591/2/3, fax 09-710 293), which is part of a large sports and leisure development. Hotel guests can use the facilities such as the swimming pool, tennis and squash courts, although there is a small extra charge for these facilities. The hotel also has its own ski lifts up to the pistes. Double rooms cost US$227 (high season) and from US$122 in the low season (May/June and October/November). All prices include breakfast and the service charge. As with other resorts, this one is open in the summer and hires out mountain bikes.

On the road above the village, next to a petrol station, there is a small restaurant called *Highland Snack* which offers about the only cheap meals in the area. Further

down near the ruins is *Restaurant Faqra*, which is a bit more expensive, and about 1km past the village is *Restaurant Kanater*, also quite good.

At the top end of the scale, is the exclusive *Chez Michel* (☎ 09-988 233), which sits on its own at the end of Faqra and is the most famous restaurant in the area. It has a reputation for good food (it starts at about US$25 per person) and wild partying. If you can pull yourself away from the log fire there are also fantastic views. Reservations are essential.

The Coast

Heading up Lebanon's north coast you could be forgiven for thinking you'd never left Beirut. Uncontrolled development throughout the civil war has left much of the coastline ravaged by concrete. But appearances can (sometimes) be deceiving. With a little searching you'll find some of Lebanon's best beaches, as well as its most ancient and picturesque town, Byblos. The area's proximity to Beirut makes it a comfortable day trip from the capital.

NAHR AL-KALB   نهر الكلب

The mouth of Nahr al-Kalb, or Dog River (the Lycus River of antiquity), is on the coast road heading north between Beirut and Jounieh. Prior to the building of the huge highway that now crosses the river, the steep-sided gorge was very difficult for armies to cross, forcing them to cross in single file and leaving them vulnerable to attack. To give thanks for their successful crossing, conquering armies down the millennia have left some plaque or memorial carved into the sides of the gorge. It is a tradition which has persisted into this century, and the most recent inscriptions were left by Christian militias during the civil war.

Apart from the earlier Assyrian carvings, there are **stelae** in Latin, Greek, Arabic, French and English. All of these, except for the stele of Nebuchadnezzar II, are on the left bank, following the ancient courses of the steep roads carved along the slopes of the gorge.

Downtown Beirut at night

Dining in Beirut's reconstructed downtown area

Many buildings in downtown Beirut still show the scars of war.

Soaking up the rays in Byblos

A view across the waterside buildings of Beirut

High-rise Beirut, as seen from the city's public beach

Howling Wolf

Nahr-al Kalb got its name from a large statue of a wolf which that to guard the entrance to the river.

Legend has it that the statue used to howl as a warning against invaders. How this worked nobody has been able to explain, but it may have been due to some kind of wind trap causing an acoustic effect. In 1942 Australian soldiers, who were working on the nearby railway, apparently uncovered a large, but badly damaged, wolf statue. This has since disappeared.

Some of the oldest stelae have eroded to almost nothing, but some of the later inscriptions are still visible, if not always clearly. Unfortunately the coastal highway has destroyed any feel of what the site might once have been like, but if you're a history buff or enjoy scrambling about to the constant roar of traffic, the inscriptions are fascinating. The walk along the left bank of the river is also quite pleasant in springtime, when the river is in full flow, less so in other seasons when the dry riverbed tends to trap garbage.

Riverside Inscriptions

Starting from the motorway, the first bridge is the old 'modern' road. A hundred metres past that you see the charming, triple-arched old **Arab bridge** which now serves as a crossing point to a restaurant.

All inscriptions before 1920 have Roman numerals, and run as follows:

I – Engraved by Nebuchadnezzar II on the rocky wall on the right (north) bank near the junction of the motorway and the old 'modern' road is a cuneiform inscription from the 6th century BC recording the campaigns of Nebuchadnezzar II in Mesopotamia and Lebanon. This is very overgrown and hard to see. All the other inscriptions are on the left bank starting near the Arab bridge and following the bank of the river to the main road, then continuing up the side of the gorge. Follow the stairs up until you are on top of the motorway tunnel. The ancient Egyptian and Roman roads continue and there are further inscriptions.

II – This is an Arabic inscription lying almost at water level opposite the Arab bridge and commemorating its construction. It dates from the 14th century and was inscribed on behalf of Sultan Seif ad-Din Barquq by the builder of the bridge, Saifi Itmish.

III – A few metres down river there is a Latin inscription from the Roman emperor Caracalla (Marcus Aurelius Antonius, AD 198–217) describing the achievements of the 3rd Gallic Legion. Just above the Roman inscription is a modern obelisk which marks the French and Allied armies' arrival in Lebanon in 1942, while beyond it is another modern inscription commemorating the 1941 liberation of Lebanon and Syria from Vichy forces.

IV – A French inscription marks the French invasion of Damascus on 25 July 1920 under General Gouraud. Not far from this is a plaque with Arabic script and the date 25/3/1979; next to this another plaque with the engraving of a cedar tree and another Arabic inscription commemorating the withdrawal of French troops from Lebanon in 1946.

V – The original stele showing an Egyptian pharaoh and the god Ptah has been covered by a later inscription by the French army commemorating their 1860 expedition in the Chouf.

VI – An Assyrian king is depicted wearing a crown with his right hand raised is badly preserved.

VII – Next to VI, another Assyrian figure, now almost impossible to make out.

VIII – Further along, another Assyrian stele which again is in a very bad state of preservation.

IX – Above VI and VII, a commemoration of British led 'Desert Mountain Corps' and its 1918 capture of Damascus, Homs and Aleppo.

X – Right by the motorway, a British commemorative plaque dating from 1918 marks the achievements of the British 21st Battalion and the French Palestine Corps. Beside this, steps lead up the mountainside and over the motorway, leading to the other inscriptions.

XI – A weathered Greek inscription.

XII – Another Greek inscription, but it is very worn. Just past this and to the right is the white rock plinth where the wolf statue once stood.

XIII – About 30m further on, a stony path climbs sharply, just after some cedars carved into the rock by Phalange fighters. This next stele shows an Assyrian king in an attitude of prayer.

XIV – Next to XIII is a rectangular tablet showing Pharaoh Ramses II of Egypt (1292–1225 BC) sacrificing a prisoner to the god Harmakhis. This is the oldest inscription at Nahr al-Kalb.

XV – A little higher and only a few metres away on a dead-end path is another inscription of an Assyrian king.

XVI – About 25m further up the slope, you come to the road at the top. There you'll see a rectangular stele which shows Ramses II again, this time sacrificing a prisoner to the sun god Amun by burning him to death.

XVII – The last stele is Assyrian and shows Esarhaddon with cuneiform text describing his victory against Egypt in 671 BC.

Also worth seeing is the nearby Catholic retreat of **Deir Luwaizeh** on the north side of the gorge. It has a huge statue of Christ, which stands on top of the building, with arms outstretched.

Places to Stay & Eat

There are no places to stay in the immediate vicinity, but Nahr al-Kalb is very close to the amenities of Jounieh. *Tazka (☎ 09-830 924, cell 03-633 295)*, is a Lebanese restaurant just across the old Arab bridge. You can sit out on the river terrace and have mezze or the full works. It is open for lunch and dinner every day except Monday. An average meal will cost around US$10, an open buffet meal US$15 and an a-la-carte meal around US$25; extra for drinks. The food is well above average. The restaurant sometimes has an oriental night with belly-dancing entertainment.

If you want a cheaper bite, on the left bank there is a new complex of bars, fast-food restaurants and an adventure playground for kids called *Happy Valley/McMagic*, which obviously caters for families on a day trip.

Getting There & Away

Nahr al-Kalb is simple to get to – just take a service taxi from Beirut's Dawra bus station that is going to Jounieh and get it to drop you off. The river mouth is just past the long tunnel on the highway and is easy to spot. The fare from Beirut is LL2000. When you leave, it is easy to flag down a service taxi going in either direction on the highway.

JEITA GROTTO   مـغارة جعيتـا

It would be a pity to visit Nahr al-Kalb and not see the Jeita Grotto (☎ 09-220 840/1/2/3), a stunning series of caverns containing one of the world's most impressive agglomerations of stalactites and stalagmites. Stretching some 6km back into the mountains, these caves are the source of the Nahr al-Kalb and in winter the water levels rise so high that the lower caverns are flooded. During the civil war, the caves were used as an ammunitions store, but they were cleared and reopened to the public in 1995 and have become one of the country's biggest tourist attractions.

Perhaps because of its drawing power, the grotto has been almost over-developed. A superfluous cable car takes you about 200m up the hill from the site entrance to the upper cavern. To go the 100m or so down to the lower cavern a Disney-style train is laid on. If you can ignore the annoying tourist tack,

---

A Shot of Discovery

The Jeita Grotto caves were originally discovered in 1836 by an American named Thompson who was out on a hunting trip. He fired a shot into the blackness to judge the size of his find and realised that the cavern was enormous. He reported his discovery, but it was not until 1873 that the authorities sent a team from the Beirut Water Supply Company to investigate. They discovered a vast honeycomb of galleries and ravines with an astonishing natural spectacle of rock formations – and enough water to supply at least some of Beirut's needs.

A second survey was carried out the following year and the team named one of the huge columns in the grotto after their leader, MJ Maxwell. Team members then wrote their names on a piece of paper and placed them in a bottle, which they then left at the top of the column. Over time calcite formed over the bottle, incorporating it into the column, where it remains today.

Later expeditions – in 1902, 1927 and two further explorations in the 1950s – managed to chart over 10km into the system. In 1958 a new, dry upper chamber was discovered, large enough to seat an audience of 1000. The acoustics were found to be excellent and many concerts were given here, including, in 1969, a series by the German composer Stockhausen.

the caves themselves are spectacular. The upper cavern is open year-round and it is a surreal experience walking among its bizarre shapes. The lower cavern, which is seen by boat, is very beautiful but is closed in the winter because of the high water levels. Every half-hour a sound and light show is put on in another series of caverns.

Entrance is a steep LL16,500 for adults and LL9250 for children (no doubt the pointless transport is laid on to justify the high prices). The caves are open from 9 am to 6 pm Tuesday to Thursday and from 9 am to 7 pm Friday to Sunday. They are closed on Monday, unless it is a public holiday. There is strictly no photography allowed inside the caves, and all cameras must be handed in at the door.

The road to the caves is the first turning on the right past Nahr al-Kalb if you are heading north. You can catch a service taxi to Nahr al-Kalb and either walk from there (a stiff half-hour uphill climb), or catch a taxi to take you up from the highway – not many service taxis go up this road. It is about 5km from the highway to the grotto. A return trip to the caves from Nahr al-Kalb will set you back at least US$10. The turn-off is clearly signposted on the highway.

JOUNIEH   جونيه
☎ 09

Prior to the war, Jounieh was a sleepy fishing village. But all that changed when Beirut was sliced in half by the conflict. Prosperous Christian Beirut wanted a place to escape from the shells and Jounieh, only 21km north of Beirut, was where they came to party their troubles away. Any semblance of planning, never a Lebanese strong point, was lost in the anarchy of war and the frenzy to build. The result is a high-rise strip mall hemmed in by the sea on one side and the mountains on the other. Not content with building on every square metre of land next to the sea, developers moved up the mountain and plonked high-rise buildings gravity-defyingly high up the steep mountainside. The throbbing heart of Lebanon's nightlife has returned to Beirut now, but Jounieh still remains popular with expat

Lebanese returning for their summer holidays and Gulf Arabs, who spend their petrodollars in the town's many nightclubs.

Orientation & Information
Coming along the coast road from the south you pass through Kaslik, home to malls, restaurants and an enormous cinema complex. What's left of the old fishing town is concentrated on Rue Mina, the old road that hugs the bay. This is the only area of town that has some charm, with a few outbuildings, many in a tumbledown state, to give you an idea of how it used to look. From here, the road heads north past the municipality building and at a roundabout becomes Rue Maameltein, named after the village that used to lie a couple of kilometres to the north but has now been swallowed up by the Jounieh sprawl.

Most of the amenities such as banks, the post office and the municipality building are in the lower part of town on or around Rue Mina, as is the taxi stand. It is easy to change money here if the banks are closed; most shops and hotels will only be too happy to change US dollars.

Cafe Net has Internet facilities for LL5000 per hour, as well as coffee and cake for sale. To get there, head south down Rue Mina, turn left at the roundabout and take your first right (there's a sign to Beirut) and it's about 50m up the hill on your left.

Things to See & Do
Other than swimming in the not-so-clean sea, watching Eastern European dancers strut their stuff in nightclub spectaculars, or having a decent seafood meal, Jounieh doesn't have much to occupy you. The possible exception is the traditional Lebanese houses along Rue Mina, but a stroll along its entire length won't take more than about an hour.

If you do want to swim, you can go to any of the resorts that surround the bay. You usually have to pay between US$5 and US$10, but be warned that in order to get the most out of their parcel of seafront, all have built out over the sea, so swimming is usually from a concrete pier.

Once you have exhausted the swimming, eating and drinking possibilities, the only thing left to do in Jounieh is to take the **Téléphérique** (cable car) from the centre of town up to the dizzying heights of Harissa. This ride, dubbed the Terrorifique by some, takes about nine minutes. If you suffer from vertigo, avoid. The ascent is at a very steep angle and the cars are tiny, taking an absolute maximum of four people. The ride leaves from the Rue Maamaltein, just beyond the municipality building. Curiously, the tiny cars have developed a reputation as a place for slightly less than clean cut fun. Apparently young couples, desperate for privacy, use them for amorous trysts, begging the (frequently joked about) question of what exactly they can accomplish in only nine minutes.

The Téléphérique (☎ 914 324) operates from 10 am until 11 pm from June to October, 10 am until 7 pm from November to May, and is closed on Monday, Christmas Day and Good Friday. Return tickets cost LL7500/3500 for adults/children.

The **Casino du Liban** (☎ 932 932, 932 779) was once the most famous casino in the Mediterranean. Overlooking the northern end of Jounieh bay, it opened in 1959 and was *the* symbol of Beirut's decadence in the 1960s. The rich and famous flocked here to see extravagant floor shows, hang around the gaming tables a la James Bond or patronise the several restaurants and bars. Closed during the war, it reopened to much fanfare in 1996. But casinos are no longer the epitome of sophistication and the new incarnation has been criticised for being sterile. It was described in one magazine as looking like 'it was based on the design of a video arcade in a multiplex cinema'. If you don't mind throwing away lots of money for the sake of kitsch or curiosity, it could be worth a visit to one of the 60 gaming tables or six restaurants, the 1200-seat theatre or any of the other facilities on offer.

The casino is open seven days a week. Admission is for over-21s and there is a strict dress code. The gaming rooms are open from 8 pm to 4 am, the 300 slot machines from midnight to 4 am.

Places to Stay

The **Hotel St Joseph** (☎ 131 189, Rue Mina) is in the old part of town, about 50m north of the municipality building. It is more of a pension than a hotel with only 12 increasingly shabby rooms in a lovely 300-year-old house. The main rooms have high vaulted ceilings and there is a great roof terrace with views over the street on one side and the sea on the other. The hotel attracts long-stay guests and it is difficult to get a room in summer. It charges US$20/30 for a single/double with shower and toilet.

Holiday Suites Hotel (☎ 933 907, 639 038, ✉ holidaysuites@usa.net, Rue Mina), behind the British Bank, is friendly and has some nice rooms overlooking the sea. Singles/doubles/suites (sleeping three) are US$55/65/85, plus 14% service and 5% tax.

At the beginning of Rue Maameltein is *Arcada Marina* (☎ 915 546, 832 250, fax 935 956). The hotel is a converted and extended old building. The entrance is tacky, but the hotel has a bar and nightclub downstairs with brick-vaulted ceilings. There are 70 rooms with air-con, bathrooms and TV, plus a swimming pool. Singles/doubles cost US$70/80 including breakfast and service but can be bargained down considerably out of season.

Further north along Rue Maameltein is *Lamedina Hotel* (☎/fax 918 044, cell 03-274 011, ✉ lamedina@libancom.com.lb). Also on the seafront it too has a kitsch factor but has more character than some of the rather plastic hotel chains along the strip. The back of the hotel is on the sea and the rooms have TV, air-con and bathroom facilities. Off-season singles/doubles go for US$50/75, including breakfast. Add another US$15 per room in the summer.

Places to Eat

There are so many places where you can eat in Jounieh that your best bet is to look around until you find one that suits you and your budget. There are plenty of snack bars and restaurants serving the standard shwarma and felafel-type dishes places along Rue Mina and further north on Rue Maameltein.

Jus Cocktail, about 100m south of the British Bank on Rue Mina, has a terrace overlooking the sea and excellent fresh fruit juices starting at LL3000 for a (very large) small glass. *J Kabab*, also on Rue Mina, 220m south of the British Bank, serves toasted sandwiches, mezzes, salad and grills at reasonable prices.

Another very good place is *La Crêperie* (☎ 912 491), where you can have a selection of savoury and sweet crepes at reasonable prices (US$6 on average), as well as other dishes for US$5 to US$15. The restaurant is in an Ottoman-era house set on a cliff with a magnificent view of Jounieh bay. It is on the old Jounieh road in Kasklik, just before you enter the centre of town.

The restaurant at *Al-Medina Hotel* (☎ 918 484) serves decent mezze in a stone-vaulted dining room. Individual dishes start at US$2 and you can expect to pay at least US$20 for a full meal.

Chez Sami (☎ 910 520, cell 03-242 499, Rue Mina) is a rare oasis of taste among the seafront sprawl and is reputed to be the best fish restaurant in the country. Set in an old stone house with a terrace overlooking the beach, it is also famous for its excellent mezze, which includes unusual (for Lebanon) treats such as squid in its own ink. Most of the fish are chosen as they swim around a large tank (no worries about freshness) and are sold by weight. If you haven't already guessed, this is not for anyone on a budget. But if you're not financially challenged, this place alone is worth the trip to Jounieh. Reservations, particularly on weekends, are essential.

Entertainment

Jounieh is famous for its nightlife, but since Beirut's renaissance most of it consists of tacky floorshows that often slide into sleaze. There are a couple of exceptions, though. *Amor Y Libertad* (☎ 640 881), below Kaslik Cinema in Kaslik, is an amazing Cuban club-restaurant. It's expensive at US$20 for the cover charge (which entitles you to two drinks) but it's an unforgettable experience. There's a live band playing Latin American and world music, a Blues Brother lookalike singing and dancing on the bar, and a trendy 25- to 40-year-old crowd. The highlight is Musbah, a gay male belly-dancer who is absolutely sensational and has to be seen to be believed. He performs at 11.30 pm on Thursday, Friday and Saturday.

Oliver's (☎ 934 616, Rue Maamaltein) is another popular venue for young locals and has good food, drink and music, as well as a lively atmosphere.

Getting There & Away

You can get to Jounieh by bus (see Getting Around in the Beirut chapter for details) for LL1000. Service taxis leave from Beirut's Dawra bus station and cost LL2000. If you catch a taxi that is going further north, you will be dropped off on the highway. Ask to be let out near the Téléphérique, where there is a pedestrian bridge across the highway which leads to the centre of town (about a five-minute walk). A private taxi from Jounieh to Hamra costs LL20,000.

HARISSA

High above Jounieh bay is the gigantic white statue of the **Virgin of Lebanon** with her arms outstretched, where she has stood since the end of the last century. Around her are the churches and cathedrals of various denominations, the latest being the modernist Maronite cathedral whose outline can be seen from Jounieh below.

During religious festivals, such as Easter, there are often rather colourful **religious parades** which attract the crowds. At other times, pilgrims climb the spiral staircase around the statue's base. Others just enjoy the fantastic view from the top. There is a restaurant at the Téléphérique terminus which serves mezze, grills and great views for about US$15 per person.

To get to Harissa from Jounieh you have two death-defying options: either you take the cable car or you go by road. If you want a taxi, you can pick one up at the main taxi stand just off Rue Mina, not far from the Hotel St Joseph. The road to Harissa redefines the term 'hairpin bend'. The road twists alarmingly with sheer drops along part of the route, but the ride takes only 15 minutes. The fare is about US$5. For details about the cable car, see Things to See & Do under Jounieh.

BYBLOS (JBAIL)

جبيل

☎ 09

The name Byblos is known as one of the world's oldest continually inhabited towns. Old before the great civilisations of the Middle East were even thought of, archaeologists believe that the site has been occupied for at least 7000 years – perhaps even more.

Byblos is 36km north of Beirut and still relatively unspoiled and very picturesque. In its tourist heyday before the war, it was a favourite watering hole for the crews of visiting private yachts, international celebrities and the beautiful people of the Mediterranean jet set. It still retains the rather chic air of a place to see and be seen in, although the new generation of locals has grown up without the benefit of a tourist economy and the original town has spilled over its historic boundaries in an unlovely jumble of modern styles. But the slow postwar recovery has begun to breathe new life into the resort. Smart Beirutis come here to linger over arak and mezze on weekends and give the town something of its old glamour.

History

To describe Byblos' history requires a trip back into prehistoric times. The earliest occupation dates from the 5th millennium BC when the first settlers fished and tended their animals. This was also the era of early agriculture, and the remains of cultivated grains have been found at a site that has been partially excavated on the promontory. This Neolithic community lived in houses of a single room with crushed limestone floors. Many tools and primitive weapons have been discovered at the site, some of which are on display at Beirut's National Museum. By the Chalcolithic period (around the 4th millennium BC), the use of metals and ceramics had become commonplace. These Chalcolithic inhabitants of Byblos buried their dead in distinctive terracotta storage jars which have been found in great numbers at the archaeological site.

By the mid-3rd millennium BC, Byblos, as well as other areas along the coast, was colonised by the Phoenicians. The city-state of Byblos became a significant religious centre in the area. The temple of Baalat Gebal was famous in antiquity. It was probably built on the site of an early sacred grotto, and it underwent several rebuildings during the course of time due to both natural and military catastrophes.

Close links with Egypt encouraged the development of Byblos, both culturally and religiously. The temple received generous offerings from several pharaohs during this prosperous era and Byblos evolved its hybrid style of art and architecture: part Egyptian, part Mesopotamian, and later showing some Mycenaean influences.

Around 2150 BC the Amorites invaded and took the city. Culturally they were a less-developed people who ruined much of the city's well-ordered layout as well as its settled and prosperous wellbeing. This is the period of the underground royal tombs and of the Obelisk Temple dedicated to Resheph, god of burning and destructive fire. Amorite rule lasted until 1725 BC, but the people of Byblos were resilient enough to keep something of their own identity throughout this occupation and a continuity of their art can be seen throughout this and subsequent periods.

The Amorite occupation was ended by another invasion, this time by the warlike Hyksos people from western Asia. The Amorites were shocked into a quick submission by the Hyksos army who arrived with horses

TRUDI CANAVAN

Pectoral set buried in King Ibshemuabi's tomb, Byblos, more than 3800 years ago

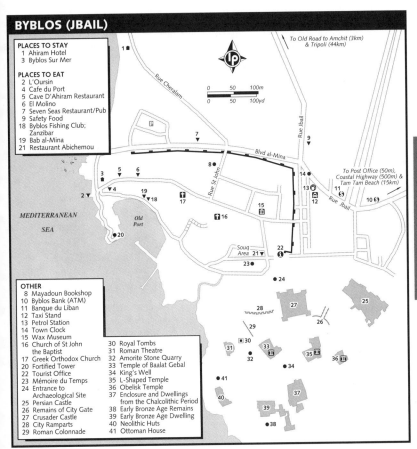

BYBLOS (JBAIL)

PLACES TO STAY
1 Ahiram Hotel
3 Byblos Sur Mer

PLACES TO EAT
2 L'Oursin
4 Cafe du Port
5 Cave D'Ahiram Restaurant
6 El Molino
7 Seven Seas Restaurant/Pub
9 Safety Food
18 Byblos Fishing Club;
Zanzibar
19 Bab al-Mina
21 Restaurant Abichemou

OTHER
8 Mayadoun Bookshop
10 Byblos Bank (ATM)
11 Banque du Liban
12 Taxi Stand
13 Petrol Station
14 Town Clock
15 Wax Museum
16 Church of St John
the Baptist
17 Greek Orthodox Church
20 Fortified Tower
22 Tourist Office
23 Mémoire du Temps
24 Entrance to
Archaeological Site
25 Persian Castle
26 Remains of City Gate
27 Crusader Castle
28 City Ramparts
29 Roman Colonnade

30 Royal Tombs
31 Roman Theatre
32 Amorite Stone Quarry
33 Temple of Baalat Gebal
34 King's Well
35 L-Shaped Temple
36 Obelisk Temple
37 Enclosure and Dwellings
from the Chalcolithic Period
38 Early Bronze Age Remains
39 Early Bronze Age Dwelling
40 Neolithic Huts
41 Ottoman House

*To Old Road to Amchit (3km)
& Tripoli (44km)*

*To Post Office (50m),
Coastal Highway (500m) &
Tam Tam Beach (15km)*

MEDITERRANEAN
SEA

Old
Port

Souq
Area

MT LEBANON

and chariots, hurling javelins and carrying lances, all new to the people of this region. The Egyptians, also suffering from the Hyksos invasion of their country, soon retaliated and, from 1580 BC, claimed the coast of Phoenicia as their own.

A long period of good trade and development followed, during which time the kings of Byblos were the subservient partners of their Egyptian masters. Many Egyptian customs were adopted, with temples and burial chambers being decorated in the Egyptian manner. The cult of Isis was very strong during this time.

The linear alphabet, perhaps the most significant achievement of the Phoenicians that has been handed down to us, was also developed during this period. It is thought that the alphabet may have originated in Byblos, and was invented as a more practical way of recording trading transactions than the cuneiform script that was previously used. This new system of writing quickly spread throughout the civilised world.

The Egyptian-dominated period of prosperity did not last and between 1100 and 725 BC Byblos was eclipsed by Tyre as the most important Phoenician city-state. Byblos then became a pawn in the power struggle between the Greeks and the Assyrians between 725 and 612 BC, eventually being ruled by the Assyrians and then the Neo-Babylonians.

Following the conquest of Babylon by Cyrus the Great in 539 BC, Byblos was regenerated as a trading link to the east under the Persian Empire. During the Hellenistic period, Byblos, unlike Tyre, voluntarily became an ally of Alexander and continued to flourish under its own royal dynasty.

When the Greek Empire waned and the Roman Empire waxed, Byblos concentrated its trading efforts to the west. From 63 BC onwards, the Roman Empire became a market for Phoenician goods. Byblos had long ago burst its original confines and now the city boasted lavish public architecture and suburban farming developments.

Unfortunately, Byblos had sowed the seeds of its own downfall by not regulating the pace of deforestation – the very resource that had made this boom town wealthy was in short supply. When the Roman Empire split into east and west in AD 395, Byblos allied itself to Constantinople (later Istanbul) and became increasingly important as a religious centre. Pagan religion gradually gave way to Christianity and the city became the seat of a bishopric under Emperor Diocletian. It was protected by the Eastern Roman Empire until the Islamic invasion in AD 636.

Under the Muslims the focus turned eastwards and Byblos' sea port dwindled into insignificance along with the city's defences. Damascus and Baghdad were not interested in cultivating trade with Europe, and Byblos, now called Jbail, was left vulnerable. During the Crusader offensive, which began in 1098, Jbail fell to the Count of Tripoli, Raymond de Saint-Gilles. Despite resuming trade with Europe, the city never regained its former power. The subsequent power struggles between the Crusaders and the Muslim forces continued until August 1266 when Emir Najibi, lieutenant of Sultan Beybars, laid siege to the town. The defenders withdrew to Tripoli under the cover of night.

The next few centuries were relatively uneventful; the Turks took control of the city in 1516 and Byblos passed into insignificance until Ernest Renan, a French historian and philosopher, began to excavate the site during his stay in Lebanon from 1860 to 1861. It wasn't until the 1920s that a proper survey of the site was carried out, work that is still incomplete. Excavations at Byblos came to a standstill during the civil war and have yet to resume.

Ernest Renan (1823–92)

The name of Ernest Renan turns up frequently in Lebanon. His early life in France prepared him for a career as a Roman Catholic priest, but he later broke away from the church. He is famous as a theological writer and critic. His best-known work, *Vie de Jesus* (Life of Jesus), was published in 1863 and formed part of an eight-volume work *History of the Origins of Christianity*. More relevant to Lebanon, he also published the *Mission de Phénicie*, a painstaking survey of Phoenician ruins in Lebanon (reprinted in Beirut by Terre du Liban et Cellis in 1998), as well as numerous philological works that have earned him the not-entirely complimentary designation as one of Orientalism's founding fathers.

He lived in Amchit with his beloved sister, Henriette, during his research of the site at Byblos. She died after an illness and is buried in the churchyard in Amchit, where you can still see her mausoleum. Renan described the spot in his preface to *Vie de Jesus*: 'beneath the palms of Amchit near sacred Byblos, not far from the river Adonis to which the women of the ancient mysteries came to mingle their tears … '.

Papyrus City

Byblos was called Gebal in the Bible and Giblet by the Crusaders. Today, in Arabic, it is known as Jbail. However, its ancient name, the one by which anyone paying attention in class knows it, is Byblos, thought to derive from *bublos*, the Greek word for papyrus. In Phoenician times the town was a stopping-off point for papyrus shipments en route from Egypt to Greece. A collection of papyrus sheets were called *biblion*, or book, and from the Greek *ta b blia*, or 'the books', the English word 'Bible' was derived.

Orientation

The town radiates uphill to the east of the harbour and is flanked on the south by a promontory which is the site of the Crusader castle and ancient ruins. The older part of the inhabited town stops at the medieval city wall at the top of the hill, and from there to the main highway is the modern part of town. Back down at the entrance to the harbour there is a defensive tower which you can climb for a good view of the harbour and the ancient ruins.

Information

Tourist Office The tourist information office (☎ 540 325) is beside the main entrance to the archaeological site.

Money The main road in and out of the town, Rue Jbail, has several banks including a Banque du Liban and a Byblos Bank, the latter with an ATM. Both are on the left as you follow the highway out of town. There are some bureaux de change as well – look out for signs in the shop windows. You can also change money in the hotels.

Post & Communications There is a post office tucked away on the first floor of a building just off Rue Jbail. Look for a large, modern building with the sign 'Diab Brothers' on the corner of Rue Jbail. The entrance to the post office is a few metres along this road on the right. It is open Monday to Saturday from 8 am to 1.30 pm.

Bookshop Mayadoun Bookshop in the old town, on Rue St John, sells a reasonable selection of books in English and French, as well as a small selection of international magazines and newspapers. It is open from Monday to Saturday.

Walking Tour

Byblos is ideal to explore on foot. Starting at the taxi stand on Rue Jbail, head north and take the road that follows the medieval walls. This curves around to the left and you come out by the Byblos Sur Mer hotel. A quiet stroll around the harbour brings you to a turn on your left leading uphill. Take this road, which leads up to the **Church of St John the Baptist**. Half a block up the road on the opposite side of the street is the **Wax Museum** with its kitsch tableaux of Lebanese culture. From here, turn right and walk past the **souq**. You will see the entrance to the **archaeological site** ahead of you, slightly to the left. Allow a couple of hours to explore the site. When you leave by the same entrance, head back to the small souq area. Next, head west back down to the harbour and end up at the **Byblos Fishing Club** for a well-earned drink and a look at the private collection of antiquities.

The Ruins

The site is open 8 am to sunset daily and entrance costs LL6000 (children under six are free). Guides who speak English, French, German, Italian or Japanese are available. They seem to rely on gratuities, but figure on paying at least LL10,000 (more if there are several of you).

Crusader Castle The most dominant monument at the archaeological site is the castle built by the Franks in the 12th century and constructed out of monumental blocks, no doubt pillaged from the classical ruins. Some of the blocks are the largest used in any construction in the Middle East (apart from one or two at Baalbek). The castle measures 49.5m by 44m with a deep moat around it. You can see the nearby Phoenician ramparts on either side of the entrance.

The structure is far from elegant but has some points of interest.

The whole of the basement area is a huge water cistern that is largely intact. The best part of a visit to the castle (unless you are passionate about Frankish architecture) is to climb to the ramparts and see the whole of Byblos spread out with the sea behind. Apart from a glorious view, it gives you a very clear idea of the layout of the ancient city. It's worth noting that because of the many layers contained in the small site, later monuments were moved and reconstructed in order to gain access to those underneath. So while the Roman theatre is now at western edge of the site, it was originally between the town's north-east entrance and the Temple of Resheph. Access to the roof is via a staircase. A word of warning: there are no safety rails on either the staircase or the roof and there are some sheer drops. (For more about the architecture of Crusader castles see the special section 'The Architecture of Lebanon' in the Facts about Lebanon chapter.)

Ramparts The defences of Byblos have been maintained and added to since the foundation of the city. They date from the 3rd and 2nd millenniums BC. Six different constructions have been discovered forming a 25m-thick wall. The ramparts curve around from the castle to the shore and on the other side of the castle curve west and then south, blocking access to the promontory where the original city was confined.

Temple of Resheph This 3rd-millennium BC temple was burned and rebuilt during the Amorite occupation. The later temple (known as the Obelisk Temple) was removed to a nearby site so that Dunand, an archaeologist, could excavate the original structure. It consists of a sacred enclosure. In the middle is a tripartite sanctuary facing east.

Temple of Baalat Gebal This is the oldest temple at Byblos with parts dating back to the 4th millennium BC. The temple underwent major rebuilding after being destroyed by fire during the Amorite period. A

few centuries later the site was levelled and a new sanctuary was built. It later became a symbol of the close relations between Egypt and Byblos. Numerous alabaster fragments of votive vases, many inscribed with the name of Old Kingdom pharaohs, were discovered here and can be seen in Beirut's National Museum. The temple remained an important religious centre through the centuries. A colonnade of six standing columns from around AD 300 lines the route to the temple and testifies to its use in Roman times, when it was thought to be dedicated to the goddess Astarte.

Obelisk Temple Despite being rebuilt on this new site, the Obelisk Temple is one of the more interesting places to visit at Byblos. The temple consists of a forecourt and a courtyard which houses the slightly raised sanctuary. The cube-shaped base of an obelisk stands in the middle of the sanctuary and is thought to have been a representation of Resheph. In the courtyard is a collection of standing obelisks, including one built at the command of Abichemou, king of Byblos at the end of the 19th century BC. They were thought to have been originally 'God boxes' where the gods would live and be worshipped. Several votive offerings have been found here, including bronze figurines. Other schools of thought suggest that they may be connected to the rites of Adonis and Astarte.

King's Well In the centre of the promontory is a deep depression which is the site of the King's Well (Bir al-Malik). According to legend, Isis sat weeping here when she came to Byblos in her search for Osiris. Originally a natural spring, the well supplied the city with water until the end of the Hellenistic era. By Roman times it was used only for religious rituals as the city's water came from the surrounding mountains and was transported through a network of earthenware pipes. The stone walls were built as the rising ground level threatened to close over the spring. Access was via steep steps which have been rebuilt many times over the course of the centuries.

Roman Theatre This charming reconstruction of the theatre is only one-third its original size and has been sited near the cliff edge, which gives it marvellous views across the ocean. First built in AD 218, its orchestra had a fine mosaic floor depicting Bacchus (now in Beirut's National Museum). One notable feature is the series of miniature porticos in front of the stage.

Royal Necropolis This series of nine royal tombs are cut in vertical shafts deep down into the rock and date from the 2nd millennium BC. These **well tombs** are not found elsewhere and attempts to protect the tombs from plunder proved fruitless – all of them have been raided for treasure. The most important tomb is that of King Hiram (1200 BC) who was a contemporary of Ramses II of Egypt. The shaft containing his grave was inscribed with early Phoenician script and said '*Warning here. Thy death is below'*. Hiram's sarcophagus has been removed to Beirut's National Museum. There are steps leading down into one of the tombs, and a tunnel leads to another containing a stone sarcophagus of a 19th century BC prince, Yp-Shemu-Abi.

Early Settlements To the south of the site are the Neolithic (5th millennium BC) and Chalcolithic (4th millennium BC) enclosures. Unfortunately, it is almost impossible to see the crushed limestone floors and low retaining walls through the thick undergrowth that has overtaken this part of the site. Throughout the area, large burial jars were found in which the bodies were curled up in a foetal position. In the earlier period the dead were buried beneath the floors of the houses.

The Medieval Town
Church of St John the Baptist In the centre of this Crusader town is the Romanesque-style Church of St John the Baptist, which was begun in AD 1115 but badly damaged by an earthquake in 1170. Ancient columns were used in the doorways and the heavy buttressing on the western side is thought to have been an effort to prevent

further earthquake damage. One of its most unusual architectural features is the open-air baptistry, which sits against the north wall. Its arches and four supporting pillars are topped by a dome.

The church also has an unusual layout: the apses are facing north-east, but a sharp change in direction brings the northern half of the church back into its more conventional east-west alignment. Apparently, this is because a mistake in orientation was only discovered after the apses had been built and was corrected halfway through construction. The south portal is purely Romanesque, but the north doorway is of an 18th-century Arab design.

To the west of the church is a single standing column and overgrown mosaic floor, remnants of an earlier Byzantine church.

Wax Museum Almost opposite the Church of St John is a small museum (☎ 540 463) containing wax figures in various tableaux representing the history of Byblos from earliest times. The tableaux and design are high kitsch. If that's your thing, it is open 9 am to 6 pm daily and admission is LL5000.

Souq Area The medieval part of the city has a beautifully restored souq area. Unfortunately, most of the shops specialise in tourist trinkets. One interesting shop, although it should really be a museum, is *Mémoire Du Temps* (☎ 547 083). Here you can buy 100,000-year-old fossilised fish remains, set in the rock in which they were found. Excavated from a site near Hjoula, in the mountains above Byblos, not all of the exhibits are for sale and the owners have worked with archaeologists from the British Museum, so they know their stuff. The shop is open from 9 am until 9 pm every day except Sunday.

The Harbour It seems hard to believe that the small harbour, with its fishing boats and posing cafe society, was once a nerve centre of world commerce, but this small port was where the cedar, and other wood for which Byblos was famous, was shipped to the capitals of the ancient world. Much later the Crusaders left their mark here, building defensive towers on either side of its mouth. A chain between the towers could be raised to prevent boats from entering. The northern tower was restored in Mamluk times and is still in fairly good condition. From the top you can look down and see the remains of ancient quays in the clear water below.

Boat Rides

A cluster of long motor boats in the harbour take visitors on 15-minute rides for LL5000 per person from spring until autumn.

Beaches

Near the promontory is a one of Lebanon's rare public beaches, Tam-Tam Beach, which turns into Paradise Beach (a well-known gay hangout) at its northern end. Tam-Tam Beach is about a kilometre south of the centre of town. Follow the road which runs parallel to the coastal highway and look for the hand-painted sign on the right. There is a small road leading down to a parking lot. This is one of the better beaches in Lebanon and has soft sand and clean water. It can get very crowded with young Beirutis on summer weekends, but surveying the scene is part of the fun. Take care when swimming, though; thanks to a strong undertow, lifeguards are regularly plucking people out of the water. There is a small snack bar that sells sandwiches, beer and soft drinks. The taxi fare from the centre of town is about LL2000. If you want to brave the traffic, you can also get the bus or service taxi to/from Beirut to drop you off on the main highway.

Places to Stay

There are only two hotels in town. The cheaper of the two is *Hotel Ahiram* (☎ 540 440), which is a five-minute walk from the harbour heading north (signposts point the way). This is a mid-range hotel with 25 rooms and is just above a stretch of beach belonging to the hotel. It also has a pool, a bar and a small restaurant. Singles/doubles/triples start at US$45/65/75. The rooms are small and the bathrooms do need attention, but there are some terrific sea views. All the rooms have TV, air-con and room service. The price includes the service charge

and a basic breakfast. Lunch or dinner costs about US$10.

Byblos Sur Mer (☎ 540 356, 548 000, fax 944 859, ✉ byblos.mer@inco.com.lb) is right on the harbour and has wonderful views both across the sea and the harbour. For the price the rooms are small and uninspiring but they are comfortable (as they should be). There are two restaurants, including one, *L'Oursin*, which specialises in fish, right across the road on a private jetty next to the hotel swimming pool. Singles/doubles, including the service charge, cost US$90/108 in the high season and US$66/79 in the low season. Breakfast is an extra US$7. There is a fixed-price lunch available for around US$20 and dinner costs between US$20 and US$50.

Places to Eat

Fast Food There is no shortage of small places selling shwarma sandwiches and felafels, as well as the usual pizza and burger joints, along the main street, Rue Jbail. A good place to try, near the junction with the road down to the harbour, is the reassuringly named *Safety Food* (☎ 943 017), where you can get a filling sandwich or a variety of burgers for about US$2.

Along Blvd al-Mina is a cluster of three cafe/restaurants. Although it is lacking in sea views, the *Seven Seas Restaurant/Pub* (☎ cell 03-686 248) is recommended for its friendly management and reasonably priced mixture of Lebanese and Western food. It has a selection of sandwiches starting at LL3500 and mezzes from LL2500 to LL3500. There is also draft beer at LL2500.

Restaurants The *Restaurant Abichemou* (☎ 540 484) has been running for 25 years and commands an impressive view over the castle from its 1st-floor terrace. It is right outside the entrance to the ruins. The menu is Lebanese and there is a special fixed-price menu at lunch time. A selection of mezze dishes and a main-course grill, plus fruit and coffee, costs US$10. If you want fish instead of meat, the price is US$15. In the evening, an a-la-carte dinner will cost around US$20.

If you're sick of mezze, *El Molino*, next door to Cave d'Ahiram Restaurant, offers Mexican food and commanding views of the harbour. It has tacos, tortilla dishes and Mexican dips and salsas. Expect to spend US$15 to US$25 per head (a lot more if you have a taste for margaritas!).

Byblos has no shortage of smarter places to eat, especially around the harbour area. The most famous is the *Byblos Fishing Club* (☎ 540 213). This place was once described as the most fashionable restaurant in the Middle East, and anyone who was anyone in the world of showbiz or politics in the 1960s seems to have passed through here and sat at the bar made from an old fishing boat. The bar is still here, but the celebrities are a bit thin on the ground these days. Never mind, owner Pepe Abed (see the boxed text 'Pepe the Pirate') still keeps his amazing collection of antiquities on display in a museum-cum-bar downstairs. The restaurant specialises in fish and Mexican cuisine, and has a set fish menu of US$20 per person. Expect to pay more if you order a la carte. It is open from 11 am to midnight.

Next door to the Byblos Fishing Club is *Bab al-Mina* (☎ 540 475), where designer-clad families come on weekends to view the harbour and each other. Many reckon the fish here is better than at the Fishing Club; certainly the terrace is fantastic and, for most Lebanese, this tips the balance in its favour. Expect to pay at least US$30 per person for a fish meal. Reservations are essential for weekend lunch.

Should these two restaurants be full, the *Cave d'Ahiram Restaurant* (☎ 540 206), next door to the Byblos Sur Mer hotel, has the usual mezze and grill menu. Starters here cost from LL2000 to LL6000 and main courses about LL15,000. There is a harbour view from the terrace.

If you are looking for entertainment as well as food, *Zanzibar* (☎ 541 516), just beside the Fishing Club, is a popular nightclub decorated with a melange of ethnic objects from South America and Lebanon (East Africa

Pepe the Pirate

Known as the Pirate of Byblos, Pepe Abed is a tourist attraction in his own right. Restaurateur, jewellery designer, marine archaeologist – these are just some of the things which have brought the beautiful people of the prewar jet set to his bar, the Fishing Club, at Byblos.

Born in Mexico of Lebanese parents, he took off around the world with his playboy cousin and, having mixed with the glitterati of the day, he ended up in Byblos. He opened the Fishing Club in 1963 and it soon became one of the most fashionable restaurants in the Mediterranean. His regular visitors included Marlon Brando, David Niven, Brigitte Bardot and Anita Ekberg, and their pictures, along with those of dozens of other celebrities, line the walls of the bar.

Pepe, now in his 80s, lives in an apartment at the Fishing Club, where he houses an impressive collection of antiquities that he has found over the years on diving expeditions. A marble knight's head sits across his table. 'He is my best friend – he never speaks', says Pepe.

Visitors can see his collection as some of it is housed in the basement museum, but his collection of stunning jewellery, designed and made by himself, is a more private matter. He never sells his work, but he may be persuaded to let you have a look – if he is in the mood. Otherwise, content yourself with a look around the 'hall of fame' and have a cool beer.

being strangely absent). You can eat (expect to pay about US$15 per person) but most people come here to dance the night away.

Getting There & Away

Bus Minibuses ply the route between Beirut's Dawra bus station and Byblos for LL500, one way. On weekends they will often drop you at Tam-Tam or Paradise Beach, but check with the driver. You can also take the Tripoli Express from Charles Helou and get dropped off on the highway, although this is slightly more expensive.

Service Taxi Service taxis leave from Cola or Dawra bus stations in Beirut and charge LL3000 to Byblos. Ask for Jbail, which is the Arabic name for the town. If this is not the final destination of the service taxi, you will be dropped at the side of the highway, but it is only a five- to 10-minute walk into town.

Taxi A private taxi to Byblos will cost around US$15 from the centre of Beirut. A return journey will cost the same again. There is a taxi stand on Rue Jbail.

Getting Around

Everywhere in Byblos is easily reached on foot, but if you need to use a taxi, they congregate at the junction of Rue Jbail and the road down to the harbour, and also at a point halfway along Rue Jbail heading east towards the highway. A short ride of up to 5km will cost around US$5 (to destinations within the town US$2). The local service taxis, which leave from the same places, charge from LL1000 to LL2000, depending on your destination, or you can flag one down on the highway, which is a five-minute walk from the centre of town.

AMCHIT   عمشيت
☎ 09

The town of Amchit, 3km north of Byblos, is a well-preserved relic of Lebanon's past. Once again, do not let the general view of low-rise concrete chaos put you off. Amchit is famous for its collection of **traditional townhouses**, which were built originally by wealthy silk merchants in the 19th century.

They are now nearly all privately owned – some are fully restored, others are in need of work.

There are 88 old houses in total, which are now under a preservation order. The houses were constructed using the old stones of the area and you can often spot an ancient piece of carving being used as a lintel. The architecture is influenced by both the Oriental and Venetian styles, with double-arched mandolin windows and covered courtyards. This Italian influence was due to the trade agreement between Lebanon and the Duke of Tuscany.

The houses are not officially open to the public, but if you ask around, often the owners are happy to show visitors inside.

It was in Amchit that Ernest Renan lived for a while; it was also here that he lost his sister, Henriette, whose tomb can still be seen outside the small church at the top of the village. The church here was built on the site of an earlier temple of which some remains are still visible.

A more up-to-date celebrity in Amchit is **Bechara Karam** who is a well-known artist and herbalist with his own very popular TV show. Ask for directions to his house and he may treat you to a glass of his herbal elixir.

Places to Stay

Les Colombes (☎ 943 782, 940 332), known locally as Camping Amchit, is just off the old coast road in the lower part of Amchit. The mother of the current owners, François Matta and his wife Pascale, started the camp in the grounds around the family house back in the 1960s. The camp is on a cliff-top site overlooking a beautiful stretch of coast. There is a private pathway down to the sea where you can bathe from the rocks (with excellent snorkelling). Unfortunately, all but one of the tents that used to dot about the camp site have now disappeared in favour of tiny, pre-fab 'tungalows' – bungalows in the shape of a tent with two beds and a shower. You can pitch your own tent for US$3 per person or sweat in one of the tungalows for US$20. There are also a few chalets, which should be booked ahead, for US$30. While there are quite a few facilities on the site, in general it is rundown and readers have complained about its shabby, non-too-clean bathrooms. Apart from the view and the lack of any other affordable accommodation nearby, there is little to recommend it.

Getting There & Away
A local taxi from Byblos costs LL8000 or you can catch a service taxi from Beirut heading north (past Byblos) and get them to drop you at the Amchit turn-off. The highway dissects the town and if you're coming from the south you must turn off and head up the hill for a couple of hundred metres before being able to turn left towards the sea (where the camping ground is located). It is about a five-minute walk to the upper part of town and 10 minutes to walk down to the camping ground.

RACHANA راشانا
About 17km north of Amchit, is a turn off to Rachana – the 'Museum Village'. This place is worth visiting for the family of artists who have their homes and studios there. You know you are in the right place when you come across great **modern sculptures** lining the road side.

The Basbous brothers have created an extraordinary artistic community in the village. Of the three brothers, Michel, Alfred and Yusuf, only two are still alive; Michel died some years ago. Both of the surviving brothers are still working prolifically in stone, wood and metal, creating striking and sometimes bizarre figures. They are very welcoming to visitors and will happily show you around. They have become something of a tourist attraction in their own right and at the weekend many visitors pass by their studios to look or buy.

When Michel was alive, he built an amazing house in organic shapes, reminiscent of Gaudi. He used all manner of found materials, such as the curved windscreen used as a window. The tiny house is now used as a workshop by Yusuf, who works in an instinctive primitive style. His brother Alfred, who has a house and large studio down the road, has been sculpting for 37 years and has exhibited internationally.

To find the studios, turn left at the junction of the main street in Rachana, by a small shop selling cold drinks. A few hundred metres along the road you will come to a bend and Yusuf's house. Alfred's is a short distance around the corner.

The turn-off to Rachana is about 5km south of Batroun at a Lebanese army post. The village is a further 3km to the northeast. If you do not have your own transport, you will need to get a taxi from Amchit or Byblos and get it to wait for you while you visit the studios. The return trip will cost about US$15.

BATROUN بترون
☎ 06
Batroun is a small Maronite town on the coast about 22km from Byblos and 56km north of Beirut. This was the Graeco-Roman town of Botrys, but its foundation was much earlier than this. It is mentioned in the Tell al-Amarna tablets (Tell al-Amarna is the modern name of Akhetaten, an ancient Egyptian city) as a dependency of the king of Byblos. Called Butron in medieval times, it fell under the diocese of the County of Tripoli and was famous for its vineyards.

Today, behind the usual coastal sprawl, the town has a small fishing port with two interesting old churches.

Things to See & Do
St Georges Orthodox Church is just behind the harbour and was built in the late 18th century. It has 21 fine, painted panels and carved, wooden doves above the altar screen. Close by is the larger **St Estaphan (Stephen) Church**, also known as the fisherman's church. Its old stonework has recently been restored.

The **old harbour** has a small section of an extraordinary natural sea wall creating a pool on the land-side. This natural feature was reinforced by the Phoenicians and the remains of their harbour are visible. Around the old harbour is a small area of well-preserved Ottoman-era stone houses and souqs, which make for a pleasant walk.

In the garden of a private house north-east of the town centre are the remnants of a

Roman theatre. Visitors are welcomed, or you can just look over the wall. To find it, head north along the main street, Rue Principe, and walk 200m past the Badawni Restaurant and turn right at the pharmacy. The Roman theatre is about 50m along on your right near a restaurant called Studio Jamal.

A local speciality of Batroun is **lemonade**, made using water soaked in fresh lemon peel. You can find it at the several juice shops and cafes along the main street.

Just south of Batroun is **White Beach**. Although covered with fine white pebbles (hence the name) rather than sand, it is spotlessly clean and the water is crystal clear. There is also a beachside cafe and a restaurant. Entry costs LL5000, but be warned: it gets crowded on summer weekends.

Places to Stay & Eat

All the hotels are resort-style complexes along the beach south of the town centre. *San Stephano Beach* (☎ 640 366, 642 366) is a whole resort complex with a large swimming pool, restaurant and beach snack bar. Double rooms cost US$70.

Aqualand (☎ 742 760) is the newest resort along the strip and, architecturally, is slightly more tasteful. It has all the resort staples and a double room costs US$90, not including breakfast.

Restaurant al-Mina (☎ 740 188) is in a restored Ottoman house overlooking the old harbour. Mezze starts at LL2500 and fish is sold by weight – expect to pay at least US$15 per person for a full meal. A good fruit juice place is *Mango's Cocktail*, also on Rue Principe. For the traditional lemonade, try *Hilmi Sweets* further north along Rue Principe, close to the souq area.

Beside the sea just south of Batroun is the *White Beach Restaurant* (☎ 742 404), a very pleasant lunch place overlooking the sea and offering traditional mezze and fish meals for about US$15 to US$20 per person.

Getting There & Away

As Batroun is a coastal town just off the highway, you could easily get a service taxi from Beirut or Byblos heading for Tripoli to drop you at the turn-off and walk the short way into town. The cost from Beirut should be LL4000. Alternatively take the Tripoli bus from Beirut and get the driver to drop you off. The price will be the full fare to Tripoli, LL5000.

MOUSSALAYHA CASTLE

قلعة المسيلحة

About 3km beyond Batroun, in the narrow valley at Ras ech-Chekka, is the fairy-tale Moussalayha Castle, which used to defend the only land route between Beirut and Tripoli. Unfortunately the highway runs right beside it, diminishing the drama of its craggy setting. It stands on a rocky outcrop and is built on the summit in such a way as to look like part of the living rock itself. Although dramatic looking, it is restricted by its rocky foundation and its proportions are almost miniature. The entrance is at the top of a steep, rock-cut stairway.

Although the site is very ancient (it is probably the ancient Gigarta mentioned by Pliny), the castle is not and probably dates back to the 16th century. It seems that the site was abandoned until the present castle was constructed.

Beneath the castle runs a small river with an ancient stone bridge crossing it. The whole scene would be incredibly picturesque if it wasn't for the din of the traffic.

If you are using a service taxi heading for Tripoli, simply get them to drop you off at Moussalayha and then flag down another service taxi when you want to continue your journey (there are plenty of service taxis serving this route). The castle is within easy walking distance from the highway. If you have a taxi to yourself, it is probably better to get it to wait for you. To drive down, take the small dirt track to the right of the highway, just before you can see the castle. Cars can only approach as far as the old bridge.

QUBBA

قبّة

This is a small village built in tiers just north of Batroun. Its name probably derives from the Italian Qobba family, who settled here in the time of the Crusaders. The main reason for visiting this village is to see the newly restored Crusader **Church of the Holy Saviour**, which is perched high on the east and south faces of the hill. There are also some **rock-cut grottoes** and **burial places** nearby, one of which was used by a hermit as a dwelling. The church is still used occasionally for services – on saint's days, for instance.

There is another Crusader monument in the village. High on the headland is a **Crusader watchtower**, the Bourj as-Salla, from which fires were lit as warnings, and sometimes for celebrations as well.

Qubba is set back from the old coast road to the east, but is visible from the road if you keep your eyes open. If you are travelling by service taxi, it is a walkable distance from the highway turn-off. Otherwise you can drive up to the village and then walk up to the church. Access is by a winding pathway.

Adonis Valley & Jebel Tannourine

جبل تنورين وادي أدونيس

Famed for its romantic legends as much as for its dramatically beautiful scenery, the Adonis Valley is a deep, jagged cut forged in the coastal mountains by the Nahr Ibrahim (also known as the Adonis River) as it flows out to sea. The river's source, the Afqa Grotto, is at the head of the valley and in ancient times its northern side was a pilgrimage route. Now the road is dotted with ancient remains as well as breathtaking views. To the north lie villages perched on the side of Jebel Tannourine and the ski resort of Laklouk.

The entire area is easily visited as a day trip from Beirut. If you don't have your own car, it would be worth getting a group together and renting one, or a taxi, for the day. Otherwise, you can try your luck hitching. If you don't mind crowds, your best bet for finding a ride is at the weekend, when large numbers of Lebanese head up to the grotto for picnics.

MASHNAQA   مشنقة

The small village of Mashnaqa (pronounced mashna-ah) has some isolated **temple ruins** with fabulous views. They sit on a hilltop off to the right of the road heading east from Byblos towards Afqa and Laklouk and are easily missed (keep your eyes open for a glimpse of a temple above the tree tops); look for the sign marking the entrance to the village, just before the turning to Ehmej. There you will find steps leading up the hill. At a cleft in the rock below the temple are carved funerary niches, depicting hunting scenes and funerary rituals.

The temple, just beyond the rocks, is thought to have been a Phoenician site, later adopted by the Romans. It was likely dedicated to Adonis (is there a temple around here that wasn't?), and appears to have been fairly substantial. Most of what remains today are the lower courses of the temple's outer walls and its main entrance. Even with the modern (if modest) stone house that has encroached on one end of the site it has a feeling of isolation and drama.

Opposite the temple entrance is the partially preserved altar, with four columns still supporting the part of the original entablature. The bases of two earlier altars are enclosed within the structure. Column sections and massive stone blocks are scattered in the grass around the building. From here you have stunning views over the dramatic landscape below and the temple's isolation makes it an ideal picnic spot.

QARTABA   قرطبا

The village of Qartaba is 11km beyond Mashnaqa and is built on the south slope of Jebel Wardiye, overlooking the Nahr Ibrahim. With its pleasant main square, red-tiled roofs and beautiful views, it makes a picturesque stopping-off place on the way to Afqa.

On a small plateau to the south of the village you can see the remains of a **ruined village**, including the remnants of a fairly large monument. Slightly higher up, there is a small temple which was converted to a church in the Byzantine era. This is called locally **Mar Jurios Azraq**, meaning St

George the Blue, thought to have been named after the blue-grey stone used to build the temple.

AFQA GROTTO مـغـارة أفـقـا

Ernest Renan thought Afqa Grotto was one the most beautiful sights in the world – this is not necessarily a recommendation, but in this case he was on the right track. The huge cavern dominates the rocky mountainside at the head of the valley and water roars down under a stone Roman bridge before snaking its way towards the sea. This is the sacred source of the Nahr Ibrahim where, mythology tells us, Adonis (or Tammuz, to give him his Phoenician name) met his death; he was gored by a wild boar while out hunting. The grotto is also intertwined with the legendary love story of Adonis and Aphrodite. Legend has it that this is where they exchanged their first kiss, and the Greek word for kiss, *aphaca*, would appear to reinforce the romantic connection.

The area is riddled with ancient shrines and grottos dedicated to the tragic youth. His story has come to symbolise life, death and rebirth, the theme echoed in the stories of Osiris and Christ. Each spring the river runs red, and in antiquity it was believed to be the blood of Adonis. In reality, the force of the water flowing down the valley picks up ferruginous minerals from the soil and stains the water the colour of red wine.

Afqa today is a very popular weekend excursion for Lebanese families (something to keep in mind if you like your vistas peaceful). In the winter and spring a torrent rages down from the grotto 200m above. When the flow isn't too strong, you can enter the cave by walking up a set of steps on the right-hand side of the bank of the river (steep but not too difficult). Inside, the cave is enormous and the freezing water surges out of an unseen underground source. When the flow of water slows in the summer it is possible to explore the extensive tunnels and caverns further into the mountain.

Thammuz came next behind
Whose annual wound in Lebanon allured
The Syrian damsels to lament his fate
In amorous ditties all a summer's day

Lovers Forever

According to Greek mythology, Adonis was the most beautiful baby in the world, the fruit of an incestuous union between King Cinyras and his daughter Myrrha (who was turned into the Myrrh tree for her sin). The goddess Aphrodite (Venus to the Romans) took the baby and left him in the care of Persephone, goddess of the underworld. When she gazed upon Adonis' beauty, Persephone refused to return the child. Zeus mediated between the two goddesses and decreed that Adonis was to spend half the year with Aphrodite, and the other half in the underworld.

Aphrodite and Adonis eventually became lovers, incurring the wrath of Aphrodite's husband, Ares, who turned himself into a boar and attacked Adonis at Afqa. Aphrodite tried in vain to heal his wounds but her lover bled to death in her arms. In the places where his blood fell to the ground, red anemones sprang up. But the decree of Zeus remained in force and Adonis was permitted to return to his love every six months. Each spring the red anemones (*naaman* or 'darling' in Arabic – also an epithet for Adonis) return, symbolising his return to the world.

Apart from being a racy tale of incest, jealousy, sex, murder and the triumph of true love, the Adonis and Aphrodite myth symbolises those most ancient of themes: fertility and rebirth. In the myth's earlier Semitic form, Aphrodite was Astarte, the great goddess of fertility; her lover was Tammuz, (called 'Adon' by his followers, transformed into Adonis by the Greeks) a god associated with vegetation who journeyed to the underworld each year. Astarte would follow to retrieve him, and while she was gone the world would become barren, reproduction would stop and life itself would be threatened. Followers of Adonis would spend seven days lamenting his death; on the eighth day, in a practise echoed in Christianity, his rebirth was celebrated.

While smooth Adonis from his native rock
Ran purple to the sea, supposed with blood
Of Thammuz yearly wounded

Milton, *Paradise Lost*

At the foot of the main fall is a Roman bridge. If you walk down beneath the bridge, there is a cafe on a terrace with soothing views of the water as it crashes and tumbles over the rocks (or, in summer and autumn, slowly trickles) to the river below.

On a raised plateau nearby, above the left bank and just below the village of Khirbet Afqa, are the ruinous remains of a **Roman temple** which is dedicated to Astarte (Aphrodite/Venus). Its broken columns are made of granite from the famous Pharaonic-era quarries at Aswan in Egypt. The cost involved in bringing the stone several hundred kilometres down the Nile, shipping it to the Lebanese coast and then dragging it up the valley must have been astronomical, and is a testament to the temple's importance as a pilgrimage site. In the foundations, on the riverside, is the entrance to a sort of tunnel that is thought to have carried water into a sacred pool in the temple into which offerings may have been thrown or devotees carried out their ablutions. Constantine destroyed the temple on account of its licentious rites, but the power of legend has stayed with the place. Both Christians and Shiite Muslims attribute healing powers to the place and strips of cloth are still tied to the nearby fig tree in a ritual which dates back to antiquity.

Places to Stay
Just after the turn-off to Afqa is *La Reserve* (☎ 01-498 744/5/6, fax 01-492 660, ✉ info@lareserve.com.lb), a well-appointed camp site and eco-resort encompassing hundreds of square kilometres in the mountains surrounding the Adonis Valley. The resort organises a huge range of outdoor activities all over Lebanon, including rafting, caving, hiking, mountain biking and horse riding. Check out their Web site (www.lareserve.com.lb) for more information and the prices of individual activities. Accommodation in canvas tents, sleeping

up to four people, costs US$10 per person. Mattresses and pillows are provided but you will need your own sleeping bag. In the summer La Reserve organises a two-week summer camp for children aged six to 15. See Travel with Children in the Facts for the Visitor chapter.

Places to Eat
The cafe/restaurant, *Ash-shalal*, beneath the bridge, is the only place to eat in the vicinity. It serves tea, coffee and cold drinks (including beer). Light meals and snacks of the kebab-and-chips variety are available quite cheaply. It is only open during the spring and summer months. Lunch costs from US$6 to US$8.

Getting There & Away
Without a private car, the only way to get to Afqa is by taxi. It is not on a service taxi route, so this will cost around US$20 from Byblos. Hitching might work at the weekend when there is enough traffic on the road, but during the week, you could easily wait quite a while for a lift.

AAQOURA
Aaqoura is famous for its spectacular location, its devotion to Maronite Christianity and its cherries. Reputed to be one of the first villages in the area to convert to Christianity, some 42 churches lie within its confines. The most famous is **Mar Butros**, or St Peter, which sits in a grotto in the towering cliffs that surround the village and can be reached by steps carved out of the rock. The hollowed-out tombs inside the grotto may originally have been part of a Roman necropolis, but what is particularly noteworthy here is the faint traces of writing at the back of the cave. This is thought to be a rare extant example of a Chinese-influenced vertical Syriac script brought back by Christian missionaries to China in the 7th century.

Down in the village there is also the remains of a Roman road, which was part of the pilgrimage route that would lead devotees of the Adonis cult over the mountains and into the Bekaa Valley.

MT LEBANON

La Reserve organises caving excursions in the Aaqoura cliffs. See Places to Stay in the Afqa Grotto section earlier.

Note that the mountains around Aaqoura were heavily mined during the war and hiking without a local guide is not advised.

LAKLOUK
لقلوق

☎ 09

Laklouk is one of the main ski resorts in Lebanon during the winter season. It is set in an attractive rocky location at 1920m above sea level, 28km east of Byblos. It is also a pleasant summer resort. The place consists of a few hotels and restaurants – there isn't a village as such.

Things to See & Do

Apart from enjoying the scenery, there are a few places of interest nearby. A couple of kilometres from the resort on the Chatin-Balaa road are the unusual **Balaa rock formations**, which consist of several houses or chapels carved into the rock. They are known as the 'bishop's house'. The landscape here, with its otherworldly shapes, is reminiscent of that at Cappadocia in Turkey.

Further along the same road, about 6km from Laklouk, is the **Balaa Gorge**. There is

---

Ski Facts: Laklouk

Altitude: 1650m to 1920m
Number of Lifts: Nine lifts and nine slopes
Opening Hours: 8 am to 4 pm
Phone Numbers: ☎ 441 112, cell 03-256 853
Adult Day Pass: US$20 (weekends); US$10 (weekdays)

Originally one of Lebanon's smaller ski resorts, Laklouk was expanded in 1996. There are now three chairlifts, three ski lifts and three baby lifts. It is also possible to do cross-country skiing and snow-shoeing here. More family-oriented than some of the ski resorts closer to Beirut, Laklouk is best suited to beginner and intermediate skiers, although there is one slope that has been approved for by the International Ski Federation for international competitions.

---

a small turning on the left if you are coming from Laklouk and, after about 400m, the road ends. This is the beginning of the descent on foot to the gorge. The walk down is easy and takes about 15 minutes. At the bottom is an extraordinary natural rock formation – a rock bridge spans the chasm and a waterfall crashes down into a deep hole behind. It is really worth the effort to visit, but be warned: there are no fences or barriers and the drops are sheer. The return walk takes about 25 minutes.

Places to Stay & Eat

The **Shangrila Hotel** (☎ 945 521, 01-200 019, fax 01-336 007) is a pleasant, old-world place, built in the 1950s, right in the centre of the resort and close to the ski lifts. It is open all year and in summer has a sun room and pool. Staff at the hotel can organise horse-riding excursions and mountain bikes for hire. Singles/doubles/triples cost US$70/100/135. If you want to sleep four in a room, the cost is US$170. All prices include breakfast. The restaurant has a daily menu for a fixed price of US$20 with a range of European and Lebanese dishes.

You will find rooms slightly cheaper at the **Nirvana Hotel** (☎ 945 521), which is an annexe of the Shangrila Hotel, but it is only open when the Shangrila is fully booked.

The **Motel La Vallade** (☎ 904 140, cell 03-205 901, fax 01-904 376) is the first hotel on the left as you enter Laklouk. It is open all year and has a swimming pool and tennis courts open in the summer. It has large rooms that can sleep up to six, as well as chalets. A double room costs US$45.

For cheap eats, there are a couple of simple snack places close to the slopes (and only open in the winter). The **Auberge** and **Terra E** both do the usual sandwiches and snacks for between LL4000 and LL5000 per person. Other than that you are limited to the hotel restaurants.

Getting There & Away

Laklouk is not on any bus or service taxi route, so you will need your own transport or pay for a taxi from Byblos. A one-way trip will cost in the region of US$25.

DOUMA دوما
☎ 09

This is another traditional, but very well-preserved red-roofed village, famous for being in the shape of a scorpion – this can be seen from the hillside overlooking the village. It is about 22km north-east of Byblos and is a quiet and peaceful place that is said to have been named after the wife of Roman Emperor Septimus Severus, who came here to escape the summer heat on the coast. Under the Ottomans it was famous for the production of swords and guns, a lucrative business in the always-troubled Lebanon, and this paid for the grand houses that can be seen around the village.

Apart from wandering around, there's not a lot to see: the main square has a **Roman sarcophagus** and there are two churches. Above the village there are some Roman inscriptions from the reign of Hadrian. There is also a small souq and some local cafes clustered around the main village square from which you can watch the world go by while sipping a tea or smoking a nargileh.

The Douma Hotel arranges hiking expeditions – there are eight different walks from Douma of varying difficulty.

Places to Stay & Eat

There is one pretty good hotel, the **Douma Hotel** (☎ 520 106, 520 202, fax 01-351 598), which is about 1km from the main square along the main road. It is a pleasant place and its 36 rooms each have a TV and bath. The hotel is open all year and singles/doubles cost US$35/50, including breakfast. A suite costs US$70. There is restaurant serving Lebanese or continental food for US$10 to US$15 per person.

Apart from the hotel, there are a number of snack bars around the village square.

Getting There & Away

There are no buses to Douma and very few service taxis from Byblos. You can take a service taxi to Batroun on the coast and pick up a taxi from there, which would cost about US$15, or get a taxi from Byblos, which would cost about US$20.

MT LEBANON

The Chouf Mountains جبل الشوف

History

The Druze stronghold of the Chouf Mountains lies south-east of Beirut and forms the southern part of the Mt Lebanon Range. In places, the mountains are wild and beautiful; in others they are peppered with small villages and terraced for easy cultivation. Olives, apples and grapes, the main crops, are fed by numerous springs and wells. There are several rivers that run from east to west and divide the land into steep canyons. Most people travel here to see the village of Deir al-Qamar and the nearby Beiteddine Palace, but it is also pleasant to simply wander among the mountain villages of the area.

The main road runs from Damour on the coast, almost parallel to the Nahr ad-Damour, and up into the mountains. Along with the Qadisha Valley in the north, this is probably the best area in Lebanon to explore on foot, but whether you are travelling by car or hiking, you will find the whole area very scenic.

THE CHOUF MOUNTAINS

To Beirut (15km)
Bhamdoun
Sofar
Khalde
Aaramoun
Ain Dara
Baissour
Chouf Cedar Reserve
Damour
Kfarhim Grotto
Aabey
Ain Zhalta
Chouf Mountains
Deir al-Qamar
Majdel Meouch
Barouk
Beiteddine
Samqaniye
Baaqline
Kefraya
Barja
Moukhtara
Maasser ech-Chouf
Gharifé
Mazraat ech-Chouf
Bekaa Valley
Chhime
Ketermaya
Jbaa
Joun
Niha
Lake Qaraoun
Nahr al-Aweli
Bkassine
To Sidon (15km)
Jezzine
Qaraoun
Jbaa
Kfar Houné
Sarba
0   5   10km
0   3   6mi

Highlights

- Visit stone palaces and khans at Deir al-Qamar, one of Lebanon's best-preserved traditional villages.
- See one of the world's finest collections of Byzantine mosaics at the magnificent Beiteddine Palace.
- Hike among ancient cedar trees in the Chouf Cedar Reserve.

The Chouf Mountains were historically a Druze area, but following an invitation from Fakhreddine (Emir Fakhr ad-Din al-Maan II), in the 17th century, increasing numbers of Maronite Christians settled in the area and the two religions lived side by side. By the mid-19th century, Christians formed a majority in the area and violence erupted between the two groups. A particularly severe massacre took place in 1860 in which hundreds of Maronites at Deir al-Qamar were killed by the Druze. Not surprisingly, the event sparked an exodus of Maronites from the Chouf.

During the civil war, the Chouf was occupied by the Israeli army, which in turn brought in members of the Lebanese Forces, the militia of the Christian Phalangist Party, sparking anti-Christian feeling. When the Israelis withdrew in 1983, fierce fighting once again broke out between the Christian militias and the Druze. The latter eventually won the 'Mountain War' and large numbers of Maronites left the area. Nowadays, some efforts are being made to restore harmony between the two communities and Christians are returning to their former homes.

DEIR AL-QAMAR دير القمر
☎ 05

In the Middle Ages, Lebanon was divided into fiefs, each ruled by an emir. By the early 17th century, Fakhreddine had extended his power throughout the territory, which roughly corresponds to modern Lebanon, and united the small fiefdoms into one. His first capital was at Baaqline, but because of water shortages, he moved to nearby Deir al-Qamar, which is fed by numerous springs. Three centuries later the village is one of the best preserved examples of 17th- and 18th-century provincial architecture in the country and, with its great views over the valley to the Beiteddine Palace, is an extremely picturesque spot to spend a few hours. The focal point of the old town is a large square with a fountain, around which most of the historic buildings are grouped.

Mosque of Fakhreddine

To the east of the fountain is the mosque of Fakhreddine, with its distinctive octagonal-shaped minaret. The original building dates back to 1493, but it was restored under Fakhreddine, from whom it takes its name. Built in Mamluk style, the mosque has a vast square room with high arches resting on a central pillar. Quranic verses, along with the date of construction, are carved into the western facade.

Steps behind the mosque lead up to what was once the town's **souq**, which still houses a few shops and a cafe.

The Palace of Younes Maan

Younes Maan governed Deir al-Qamar when his brother, Fakhreddine was in exile in Italy. His palace dates back to the 18th century, but is now a private house and closed to visitors. However, the elaborate entrance is particularly fine and definitely worth a look.

Silk Khan

Dominating the main square is the huge silk khan and its warehouse. It dates back to 1595 and takes the form of a huge rectangle, incorporating an open courtyard surrounded by arcaded galleries that were once used as stables and servant quarters. Part of the first floor, which originally housed the main part of the khan, is now the **French Cultural Centre** and can be visited.

Palace of Fakhreddine

Next to the silk khan and warehouse is Fakhreddine's palace, dating back to 1620. It is built on the site of an earlier palace that was destroyed during a battle with Youssef

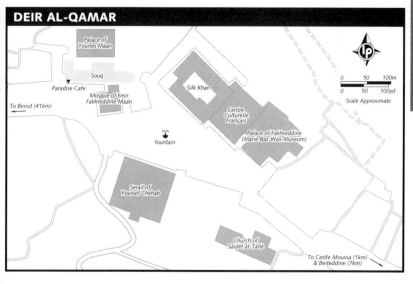

DEIR AL-QAMAR

Palace of Younes Maan

Souq

Paradise Cafe

Mosque of Emir Fakhreddine Maan

To Beirut (41km)

Silk Khan

Centre Culturelle Français

fountain

Palace of Fakhreddine (Marie Baz Wax Museum)

Serail of Youssef Chehab

Church of Saidet at-Tallé

To Castle Moussa (1km) & Beiteddine (7km)

0   50   100m
0   50   100yd
Scale Approximate

Fakhreddine

Nationalist hero, brilliant administrator, connoisseur of fine architecture and all-round Ottoman-era gentleman, Fakhreddine is credited with being the first to unify Mt Lebanon with the coastal cities, foreshadowing the modern state of Lebanon.

Appointed by the Ottomans in 1590 to pacify the unruly Druze of the Chouf Mountains (many of whose ringleaders were members of his own family, the Maans) he proved more than up to the job. Initially his fief was confined to the district of Sidon and the Chouf, but he was soon granted Beirut and eventually extended his rule to include the Qadisha Valley and Tripoli. While it became clear that their governor was not the subservient puppet they had hoped for, the Ottomans were occupied with revolt in Anatolia and Persia and initially left him more or less to his own devices.

Fakhreddine did more than simply grab territory. He began an ambitious program of development in Lebanon. From 1613–18, for entering into an alliance with one of the Medicis, he was exiled to Tuscany. He returned, inspired by his time abroad, and set about modernising his dominions, developing a silk industry and upgrading olive-oil production with the help of Italian engineers and agricultural experts. Their influence can still be seen in some of his buildings in the Chouf town of Deir al-Qamar. Trading links with Europe were also strengthened and European religious missions were allowed to settle in the areas under his control.

Consolidating his power at home, Fakhreddine developed links with the Maronite Christians in the north and encouraged their migration to the south, where they provided labour for silk production. He modernised the ports of Sidon and Beirut, turning them into busy trading centres. In all, the economy flourished under his rule and his power grew to the extent that he controlled areas of what are now Jordan and Israel.

Alarmed at their vassal's growing independence, the Ottomans reacted, sending their Syrian and Egyptian governors to attack his territory and bring it back under Istanbul's control. After fleeing to a nearby cave he was captured in 1633 and taken to Istanbul. Two years later he was executed.

Sifa, Pasha of Tripoli, in 1614. According to local lore, Fakhreddine vowed his revenge and took Youssef's castle at Akkar near Tripoli. He tore down the castle and brought the stones back to Deir al-Qamar. He then brought in Italian architects, who rebuilt the palace in Italian Renaissance style. See also the Castle of Akkar section in the Tripoli & the North chapter.

The palace has been converted by its present owners, the Baz family, into the **Marie Baz Wax Museum**. The collection is a slightly eccentric jumble of figures relating to Lebanese history, including Lady Hester Stanhope wearing a fanciful costume and flanked by the French poet Lamartine. The modern history section is interesting, with a jovial-looking George Bush standing next to a grim-looking General Aoun. Conspicuously absent from the assortment of local political leaders are any representatives of Hezbollah. Unfortunately, apart from tanta-lising glimpses of other parts of the palace from the pleasant cafeteria in the courtyard, only four rooms of the palace are accessible and the 10 minutes or so it takes to view the waxworks hardly make the museum worth the price of admission. It is open from 9 am to 6 pm in the summer (5 pm in winter). Entry to the museum costs LL6000, LL4000 for children under 12.

Serail of Youssef Chehab

On the lower (south) side of the square is the Serail of Youssef Chehab, which is built on the hillside on several levels. Built in the 18th century, it has a somewhat grisly past: not only did Emir Youssef Chehab assassinate several of his relatives here, but the central courtyard was the site of a massacre during the anti-Christian violence in 1860. Nowadays the building is noteworthy for its beautiful stonework. Just above the entrance there are two carved lions, symbolising, ironically enough, justice. Beyond the massive doorway is a large central courtyard. On the south side, overlooking the valley, is the former royal apartment, which has an elegance that belies the ruthlessness of some of its former inhabitants. There is a dome above the centre of the room, and a beautifully restored, painted wooden ceiling to the side. The window's exterior, which can be seen by walking down the steps to the left of the entrance, is also perfectly restored. Although it houses municipal offices, visitors can wander through some parts of the building during office hours (from 8 am to 1 pm, every day except Sunday).

Church of Saidet at-Tallé

The words *deir al-qamar* mean 'monastery of the moon', and the lunar motif can be seen carved in stone on a figure of the Madonna in the Church of Saidet at-Tallé, which sits on the lower slopes of the town. The crescent moon was a symbol of Phoenicia's pagan cult and the Madonna standing on it could be taken as a symbol of Christianity superseding the pagan religion; on the other hand it could simply be incorporating the old religion into the new. The original church was built in the 7th century on a temple dedicated to the goddess Astarte, but was destroyed by an earthquake a century later. Fakhreddine reconstructed the building in the 16th century and it was enlarged again in the 17th century. The nave stretches some 26m in length and is covered by an impressive vaulted stone ceiling. The site also houses a Maronite convent.

Castle Moussa

About 1km out of the town in the direction of Beiteddine is the extraordinary Castle Moussa (☎ 500 106, 501 660), a monument to kitsch and the dream-child of a Mr Moussa, who as a child was beaten by his teacher for dreaming of living in a castle. After becoming a successful businessman he built this castle to fulfil his fantasy. He then filled it with waxwork and mannequin tableaux depicting everything from traditional Lebanese life to Santa's grotto, including a depiction of himself as a child

being beaten by his teacher. An added bonus is that the models are mechanised. There is a shop at the end of the tour and a man who makes Arabic coffee on a brazier for guests. Very popular with Lebanese groups, who visit by the bus load, the castle is open daily from 7 am to 9 pm in summer, 7 am to 6 pm in winter; the entrance fee is LL5000.

Places to Stay & Eat

There are no places to stay in Deir al-Qamar, but there are several cheap restaurants and snack bars in the main square. The *Paradise Cafe* sells simple meals and snacks and there is a pleasant cafe below the old souq. A *furn* (oven) below the entrance to the Marie Baz Museum has tables and makes the usual *zaatar* (thyme), *jibna* (cheese) and *lahma bi ajeen* (spicy meat) on demand for about LL1500.

Next to Castle Moussa, ***Restaurant Farah*** (☎ 500 509) serves mezze and has spectacular views. Lunch or dinner will cost about US$15 to US$20.

Getting There & Away

Service taxis en route to Beiteddine go through Deir al-Qamar and can drop you off there. The fare from Beirut's Cola bus station is LL4000. If you are planning to visit both places in the same day, you could continue to Beiteddine and then walk back (6km) to Deir al-Qamar, a pleasant, downhill walk. Keep in mind that service taxis are scarce after dark.

BEITEDDINE بيت الّ ين
☎ 05

Some 50km south-east of Beirut, Beiteddine is the name of both a village and a magnificent palace complex that lies within it. The palace can be seen from across the valley as you approach and looks almost like a vision from a fairy tale. The style is a cross between traditional Arab and Italian baroque (the architects were, in fact, Italian) with its grounds descending over several terraces planted with poplars and flowering shrubs.

The village is also picturesque. Many of the houses are built in the traditional stone style with graceful arches. This area was the scene of fierce fighting during the civil war and traces of the severe damage sustained by the buildings can still be seen here and there, although they are rapidly disappearing.

There were three other palaces in the vicinity, built for the emir's sons. Of these only one, the **Mir Amin Palace**, still stands and is now a luxury hotel above the main part of the village. Nearby is Emir Bashir's **country house**, which now houses the arch-bishopric. There are still some remains of the original building including a beautiful stone doorway, which leads onto a roof shaped like a Chinese pagoda.

A **festival** is held in Beiteddine every summer in July and August. It features an eclectic mixture of international and Arab musicians, singers, dancers and actors. Check out their Web site (www.beited dine.org.lb) or contact the tourist office in Beirut for further details.

Beiteddine Palace

This beautifully restored early 19th-century palace complex (☎ 500 045/78) was built over a period of 30 years, starting in 1788, and became the stronghold of Emir Bashir, the Ottoman-appointed governor and leading member of the Shihab family. It is the greatest surviving achievement of 19th-century Lebanese architecture and an impressive symbol of Bashir's power and wealth.

The name Beiteddine means 'house of faith' and the original site was a Druze hermitage, which was incorporated into the complex. The palace was built after the Shihab family took over from the Maan dynasty. Partly due to family disagreements, Emir Bashir decided to move from Deir al-Qamar and build his own palace, which would reflect the increasing power and glory of his reign. Architects from Italy and the most highly skilled artisans from Damascus and Aleppo were hired and given free rein to try out new ideas. The result was a huge edifice over 300m in length built high on a mountain overlooking the valley. The grounds below the palace are terraced into gardens and orchards.

During the French mandate the palace was used for local administration, but after 1930 it was declared a historic monument and placed under the care of the Department of Antiquities, which set about restoring it. In 1943 Lebanon's first president after independence, Bishara al-Khouri, made it the official summer residence and brought back the remains of Emir Bashir from Istanbul, where he'd died in 1850.

The palace suffered tremendous losses following the Israeli invasion, when as much as 90% of the original contents are reckoned to have been lost. Once the fighting ended after 1984, the Druze leader Walid Jumblatt ordered its restoration and declared its to be a 'Palace of the People'. As such, it contains several museums housing various collections, including some magnificent mosaics and a small exhibition dedicated to Walid Jumblatt's father, Kamal, who was assassinated (probably by the Syrians) in 1977. Most of the items on display are there courtesy of the Jumblatt family.

The palace consists of three main courts: **Dar al-Baraniyyeh** (the outer courtyard to which passing visitors were admitted freely), **Dar al-Wousta** (the central courtyard, which housed the palace guards and offices of the ministers) and **Dar al-Harim** (the private family quarters). Beneath Dar al-Wousta and Dar al-Harim are huge vaulted **stables**, which held 500 horses and their riders in addition to the 600 infantry that formed the emir's guard. Part of the stables now houses the mosaic collection.

From the entrance to the palace, you pass through a passage that leads into the small **Kamal Jumblatt Museum**. The former Druze leader was born in 1917 and established the Progressive Socialist Party in 1949. Exhibits include photographs, some personal possessions and documents chronicling his life.

The museum exit leads into to a 60m-long courtyard where public festivals and gatherings took place. It was from here that the emir would leave for his hunting expeditions or to fight wars. Along the north side of this courtyard are the guest apartments. It was the custom of noble houses to offer hospitality for three days to visitors before asking their business or their identity. The

BEITEDDINE PALACE

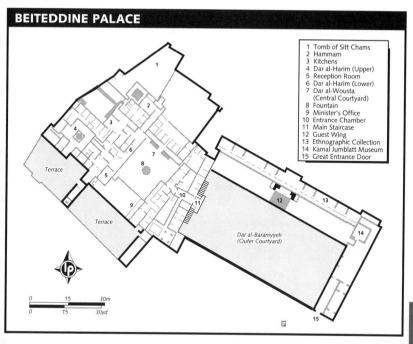

1 Tomb of Sitt Chams
2 Hammam
3 Kitchens
4 Dar al-Harim (Upper)
5 Reception Room
6 Dar al-Harim (Lower)
7 Dar al-Wousta
   (Central Courtyard)
8 Fountain
9 Minister's Office
10 Entrance Chamber
11 Main Staircase
12 Guest Wing
13 Ethnographic Collection
14 Kamal Jumblatt Museum
15 Great Entrance Door

Terrace

Terrace

Dar al-Baraniyyeh
(Outer Courtyard)

0   15   30m
0   15   30yd

French poet, Lamartine, who was a guest at the palace, wrote the following description:

> Magnificently dressed black slaves armed with silver-plated pistols and glittering finely chased gold Damascus sabres stood on either side of a door carved in woods of various colours with marble all around and Arabic inscriptions above. The vast courtyards facing the palace swarmed with a host of servants, courtiers, priests and soldiers wearing all the variety of picturesque costumes characteristic of the five peoples of the Lebanon... Five or six hundred Arab steeds were saddled and bridled, covered in brilliant drapery of every hue...

The restored upper floor of this wing is used as museum space to exhibit the **Rachid Karami Ethnographic Collection**. This large collection includes pottery from the Bronze and Iron Ages, Roman glass, Islamic pottery, lead sarcophagi and gold jewellery. There is also a scale model of the palace

and, in other rooms, a collection of weapons and costumes.

At the far end of the outer courtyard is a double staircase leading up to the entrance of the central courtyard. This is known as the 'tumbling staircase' on account of the tale of a sheep that escaped the butcher's knife and head-butted an eminent pasha down the stairs. These days the head of the stairs is decorated with a bust of Kamal Jumblatt.

Through an arched passageway is the central courtyard. The entrance is decorated with an inscription of welcome and a decorative **marble portal**. Inside is a charming courtyard with a fountain; the open side overlooks the valley. The apartments and offices off the courtyard are set along graceful arcades. The rooms are luxurious and richly decorated with marble, mosaics and marquetry, with furnishings in traditional oriental style. The walls and ceilings are of painted, carved cedar wood embellished with Arabic calligraphy. In the richly decorated room on the south side of the courtyard an inlaid marble **water fountain** is built into the wall, serving both as a way of cooling the room while at the same time making conversation inaudible to eavesdroppers.

The **entrance to the third court** is a beautiful facade which leads through to the lower court (the kitchens and famous bathhouse) and the upper court (the reception rooms). The rooms are lavishly decorated. On the ground floor, immediately beyond the entrance is the waiting room, known as the **room of the column**, named for the single column supporting the vaulted ceiling. Beyond this is a two-level **reception room** *(salaamlik)* with a mosaic floor and inlaid marble walls.

The huge **kitchens** are also well worth a look. In their heyday they catered for 500 people a day. Endless trays of food would have been carried on vast trays to set before the divans and sofas of the court and the visitors. To the north of the kitchen is the large **hammam** or bathhouse, a series of domed rooms luxuriously fitted out in marble with carved marble basins and fountains. Bathers would move between the cold, warm and hot chambers before reclining to rest in the anteroom. In a small shaded garden to the north of the hammam is the **Tomb of Sitt Chams**, the emir's first wife. The ashes of Bashir are also reported to be in the tomb.

In the lower part of the palace, is the one of the most spectacular collections of **Byzantine mosaics** in the eastern Mediterranean, if not the world. These were mostly excavated from a former church at Jiyyeh, the ancient city of Porphyrion, which was discovered by workmen digging on the coast in early 1982. The area was then under the control of Walid Jumblatt, who had the well-preserved mosaics brought to him and kept them safe from looters throughout the war. The magnificent collection includes some 30 room-sized mosaics and many smaller ones. The designs are often geometric and stylised, reflecting the austere nature of early Christianity in the area, but there are also depictions of animals, including leopards, bulls, gazelles and birds, as well as religious figures. Set among the graceful stone arches and vaulted ceilings of Beiteddine's former stables, and along the walls of the palace's lower gardens, the mosaics are a stunning visual treat.

The palace is open from 9 am to 6 pm in summer (4 pm in winter) every day except Monday. Admission is LL7500, and there are multilingual brochures available. Guides can also be hired to take you through the palace (price dependent on your negotiating skills, but expect to pay at least LL10,000), which can gain you access to areas that are usually kept locked.

Places to Stay & Eat

There are no cheap hotel options in the area, but the furnished apartments at the *Motel SJS* (☎ *501 567 or cell 03-747 481)*, on the main road at Samqaniye, about 3km south of Beiteddine on the road to Moukhtara, can be rented for US$35 per night.

The only hotel in Beiteddine itself is the luxurious and expensive *Mir Amin Place* (☎ *501 315/6/7/8)*. Set on the hill above Beiteddine and overlooking the palace below, this is the restored palace of the emir's eldest son, and the second of the three palaces built by Bashir (the third is no longer standing). With singles/doubles starting from US$123/146 (plus 5% tax), it is not for travellers on a budget, although prices can drop by as much as 40% out of season. Whatever your budget, it is well worth dropping by for a drink on the terrace, where the pool is decorated like an oriental carpet and the views are spectacular. The hotel has three restaurants: *Al-Diwan* (oriental food), *Arcadia* (European food) and *Le Jardin* (a mixture of the two). Expect to spend at least US$30 to US$40 per person for a meal.

Down in the town there are a few simple cafes and snack places. Near the main square is *Hatemia Restaurant* which is OK, but a bit overpriced with pizzas and burgers starting at about US$5. On the road above the palace there are a couple of good places next to each other. The first is *Al Wasr Restaurant & Snacks* where you can have a good lunch for about US$8. The other, *Nasr Khan al-Mir*, is a bit more upmarket, but both have good views across to the palace. In the village

THE CHOUF MOUNTAINS

of Baqaline, just off the road to Mir Amin, the ***Restaurant New Garbatella*** (☎ *301 411)* has good views over the valley and has a selection of European style food and a few mezze choices. Pizzas start at LL6500 and steaks at LL11,000. To get there, take the right fork just before the turn-off to Mir Amin and follow the road for about 1km.

Getting There & Away

The route to Beiteddine runs south from Beirut along the coast to Damour and then east. Service taxis from Beirut's Cola bus station serve the route and the fare to Beiteddine is LL4000.

It is feasible to visit several places and get dropped off along the way, hailing a passing service taxi when you want to move on, but along the quieter stretches you may have a bit of a wait. The service-taxi stand in Beiteddine is close to the palace on the main square. Keep in mind that you're unlikely to find service taxis running after dark.

MOUKHTARA مـختـارة

About 9km south of Beiteddine is the town of Moukhtara. This is the seat of the Jumblatt family and defacto capital of the Chouf. The Jumblatt's 19th-century stone palace dominates the town. Consisting of three large buildings it has its own hammam, a garden with a collection of Roman sarcophagi and a waterfall that tumbles into an ornamental pool. There are public reception rooms that are open to visitors.

Each weekend that he is in residence, Walid Jumblatt, head of the family and leader of the Druze, spends his mornings listening to the complaints of his mostly Druze followers. If you happen to be there then, you will see the long line of petitioners as they wait to see their leader.

Apart from the overwhelming Jumblatt presence, the town is picturesque and has a number of traditional red-tiled buildings that make for a pleasant wander.

Getting There & Away

Service taxi to Moukhtara leave from Beirut's Cola bus station and cost LL5000 each way. Keep in mind, especially when planning your

---

> ## Jumblatt Feminism
>
> The Jumblatts have long been prominent in the Chouf and have headed the Druze community in Lebanon for the past century. Back in the 1920s their position was threatened when Fouad Jumblatt, great-grandfather of Walid Bey, was assassinated. His son, Kamal, was too young to assume power and the Druze community came to Fouad's wife to help them decide what to do. She took the initiative and assumed leadership of the community herself until Kamal came of age. The unprecedented spectre of a woman leader was difficult for many to accept (particularly close male relatives), but eventually she won them over and remained in power until Kamal grew up.

return trip, that because the town is small, service taxis can be infrequent.

CHOUF CEDAR RESERVE

محميّة أرز الشوف

The largest of Lebanon's three natural protectorates, the Chouf Cedar Reserve, covers some 50,000 hectares, 5% of Lebanon's entire area. Seventy percent is in the Chouf itself, while the remaining 30% is in the western Bekaa. The reserve marks the southernmost limit of Lebanese cedar *(cedrus libani)* growth, and incorporated within the protectorate are six cedar forests, of which the Barouk and Maaser al-Chouf forests have the largest number of ancient trees – some are thought to date back 2000 years. Although nine villages, with a population totalling around 30,000, border the reserve, hunting and livestock grazing bans are strictly enforced and a number of species of flora and fauna have returned to the area in recent years. According to the Chouf Cedar Society, which runs the reserve, more than 200 species of birds and 26 species of wild mammal (including wolves, gazelles and wild boar) either live in or pass through the area.

Also within or just outside the reserve's boundaries are a number of historical sites. These include the remains of the rock-cut

THE CHOUF MOUNTAINS

fortress of **Qab Elias** and **Qala'at Niha**, in addition to the **Shrine of Sit Sha'wane**, a woman saint venerated by the Druze and still a site of pilgrimage for local residents.

Apart from hiking, the reserve's **trails** are also ideal for mountain biking and, in winter, snow-shoeing. Lebanese Adventure organises all of these activities (see Organised Tours in the Getting Around chapter). Or you can call the Chouf Cedar Society in Moukhtara (☎ 05-503 230 or cell 03-682 472) for more information. You can also check out their Web site (www.shoufcedar.org). At the time of writing, camping was not allowed in the reserve.

Getting There & Away The reserve can be reached either from the road leading from Beiteddine to Sofar, or via Ain Zhalta from the Beirut-Bekaa Highway. There are three entrances into the reserve, although only two, near the villages of Barouk and Maasar ech-Chouf, can be accessed without calling ahead. The latter is the best place to view the old growth cedars and is marked by a small visitors centre that sells delicious local produce, including honey, dried fruit and jam. Because both villages are out of the way, you're unlikely to find frequent service taxis there. If you don't have your own vehicle, the best way is to get a taxi from Beiteddine, some 10km away. If you have a four-wheel drive, there is also a track that leads from Maasar al-Chouf through the mountains and down to the village of Kefraya in the Bekaa Valley. It can sometimes be blocked with snow in winter, so check the accessibility with the Chouf Cedar Society office.

KFARHIM GROTTO مـغـارة كفرحيم

About halfway between Damour and Deir al-Qamar is the village of Kfarhim where a small, natural cave was discovered over 80 years ago. The grotto has stalagmites and stalactites, but is nowhere as large or impressive as the Jeita Grotto. It is open to the public from 7 am to 7 pm daily; admission is LL2500. There's a souvenir shop here where you can buy slide film.

Getting There & Away

Service taxis en route to Deir al-Qamar from Beirut's Cola bus station (see Deir al-Qamar Getting There & Away section earlier this chapter for more details), will drop you at the turning to Kfarhim on the main road, which is some 3 km from the grotto. If you don't have a private taxi or car, you'll have to walk this (uphill) road and back.

Tripoli & the North

Northern Lebanon is dominated by the city of Tripoli, with its well-preserved medieval souqs and bustling port of Al-Mina. In the mountains behind lies one of the most beautiful areas of Lebanon, the Qadisha Valley. At the far north of both is Akkar, a poor, largely agricultural region which sits against the Syrian border. Once again, Lebanon's contrasts are apparent, with the very Middle Eastern feel of Tripoli and the Akkar giving way to an almost entirely Christian Qadisha.

Tripoli (Trablous)

طرابلس

☎ 06

Tripoli, or Trablous in Arabic, is the second-largest city in Lebanon and, with its bustling souqs and rich Islamic architectural heritage, feels more in sync with neighbouring countries than the country's other coastal towns. The architectural remains of the city's medieval past survived the civil war more or less intact, making the Old City a fascinating place to wander.

Joined to the medieval town centre is Al-Mina, the port area that is a second centre, with its own small souq and a long seafront filled with restaurants and cafes.

History

Although much of Tripoli's early history is lost to us, the city is thought to be the Kadytis of Phoenician times. There is some evidence of a settlement here as far back as 1400 BC but its past is likely to go back even further. By the 8th century BC, what had been a small trading post by the sea grew with the arrival of traders from Sidon, Tyre and Arwad (Aradus, which became Tartus in Syria). Each community settled within its own walled area, giving rise to the Greek name Tripolis, which literally means three cities

During the rule of the Seleucids and, later, the Romans, Tripoli prospered and was embellished with many sumptuous temples and

other buildings. A huge earthquake in AD 543 changed the geography of the port area completely and destroyed most of the town. It was quickly rebuilt but, by AD 635, a general of Mu'awiyah, the governor of Syria and founder of the Umayyad dynasty (AD 661–750), besieged the city and attempted to starve it into submission. The inhabitants of Tripoli escaped by sea with Byzantine help and when the general entered the town, he found it deserted. He resettled it with his military garrison and a Jewish colony.

The garrison's frequent absences were taken advantage of by the Byzantines and between 685 and 705 they captured and settled the city. It was then recaptured by the Muslims and incorporated into the Umayyad and, later, Abbasid caliphates. By the end of the 10th century, as the Abbasids were losing their grip on the region, the Shiite Fatimids took control of Tripoli. They held on to it until 1069, when one of the city's judges, from a family named Banu Ammar, declared its independence. The already prosperous city grew steadily under Ammar rule, and became a centre of learning renowned for its school, the Dar al-Ilm (literally, 'Abode of Knowledge'), which had a library reputed to contain some 100,000 volumes.

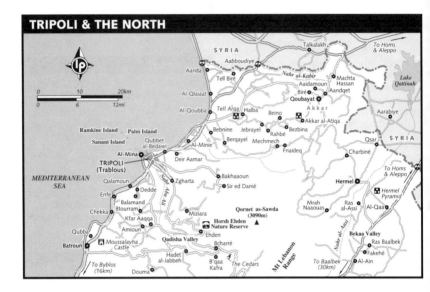

TRIPOLI & THE NORTH

When the Crusaders, led by Raymond de Saint-Gilles of Toulouse, initially arrived on the scene in 1099, the Ammars persuaded them to bypass Tripoli, bribing them with lavish presents. However, Tripoli's agricultural wealth was too glittering a prize and Raymond returned some three years later with only 300 men. Tripoli's rulers brought in reinforcements from Damascus and Homs, thinking that victory would be easy, but Raymond defeated the three armies. He then built a fortress, the Citadel of Raymond de Saint-Gilles, on a hill inland from the Tripoli (which was still concentrated around the port area) and controlled all land trade coming into the city.

Tripoli's leaders launched repeated raids on the fortress, eventually mortally wounding Raymond. Just before he died he signed a truce guaranteeing safe passage in and out of the city for its inhabitants and this lasted until his successor, Guillaume Jourdain, took over and once again imposed the blockade. This time, however, he enlisted the help of the Genovese fleet, which blocked the city from the sea. After four increasingly desperate years under siege, the city finally fell to the Crusaders in June

1109. The victors sacked the city and set fire to the magnificent library at Dar al-Ilm.

Tripoli became the capital of the County of Tripoli and the Crusaders managed to hang on to the city for 180 years, during which time the economy, based on silk weaving and glass making, prospered. Academic traditions were revived too, although this time it was Christian schools, rather than Muslim, that led the way.

The Mamluk sultan Qalaun took the city of Tripoli in 1289, massacring most of the population as he did so. Muslim historian Abu'l-Fida describes how desperate citizens swam to an offshore island in hope of escape, but Muslim troops jumped into the water and swam out, killing all the men and taking the women and children captive. When the chronicler himself tried to visit the island, his boat could not land, so strong was the smell of putrefying corpses.

Qalaun had the port city razed and built his new city around the Citadel of Raymond de Saint-Gilles. Once again the area flourished: the souqs, mosques, madrassas (theological schools) and khans (inns) that form the bulk of present-day Tripoli's monuments are testament to the city's economic and cultural prosperity in Mamluk times. The Turkish Ottomans took over the town in 1516 under the ruling sultan Selim I. When the *mutasarrifa*, administrative district, of Mt Lebanon was created in 1860, Tripoli was still ruled by the Ottomans; however, it fell within the boundaries of the French Mandate of Greater Lebanon in 1920.

Since independence in 1946, Tripoli has been the administrative capital of northern Lebanon. Fairly conservative and predominantly Sunni Muslim, it was perhaps natural that the pro-Arab nationalist forces, led by Rachid Karami, based themselves here in the civil war of 1958. The labyrinthine Old City was almost impossible for outsiders to penetrate and Karami's men held out for several weeks. The Karami name remains prominent in Tripoli and many of city's main thoroughfares are named after family members.

In the 1975 to 1991 round of fighting, Tripoli suffered a lot of damage – especially during the inter-Palestinian battles of 1983 – but it still fared better than the south. Both during and after the war, the city's population grew rapidly, swelled both by refugees (including large numbers of Palestinians) and natural increase. Today it is concentrating on rebuilding its industry and business sectors, and is also looking to tourism as a source of future income.

Orientation

There are two main parts to Tripoli: the city proper and Al-Mina. The main part of Tripoli is set slightly inland from the sea and is dominated by the Citadel of Raymond de Saint-Gilles, set on a hill overlooking the Old City and the Nahr Abu Ali (also called the Qadisha River). A maze of souqs cluster at the foot of the hill, and further afield are the modern shopping and residential districts. The centre is at Sahet et-Tall (pronounced et-tahl), a large square by the clock tower and municipality building, where you'll find the service-taxi and bus stands, cheap restaurants and hotels. The Old City sprawls east of Sahet et-Tall, while the modern centre is west of the square.

Three main avenues lead to Al-Mina, a promontory 3km to the west that contains the port area and fishing harbours, as well as high-rise apartments and upmarket shops. The shore is bordered by a long Corniche where Tripoli strolls and cruises, à la Beirut. This is where Tripoli's nightlife, such as it is, is centred. There are beaches around Al-Mina and some nearby islands that can be reached by boat from the northern shore of the promontory.

Information

Tourist Office The tourist office (☎ 433 590) is right on Abdel Hamid Karami Square, the first major roundabout as you enter Tripoli from the south. The roundabout has a large 'Allah' sign in Arabic in the middle and the office is on the right as you face north. It has a few brochures and a map of the city that lists the various monuments. The staff is very friendly and can advise you about visiting the Palm Islands Reserve, for which you need a permit.

Money There are ATMs, banks and exchange offices all around Sahet et-Tall. Al-Masri on Rue Tall will exchange travellers cheques without a problem.

Post & Communications There are two post offices in Tripoli. The main one is on Rue Fouad Chehab near the Bank of Lebanon building, just south of Abdel Hamid Karami Square, and the other is in Al-Mina on Rue ibn Sina.

There is a public telephone at both post offices and there is a public telephone office on a side street running between Jamal Abdel Nasser Square and Rue Fouad Chehab.

Email & Internet Access There are two Internet cafes on Rue Riad al-Solh (also called Rue Mina), one of the broad avenues leading to Al-Mina from central Tripoli. CompuGames1 (☎ 448 202) is in the City Complex. It is open from 11 am to midnight Monday to Friday, from 2.30 pm on Saturday and from 6 pm on Sunday; it costs LL4000 per hour for Internet access.

A little further along the same road in the Riad Bakri Centre is Magma Internet (☎ 206 083 or cell 03-446 226), which is open 10 am to 11 pm daily and charges LL3000 per hour.

Emergency The following Tripoli telephone numbers may be useful in the event of an emergency:

Ambulance	☎ 602 510, 610 861 (ext 140)
Police	☎ 430 950/1/2/3
Red Cross	☎ 602 510

Old City

The Old City mostly dates from the 14th and 15th centuries (the Mamluk era) and is a maze of narrow alleyways, colourful souqs, *hammams* (bathhouses), khans, mosques and madrassas. Some monuments were damaged during the war, others have suffered from neglect, so there is a lot of renovation work being carried out. It is a very lively place where artisans, including jewellers, tailors and coppersmiths, continue to work as they have done for centuries.

There are 40 listed monuments in Tripoli, almost all in the Old City, and they have numbered plaques (we have put the plaque number for each monument in brackets). Some are completely ruined and many are locked, but the key is almost always kept in a nearby shop or house. If you ask around someone will usually fetch it for you.

Citadel of Raymond de Saint-Gilles (No 1)

The city is dominated by the vast citadel, known as Qala'at Sanjil in Arabic. In AD 1100 Raymond de Saint-Gilles occupied the hill which overlooks the valley, the town and the coast. He decided to transform this position, which he called Mont Pelerin (Mt Pilgrim), into a fortress. The original castle was burnt down in 1287, as well as on several subsequent occasions. It was rebuilt by Emir Essendemir Kurgi in 1307–08, and was added to right up until the 19th century. As a result, the only really early parts are the foundation stones.

The layers of architectural styles become apparent as you enter the fortress. The first entrance is a huge Ottoman gateway, over which is an engraving from Süleyman the Magnificent, who ordered the restoration

(yet again) of 'this blessed tower, that it may serve as a fortified position until the end of time'. After this there is a bridge across a moat dug by the Crusaders. Following a left turn there is another huge portal, decorated with the distinctive black-and-white stone of the Mamluks. After a sharp right turn (the turns were designed to foil the battering rams of potential enemies) there is a third gateway, with the pointed arch of the Crusaders. This leads into a tunnel containing the surprising sight of Roman sarcophagi. These were brought here for safekeeping during the civil war.

Inside the castle is a confusing mixture of architectural styles and features that reflect the different occupants and stormy history of the city. Be on your guard when exploring as there are some sheer drops that are not protected by barriers or warnings.

The castle is open from 8 am to 6 pm daily. The entrance is up a steep road on the western approach to the castle mount. There is not always someone to collect the entrance fee, but the official charge for entry is LL5000.

The Tragedy of Melisinda

One of the most romantic and tragic figures who lived in the Saint-Gilles citadel was the beautiful sister of Raymond de Saint-Gilles, Melisinda. Hearing about her charm and beauty, the emperor of Constantinople asked for her hand and Raymond delightedly accepted. It was to be a very advantageous alliance. A splendid dowry was prepared and 12 galleys made ready to conduct Melisinda to Byzantium in a manner fitting a future empress.

At the last minute the emperor decided it was more politically fitting to ally himself with the house of Antioch and asked Maria, sister of Prince Bohemond I, to marry him instead. Raymond was furious at the insult to him and his sister. He loaded the 12 galleys with thugs who were sent to pillage the emperor's territories.

Meanwhile, Melisinda was heartbroken and died soon afterwards of grief. Her tragic story is remembered in the sad songs of the wandering troubadours.

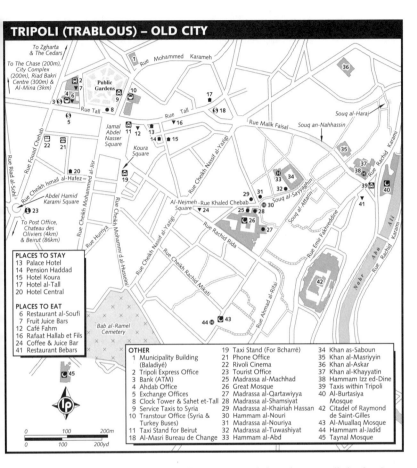

TRIPOLI (TRABLOUS) – OLD CITY

PLACES TO STAY
13 Palace Hotel
14 Pension Haddad
15 Hotel Koura
17 Hotel al-Tall
20 Hotel Central

PLACES TO EAT
6 Restaurant al-Soufi
7 Fruit Juice Bars
12 Café Fahm
16 Rafaat Hallab et Fils
24 Coffee & Juice Bar
41 Restaurant Bebars

OTHER
1 Municipality Building (Baladiyé)
2 Tripoli Express Office
3 Bank (ATM)
4 Ahdab Office
5 Exchange Offices
8 Clock Tower & Sahet et-Tall
9 Service Taxis to Syria
10 Transtour Office (Syria & Turkey Buses)
11 Taxi Stand for Beirut
18 Al-Masri Bureau de Change
19 Taxi Stand (For Bcharré)
21 Phone Office
22 Rivoli Cinema
23 Tourist Office
25 Madrassa al-Machhad
26 Great Mosque
27 Madrassa al-Qartawiyya
28 Madrassa al-Shamsiyat
29 Madrassa al-Khairiah Hassan
30 Hammam al-Nouri
31 Madrassa al-Nouriya
32 Madrassa al-Tuwashiyat
33 Hammam al-Abd
34 Khan as-Saboun
35 Khan al-Masriyyin
36 Khan al-Askar
37 Khan al-Khayyatin
38 Hammam Izz ed-Dine
39 Taxis within Tripoli
40 Al-Burtasiya Mosque
42 Citadel of Raymond de Saint-Gilles
43 Al-Muallaq Mosque
44 Hammam al-Jadid
45 Taynal Mosque

When you have explored the castle, walk down to the bridge and cross the river. The east bank is the best place to view the castle with its sheer walls and picturesque Arab buildings nestling at the foot of the mount.

Great Mosque (No 2) Construction of the Great Mosque was begun in 1294 and completed 21 years later. It was built on the ruins of a 12th-century Crusader cathedral, St Mary of the Tower, which was destroyed by the Mamluks, although parts of the cathedral were incorporated into the mosque's construction. The mosque's northern en-trance and the minaret, a distinctive Lombard-style tower, are likely remnants of the original building. Inside, a large courtyard is surrounded by porticos on three sides, and a domed and vaulted prayer hall on the fourth.

The adjacent 14th-century madrassas of **Al-Machhad** and **Al-Shamsiyat** reveal details of daily life under the Mamluks. Opposite its northern entrance are two more 14th-century madrassas, **Al-Khairiah Hassan** and **Al-Nouriyat**. The latter is still in use and has dis-tinctive black-and-white stonework around its doors and windows, and a beautiful inlaid mihrab (prayer niche). Across from them is the **Hammam al-Nouri**, a large public bath built around 1333, but which is now completely derelict.

Madrassa al-Qartawiyya (No 3) Attached to the east side of the Great Mosque is the Madrassa al-Qartawiyya, which was built by a Mamluk governor of the same name between 1316 and 1326. Famed for its fine workmanship, the madrassa has an elegant facade of black-and-white stone facings, topped by a honeycomb-patterned half-dome above the portal. The back wall is also made with black-and-white stone and has some beautiful Arabic inscriptions. Inside, the prayer hall is topped by Tripoli's only oval dome and has a finely decorated south facing wall and minbar (pulpit).

Al-Muallaq Mosque (No 29) To the south of the Great Mosque is the Muallaq, or hanging, mosque, a small, 14th-century mosque which is unusual because it is built on the second floor of the building. It has a simple interior and leads down to a courtyard garden.

Hammam al-Jadid (No 30) Almost opposite the Muallaq Mosque is the Hammam al-Jadid, the 'New Baths'. The word 'new' is a bit of a misnomer given that it was built around 1740 and is no longer operational, but it is worth seeing. It was in use until the 1970s and is the city's best-preserved hammam (with the exception of the still-functioning Hammam al-Abd). It is also the city's largest hammam and retains its sense of grandeur. It was donated as a gift to the city by As'ad Pasha al-Azem of Damascus and no expense was spared in its construction. Draped over the portal is a 14-link chain carved from a single block of stone. A huge, glass-pierced dome dominates the main chamber and brings a dim light to the pool and fountain below. The floor and fountain are laid with slabs of marble in contrasting colours. Several smaller chambers, also with glass-pierced domes, lead off the main room.

Madrassa al-Tuwashiyat (No 9) Back in the heart of the old town, along the main street in the gold souq (Souq al-Sayyaghin), is the Madrassa al-Tuwashiyat, a law school with an attached mausoleum which dates back to the early 1470s. Built of sandstone in alternating black-and-white patterns, it has an unusual, finely decorated portal that towers above the building's ornate facade.

Hammam al-Abd Close by the Madrassa al-Tuwashiyat is Tripoli's only functioning bathhouse, Hammam al-Abd. For some reason it is not a listed monument, despite being some 300 years old. With the pierced domes that are typical of Mamluk- and Ottoman-era public baths, stone arches, cushioned benches and oriental carpets on which to recline and smoke a nargileh (water pipe) after the rigours of bathing, it fulfils everyone's hammam fantasy. Unfortunately, you have to be male to indulge, unless you can get a group of women together and book the entire place in advance. The hammam is open from 8 am to 11 pm daily, and a basic bath costs LL10,000; add at least LL6000 if you want the full works.

Khan as-Saboun (No 10) Situated off the gold souq, near Hammam al-Abd, the Khan as-Saboun was built in the 16th century and was first used as an army barracks. After 70 years it was abandoned and later came back to life as a market where local farmers sold their olives and olive-based products – soap, in particular – from the small shops surrounding the courtyard. The khan became famous for its high-quality scented soaps and when the soap industry took off in the 18th century (see the boxed text 'Suds in History') the khan was at its centre. Now the khan is occupied by only about five shops, including one, Bader Hassoun (☎ 438 369), that sells more than 100 types of traditionally made soaps. All have an olive oil base and come in a bewildering array of naturally dyed colours and flower- or herb-based scents. The more elaborately scented soaps sell for around LL5000 each

Khan al-Misriyyin (No 14) On the northern side of the old town is the Khan al-Misriyyin, or the Khan of the Egyptians, which

Suds in History

Tripoli's Khan as-Saboun may only have one or two traditional soap makers nowadays but historically soap was an important part of the city's economy. Some local patriots claim that soap was invented here, but whether or not this is true, by the 18th century Tripoli soap was a prized product in Europe. Some say that the world-renowned Marseilles soap may well have had its origins here.

Soap was traditionally made with olive oil, honey, glycerine and other natural ingredients that were melted together in a huge vat, coloured with saffron and other natural dyes, and scented with essential oils. The soap supplied the local hammams as well as households. A collection of differently shaped soaps, symbolising purity, would also be given to brides as part of their trousseau.

Cheap mass-produced soap all but killed traditional soap making in Tripoli a generation ago, although olive-growing villages continued to make their own until recently. One of the only hopes for the survival of the craft, say soap makers, is tourism, and for this reason they are rebranding their old-fashioned wares with words like 'aromatherapy', and betting that the trend for all-natural, handmade beauty products in the West will result in higher sales.

is thought to have been built at the beginning of the 14th century and is in need of restoration. Used by Egyptian merchants, the building has a traditional khan design, with two arcaded storeys built around an open courtyard.

Hammam Izz ed-Dine (No 11) Izz ed-Dine Aybak was the Mamluk governor of Tripoli at the end of the 13th century, and he not only donated this bath to the city but gave orders to be buried beside it (his mausoleum can be seen next to the hammam). The building incorporates remains from an earlier Crusader church and hospice. It was heavily damaged during the civil war and derelict at the time of writing (although it could be visited), but is slated for restoration.

Khan al-Khayyatin (No 12) Beside Hammam Izz ed-Dine is the beautifully restored Khan al-Khayyatin, or Tailors' Market, which was built in the first half of the 14th century, making it one of the city's oldest khans. It was probably built on top of an earlier Byzantine and Crusader building that was part of the commercial suburb built by Raymond de Saint-Gilles to control trade into the area. Because of this it has a different plan to most of the other khans in the city: consisting of a long east-west passageway with tall arches on either side and ten transverse arches. The eastern end opens onto the street running along the Nahr Abu Ali.

Burtasiya Mosque & Madrassa (No 19) Situated by the river, across the street from the eastern entrance to the Khan al-Khayyatin, is the Burtasiya Mosque and Madrassa. Built by the Kurdish prince Sharafeddin Issa ben Omar al-Burtasi in 1315, its square, tower-like minaret and black-and-white stonework are particularly fine. Inside, the intricately decorated and inlaid mihrab makes the visit worthwhile. Look for the mosaic in its half-dome.

Souq al-Haraj (No 21) At the northern end of the old town is the Souq al-Haraj, which is thought to have been built on the site of a Crusader church. Its high, vaulted ceiling is supported by 14 granite columns, two in the centre and the other 12 around the side, which probably came from the earlier structure. Today the souq specialises in mats, pillows and mattresses.

Khan al-Askar (No 33) Just around the corner from the Souq al-Haraj is the Khan al-Askar, or Soldiers' Khan, which consists of two buildings joined by a vaulted passage. It is thought to have been built in the late 13th or early 14th century and was restored in the 18th century.

Taynal Mosque (No 31) Standing on its own to the south of the souqs, but well worth the few minutes walk it takes to get there, is one of the most outstanding examples of

Islamic religious architecture in Tripoli, the Taynal Mosque. Built in 1336 by Sayf ed-Din Taynal on the ruins of an earlier Carmelite church, it still has a partially preserved Carmelite nave in the first prayer hall. Other recycled elements, including two rows of Egyptian granite columns topped with late Roman capitals, were taken from an earlier monument. The simplicity of the bare stone walls contrasts beautifully with some of the Mamluk decorative elements, in particular the entrance to the second prayer hall, a masterpiece of alternating black-and-white bands of stone with Arabic inscriptions, marble panels with geometric designs and a honeycombed semidome.

Al-Mina

Al-Mina is situated on a headland and three main avenues run from the old part of Tripoli down to the port. Until a few decades ago the avenues ran between orange groves, but these have now been built over, mostly with residential developments and shops – testament to the city's rapidly expanding population. Although the history of the port area stretches back far further than the medieval city, there is almost noth-

ing of this earlier occupation left today. Instead, the area has a seaside air, with families promenading along the Corniche or eating at the seafront restaurants.

Burj es-Sabaa (Lion Tower) The only monument of real interest in Al-Mina is the miniature fortress at the eastern end of the harbour called the Lion Tower. It is separated from Al-Mina proper by old railway sidings. Named after the bas-relief decorations of lions that used to line the facade, the building dates from the end of the 15th century and was probably built by Mamluk sultan Qaitbey to protect the coastline against attack from the Ottomans. It is an exceptional example of Mamluk military architecture with a striking black-and-white striped portico. The whole of the ground floor is one vast chamber that used to be decorated with paintings and armorial carvings, traces of which you can still see. The upper floor has eight rooms opening onto a central hall. At the top there is a terrace, which has views over the city and a harbour area. The only other remains of ancient Tripoli are a few dejected-looking Roman columns in a park close to the seafront and

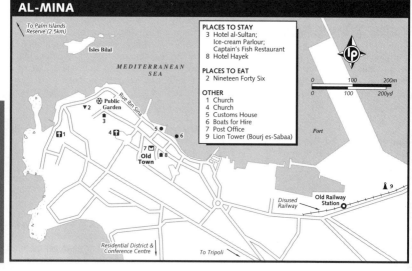

AL-MINA

PLACES TO STAY
3 Hotel al-Sultan;
   Ice-cream Parlour;
   Captain's Fish Restaurant
8 Hotel Hayek

PLACES TO EAT
2 Nineteen Forty Six

OTHER
1 Church
4 Church
5 Customs House
6 Boats for Hire
7 Post Office
9 Lion Tower (Bourj es-Sabaa)

To Palm Islands Reserve (2.5km)

Isles Bilal

MEDITERRANEAN SEA

Rue Ibn Sina

Public Garden

Old Town

Port

Disused Railway

Old Railway Station

Residential District & Conference Centre

To Tripoli

the remains of an Ottoman khan that has been converted into apartments.

Boat Rides Along the seafront there are many boats available to take people to the small islands just offshore. A return trip takes about two hours (with time for a swim). The fare for a return trip is LL5000 or, if there is a group, you can hire the entire boat (10 to 12 persons) for LL50,000.

Palm Islands Reserve The Palm Islands Reserve consists of three islands, Palm, Sanani and Ramkine, that lie 5km off the shore of Al-Mina. The protected area covers almost 5 sq km of land and sea and represent an eastern Mediterranean marine ecosystem. The site is particularly significant as a resting and nesting place for migratory birds. Over 300 species have been observed here, including seven that are threatened worldwide, and 11 others that are rare in Europe. In recent years, the threatened Mediterranean turtle has also come here to lay eggs.

As well as providing a haven for fauna, the islands are rich in wildflowers and biologists hope that the area could serve as a natural botanical conservatory for eastern Mediterranean coastal species under threat from the area's coastal development.

On Palm Island there are some 2500 palm trees, and paths have been laid out for visitors. There are also beaches and you can swim from one island to the other, or have a picnic while you watch the birds and wildlife.

Although the islands are open to the public, you need a permit, which you can get from the tourist office in Beirut or Tripoli. You will have to negotiate with one of the boat owners to take you there and back; expect to pay about LL20,000.

Places to Stay

Compared to other parts of Lebanon, Tripoli has quite a few cheap hotels, mostly clustered around Rue Tall.

Places to Stay – Budget

Palace Hotel (☎ 432 257, Rue Tall) is in a beautiful old building with high ceilings and stained glass windows. The inside doesn't quite live up to the exterior's promise, but the management is friendly and charges US$10 per person for doubles with shared bath and US$15/25/30 in singles/doubles/triples with private bathroom and air-con.

By far the best place in town is the *Hotel Koura (☎ cell 03-326 803, Rue Izz ed-Dine)*. Run by a brother and sister, the Koura is more a pension than a hotel and has a homey feel. Singles/doubles cost US$10/20 with shared bath. Two rooms have been nicely renovated, their old stone walls exposed and new wooden ceilings built. They have private baths and air-con, and cost US$30 for the double, US$45 for the triple.

Pension Haddad (☎ cell 03-507 709, 03-361 349) is on a side street off Rue Tall. It is small, friendly and kept spotlessly clean by the Haddad family, who live here. Rooms with shared bath cost US$7/10.

Hotel al-Tall (☎ 628 404, Rue Tall) is clean, if somewhat tacky with smoked mirrors and embellished furniture. Rooms come in several permutations. The cheapest are US$10 per person without bath or breakfast. Doubles with bath and air-con go for US$26. Breakfast is US$5.

The family-run *Hotel Hayek (☎ 601 311, Rue ibn Sina)* in Al-Mina is in a charming old (pink) house on the Corniche. It has clean rooms and seaviews at US$20 for double or triple rooms with baths, including breakfast. There's a supermarket and a cafe with a billiard table on the ground floor. The hotel entrance is around the back; if the door is shut, ask at the supermarket.

Hotel Central (☎ 441 544) is on the 6th floor of a dilapidated modern block on a side street close to the tourist office. If you can ignore the filth of the stairwell, the rooms are large and are not bad for US$10 per person.

Places to Stay – Mid-Range

Hotel al-Sultan (☎ 601 627, 611 640, Rue ibn Sina) is in a great location, right on the Corniche, on the corner of Rue al-Meshti. Unfortunately the rooms are shabby and are not worth the price (US$30/46 for singles/doubles, including breakfast) even with TV, minibar and air-con.

Places to Stay – Top End

Tripoli's most expensive hotel is *Chateau des Oliviers*, more commonly known as the *Villa Nadia* (☎ 629 271, cell 03-228 432, fax 440 981, ✉ info@villanadia.com). This is a modern mansion converted into a hotel by the owner Nadia Dibo. It is set high on a hill a few kilometres south of the city in the Haykalieh region and has 22 rooms and six suites, as well as a garden and a swimming pool. But the reason to come here is Madame Nadia herself. She somehow manages to be flamboyant, charming and maternal all at once, and she is a larger-than-life repository of fascinating tales (ask her about the fighting in Tripoli in 1982–83). She has a book with the names of what seem like hundreds of journalists who've stayed here (she calls them her 'children'), many of them now household names. The hotel has suffered with the lack of tourism over recent years, but the redoubtable Nadia carries on anyway, hopeful that the new political situation will reopen the floodgates of visitors. A night here costs you between US$90 and US$300, including breakfast, but discounts are sometimes available so it's always worth asking. Fixed-price lunch or dinner is available from US$20.

Places to Eat

On and around Rue Tall there are several simple restaurants serving *shwarma* (meat sliced off a spit and stuffed into bread) for LL1500 and felafels for only LL750. You can also get a plate of *fuul* (fava bean paste) or hummus for LL1500. *Restaurant al-Soufi* on the corner of Rue Tall and Rue Mohammed Karameh, is one of the better fast-food places and has some tables where you can sit and eat. This area also has a number of juice stands, where you can get a glass of freshly squeezed fruit and vegetable juice for about LL3000. There's a good hummus shop in the souqs, right by Al-Muallaq Mosque. There is also the fantastic, traditional and cavernous *Café Fahim*, which has a terrace overlooking Jamal Abdel Nasser Square and serves tea and nargileh.

The best place to eat in the Old City is *Restaurant Bebars* (☎ 443 445, cell 03-258

163, *Rue Rachid Karami*), in a restored 800-year-old stone house just down the hill from the Citadel of Raymond de Saint-Gilles. It serves reasonably priced Lebanese food. There is a small selection of mezze (starters), and *shish tawouq* (marinated chicken on skewers) or shwarma platters are a reasonable LL5000. Although the menu is essentially Lebanese fast food, it is freshly prepared, and sitting under a stone vault while listening to traditional oud music only adds to the taste. Afterwards you can smoke a nargileh while reclining on carpeted benches.

If you're hankering after Beirut-style sleek surroundings, there's a branch of *The Chase* (☎ 442 469) on the main road beside the City Complex on Rue Riad al-Solh (Rue Mina). Like its counterpart in Beirut, it serves international dishes (a meal costs about US$15) and is open until 24 hours a day.

In Al-Mina, *Captain's Fish Restaurant* (☎ 613 031, Rue ibn Sina), places the catch of the day on ice and sells it by weight. Fish is not cheap so expect to pay about US$20 to US$30 per person for two, with reasonable mezze. There's an *ice-cream parlour* downstairs that does a roaring trade with families out for an evening stroll along the Corniche.

If you're sick of mezze and grills, *Nineteen Forty Six* (☎ 212 223, Rue ibn Sina) is a trendily decorated restaurant/cafe with great views over the Corniche. It serves Western-style pastas and steaks, with mains starting at US$5. Expect to pay about US$12 for a steak meal. It is open until 11.30 pm daily.

Tripoli is famous for its pastries. *Rafaat Hallab et Fils* (☎ 432 295, Rue Tall and branches throughout the city) is one of the best patisseries in Lebanon and is *the* place to try Tripoli's sweet specialties. *Halawet ej-jibna* is a sinfully sweet concoction of a special cream cheese drenched in sugar syrup, rose-water, ground pistachios, preserved lemon peel and (amazingly) cream. Another regional speciality is *mafrouqeh*, a sugar and butter mixture covered with rose-water and sugar syrup and topped with cream, almonds and pine nuts. *Zinoud is-sitt* are long, plump white pastries stuffed with cream that are supposed to resemble a woman's upper arms. Rafaat Hallab also has a Web site (www.hallab.com) and delivers its famed pastries all over the world.

Entertainment

A far more conservative town than Beirut, Tripoli is pretty dead at night. There are, however, a couple of cinemas: *The Rivoli*, a sleazy-looking place on Rue Fouad Chehab, close to Rue Tall; and the far better *Ciné Planéte (☎ 442 471, Al-Mina Ave, City Complex)*, which shows the latest release English-language movies with Arabic subtitles. Tickets are LL10,000 per person (half price on Monday).

Shopping

Exploring the old souqs is the best way to shop in Tripoli. If you are looking for jewellery, there is a whole souq devoted to gold (Souq as-Sayyaghin). If you are looking for a more modest souvenir, then head for the brass souq (Souq an-Nahhassin). Even if you don't want to buy, it is well worth a visit just to see the metalworkers making pieces by hand in the same way that they have done for centuries. For traditional handmade soap, head to Khan as-Saboun at the end of the gold souq. Note that many shops in the souqs close on Friday.

Getting There & Away

Bus & Service Taxi   Buses to Charles Helou and Dawra in Beirut leave from the area around the public gardens. Ahdab Co (☎ 433 656) has buses leaving every 15 minutes from 5 am until 7 pm. Tickets cost LL1500 for regular service, LL2000 for buses with air-con and video. You can get off on the highway for Byblos or any other coastal town along the way.

Tripoli Express (☎ cell 03-575 844) has buses to Beirut's National Museum as well as Charles Helou starting at 5.30 am. The small buses (nonsmoking) depart roughly every 15 minutes and tickets cost LL1500.

The service taxi stand for Beirut is on Rue Tall by the clock tower and public gardens. There are frequent departures to Beirut and the fare is LL5000.

Tripoli is a good place from which to visit Bcharré, the Cedars and the Qadisha Valley.

The taxi stand to this area is on Koura Square. Service taxis to Bcharré (about 40 minutes) charge LL5000 and to the Cedars LL6000 (almost an hour). With a private taxi you can get to the Cedars for LL15,000 or to Ehden for LL20,000.It is possible to get a service taxi to Baalbek from Tripoli, but departures are infrequent. If you are lucky enough to find one, it should cost LL8000. Otherwise a taxi will charge at least LL40,000, if you negotiate hard.

To Syria & Turkey Transtour (☎ cell 03-411 015) offers a bus service to Syria and beyond to Turkey. They leave when full from the Transtour office. Fares range from LL5000 to LL8000 for Syria (see the Fares to Syria table in the Getting There & Away chapter). Buses to Homs, Hama and Aleppo (Halab) leave hourly between 9 am and 12 noon. There are two departures to Damascus, one at 5 am and the other at 3 pm. There is a daily bus to Lattakia and Tartus at 3.30 pm. Services to Turkey range from US$30 to US$35 and take about 24 hours. There are service taxis to Syria all around Sahet et-Tall and fares range from LL7000 to Homs and LL16,000 to Damascus.

Getting Around

Local taxis can be flagged on the street and charge LL500 for a short hop within the city (LL1000 to Al-Mina). Private taxis within the city cost LL2500. There is a stand beside the Burtasiya Mosque, close to the river at the northern end of the medieval town.

Around Tripoli

QUBBET AL-BEDDAWI

قبّة البدّاوي

This sanctuary, built upon the site of the Crusader Priory of St Anthony of Padua, is only 3km east of Tripoli near the main Lattakia highway. It is famous as a small **monastery of dervishes** (that's right, the whirling variety), but people visit mainly to see the **sacred pool** of fish which is thought to have originated in antiquity as a pool sacred to Astarte, goddess of fertility. The crescent-shaped pool has thousands of carp which have been worshipped since ancient times. A nearby spring keeps the water clear. Fish were considered sacred by the Phoenicians, being connected to the idea of the egg from which Tanit, the chief goddess of Carthage, hatched. These carp, some of which live to be 200 years old, are often fed chickpeas by visitors.

It is a short ride by taxi from central Tripoli – only about 10 minutes. The fare should be about LL3000.

ENFE
أَنْفَا

☎ 06

On the coast 15km south of Tripoli is the village of Enfe (the name means 'nose' in honour of the shape of the coastline). Nowadays this is a largely Greek Orthodox town, but during the Crusades, this was the town of Nephim, a fief of the County of Tripoli. The lords of Nephim played an important role here and later moved to Cyprus in the 13th century. There is very little left of the Crusader castle, except for a few ruined stone walls. Several vaults carved into the rock remain, and the most interesting relics are two **Crusader moats**, one of which is over 40m long.

The castle had a sadistic history: the lord of Nephim, Count Bohemond VII, walled up his rivals, the Embiaci, in the castle. This grisly scene was later recalled in Edgar Allan Poe's story, *The Cask of Amontillado*.

There are also four **churches**, one of which is Byzantine with the remains of painted murals. It is romantically named 'Our Lady of the Wind'. The Church of the Holy Sepulchre dates from the time of Bohemond in the 12th century and is still very much in use.

As the coast is clean and attractive in this part of Lebanon, it has not escaped the developer's meddling. ***Marina del Sol (☎ 541 301, cell 03-331 466/77)*** is yet another big resort, with apartments that are rented or leased, usually by the season. A family apartment costs from US$125 per night without breakfast, and US$150 with breakfast. Nearby is ***Las Salinas (☎ 540 970)*** with the same resort facilities at similar prices.

Enfe is on the service taxi route between Tripoli, Byblos and Beirut, so it is easy to get to; simply ask the driver to drop you at the turn-off. You will probably be charged the full service-taxi fare to Tripoli (LL5000). Alternatively, a taxi from Tripoli will cost about LL7000.

CHEKKA
شِكَّا

☎ 06

A coastal town just south of Enfe, Chekka seems at first glance to be a place to be avoided at all costs. The town is dominated by a hideous cement works that does nothing for its ambience. Amazingly enough, there are a few quite upmarket hotels here. The reason is a sandy **beach** and good, safe bathing. Along the coast in this region are also many saltpans where sea water evaporates in shallow pools by the sea to leave behind salt crystals.

A road climbs to a wooded headland to the south of Chekka, where an old **monastery** nestles at the top. The views from here are great.

QALAMOUN

Yet another small village north of Enfe, this one is worth mentioning for one reason: the stretch of shops selling really good copper and brass ware. You can't miss them as they are all together on the main road which runs through the village. There are old and new pieces on sale and the prices are reasonable. This is the place to practise your haggling skills.

BALAMAND
بَلَمَند

☎ 06

High above the village of Qalamoun, overlooking the old Tripoli to Beirut road, is the **Greek Orthodox abbey** of Balamand (or Belmont). This started out as a Cistercian abbey founded in 1157. It is possibly even older than this, as it was built on the site of a Byzantine monastery. The Cistercians either abandoned it or were driven out, possibly in 1289 when the Mamluk sultan Qalaun took Tripoli.

The monastery underwent major restoration work several centuries ago and the

Crusader buildings are all but lost to later designs. The Church of Our Lady of Balamand is very pretty with its bell tower intact. The church interior has been carefully restored and is worth seeing for the fine icons set into a carved screen behind the altar. The great hall of the abbey with its vaulted ceiling is now used for concerts and recitals.

These days the abbey is a university. It is the principal seat of learning in the north of Lebanon as well as a cultural and religious centre. You can ring the abbey for information (☎ 400 740, 400 742).

Balamand is 12km south of Tripoli. Taxis leave from the main stand on Rue Tall.

Qadisha Valley   وادي قاديشا

One of the most beautiful spots in Lebanon, the Qadisha Valley is a long deep gorge that starts near Batroun in the west and rises dramatically to its head just beyond the town of Bcharré. Villages with red-tiled roofs perch atop hills or cling precariously to the mountainsides. The Qadisha River, or Nahr Abu Ali, with its source just below the

Cedars, runs along the valley bottom and Lebanon's highest peak, Qornet as-Sawda towers overhead.

The word Qadisha comes from the Semitic root for 'holy' and the valley's steep, rocky sides have made it a natural fortress for persecuted religious minorities for millennia. From the 5th century onwards, the Maronites made this area their refuge and the valley is scattered with rock-cut monasteries, hermitages and churches. Today, the villages perched atop the cliffs surrounding the valley are almost exclusively Maronite.

Because of its natural beauty and unique history the Qadisha Valley has been recognised as a world heritage site by Unesco, although this hasn't prevented its environment from coming under threat. Until recently, local visitors would drive their cars down into the valley and hunt. Garbage was often dumped in the area (there are still huge piles of rubbish higher up on the road between Bcharré and the Cedars) and sewage was pumped into the river from the surrounding villages. But the construction of a waste-water treatment plan, enforcement of driving and hunting bans and clean-up efforts are all paying off.

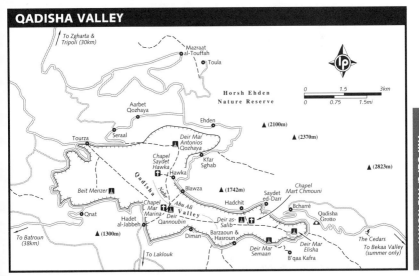

QADISHA VALLEY

Map locations include: To Zgharta & Tripoli (30km), Mazraat al-Touffah, Toula, Horsh Ehden Nature Reserve, Aarbet Qozhaya, Ehden, Tourza, Seraal, Deir Mar Antonios Qozhaya, Chapel Saydet Hawka, Hawka, Kfar Sghab, Beit Menzer, Blawza, Chapel Mart Chmouni, Saydet ed-Darr, Bcharré, Qnat, Chapel Mar Marina, Deir Qannoubin, Hadchit, Qadisha Grotto, Hadet al-Jabbeh, Diman, Deir as-Salib, Barzaoun & Hasroun, To Batroun (38km), To Laklouk, Deir Mar Semaan, Deir Mar Elisha, B'qaa Kafra, The Cedars, To Bekaa Valley (summer only). Peak elevations: (2100m), (2370m), (2823m), (1742m), (1300m). Scale: 0 – 1.5 – 3km / 0 – 0.75 – 1.5mi.

Although the valley is nearly 50km long, the main area of interest is the higher 20km section from Tourza up to the Qadisha Grotto. This is a hiker's paradise with numerous waterfalls, rock-carved tombs and monasteries, and stunning scenery.

EHDEN أهدن

☎ 06

Easily reached from Tripoli via a brief stretch of highway that runs as far as Zgharta, Ehden, on the northern rim of the Qadisha Valley, is a popular summer resort with a picturesque old centre dominated by a lively main square lined with cafes.

Opposite the square, a small street leads up to St George's Church, where there is an equestrian **statue** of Youssef Bey Karam, a 19th-century nationalist hero who led rebellions against Ottoman rule with the support of other religious communities, as well as his fellow Maronites. He was killed by the Turks near Ehden and his mummified body, dressed in a gold-braided traditional costume, lies in a glass-topped sarcophagus against the southern wall of St George's Church. His descendants remain prominent in the area

To the north-west of the village on a hill is the tiny **chapel** of Our Lady of the Castle, which is thought to have been a Roman lookout post originally. Now the chapel is dwarfed by the enormous modernist eyesore of the same name.

Places to Stay & Eat

Most people who visit the Qadisha Valley stay in either Bcharré or the Cedars, but there are alternatives in Ehden. The *Grand Hotel Abchi* (*☎ 560 001, fax 561 103*) is a modern hotel with a UFO-like disco, which overlooks the village from the west. A double room costs US$54 and a suite costs US$80.

Hotel La Mairie (*☎ 560 108, Rue Dawalib*) is on the main road of the village and is open all year. Singles/doubles with breakfast cost US$50/60, including breakfast.

Ehden is famous for its restaurants that overlook the Nebaa Mar Sarkis, or Mar Sarkis Spring, as it emerges from the hillside to the north-east of village. About four restaurants cluster around the source, and they all serve traditional Lebanese food with huge mezze spreads. The most famous are *Al-Arze* (*☎ 560 226*) and *Nabeh Mar Sarkis al-Asmar* (*☎ 560 150*). On summer evenings, many also lay on live music and dancing. Expect to pay at least US$20 per head.

There are several other cheaper restaurants. *Au Père Loup* (*☎ 662 413, Dawalib St*) and *Restaurant al-Rabiah* (*☎ 661 806, Rue Dawalib*) both serve Lebanese food for slightly less (US$10 to US$20 per person) than the restaurants overlooking Nebaa Mar Sarkis; Al-Rabiah also offers entertainment in the summer.

For Lebanese fast food, there are a number of cafes around the main square in the old part of town where you can sit under the trees and order *lahma bi ajeen* (spicy meat pizza) or shwarma for about LL1500 while you sip your tea or beer.

The Darker Side of Eden

With its well-kept buildings, bustling square and beautiful scenery, Ehden and its environs do not bring mafia-style violence to mind. Yet the pastoral bliss of the Qadisha can be deceptive. Although the Maronites may have sheltered here from the persecution visited on them by other sects, both Christian and Muslim, they have recently managed to visit some pretty impressive violence upon themselves too, based upon the local proverb 'the enemy of my grandfather can never be my friend'.

In one of the most notorious events of the civil war, Samir Geagea, of Bcharré amassed several hundred militiamen, went into the home of Tony Franjieh (son of President Suleiman Franjieh) in Ehden and killed him and his entire family as he slept. While this was explained by political differences between the two families, in fact it had its roots in a Hatfield and McCoy-like feud between the Geageas and the Franjiehs that dates back to the 19th century. At that time, according to local (Bcharré) lore, a Geagea woman was killed by two Ehden men after offering them water and food. In response Bcharré's residents burned down the town of Ehden and killed many of its inhabitants.

Getting There & Away

If you are taking a service taxi from Tripoli to Bcharré, you can ask the driver to drop you at Ehden or any other point en route along the north side of the valley. If you want to get to the south side of the valley, you will have to go to Bcharré and get a taxi from there. A service taxi to any point from Ehden to Bcharré will cost LL5000. There are also microbuses that ply the rim of the valley; they pass by about six times a day and cost LL2500.

You would be better off with your own transport to explore this part of Lebanon. If you don't have a car, it might be worth hiring a car and driver for the day. Your hotel can arrange this. Expect to pay from US$80 to US$100 for a whole day, which is not too bad if there are a few of you to share the cost.

HORSH EHDEN NATURE RESERVE محميّة حرش أهدن

Just over 3km from Ehden is the nature reserve of Horsh Ehden, a 17 sq km mountainous ecosystem. Run by the Ehden municipality you can arrange a visit by calling the reserve manager Sarkis Khawaja (☎ cell 03-389 973).

Although the reserve covers less than 1% of Lebanon's total area, some 40% of the country's plant species have been found within its borders. There are 1058 species of plants, 12% of which are threatened. Ten species are unique to the reserve. The reserve also has one of the largest stands of native cedar in Lebanon, mixed with varieties of juniper, conifer, wild apple and others.

Like much of Lebanon, it is a nesting place for birds and also provides a refuge for some of Lebanon's endangered mammals, which include a species of squirrel (*Sciurus anomalus syriacus*), martens (*Martes foina cyriaca*), weasels (*Mustela nivalis*) and badgers (*Meles meles canescens*). Wolves and hyenas have also been spotted here, as have wild boars. The latter are thought to have been introduced to the area from France as recently as the mid-1990s. They have nol predators and have been damaging the reserve's flora and the reserve's management is thinking of organising expensive hunting trips to raise revenue and cull the growing numbers

KFAR SGHAB كفر صغاب

The small village of Kfar Sghab is 4km east of Ehden. Australians, particularly Sydney-siders, passing through here might be surprised to see a sign announcing Parramatta Rd on the main street. More surprising still, if you say hello to almost any of the 750 inhabitants of the village you're likely to hear 'g'day mate' thrown back at you. There's even a Para Cafe just off the main road in the centre of the village.

The reason for this surreal connection between a village in the Qadisha and a used-car strip in Sydney? A staggering 15,000 Australian Lebanese trace their roots back to this area. Many have returned to Lebanon since the war ended and are building summer homes here.

HADCHIT حدشيت

This village is 3km west of Bcharré, about 1km off the main valley road on the north side. The **Church of St Raymond** is its dominant feature. Outside is a headless Roman statue which used to be inside until one day somebody realised it was a pagan idol and smashed off its head and arms. Starting on the last Sunday of August each year the village celebrates the feast of St Raymond.

There is a very steep path that descends from here to **Deir as-Salib**, a tiny monastery cut into the cliffs below the village.

BCHARRÉ نشرّي و
☎ 06

The main town in the Qadisha Valley is Bcharré, a quaint, red-roofed town perched on the side of the valley and famous as the birthplace of the 19th-century poet and artist, Khalil Gibran. In Phoenician times the town was known as Beit Chari and later, during the Crusades, as Buissera, when it was one of the fiefs of the County of Tripoli.

Apart from the lush natural scenery, the town is dominated by three large churches, which were built and subsequently rebuilt by the leading families of the town in ever more imposing styles. The largest, St Saba

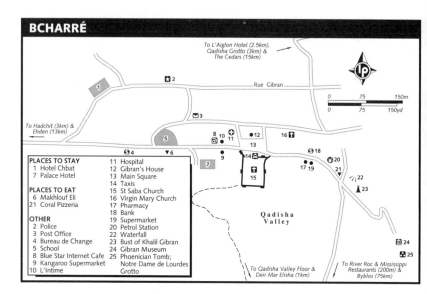

BCHARRÉ

To L'Aiglon Hotel (2.5km),
Qadisha Grotto (3km) &
The Cedars (15km)

Rue Gibran

To Hadchit (3km) &
Ehden (13km)

PLACES TO STAY
1 Hotel Chbat
7 Palace Hotel

PLACES TO EAT
6 Makhlouf Eli
21 Coral Pizzeria

OTHER
2 Police
3 Post Office
4 Bureau de Change
5 School
8 Blue Star Internet Cafe
9 Kangaroo Supermarket
10 L'Intime

11 Hospital
12 Gibran's House
13 Main Square
14 Taxis
15 St Saba Church
16 Virgin Mary Church
17 Pharmacy
18 Bank
19 Supermarket
20 Petrol Station
22 Waterfall
23 Bust of Khalil Gibran
24 Gibran Museum
25 Phoenician Tomb;
Notre Dame de Lourdes
Grotto

Qadisha
Valley

To Qadisha Valley Floor &
Deir Mar Elisha (1km)

To River Roc & Mississippi
Restaurants (200m) &
Byblos (75km)

Church, is more like a small cathedral perched on the edge of the gorge.

Opposite St Saba is a small village square where you will find Khalil Gibran's house, which is empty inside.

Information

There is a post office and public telephone bureau on Rue Gibran in the centre of town, north of the main square. It is open from 8 am to 1 pm daily. The Blue Star Internet cafe on the main street charges LL4000 per hour for Internet use. Next door is a shop, L'Intime, that doubles as a private telephone office and charges US$1 per hour for overseas calls. Across from here is the Kangaroo Supermarket, where the Australian connection (see Kfar Sghab) continues with the owner, a returnee from Sydney who stocks a few Australian goodies.

Gibran Museum

Bcharré's most famous citizen is Khalil Gibran, the poet and artist whose tomb and museum are just outside the town. To get there, drive through the main street and turn right at the huge bust of Gibran that sits on a cliff (unfortunately overshadowed by a

huge concrete structure that looks suspiciously like it will be large hotel).

The museum is in a beautiful stone building that has an interesting history of its own. It was originally a hermitage, beside which a residence was built for the papal nuncio in the 15th century. Eventually, the hermitage and residence, and some adjacent hermits caves, were incorporated into a monastery. In the 16th century the French consul spent his summers taking in the building's stunning views over the valley and, in the 17th century, it was donated to some local Carmelite monks. Gibran bought it from the monks with the idea of retiring here, but he died a short time later.

The museum has brought together a huge number of Gibran's paintings, as well as his personal effects. The air of hushed reverence, enhanced by new-agey flute music is a bit much, but seeing Gibran's work in the beautiful setting is worth the annoyance. His talent as a visual artist is a pleasant surprise for those who only know him as a writer and his work is reminiscent of William Blake. Some of his charcoal portraits are particularly fine.

The museum is about 15 minutes walk from the centre of town up a steep hill and is open from 9 am to 5 pm daily, except Monday. Entrance costs LL3000 and there are booklets available in English and French.

Notre Dame de Lourdes Grotto

Part way up a small path near the museum is a small cave with a spring dedicated to the Virgin Mary. Local legend has it that she took pity on a Carmelite gardener-monk who had to carry water up to the monastery each day to water his vegetable patch. Small candles and statuettes sit on an altar that has been built around the spring.

Phoenician Tomb

Just up the hill from the grotto is a large stone obelisk thought to date back to 750 BC. At the base of the obelisk is a burial chamber and ledges for four coffins.

Qadisha Grotto مفارة قادشيا

On the road to the Cedars at the L'Aiglon Hotel is a signposted path that leads to the cave where the Qadisha River originates. The gushing water has carved a tunnel out of the rock and behind this is a larger cavern with stalagmites and stalactites. The cavern isn't as awesome as Jeita, but is worth a look for its stunning views over the valley, as much as for the grotto itself. The grotto is open from 9 am to 7 pm during summer. Entry costs LL2000.

Places to Stay & Eat

In the centre of town, is the *Palace Hotel - (☎ 671 460)*, which is a smallish place with 24 rooms, all with bath and air-con. Singles/doubles/triples cost US$30/40/48 including service tax. Breakfast is an extra US$4.50.

L'Aiglon Hotel (☎ 671 529) between Bcharré and the Cedars, was closed at the time of writing.

The best hotel in town is the *Hotel Chbat (☎ 671 237, 671 270)*, built in 1955 on the side of a hill in the upper part of Bcharré and with views across the Qadisha Valley. It has a relaxed and homely atmosphere with big open fires and a Lebanese cook who has been with the hotel since it opened. Rooms cost US$65/78/88 plus

Khalil Gibran (1883–1931)

Gibran Khalil Gibran is Lebanon's most famous and celebrated literary figure. He was a philosophical essayist, novelist, mystic poet and painter whose influences were the Bible, Nietzsche and William Blake. He's mostly known in the West as Khalil Gibran, author of *The Prophet*.

He was born in Bcharré on 6 January 1883. Having received his primary education in Beirut, he emigrated with his parents to the US where he lived in Boston. Returning to Beirut in 1898 he continued his studies with an emphasis on classical Arabic. On his return to Boston in 1903 he published his first literary essays and met Mary Haskell. She became his benefactor and remained so for the rest of his life.

His artistic tutelage came under Auguste Rodin during a stay in Paris in 1909, and it was during this period that he developed his visual art skills. In 1912 he went to New York and continued to write literary essays and short stories. He began painting in a highly romanticised, mystical style strongly reminiscent of William Blake.

When he died in 1931, his body was returned to Lebanon and he now lies in a casket at the Gibran Museum in Bcharré. Some of his personal possessions are with him in the former monastery building, including an ancient Armenian tapestry portraying the crucifixion scene in which Christ is smiling.

14% service, with discounts of about US$12 in the off season. The price includes breakfast. Unusually, the hotel also has a couple of dormitories for groups and students who want budget accommodation. To qualify, there needs to be at least 10 people in your party and you need to book in advance. This is popular with school skiing groups in winter. In summer there is a swimming pool. Lunch or dinner in the restaurant costs from US$10 to US$15.

There are a couple of restaurants in town. *Makhlouf Elie*, on the western side of town, is a small restaurant with a rooftop terrace and fantastic views. It serves mezze and sandwiches for about US$5. *Coral Pizza* is an outdoor cafeteria which is just below the waterfall at the eastern edge of town and has pizzas and snacks (summer only).

Along the road at the head of the valley, just outside Bcharré, are several restaurants which take advantage of the views along the gorge. *River Roc* is a restaurant/nightclub with Lebanese food for about US$20 per person. *Mississippi*, next door, has similar prices but also sells snacks.

THE CEDARS
أرز بشرّي

☎ 06

'The Cedars' is a name used for both the small grove of trees which stands at an altitude of more than 2000m on the slopes of Jebel Makmel and the ski resort a couple of kilometres further up the road. The famous trees, about 4km from Bcharré, are the remnant of a vast forest of cedar which once covered the mountains of Lebanon (see the boxed text 'The Cedar Tree' opposite).

A few of the trees are very old; all are at least 200 years old and it's thought that some may reach an age of 1500 years. Three centuries ago there were more trees: in 1550 there were 28 trees over 1000 years old; in 1660 there were 22; and in 1696, only 16. Today there are 12. These days it is strictly forbidden to cut down the trees, which are known locally as Arz ar-Rab (Cedars of the Lord). They are under the protection of the Patriarch of Lebanon, who built a chapel in the cedar grove in 1848. Each year in August there is a festival here presided over by the patriarch himself.

The grove of cedars is protected by a fence and you can visit every day all year. They look particularly dramatic against a backdrop of snow. Occasionally, access to the grove is restricted, for example when the snow is melting, so as not to cause damage to the roots from people walking on them when the ground is too soft.

About 2km further up the road is the ski station which has a small village of shops and hotels around the ski lifts. There are also equipment-hire shops. See the boxed text 'Ski Facts: The Cedars' for more details. The road which continues beyond this

---

Ski Facts: The Cedars

Altitude: 1850m to 3087m
Number of Lifts: Eight
Opening Hours: 8.30 am to 4 pm
Phone Numbers: ☎ 671 072/3, cell 03-342 762
Adult Day Pass: US$23 (weekends); US$16.50 (weekdays)

People first started coming to ski at the Cedars in the 1920s and the first lift was installed in 1953, making it Lebanon's oldest ski resort. While it is less developed than many of the other resorts, it is the second most-popular, particularly for those who actually ski (rather than pose). The runs are longer here and the quality of the snow better than at Lebanon's other resorts. At the moment there are four adult runs, two advanced, one intermediate and one beginner. There are also four nursery slopes for children. Equipment can be rented from a number of locations and there are Red Cross teams on hand at weekends.

---

point leads to the Bekaa Valley, but is only open during the summer months.

Hiking

Just north of the Cedars, near the ski hill entrance, is Makmel Park. A sign at the entrance says, 'This is Lebanon's last wild frontier and its natural water reservoir'. Distances and approximate times are written on the sign. They are: Dahr al-Kadib (3003m), 45 minutes; chairlift shelter station (2800m), one hour; Znanir (3075m) 1½ hours; Tem al-Mezreb (2971m), two hours; Qornet al-Mekfieh, 2½ hours; and Lebanon's highest peak, Qornet as-Sawda (3090m), three hours. The views from up here are spectacular and the hiking is not too difficult, although there are no set paths to follow. Also, the signs for each peak have blown off and only the posts remain. Remember to dress warmly; the peaks are windy and there can be snow up here as late as May.

Places to Stay & Eat

On the road between Bcharré and the Cedars is the *Alpine Hotel* (☎ 671 517),

The Cedar Tree

There are three or four species of cedar tree *(Cedrus Libani)* throughout North Africa and Asia. The most famous of these is the Cedar of Lebanon, which was mentioned in the Old Testament, although today only a few of the original groves still exist. In antiquity the cedar forests covered great swathes of the Mt Lebanon Range and provided a source of wealth for the Phoenicians who exported the fragrant and durable wood to Egypt and Palestine.

The original Temple of Solomon in Jerusalem was built of this wood, as were many sarcophagi discovered in Egypt. A slow but sure process of deforestation took place over the millennia, and although new trees are now being planted, it will be centuries before they mature.

Of the few remaining ancient trees, most are in the grove at the Cedars, above Bcharré, and in Barouk, in the Chouf, south of Beirut. Some of the trees at the Cedars are thought to be well over 1000 years old. Their trunks have a huge girth and their height can reach 30m. Naturally, there are strict rules about taking any timber from these remaining trees and the souvenirs for sale nearby are made from fallen branches.

which is cosy and quite simple. Bed and breakfast costs US$30 per person. If you are staying a few days, the Alpine offers half board for US$40 per day. Lunch or dinner costs from US$10 to US$15.

***St Bernard Hotel** (☎ cell 03-289 600)* is right by the forest grove and has 33 rooms that cost US$84/115 for singles/doubles with breakfast between December and April. The rest of the year, rooms are US$54/80. They offer a free shuttle service to the slopes.

Handy for the slopes is ***Hotel La Cabane** (☎ cell 03-321575)* which has a restaurant and bar. Rooms start from US$24 per person.

***Hotel Mon Refuge** (☎ 671 438)* has pleasant small single rooms for US$15 and doubles for US$30. Breakfast is US$5 extra. There are also apartments that sleep twelve and have fireplaces for US$120. Downstairs is a restaurant and bar that serves a mixture of Lebanese and Western food for around US$8 to US$15 per head.

Next door is ***Centre Tony Arida** (☎ 671 195)*, which has everything from apartments

that sleep up to eight people for US$300 per night (half price in spring and autumn) to a nightclub, a restaurant and a large selection of ski equipment to rent. Tony is a former ski champion turned jovial host, and he presides over his empire with good-natured gusto.

Getting There & Away

There are service taxis to Bcharré and the Cedars from the Rue Tall taxi stand in Tripoli. They charge LL6000 to Bcharré and LL10,000 to the Cedars. Outside the ski season there are only a few service taxis to Bcharré and you will have to take a regular taxi from there to the Cedars. The fare is about LL15,000 but you may be able to haggle the price down. In Bcharré, the taxis congregate by the St Saba Church and charge US$20 for a half-day tour around the Qadisha. There is a minibus at 7 am to Beirut's Dawra bus station for LL4000 (double-check beforehand). When the road is open you can also get a taxi to take you to Baalbek for US$40.

TRIPOLI & THE NORTH

THE QADISHA VALLEY FLOOR

The best way to hike into the valley is to take one of the steep goat tracks that leads out of Bcharré and into the valley below. If that's too strenuous, you can also drive your car to Deir Mar Elisha and park it there while you walk along the valley floor. A hike from Bcharré to Deir as-Salib takes about six hours, there and back. A hike from Bcharré to Deir Mar Antonios Qozhaya will take you the whole day. Remember to bring plenty of water; the river water is not clean enough to drink.

Deir Mar Elisha

Dramatic and beautiful, the monastery of Mar Elisha (St Eliseus) is built into the side of the cliffs below Bcharré. The Lebanese Maronite Order, the first order to be officially recognised by the Roman Catholic Church, was founded here in 1695. The building goes back much further – by the 14th century it was already the seat of a Maronite bishop. It was restored in 1991 and turned into a museum, and has displays of books and other artefacts relating to the monastery's history. The museum is on two storeys and to the right is a chapel containing the tomb of the Anchorite of Lebanon, François de Chasteuil (1588–1644).

You can get to the monastery from one of the tracks below Bcharré or take the main road heading east from Bcharré and, after 3km, turn off at the small blue sign for the Qadisha Valley. A narrow road winds down to the monastery.

If you follow the track west through the lush vegetation, after about 20 minutes you'll come to a picturesque riverside restaurant, *Greenland* (sign in Arabic only) that is only open during the summer months.

Chapel of Mart Chmouni

Built under a rocky ledge in the Middle Ages, this chapel has two constructed naves, one in a natural rock formation. Sadly the 13th-century paintings which adorn the walls have been covered with a layer of plaster.

The chapel is at the eastern end of the valley at the point where Wadi Houla and Wadi Qannoubin meet. You can follow a steep path down from Hadchit or you can get there along a path on the valley floor.

Deir as-Salib

This rock-cut monastery can be reached by a steep path to the right from the valley floor or from the village of Hadchit. As well as a chapel, there are a number of caves that were used as hermits' cells. Derelict and increasingly ruined, there are nevertheless still traces of Byzantine-era frescoes inside.

Deir Qannoubin

Continuing along the valley bottom, you will eventually come to a track to the left with signpost to Deir Qannoubin. The name Qannoubin is derived from the Greek *kenobion*, which means 'monastery'. This is a very ancient site. Some sources say that it was founded by Theodosius the Great in the late 4th century. Local legend has it that at the end of the 14th century, the Mamluk sultan Barquq (who was briefly overthrown in 1389) escaped from imprisonment in Karak Castle (now in Jordan) and sought refuge in the Qadisha before returning to Egypt to reclaim his throne. Such was the hospitality shown him that he paid for the restoration of the monastery. From 1440 through to the end of the 18th century, Deir Qannoubin was the Maronite patriarchal seat. Nowadays it is a working convent.

The church is half-built into the rock face and is decorated with frescoes dating from the 18th century. Near the entrance is a vault containing the naturally mummified body thought to be that of Patriarch Yousef Tyan. Deir Qannoubin can also be reached by a path leading from the village of Blawza, on the valley's northern rim. The hike takes about an hour each way.

Chapel of Mar Marina

Just to the west of the monastery is the chapel-cave of Mar Marina where the remains of 17 Maronite patriarchs are buried. Inside the grotto are several faded 13th-century frescoes depicting the life of the saint. See the boxed text 'The Marina Grotto' for more information.

The Marina Grotto

Just 4km north of Enfe, past the village of Qalamoun, is the Marina Grotto. It is about a 20-minute walk to the east of the village over stony slopes (you may need to ask directions). The grotto, with its orange-coloured rear wall, stands out against the grey rock of the rest of the escarpment.

The grotto was a sanctuary and has painted murals from two periods; the older inscriptions are in Greek. The pictures show scenes from the life of Saint Marina, whose story is a curious one.

Legend has it that Saint Marina was raised as a boy in a Maronite monastery where her father, a widower, became a monk. She grew up with the name Marinos and only her father and the abbot knew that she was female. When they died, she remained in the monastery as a monk. When a local girl bore a child (fathered by one of the monks), Marinos was accused of being responsible and banished from the monastery. She kept silent and took the abandoned child to live in the grotto where she miraculously nursed the child with her own milk. When she died, the truth of her sex became known and she was canonised. Her body was taken for burial in Constantinople where it lies in the Saint Marina Chapel.

The grotto became a place of pilgrimage for women who could not nurse their children and it is known locally as the Milk Grotto.

Chapel of Saydet Hawka

Continuing on the main track past the signpost for Deir Qannoubin and bearing right at the fork, you will eventually see Deir Saydet Hawka on the right. This is a small monastery consisting of a chapel and a few monks' cells within a cave. It is thought to date from the 13th century. It is associated with an attack by armed Mamluks against the natural fortress of Aassi Hawka, which is in a cave high above the monastery. The cave is only accessible to experienced rock climbers.

The monastery is deserted for most of the year but is used to celebrate the Feast of the Assumption of the Virgin with a high mass on the evening of 14 August. You can get there via a path from Hawka (about 30 minutes one way) or via the valley-floor path.

Deir Mar Antonios Qozhaya

Continuing on the main track, you will eventually come to Deir Mar Antonios Qozhaya. This hermitage is the largest in the valley and has been continually in use since it was founded in the 11th century. It is famous for establishing the first-known printing press in the Middle East in the 16th century. A museum houses a collection of religious and ethnographic objects as well as an old printing press which was used to publish the Psalms in Syriac, a language still used by the Maronites in their services. A popular place of pilgrimage, the hermitage also has a souvenir shop which sells all manner of kitsch religious knick-knacks. To see the museum you need to knock at the main building and get one of the monks to open it up for you.

Near the entrance to the monastery is the **Grotto of St Anthony**, known locally as the 'Cave of the Mad', where you can see the chains used to constrain the insane or possessed who were left at the monastery in the hope that the saint would cure them.

If you're not hiking, you can reach the monastery by car from Aarbet Qozhaya on the northern valley rim.

B'QAA KAFRA   بقاع كفرة

Back up above the valley, on the road between Bcharré and Hasroun, is B'qaa Kafra, the highest village in Lebanon (elevation: 1750m) and the birthplace of St Charbel. The saint's house has been turned into a **museum** which commemorates the saint's life in paintings. It is open daily, except Monday, and there is a shop and cafe at the entrance. The village now has a new convent named after St Charbel and there is a church, Notre Dame, across the way from the museum. St Charbel's Feast is celebrated on the third Sunday of July.

DEIR MAR SEMAAN   دير مار سمعان

Just past the turn-off for B'qaa Kafra, as you head east, is a small path leading to Deir Mar Semaan, a hermitage founded in 1112 by

Takla, the daughter of a local priest called Basil. Concrete paths lead down to the spartan four-room hermitage carved into the rocks, where Mar Samaan (St Simon) supposedly lived. Access to the caves involves squeezing through doorways. Inside there are votive candles and offerings. There are also traces of frescoes, and remains of water cisterns. The walk takes about 15 minutes.

BARZAOUN & HASROUN
بزعون وحصرون

☎ 06

These two small villages on the southern rim of the valley run into one another and are famous for their traditional red-tiled roofs. There are a number of well-preserved Ottoman-era stone houses and buildings, and the quiet, winding streets make for a pleasant stroll. In the centre of Hasroun is the Church of the Virgin Mary, which has an unusual clock tower with two faces.

On the main road the *Hotel Restaurant Karam* (☎ 590 117) serves home-cooked meals on its terrace. A lunch of home-made fries, mezze and salads will cost about US$6. The small, family-run hotel also has double rooms for US$35, including breakfast.

There is a path leading down into the valley from Hasroun which leads past the old church of Mar Mikhail and the monastery of Mar Yaaqoub.

DIMAN
ديمان

In Diman on the south side of the valley is the Maronite Patriarchy which took over from Deir Qannoubin in the 19th century. It is the summer residence of the patriarch. You can't miss it – it is a large modern building on the valley side of the road. The church is not old but is well worth looking at for the panoramic paintings of the Qadisha Valley and religious scenes by the Lebanese painter, Saliba Doueihy. These date from the 1930s or 1940s when the spire of the church was built. The grounds behind the building lead to the edge of the gorge with views across the valley.

AMIOUN
أميون

Back down towards the coast, Amioun stands above the highway to/from Chekka

and is easily noticeable from the road for the rock-cut tombs that have been hewn out of its southern cliffs. These are either Phoenician or Roman burial vaults. Perched atop these cliffs is the old part of the village, a beautiful mixture of Ottoman stone buildings and narrow winding streets. Walking through the peaceful alleyways gives a glimpse of village life a century ago. The economy of the area used to be based on olives and, judging by the size of some of the houses, was very prosperous.

High up in the centre of the village is the 15th-century Cathedral of St George, which was built on the ruins of a Roman temple (itself built on Neolithic remains). The site was an important place of worship under the Romans and pagan rites were reputedly practised well into the Christian era. The temple was destroyed by an earthquake in the 4th or 5th century AD but elements, including a couple of columns, have been incorporated into the church. A stone iconostasis (screen) with fine painted icons contrasts with the fairly plain vaulted interior of the church.

AKKAR
عكّار

Akkar, the area in the extreme north of Lebanon beyond Tripoli, is usually only visited if you are driving to Syria. The coastal plain here widens out; inland the landscape is still mountainous, but more rounded than jagged. This is the end of the Mt Lebanon Range. The area is noticeably poorer than Tripoli and many villages do not have electricity. Although agriculture dominates the landscape, the army is the main employer.

In this area there is only one town of any size, Qoubayat, with little there for tourists to see. The main reason for visiting the north is to drive around the unspoilt villages where a more traditional agricultural life still exists. Once you leave the main highway there are virtually no restaurants, apart from simple cafes in the villages, and no hotels.

Heading north to the Syrian border crossing at Aabboudiye, the narrow coast road runs alongside several refugee camps and some military installations. The sea runs close to the road and there is no development; the general impression is bleak.

Qoubayat   قبيّات

Built at the foot of wooded mountains, Qoubayat was on the overland route from Tripoli to Homs in Syria before the new highway was built. Once a centre of the silk industry, it is now the administrative centre of the Akkar region. Qoubayat has an old shrine called the **Lady of Shahlo** and a large old church, **St Georges**. The town has a number of traditional houses with mullioned windows and is pleasant to wander around.

The villages of Aydamoun, Kouachra and Machta Hassan in the area around Qoubayat are famous for being the home of the Turkoman, one of Lebanon's tiniest minorities. They are thought to have arrived here in the 16th century, in the wake of the Ottoman conquest of Syria, as a type of rearguard to ensure some areas of loyalty to the new overlords in Istanbul. While the Turkomans have now Arabised their names and are Lebanese citizens, many still speak Turkmen.

Three kilometres further along the road is the village of **Aandqet**, which has a few surviving silk spinning mills. A further 1km down a track is the tiny village of **Aaidamoun** where Akkar carpets are traditionally made by the local women. Nearby is the Roman temple of **Maqam** which is constructed in a simple style.

Service taxis leave from the Rue Tall stand in Tripoli. The fare to Qoubayat is LL4000.

Akkar al-Atiqa   عكّار العتيقة

The village of Akkar al-Atiqa is famous for the **Castle of Akkar**, which stands on a rocky promontory at an altitude of 700m. It is in a pretty remote spot, about 45km from Tripoli, off the highway heading north. The castle was named after its supposed founder Muhriz ibn Akkar, whose family owned the castle until 1019. It was conquered by the Fatimid caliphs of Egypt and then by the Seljuk Turks. When the Frankish Crusaders took Tripoli in 1109, they were given Akkar by treaty. There followed the usual tug-of-war between the Crusaders and the Arabs, until the latter finally took it over for good after a siege in 1271. It is easy to see why it was such a prize; from this position the castle dwellers could make raids on the main highway between Homs and Baalbek and then retire to an impenetrable lair.

The castle is now in ruins, reputedly destroyed in the 17th century by Fakhreddine (Fakhr ad-Din al-Maan II) in a revenge attack on the area's Ottoman ruler. Fakhreddine is supposed to have used the stones from Akkar castle to build his own palace at Beiteddine in the Chouf.

Although the building is in ruins, it is worth the hour-long climb from the village for the fantastic views of the surrounding area. On a clear day you can supposedly see Krak des Chevaliers in Syria.

Getting There & Away Reaching Akkar is tricky without your own transport. Apart from a few small villages en route the road leads nowhere, so hitching is out. The nearest transport point is Halba on the Tripoli to Qoubayat road. A service taxi will drop you off at Halba (LL4000) and from there you will need a taxi to take you to the Castle of Akkar and back again.

Tell Arqa   تل عرقة

Close to Halba on the highway leading from Tripoli towards Qoubayat lies the hill (or 'tell') which conceals the remains of the Roman city of Arca Caesarea (Caesarea in Lebanon). This is an ancient place. Evidence of settlement goes back to Neolithic times. The town was already old when, centuries later, the Romans established their settlement here. Later it was fought over by the Crusaders. Now, however, it is a partially excavated archaeological site, interesting for its layers of history and its panoramic views.

Finding Tell Arqa can be a challenge. Just before arriving at Halba, the highway passes over a small bridge, where there is a turn-off to the right that takes you through the very poor village of Arqa. Carry on for about 150m and you will find a very rough track leading to the tell.

Tell Arqa is just off the main road so you can get a service to Halba (LL4000) and ask the driver to drop you at Arqa. You can flag down a service taxi on the highway to take you back to Tripoli or onwards to Qoubayat.

The Bekaa Valley سهل البقاع

The Bekaa Valley is a high plateau between the Mt Lebanon and the Anti-Lebanon Ranges. The climate is drier than elsewhere in Lebanon, as the valley falls in a rain shadow. It is very hot in summer.

For millennia the Bekaa, which the Greeks and Romans dubbed 'hollow Syria', was a corridor linking the Syrian interior with the coastal cities of Phoenicia. The many invading armies and trading caravans that passed

THE BEKAA VALLEY

Highlights

- Marvel over the spectacular temple complex at Baalbek.
- See the world's largest cut stone at Baalbek's quarry.
- Walk down the main street of Aanjar, the Middle East's only remaining Umayyad town.
- Learn to like arak and mix your mezzes at Lebanon's favourite riverside restaurants in Zahlé.
- Puzzle over the mysterious 27m-high pyramid tomb near Hermel.
- Smell the bouquet and sip the wine at the Ksara Winery, Lebanon's most famous vineyard.
- Imagine yourself a hermit in the cave cells of Deir Mar Maroun.

---

through left traces of their presence, which can be seen in a host of small sites around the valley, but particularly at the well-preserved Umayyad city of Aanjar and the magnificent, world-famous temples at Baalbek.

Fed by the Nahr al-Aasi (Orontes River) and the Nahr Litani, the Bekaa has always been an agricultural region. In Roman times it was an important grain-producing region, and was one of Rome's 'breadbaskets'. Today the Bekaa, while producing a couple of crops a year, is nowhere near as productive. Deforestation and long-term neglect have reduced the fertility of the land.

There are, however, exceptions to the downturn. One crop that flourished before and during the war was cannabis. Until quite recently 'Red Leb' was the country's most famous (or infamous) product. These days the farmers of the Bekaa have cleaned up their act and potatoes, tomatoes and grapes are the crops of choice. The dry climate and fertile soil also make the valley perfect for wine making and this is where Lebanon's burgeoning wine production is based.

Hashish Hardship

The Bekaa Valley was once the centre of Lebanon's infamous hashish production. Unfortunately for any hopeful hash smokers reading this, it no longer is.

Throughout the 1960s until the end of the civil war, no visit to the Bekaa was complete without being offered a puff of the high-quality resin. Travellers who passed through before and during the war love to reminisce about their unparalleled trips through Baalbek's Roman ruins. One French company in the 1960s reckoned that, along with prostitution, hashish was a major source of national income.

In the early days of the war, an estimated 10,000 tonnes of hashish was exported from Lebanon each year. The lucrative trade was controlled by a cartel of about 30 Lebanese families. When the Syrians arrived on the scene, they got in on the act too, and used their tanks and artillery to protect the fields.

In their bid for American respect around the time of the Gulf War the Syrians, however, put an end to the industry. Farmers were prevented from growing the crop and now produce tomatoes, tobacco, potatoes and grain. However, most of their produce cannot compete with cheaper Syrian vegetables and their incomes have plunged.

Perhaps because of its agricultural character, the Bekaa is also known for its good food, and regional specialties include fresh trout, Armenian specialties (in the Aanjar area) and hearty mezzes.

CHTAURA   شـتـورة

☎ 08

Chtaura (44km from Beirut) is the transport hub of the Bekaa, with roads heading north to Baalbek and Homs (Syria), south to Lake Qaraoun and on to Marjeyun, and east to Damascus and Jordan. The town is basically just a crossroads, although there are some pleasant orchards and small parks in the outlying areas; its function as a stopover is clear from the many cheap restaurants which line the main road. But the small restaurants are friendly and traditional, often serving local produce such as cheese and yoghurt or the local syrups, which are to be found in specialty stores all over the world. Try the almond syrup with iced milk.

Chtaura is also the main banking centre for the Bekaa and you will find many banks and bureaux de change along the main road, as well as shops selling eastern souvenirs. One of the old hotels is now a barracks for Syrian soldiers and the presence of a large hotel gives away its role as a centre for Lebanese and Syrian political conferences. Chtaura is also known as a health resort for asthma and rheumatism sufferers.

Places to Stay

The only up-and-running cheap option is the **Hotel Khater** (☎ 540 133), which is on the main road above a shop-cum-cafe. The rooms are simple and fairly clean, but there is no restaurant and you will have to wander down to a nearby cafe for breakfast. Rooms cost US$10 per person, whether single or double.

The other hotel in Chtaura is at the opposite end of the scale. The **Chtaura Park Hotel** (☎ 540 011, fax 542 686) is a super-luxury hotel with prices to match. Singles/doubles with breakfast cost from US$125/159 plus 16% service. The hotel has a sauna and other five-star amenities.

Places to Eat

The best place in town is the **Akl Restaurant** (☎ 540 699) with its two venues, one indoors and the other outdoors, close together on the main road. This long-established restaurant specialises in mezze dishes and can serve 27 different saucer-sized appetisers if you're feeling hungry. Expect to spend US$20 to US$30 depending on what you order.

Also worth trying are the **Restaurant Moutran** and **Restaurant Habre**, both on the main road near the Hotel Khater. These are also traditional Lebanese restaurants but not as fancy as the Akl.

There are a number of snack places in Chtaura. Downstairs from the Hotel Khater is a **cafe/shop** selling a bizarre combination of alcohol and ammunition. If you're not in the market for that, you can also get a half-decent sandwich and coffee.

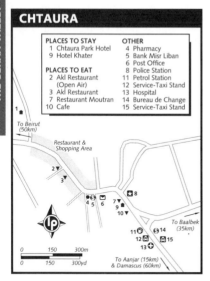

CHTAURA

PLACES TO STAY	OTHER
1 Chtaura Park Hotel	4 Pharmacy
9 Hotel Khater	5 Bank Misr Liban
	6 Post Office
PLACES TO EAT	8 Police Station
2 Akl Restaurant	11 Petrol Station
(Open Air)	12 Service-Taxi Stand
3 Akl Restaurant	13 Hospital
7 Restaurant Moutran	14 Bureau de Change
10 Cafe	15 Service-Taxi Stand

To Beirut
(50km)

Restaurant &
Shopping Area

To Baalbek
(35km)

0   150   300m
0   150   300yd

To Aanjar (15km)
& Damascus (60km)

Getting There & Away

There are frequent service taxis to and from
Beirut which cost LL4000. They congregate on the main street and you can easily
get connections onward to Zahlé (LL1000),
Baalbek (2000), and Damascus (LL6000),
as well as to some of the smaller places
along the Bekaa Valley. Microbus Nos 4
and 5 leave from Beirut's Cola bus station,
and pick up and drop off at Chtaura. To take
one on to Zahlé or Baalbek costs LL500.

ZAHLÉ   زحلة

☎ 08

Zahlé is an attractive resort town 7km
north-east of Chtaura. Known locally as
Arousat al-Beqa'a, the Bride of the Bekaa,
it is set along the steep banks of the Bir-
dawni River, which tumbles through a
gorge from Jebel Sannine. Zahlé is a predominantly Greek Catholic town with a
number of its Ottoman-era houses still intact. But it is famous for its open-air restaurants that line the river's edge in the upper
part of the town. During summer weekends
and evenings, these are usually full of locals
and Beirutis enjoying some of the finest
Lebanese cooking to be found in the country, washed down with the local firewater,
arak (see the boxed text 'Arak').

In the 19th century, Zahlé was involved
in the communal fighting between the
Druze and Christians and many of its inhabitants were killed in the 1860 massacre.
Some 25 years later, the opening of a railway line between Beirut and Damascus (no
longer operating) brought some prosperity
to the town. At the same time, more than
half the town migrated to Brazil (after
which the main street is named), from
where they sent remittances, further increasing the town's prosperity. Zahlé's gracious stone houses date from this time.

During the civil war Zahlé suffered heavy
Syrian bombardment when the Phalangists
began construction of a road linking the
town with the ski resort of Faraya. Syria was
suspicious of the Phalangists' link to the Israelis and saw the road as a threat. Fortunately, most of the town's Ottoman-era
buildings survived and the town is now
booming.

Information

Zahlé is a medium-size town with all the
basic amenities near the centre. The main
road which runs through town is Rue Brazil
with Rue St Barbara running parallel. This
is where the banks, bureaux de change and
the post office can be found. The tourist information office (☎ 802 566, fax 803 595)
is in the Chamber of Commerce building
just up the hill overlooking Rue Brazil.

Also on Rue Brazil is the Dataland Internet Cafe, which is open from 8 am to midnight daily, 2 pm to midnight Sunday.
Internet use costs LL5000 per hour.

There is a hospital on Rue Brazil towards
the head of the valley. In case of emergency
call:

Police	☎ 803 521, 824 110
Red Cross	☎ 824 892

Places to Stay

On the north-west end of Rue Brazil is the
lovely *Hotel Akl (☎ 820 701)*, a family-run
hotel in a 150-year-old house. Spotlessly
clean and friendly, rooms with high ceilings

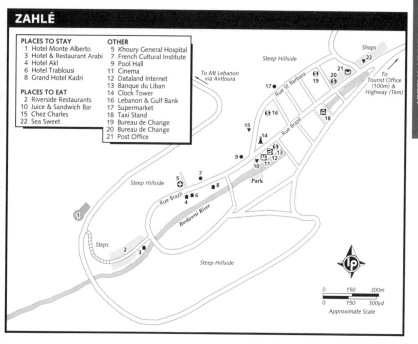

ZAHLÉ

PLACES TO STAY
1 Hotel Monte Alberto
3 Hotel & Restaurant Arabi
4 Hotel Akl
6 Hotel Trablousi
8 Grand Hotel Kadri

PLACES TO EAT
2 Riverside Restaurants
10 Juice & Sandwich Bar
15 Chez Charles
22 Sea Sweet

OTHER
5 Khoury General Hospital
7 French Cultural Institute
9 Pool Hall
11 Cinema
12 Dataland Internet
13 Banque du Liban
14 Clock Tower
16 Lebanon & Gulf Bank
17 Supermarket
18 Taxi Stand
19 Bureau de Change
20 Bureau de Change
21 Post Office

at this highly recommended place cost US$33 for a double with private bath and US$30 without. Singles pay half. There is a lounge downstairs with a TV and piano.

Next door to the Akl is the **Hotel Trablousi** (☎ 812 661), also in an old house, but slightly shabbier than its neighbour. Still, it is very charming and rooms, with single or double occupancy, cost US$20 per person.

Moving further along Rue Brazil you come to the imposing five-star **Grand Hotel Kadri** (☎ 813 920), which has 105 rooms, tennis courts, a pool and five restaurants. Singles/doubles cost US$120/145, not including service or taxes.

At the head of the valley on the river bank is the **Hotel Arabi** (☎ 821 214, fax 800 144), a small, reasonably smart hotel with rooms overlooking the riverside restaurants. Singles or doubles cost US$60, including service, but could be noisy because of their proximity to the restaurants. The hotel's outdoor restaurant is famous for its mezze.

If views are what you're after, then **Hotel Monte Alberto** (☎ 810 912, 801 451) is the place to head. Situated high above the town, but only a five-minute walk down to the river, it is very clean and comfortable. Singles/twins cost US$45 and rooms with a double bed cost US$60. Be sure to ask for a room with a view when you book. Breakfast is an extra US$5. One of the features of the hotel is its circular panoramic restaurant overlooking the gorge. Dinner costs about US$20.

Places to Eat

There is no shortage of good places to eat at all levels of spending, but one of the great treats is dinner by the river along the walkway at the head of the valley. To get there, walk through town until the road curves around the end of the valley. You will see a pedestrian street which follows the course of the river. On the land side of the walkway are various fast-food places, juice bars and entertainment arcades. Facing the water are

Arak

If there is a national drink of Lebanon, or indeed the rest of the Middle East, then this is it. An acquired taste for some westerners, this aniseed-flavoured drink has become a universal favourite in the eastern Mediterranean under several guises – ouzo in Greece, raki in Turkey – but all are fundamentally the same thing. It is a drink that doesn't travel well and somehow doesn't taste the same away from the sunny climes of the Mediterranean.

It is also curiously classless, sipped at both the smartest dinner or the humblest cafe. It manages this by being both cheap and expensive but, unlike wine, the difference between the US$4 bottle and the US$20 fancy ceramic flask is nonexistent to the untutored palate.

It comes as a bit of a surprise that arak is a by-product of wine-making, not having the least hint of 'grapiness' to its flavour. In fact it is a brandy, made from the bits left over from the wine press – the red grape skins, pips and so forth, much like the Italian grappa, but with the additional flavour of aniseed. After the first wine fermentation, the skins and solids rise to the top of the vat. These are separated and fermented into a potent but evil-smelling brew, the result of which is distilled into a lethal spirit of 92% to 94% alcohol.

One glass of this would probably kill you (or at least make you very ill). The toxins have to be carefully filtered out and the liquor refined until what you end up with is a clear and very pure form of alcohol. The methanol is separated from the brew by a further distillation and the result is a very refined product.

The distinctive flavour is added next with macerated green aniseeds from Syria, and water added to dilute it to a drinkable level of potency. After this the poisonous 'head' of the brew is removed; what remains is pure arak. The result is left to mature for six to 10 months, in the case of the finer araks, and considerably less time for the cheaper varieties.

With all the refining processes that it goes through it is not surprising that arak has the reputation for not giving you a hangover. But even so, it is surprisingly potent and even diluted can get you drunk very quickly.

Anise is not everyone's favourite flavour but diluted with ice and water arak makes a better partner for Lebanese cuisine than you would imagine. Arak, and indeed all aniseed-flavoured drinks, develops a milk opacity with the addition of water. It has a cooling and palate-cleansing effect which becomes more pleasant as you get used to the taste. So overcome any 'araknaphobia' and try it with your next mezze – you could easily become converted.

---

shoulder-to-shoulder restaurants, all with good reputations. The most famous is the *Arabi*, which is renowned throughout Lebanon for its mezze. Budget at least US$25 per person for the full treatment.

Back in the centre of town, near the clock tower, *Chez Charles* is a good eating option. Not as expensive as the riverside places, it is cosy and the food is good. Expect to pay about US$8 to US$10 for a good lunch or dinner with a few drinks. Along Rue Brazil are a number of good juice bars and snack places which serve breakfast for a few dollars. Also on Rue Brazil is a pastry shop, *Sea Sweet*, which has delicious Lebanese pastries to take away.

Getting There & Away

A service taxi from Chtaura will cost LL1000. If it is serving Baalbek and dropping you off, then keep in mind that the roundabout is over 1km from the centre of town, so it is better to get one that is going only to Zahlé. The main taxi stand in town is a square on Rue Brazil, where you can pick up a service taxi or a taxi to various points in the Bekaa. Buses en route from Beirut to Baalbek (see Chtaura earlier this chapter for details) will drop you at the roundabout on the edge of town. If you catch a local (and much slower) Bekaa bus in Chtaura it will bring you right into the centre of town. The fare is also LL500.

AROUND ZAHLÉ
☎ 08
Ksara Winery   كسارة
Lebanon's oldest and most famous winery (☎ 813 495) was originally the site of a medieval fortress (which no longer remains); vines were planted here in the early 18th century. The chalky soils and dry climate were perfect for grapes and production flourished. In 1857, Jesuit priests took over and expanded the vineyard until it was sold to its present owners in 1972. Once fermented, the wines are put into a series of ancient tunnels to mature.

The vineyard is open to visitors and you will be shown the various processes involved in wine and arak production and then taken around the cool cave-cellars by a multilingual guide. At the end you are rewarded with tastings of some of their products.

Open hours are 9 am to 4 pm daily. It is more geared up for receiving groups, so if you are an independent traveller it would be worth calling first.

Getting There & Away A service taxi from Zahlé heading south will drop you in Ksara village (LL1000), a five-minute walk from the winery. Otherwise a taxi will take you there, wait for you and drive you back for US$10. If you are driving yourself, head south along the main highway for about 2km until you come to Ksara, then look for the signposted turning on the right.

Furzol & Niha   فرزل و نيحا
Furzol Three kilometres from Zahlé, just off the road to Baalbek, is the village of Furzol, an old Christian centre that was the seat of a bishopric in the 5th century. About 0.5km up the valley from the centre is **Wadi al-Habis** (Valley of the Hermit), which has a number of early Christian **rock-cut sanctuaries** and a few Roman era **tombs**. One of the latter has a niche with a cone-shaped carving, which is thought to represent an ancient god.

After clambering about the cliffs looking at the caves you can have a drink or meal at the restaurant below, but they are open in the summer only.

Niha About 4km from Furzol is the **Roman temple** of Niha. To get here, rejoin the main road from Furzol, take the left fork after about 0.5km and carry on until you see the blue and white sign. Turn left here and carry on until you see the temple, which is clearly visible in a grove of Cyprus trees as you enter the village.

The temple complex was dedicated to Hadaranus, a Syro-Phoenician god, and is large and imposing but has been sloppily reconstructed, with concrete in evidence and original features clearly misplaced. Still, it has some interesting carvings, including, to the left of the first staircase, the faded relief of a priest or dignitary. The exterior cornice on top of the walls also has some well-preserved lions' heads. Inside the temple another set of stairs leads to where the altar would originally have stood. Small doorways on either side of the entrance lead up to the roof and give good views of the surrounding valley.

In front of the main temple are the foundations and column fragments of another, smaller temple.

Getting There & Away Neither Furzol nor Niha is on a service taxi route, so the only way to visit is by private car or taxi. From Zahlé, a trip to both sites will cost about US$20.

AANJAR & AROUND   عنجر
Only 15km from Chtaura, Aanjar (Haouch Moussa) is a small, predominantly Armenian town founded by refugees fleeing the genocide in Turkey. It is also the site of the only significant Umayyad remains in Lebanon.

The discovery of this astonishingly well-preserved early Islamic town came about by accident. In the late 1940s archaeologists were digging here in the hopes of discovering the ancient city of Chalcis, founded around 1000 BC. Instead, they uncovered a walled town with a Roman layout that dated from the first centuries of Islam. Almost all periods of Arab history have been preserved at other sites in Lebanon – but traces of the Umayyads are strangely absent, so Aanjar has great historical significance.

Lebanese Wine

Lebanon is one of the oldest sites of wine production in the world and the Bekaa Valley has always been its prime vine-growing centre. Because of its favourable climate (some 240 days of unbroken sunshine each year) and chalky soil, the Bekaa's vines need little treatment and have a high strength without added sugar.

During the war, domestic demand for wine was reduced in favour of the stronger arak or whisky (no doubt more efficient for calming jangled nerves), but wine consumption is on the increase again. In 1998 the Bekaa produced about four-million litres of juice from its grapes. Word of the quality of Lebanese wine has also spread abroad and in 1998 wine exports were worth some US$5 million.

Ksara

The oldest Lebanese wine is produced by the Ksara vineyard (see the previous page). It produces many varieties of wine, of which about 50% are red. These are based on cinsaut and grenache grapes with some of the heavier reds coming from cabernet sauvignon and syrah (shiraz) grapes. The whites are light and fruity and based on sauvignon blanc and chardonnay grapes. The estate's premier wine is Chateau Ksara, which matures in French oak casks for 18 months and stays another two years in the bottle before going on the market. The Reserve du Couvent matures over six months in each, while the table wine Clos St Alphonse is bottled straight out of the vat.

Kefraya

The Kefraya vineyard, which is 20km south of Chtaura and can be visited, is the largest producer of wine in Lebanon, turning out over a million bottles a year. Since it began production in 1979 it has won more than 60 prizes for its wine, including the Gran Prix d'Honnneur for its Lacrima D'ora, a sweet white. The estate produces an early drinking rose and a red 'nouveau'. The Chateau vintages are far more complex. For example, the Blancs de Blancs with its St Emilion, clairette, bourboulenc and sauvignon grapes have great depth and character with the earthy tang of the Levant.

Chateau Musar

This is the smallest of the commercial producers with the greatest reputation for quality. It is also the only one not working out of the Bekaa (the winery is in Ghazir, above Jounieh), although its grapes are grown in the valley and transported by truck. Wine is traditionally matured in oak casks for a full seven years before being sent to market and the high quality of its product has made it a darling of international critics. More than 90% of its wine is exported (mainly to England) where the owner, Serge Hochar, receives rave reviews. He managed to produce wines throughout the war, even though most of the 1984 harvest, ironically one of the best vintages on record, was destroyed. Even so, a few bottles survive. The winery is now increasing the production of its second wines, the lower-quality brew, and hoping to make inroads in the domestic market.

Massaya

A recent addition to Lebanon's wine producers, Massaya made its debut after the 1997 harvest and is already being quaffed in Beirut's smart restaurants. Massaya is better known in Lebanon as a brand of arak served in distinctive, tall blue bottles. Still, the new wine is doing well and its first vintage was sold out, with 80% going to export.

In addition to being a rare example of Umayyad architecture, it is a rare example of a Lebanese inland trading city, and the only site that is from a single period. Set against the backdrop of the Anti-Lebanon hills, it is a fascinating place to visit.

The Umayyad City

Aanjar is thought to have been built by the sixth Umayyad caliph, Walid I (AD 705 to 715). It is a walled and fortified city cut into four equal quarters, separated by two 20m-wide avenues, the cardo maximus and the decumanus maximus. Because it was built in the early days of Muslim rule, the influence of previous cultures was still strong and the layout is typically Hellenistic/Roman. Other influences include the reuse of columns and capitals in the colonnades lining the streets. The **tetrapylon**, a four-column structure placed where the two streets intersect, is another Roman element, although the stonework, with its alternating layers of large blocks and narrow bricks, is typically Byzantine.

The Roman effect can also be seen in the **public baths**, just inside the entrance. As with all Roman baths, and many later *hammams*, these contain three main sections: a place to change, the bathing area (consisting of chambers with cold, warm and hot water) and an area to relax and chat. In the bathing area to the left of the entrance there are two faded but reasonably intact **mosaics**.

In the south-west corner of the site is a warren of foundations that are thought to be the remains of the **residential quarters**. Across the cardo maximus from them is Aanjar's most striking building, the **great palace**, which has had one wall and several arcades reconstructed. Also interesting is the **little palace**, where you can find Greek stone carvings of leaves, shells and birds.

Because it sits on a main east-west trade route, historians have speculated that Aanjar was a commercial centre. About 600 **shops** have been uncovered here (you can still see some of them lining the southern part of the cardo maximus), which indicates that it must have been some kind of trading place. Other theories suggest that because there were two palaces and public baths here, it could also have been an imperial residence or strategic post.

But despite the obvious wealth that was behind Aanjar, it flourished for only 50 years before it was abandoned in the face of defeat at the hands of the Abbasids.

Only the northern entrance to the site is open – Aanjar is still partly occupied by the Syrian army. You can see their bunkers and mess huts on the southern side of the site. The site is open from 8 am (7.30 in summer) until sunset daily. The entrance fee is LL6000.

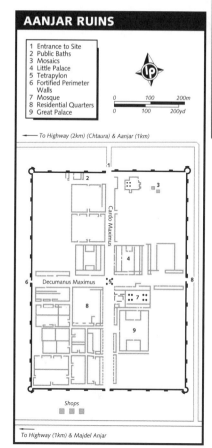

AANJAR RUINS

1 Entrance to Site
2 Public Baths
3 Mosaics
4 Little Palace
5 Tetrapylon
6 Fortified Perimeter Walls
7 Mosque
8 Residential Quarters
9 Great Palace

To Highway (2km) (Chtaura) & Aanjar (1km)

Cardo Maximus

Decumanus Maximus

Shops

To Highway (1km) & Majdel Anjar

Majdel Aanjar   مجدل عنجر

The village of Majdel Aanjar is 3km south of Aanjar. Above the village on a hill are some **Roman ruins**, including a temple and some fortifications. The cella is still intact, but the stones are heavily worn and underground passages have opened up. The temple is thought to date from the 1st century AD and in the 7th and 8th centuries it was converted to a fortress by the Abbasids.

The site is rarely visited, despite recent restoration efforts. To get there, pass through the village of Majdel Aanjar (note the 13th-century square minaret as you pass) and follow the road to the top of the hill. The last part is extremely steep and is best undertaken on foot. The views are worth the effort.

Dakweh دكوه

Three kilometres from Majdel Aanjar is another site of interest at Dakweh. Set in a yard just behind the village of the same name is a renovated Roman **temple**, with its four walls still standing and the corners of the pediment intact. A 15-minute walk up the hill behind it leads to a lovely **Roman necropolis**. There are two cave openings here, the larger one has five arched vaults and two stone sarcophagi.

Places to Eat
The area around Aanjar is famous for its Armenian food and, thanks to trout farms, its fresh fish. One of the best is **The Shams (Sun) Restaurant**, on the road to Aanjar, about 500m from the main Damascus Highway. Bread is freshly baked when you place your order and there's the usual selection of mezzes and grills, in addition to the fish. A meal without fish costs between US$8 and US$15, with fish it will be considerably more. For something cheaper, there are a few shops nearby where you can buy water and snacks, and the main Damascus highway is dotted with fast-food stalls.

Getting There & Away
If you are taking a service taxi heading south or to the Syrian border from Chtaura, you will have to get out at Aanjar town and walk from the highway (about 3km) to the site. If you don't have your own car, negotiate a return trip from Chtaura with a taxi driver who will wait for you (allow one hour for a visit – two if you are very thorough). This should cost about US$10 for a one-hour stay.

To visit the other sites you need either a strong constitution and some walking boots, or a taxi driver hired by the hour who can wait for you while you explore.

LAKE QARAOUN & THE LITANI DAM بحيرة القرعون وسدّ الليطاني

Way down south in the Bekaa Valley is the Litani Dam. This was built in 1959 and has created a lake of 11 sq km. The Litani is the longest river in Lebanon – it rises in the north of the Bekaa near Baalbek and flows into the sea near Tyre. Although the dam was built for the practical reason of producing electricity and providing irrigation, it is an attractive spot to visit and several restaurants have sprung up along its edge. Keep in mind that the waters are not safe for swimming.

There is a visitor centre at the southern end of the lake (the dam end) on the eastern side.

Aamiq Swamp عميّق

Halfway between Chtaura and Lake Qaroun, at the foot of the eastern slopes of Jebel Barouk, lies the Aamiq Swamp, Lebanon's last major wetland formed by the Nahr al-Riachi (Riachi River) and its underground source. Covering some 270 hectares, it consists of marshes, ponds, willows and mud flats. Unfortunately, intensive pumping of artesian wells in the Bekaa have lowered the level of the source and the swamp is threatened with drying up. Hunting has also taken its toll. Nevertheless, the area is a haven for migrating and aquatic birds, and more than 135 species have been observed here. At the moment the swamp is private property, but it is slated to become Lebanon's fourth nature reserve.

It is difficult to get a service taxi to the far south of the Bekaa, so you will have to negotiate hard with a taxi driver to take you. Hitching is possible, but really you need your own car.

BAALBEK بعلبك
☎ 08

Baalbek, the 'Sun City' of the ancient world, is the most impressive ancient site in Lebanon and arguably the most important Roman site in the Middle East. It enjoyed a reputation as one of the wonders of the world and mystics still attribute special powers to the courtyard complex. Its temples were built on an extravagant scale that outshone anything in Rome and the town became a centre of worship well into the Christian era.

[Continued on page 213]

BAALBEK RUINS

Main Temples

The entrance to the main site is at the south-east end of the temple complex. After passing the ticket office, you enter the ruins via the monumental staircase leading up to the **propy-laea**, which has a portico flanked by two towers and a colonnade along the facade. This would originally have been covered by a cedar roof and paved with mosaics. The column bases supporting the portico bear the inscription 'For the safety and victories of our lord, Caracalla'.

Through a central door you move into the **hexagonal court**. There is a raised threshold, which separates the propylaea from the **sacred enclosure**. This courtyard is about 50m deep. It used to be surrounded by a columned portico and to the north and south four exedrae opened symmetrically onto the portico, each with four columns. These rooms were decorated with niches that had either triangular or round pediments. To the north of the court is a famous bas-relief of Jupiter Heliopolitan which was found near the Lejuj Spring, 7km from Baalbek.

Beyond the Hexagonal Court is the **Great Court**, or Sacrificial Courtyard. It was richly decorated on its north, east and south sides

Title Page: The immense columns of Baalbek's Temple of Jupiter are the largest in the world with a height of 22.9m and girth of 2.2m. (Photo: Bethune Carmichael)

Top: Carved limestone lion's head from the Temple of Jupiter (Illustration: Sonya Brooke)

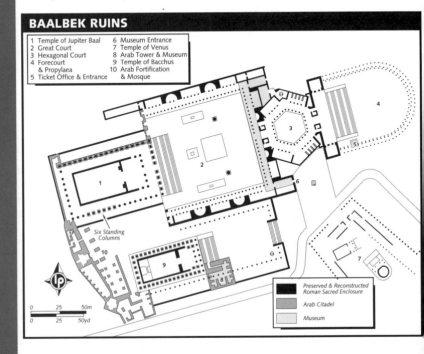

BAALBEK RUINS

1 Temple of Jupiter Baal
2 Great Court
3 Hexagonal Court
4 Forecourt & Propylaea
5 Ticket Office & Entrance
6 Museum Entrance
7 Temple of Venus
8 Arab Tower & Museum
9 Temple of Bacchus
10 Arab Fortification & Mosque

Six Standing Columns

Preserved & Reconstructed
Roman Sacred Enclosure

Arab Citadel

Museum

0   25   50m
0   25   50yd

PAUL DOYLE

GADI FARFOUR

ANDREW HUMPHREYS

Top: Niches, once used to house statuary for devotional purposes, are still visible in the well-preserved interior of Baalbek's Temple of Bacchus.

Middle: Only six massive columns remain from Baalbek's Temple of Jupiter (left). The lion's head (right) was originally part of the temple's entablature; it ⸱ides a spout that helped to drain rainwater from the roof.

Bottom: A vivid rock ⸱arving of a boar hunt at Baalbek

GADI FARFOUR

Both the Corinthian capitals and the intricate carving on the pediment are in excellent condition at Baalbek's Temple of Bacchus.

and had a double row of niches surmounted with pediments. There are a number of exedrae: four semicircular and eight rectangular. Between the exedrae there are niches, which also held statues. Above all these was a covered arcade supported by 84 granite columns. To either side of the courtyard were two pools, which still have some highly decorative carving on their sides showing Trions and Nereids, Medusas and Cupids riding dragons. In the centre of the courtyard there once stood a Byzantine basilica, which was dismantled by French archaeologists, revealing the foundations of a huge **altar** stand.

The **Temple of Jupiter** was built on an immense substructure over 300m long, and was approached by another monumental staircase

Right: A detail of Baalbek's Temple of Bacchus shows the fluted columns and statuary niches.

CHRISTOPHER WOOD

that rose high above the surrounding buildings. It consisted of a cella in which the statue of the god was housed and a surrounding portico of 10 columns along the facade and 19 columns along the side, making for 54 columns in all. These columns are the largest in the world – 22.9m high with a girth of 2.2m. Today only six of these remain standing with the architrave still in position. Their immensity has to be seen to be believed. It was thought in the old days that Baalbek had been constructed by giants and a quick look over the side of the temple to the foundation stones beneath reveals some of the largest building blocks to be found anywhere on earth. One of these megalithic blocks measures 19.5m by 4.3m and is estimated to weigh over 1000 tons – how it was moved and positioned so precisely remains a mystery. (See 'The Architecture of Lebanon' special section in the Facts about Lebanon chapter for more details.)

From the south side of the temple is a wonderful view of the so-called **Temple of Bacchus**. This was in fact dedicated not to Bacchus but to Venus/Astarte, and is the most beautifully decorated temple in the Roman world. It is also in a great state of preservation and was completed around AD 150. It is not built on the scale of the Temple of Jupiter, but more than makes up for it in style and decoration. Ironically it was called 'the small temple' in antiquity, although it is larger than the Parthenon in Athens. The entrance is up a flight of 30 stairs with three landings. It has a portico running around it with eight columns along the facade and 15 along the sides. They support a rich entablature; the frieze is decorated with lions and bulls. This supports a ceiling of curved stone which is decorated with very vivid scenes: Mars, a winged Victory, Diana taking an arrow from her quiver, a Tyche with a cornucopia, Vulcan with his hammer, Bacchus, and Ceres holding a sheaf of corn.

The highlight of the temple is the doorway, which has been drawn and painted by many artists, its half-fallen keystone forever a symbol of Baalbek (although it has been shored up since the famous 19th-century images were sketched; see the boxed text 'Sketches of

CHRISTOPHER WOOD

Left: The enormous columns of Baalbek's Temple of Jupiter were adorned with a richly engraved entablature.

Baalbek'). Inside, the cella is richly decorated with fluted columns. The 'holy place'
was at the back of the cella, which is
reached by another staircase with two ramps.
When the temple was in use this would have been
a dark and mysterious place, probably lit dramatically by oil lamps with piercing shafts of daylight
falling on the image of the god or goddess.

In the south-east corner of the Great
Court is a new **museum** (entered from the
parking area, close to the ticket office),
which is housed in a large vaulted tunnel
that may originally have been storerooms or
housing for pilgrims. As well as some beautiful
artefacts from Baalbek, the well-lit exhibits give
a thorough history of the temple under loosely
grouped themes. One fascinating display ex-
plains Roman building techniques, which shows
how the massive stone blocks used in the Temple
of Jupiter were manoeuvred into place.

In a side room is a foray into Baalbek's more
recent history, with a description of Emperor
Wilhelm II's visit to Baalbek. More interesting are
the photographs of the German photographer
Herman Burckhardt, who visited Baalbek at the
turn of the 20th century. His pictures are an
invaluable record of daily life at the time.

TRUDI CANAVAN

The site is open daily from 8.30 am to sunset. Admission is
LL10,000. For Lebanese adults/students, the entrance fee is
LL4000/2000. The museum is open from 8.30 am until 5 pm and is
free. Guided tours (of varying quality) are available in several languages, including English and French. There is no set fee so it is best to
negotiate beforehand – expect to pay around US$10. Numerous sou-
venir sellers and peddlers congregate around the entrance. You can
take a short camel ride for LL2000.

Other Attractions

Right: Bronze statue of
Jupiter Heliopolitan, now
in the Musée de Louvre,
Paris. He would usually
have held a whip in his
right hand and a
thunderbolt in his left. A
winged sun disc lies on
his chest and below are
reliefs depicting the
seven planets of Roman
astrology.

Near the main ruins about 300m from the acropolis is the exquisite,
tiny **Temple of Venus** (probably dedicated to Fortuna rather than
Venus), a circular building with many fluted columns. Inside, it was
decorated with tiers of tabernacles and covered with a cupola. During
the early Christian era it was turned into a basilica and dedicated to St
Barbara (who joined the saintly ranks when her pagan father tried to
kill her for converting to Christianity. He got his comeuppance with a
bolt of lightning that reduced him to a smouldering heap.) A copy of
this gem of a temple was constructed in the 18th century in the
grounds of Stourhead in Wiltshire, England.

Sketches of Baalbek

We have sketches and descriptions of some early travellers to Baalbek to help us understand what happened to the site over the past couple of centuries. In 1759, Constantin-François Volney observed that the central lintel in the Temple of Bacchus had slipped and hung suspended in the air as a result of the recent earthquake. The most famous picture of this was painted in the 1830s by orientalist water-colourist David Roberts. Around 1870 this was shored up by Richard Burton, the British consul in Damascus, who constructed a stone support. Burton wrote that it was not only nature but humans who destroyed Baalbek. The stones were held with metal clamps and dowels, which wereremoved to make bullets. Once that was done the great blocks were not secure and fell at the slightest tremor.

To the east of the propylaea stands the ruined Umayyad or **Great Mosque** (see the Baalbek map on page 208), which was built from the stones of the temples using many styles of columns and capitals. Lebanon's only Umayyad ruin, outside Aanjar, it was built between the 7th and 8th centuries. There is an ablution fountain surrounded by four columns in the centre of the courtyard. On the right, immediately after the entrance, are rows of arched colonnades with Roman columns and capitals, clearly taken from the temple complex. At the north-west corner are the ruins of a great octagonal minaret on a square base.

To the south-east of Baalbek's centre is the source of the **Ras al-Ain Spring**. The area has pleasant, shady parks along the spring and is the site of occasional festivities with horses and camels and side stalls. At the head of the spring is a ruined early **mosque**, which at some point was thought to be the Temple of Neptune.

The Quarry

About 1km south of the centre of Baalbek, on Sheikh Abdullah Hill, is the quarry where the huge temple stones originated. Here you can see the largest cut stone in the world lying on its side, partially submerged in the earth. The Arabs call this stone *hajar al-hubla* which means 'Stone of the Pregnant Woman'. This came about as a corruption of its original name, *hajar al-qubla*, or 'Stone of the South'. Even so, local folklore has it that women can touch the stone to increase their fertility.

This massive piece of masonry measures 21.5m by 4m by 4.5m and is thought to weigh 2000 tons. It was no doubt destined to take its place with the other outsized blocks of stone that form the foundations of the Temple of Jupiter, or perhaps for some planned but unbuilt temple of which we know nothing. In any case, it is so huge one can only wonder at the skills of the engineers who cut and moved these huge stones. Even today, with all our technology, it would still be an engineering feat to move and reposition such a monster.

[Continued from page 206]

Standing dwarf-like under the temple's colossal columns and watching the setting sun turn the stone a rich orange has got to rate as a highlight of any visit to Lebanon.

Modern Baalbek is the administrative centre of the Northern Bekaa Valley. Until recently the fame of its Roman temples was eclipsed by its notoriety as the seat of Hezbollah, or Party of God, and its association with hostage-taking and radical anti-Western politics. This is where the famous Western hostages (John McCarthy, Terry Waite, et al) were held during the civil war. There are still numerous reminders of Hezbollah's supremacy here, including the 10m-high posters of Ayatollah Khomeini, but people are friendly and welcoming.

The town is also notable for misnomers: the Temple of Bacchus was not dedicated to Bacchus, nor was the Temple of Venus dedicated to Venus. Even the main hotel is rather curiously called the Palmyra.

Baalbek's famous international **festival** takes place here every summer. If you want to watch Santana or Dame Kiri Te Kanawa perform in the floodlit temple complex, see the boxed text 'Lebanon's Festivals' in the Facts for the Visitor chapter for more details.

History
The site was originally Phoenician and settlement here is thought to have dated back as far as the end of the 3rd millennium BC. During the 1st millennium BC a temple was built here and dedicated to the God Baal (later Hadad), from which comes its name. The site was no doubt chosen for its nearby springs and ideal position between the Litani and Al-Aasi Rivers. It was also located at the crossroads of the main east-west and north-south trade routes.

The Greeks and Romans called the city 'Heliopolis', literally the 'City of the Sun', and dedicated the main temple to Jupiter Heliopolitan, who was associated with Baal/Hadad, the father of all gods and god of the sun. However, this Baal of Heliopolis was actually a triad of gods – his partners being Venus and Mercury. Venus was asso-

ciated with Astarte or Atargatis, the chief female deity, but it is not known for certain who Mercury was associated with in the Phoenician pantheon (current thought finds Simios to be the most likely candidate). This triad of gods was extraordinarily popular and altars dedicated to them have been found not only in the east but in the Balkans, Spain, France and even Scotland.

It was originally a cult of nature worship and sacrifice and the temples were a focus for all manner of sexual and licentious forms of worship. Sacred prostitution coupled with an insatiable blood-lust seem to have featured in the cult. According to ancient tablets from Ugarit, which describe the practices of the Phoenician gods in a gruesome way, Anath, the sister and wife of Baal:

> ... waded up to the knees, up to the neck in human blood. Human heads lay at her feet, human hands flew over her like locusts. She tied the heads of her victims as ornaments on her back, their hands she tied upon her belt... When she was satisfied she washed her hands in streams of blood before turning again to other things.

Following the conquest of Alexander the Great, Baalbek became known as Heliopolis, a name which was kept by the subsequent Roman conquerors. In 64 BC, Pompey the Great passed through Baalbek and was intrigued by its glade. A few years later, in 47 BC, Julius Caesar founded a Roman colony here because of its strategic position between Palmyra, in the Syrian desert, and the coastal cities. He named the new colony after his daughter Julia. The town became occupied by Roman soldiers and building works were begun. Baalbek was soon recognised as the premier city in Roman Syria.

The construction of the temples was a massive undertaking. Work is thought to have begun in 60 BC and it is known that the great Temple of Jupiter was nearing completion in AD 60 during the reign of Nero. Later, under Antonius Pius (AD 138–161), a series of enlargements was undertaken, including work on the Great Court complex and the Temple of Bacchus. They were completed by his son Caracalla,

Wine, Sex & Song

Baalbek's enthusiasm in its worship of Baal's consort, Astarte (later called Venus or Aphrodite), appears to have shocked some contemporary visitors to the town. The Roman chronicler Eusibius disapprovingly wrote in the early 4th century:

At Heliopolis in Phoenicia, the cult of Venus has given birth to luxury habits. Men and women clasp together to honour their goddess; husbands and fathers allow their wives and daughters to prostitute themselves publicly to please Astarte.

The other god associated with Baal may have been Bacchus, who added wine and song to the 'luxury habits', and all-night Bacchanalian festivals of singing, dancing and sex would be accompanied by drums and flutes. No wonder Baalbek held out against Christianity for so long.

but building was still going on when Christianity was adopted by Rome's rulers. It has been estimated that over the centuries some 100,000 slaves worked on the project.

The building of such extravagant temples was as much, if not more, a political act than a spiritual one. The Romans made efforts to integrate the peoples of the Middle East by appearing to favour their gods while in fact building the most awe-inspiring structures possible in order to impress the worshippers with the strength of Roman political rule and civilisation. Even so, the deciding factor in building on such a massive and expansive scale at Baalbek was probably the threat of Christianity, which was beginning to pose a real threat to the old order. So, up went the temples in an attempt to 'fix' the religious orientation of the people in favour of pagan worship. By this time there were no human sacrifices, but still the temple prostitution remained and probably bulls were sacrificed – a persistent theme all over the Middle East.

When Constantine became emperor, the pagan world was under threat and building work was suspended. But when Julian the Apostate became emperor in 361, he reverted to paganism and tried to reinstate it throughout the empire. There was a terrible backlash against Christians, which resulted in mass martyrdom for the Christian population. When the Christian emperor, Theodosius, took the throne in 379, Christianity was once again imposed upon Baalbek and its temples were converted to a Christian basilica. Nevertheless, the town appears to have remained a centre of pagan worship and was enough of a threat to warrant a major crackdown by the Emperor Justinian (r. AD 527–65), who ordered that all Baalbek's pagans accept baptism. In an attempt to prevent any secret pagan rites, he ordered parts of the temple to be destroyed and had the biggest pillars shipped to Constantinople, where they were used in the Aya Sofya.

When the Muslim Arabs invaded Syria, they converted the Baalbek temples into a citadel and restored its Syriac name. For several centuries it came under the rule of Damascus. It went through a period of regular invasions, sackings, lootings and devastation. The city was sacked by the Arabs in AD 748 and by the Mongol chieftain Tamerlane in 1400.

In addition to the ravages caused by humans, there was also a succession of earthquakes, in 1158, 1203, 1664 and most spectacularly in 1759, which caused the fall of the ramparts and three of the huge pillars of the Temple of Jupiter as well as the departure of most of the population. Most of what remains today lies within the area of the Arab fortifications; the Temple of Mercury further out is virtually gone. By erecting walls around some of the buildings, the Arabs unwittingly preserved the temples inside the sanctuary.

Towards the end of the 19th century the European powers became interested in the ruins and their conservation. In 1898, When Kaiser Wilhelm II visited Baalbek on a tour of the Middle East, he was immediately concerned that something should be done to excavate the site. He obtained the permission of the Sultan of Turkey to send a team of archaeologists to begin work. For the next seven years the team recorded the site in detail. By this time Baalbek was frequently visited by tourists who helped themselves to sculptures and inscriptions. They also carved their names on the temple walls.

After the defeat of Turkey and Germany in WWI, Baalbek's German scholars were replaced by French ones and they, in turn were replaced by Lebanese. Over a period of decades all the later masonry was removed and the temples restored as close as possible to their 1st-century splendour.

Orientation

The town of Baalbek is only small with around 12,000 inhabitants. It is very easy to tour the whole town on foot; the ruins are close to the centre of town. The Ras al-Ain (a spring) is about 10 minutes on foot from the centre.

Information

Money There is a branch of the Jamal Bank with an ATM on the main road into town on the left. There is another ATM just before the Palmyra Hotel. You can also change currency at the Palmyra Hotel or in various shops around the central shopping area.

Dangers & Annoyances Visiting Baalbek these days is perfectly safe for tourists, although it is prudent and considerate not to wander around in shorts (men and women) or any other kind of revealing clothes. This is a Hezbollah area whose Shiite Muslim population has close allegiance with Iran (you will no doubt notice pictures of Ayatollah Khomeini around the place) and is therefore more conservative in its dress and behaviour. Alcohol is not openly on sale in shops although, if you ask, they often have an under-the-counter supply. The Palmyra Hotel on the other hand has always served alcohol.

Places to Stay – Budget

The *Ash-Shams Hotel* (☎ 373 284, Rue Abdel Halim Hajjar) is a clean little 1st-floor place run by a tailor. It has four rooms (with washbasins) that sleep up to four people for US$6 per person, or doubles for US$7.50 per person. The toilet and shower are shared. Another budget option is the *Pension Shuman* (☎ 370 160, Ras al-Ain Blvd), near the temple ruins. It has four rooms of varying size, which cost LL10,000 per person.

A new addition to Baalbek's budget selection is the *Hotel Jupiter* (☎ 376 715, Rue Abdel Halim Hajjar), just up from the Palmyra. Owner Hani Awada has built five

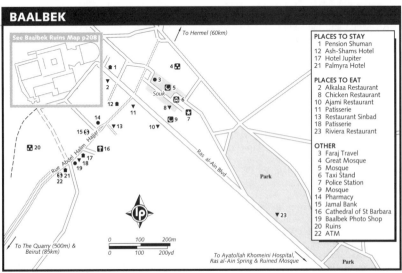

BAALBEK

To Hermel (60km)

See Baalbek Ruins Map p208

Souk

Rue Abdel Halim Hajjar

Ras al-Ain Blvd

Park

Park

To The Quarry (500m) &
Beirut (85km)

To Ayatollah Khomeini Hospital,
Ras al-Ain Spring & Ruined Mosque

| 0 | 100 | 200m |
| 0 | 100 | 200yd |

PLACES TO STAY
 1 Pension Shuman
12 Ash-Shams Hotel
17 Hotel Jupiter
21 Palmyra Hotel

PLACES TO EAT
 2 Alkalaa Restaurant
 8 Chicken Restaurant
10 Ajami Restaurant
11 Patisserie
13 Restaurant Sinbad
18 Patisserie
23 Riviera Restaurant

OTHER
 3 Faraj Travel
 4 Great Mosque
 5 Mosque
 6 Taxi Stand
 7 Police Station
 9 Mosque
14 Pharmacy
15 Jamal Bank
16 Cathedral of St Barbara
19 Baalbek Photo Shop
20 Ruins
22 ATM

rooms, each of a different size. The cheapest is US$20 for a room with four beds. There is also a single with its own bathroom for US$10 and a double without bath for US$15.

Places to Stay – Top End

The **Palmyra Hotel** (☎ 370 230, Rue Abdel Halim Hajjar) is one of those great old survivors from the days of Victorian tourism. The over 120-year-old building is right by the ruins and the former train station. It still has the air of faded grandeur, which hints at its former luxury. The staff are of the 'old retainer' school and are very friendly and helpful. The hotel is clean and comfortable but not luxurious; heating in winter is by paraffin stove and there is no air-con. Even so it is an experience to stay here.

The 1st-floor terrace overlooking the temple is a great place for a sundowner and the hotel has a lovely garden terrace dotted with antique bits of masonry and shaded by jasmine trellises, so it's worth stopping by for a drink even if you aren't staying. Like most hotels of this age it has a bit of a history. During WWI it was used by the German army and during WWII it was the British army headquarters in the area. General de Gaulle stayed here as well as General Allenby, Alfonso of Spain, the Empress of Abyssinia and the writer Jean Cocteau. Over the decades, the famous names who performed at the Baalbek festival also stayed here and signed photographs of some of them line the dining room.

Rooms here cost US$38/53 plus 15% service for singles/doubles with bath. Breakfast is US$5 extra. The hotel has a bar and restaurant where lunch/dinner will cost around US$10. The management has recently opened a new five-room wing, built in the same style as the old, for those who want a bit more comfort. Rooms here cost US$75.

Places to Eat

There are a lot of cheap restaurants on Rue Abdel Halim Hajjar, which serve good, fresh felafels and sandwiches for around LL1500. Baalbek specialises in Lebanese meat 'pizzas', *lahma bi ajeen*, which can be bought for LL1600.

There are several restaurants in town, none particularly noteworthy. The **Restaurant Sinbad**, not far from the Palmyra Hotel, has simple meals. Close to the ruins, opposite the Pension Shuman, is the **Alkalaa Restaurant**, which is quite good. Your best bet is to explore the Ras al-Ain Blvd where several restaurants with attractive eating areas outside look very promising. One of the nicest is the **Riviera Restaurant** (☎ 370 296) towards the Ras-al-Ain-end of the boulevard, backing on to the spring. You can enjoy soft drinks for LL1500 or coffee for LL1000 and choose from a good selection of mezze dishes from about LL1500 each. For a full meal of mezzes and grills, expect to pay US$10 to US$15 per person.

Closer to the centre of Baalbek is the **Ajami Restaurant** (☎ 370 051), also on Ras al-Ain Blvd. This is close to the souq area where there are a number of hole-in-the-wall eateries, but the Ajami is the only one with indoor seating. On the corner near the Ajami is a **patisserie** serving cakes and coffee.

Getting There & Away

Some service taxis go directly from Beirut to Baalbek and charge LL8000. From Chtaura the fare is LL4000 and from Zahlé, LL3000. It is also possible to pick up a service taxi to Damascus or Homs. These are quite frequent and charge LL8000 (LL5000 to Al-Qaa border crossing). The driver will ask to see a visa for Syria before taking you. There is also a minibus running from Baalbek to Beirut's Cola bus station via Chtaura for LL1000. Times seem to vary so check locally before making plans.

During the summer months there is also a road across the mountains to the Cedars and Bcharré. Another goes via Qoubayat to Tripoli. Service taxis do not run on this route, but a taxi in either direction should cost about US$33. The trip takes about 1½ hours and offers spectacular scenery.

HERMEL   هـرمـل

Hermel is the northern-most town in the Bekaa. The main economy is agriculture and it's not really for the casual visitor, but there are several places of interest in the locality. If you do not have your own vehicle, it would be the place to pick up a taxi to take you around the district. This is a painless way to see some out-of-the-way monuments if you only have a short time.

If Hermel ever gets properly excavated, it could turn out to be quite an important historical site; ancient remains have been found, the most interesting being an altar dedicated to Jupiter Heliopolitan.

Places to Stay & Eat

There are no hotels in Hermel; the nearest place to stay is on the Nahr al-Aasi. Along the main road, just past the taxi stand, you can find a few cafes and *shwarma* stands selling snacks and sandwiches. There are also one or two grocery stores selling cold drinks etc. There are no proper restaurants in Hermel.

Getting There & Away

You can get service taxis from Beirut to Hermel for LL10,000, while services run north from Baalbek to Hermel for LL3000. There are also local buses that circle the northern valley and pass on the main road almost hourly (until sunset) and cost LL500 (see Zahlé and Chtaura earlier this chapter).

AROUND HERMEL
The Hermel Pyramid   هرم الهرمل

Ten kilometres south of the town of Hermel is a 27m-high monument in the middle of nowhere sitting on the crest of a small hill. It can be seen for miles around and, although there is no signpost from the main road, you really can't miss it. It is a solid square base construction with a pyramid on top. Large sections have recently been restored but on the original stone you can see very worn depictions of hunting scenes showing stags and boars being attacked by mastiffs. One side shows a bull being attacked by wolves or bears. Nobody is quite sure what this strange monument is meant to be or why it is standing alone. It is definitely not Graeco-Roman and most closely resembles some of the tower tombs at Palmyra (in Syria) to the east. Its age is estimated at around 2000 years and it is probably a Syrian royal tomb, although some writers have suggested it may have been a hunting lodge (very unlikely). Unfortunately the inscriptions are gone, so the pyramid remains an enigma.

Getting There & Away If you are travelling to or from Hermel by service taxi, you could get the driver to drop you by the turn-off. It is about 1km from the main road to the monument along a track, which is easy to spot. If you are driving, the track is OK for a car to drive along.

Nahr al-Aasi   نهر العاصي
☎ 08

Near a bridge that crosses the Nahr al-Aasi, or Orontes River, are several restaurants, specialising in trout, and a couple of hotels. This bridge is about 7km south-east of Hermel and is near the only accommodation in the area. It is a good base to begin a walk along the river to the pools and waterfalls that lie about 5 or 6km to the north (ie, downstream). These **waterfalls** are called Shilal Heira, Derdara and Shilman. It is about a one-hour walk in the other direction to the source of the river; a large basin called **Ain ez-Zerqa** (the Blue Spring).

There is a kayaking club in Hermel that organises trips on the Nahr al-Aasi for all levels. Most trips last from four to seven hours. The club also arranges camping and trekking in the area, for about US$2 to US$4 per day for a tent and LL20,000 per day for all meals. For more information, call Francois Joubert (☎ 415 580) or Ismail Shahin (☎ 200 306 or 698 510).

Places to Stay & Eat There is a good and not too expensive hotel right by the river, about 100m from the bridge. This is the *Hotel Asamaka* (☎ 883 024) with 25 clean rooms that cost US$30 for doubles/triples. The hotel has a restaurant right by the water under awnings and serves mezze and trout (fresh from a pool) for about US$15. It also serves alcohol. Just by the bridge is another restaurant, the *Casino Restaurant*, serving much the same sort of menu at similar prices. *Shalalit al-Dardara* (☎ 828 880) overlooks the Derdara waterfalls and also serves trout and mezze for about US$20.

Offering similar standards as the Asamaka is the recently built *Al-Fardos Hotel (☎ 670 138)*. Singles/doubles cost US$15/20.

Deir Mar Maroun دير مار مارون

Overlooking the Nahr al-Aasi, about 200m from Ein ez-Zarqa sits the ancient rock-cut monastery of Mar Maroun. To reach it you can either take a 3km hike or a 12km drive. Inside the monastery are several tiers of cave-like cells connected with spiral staircases.

The monastery was established in the 5th century by St Maron, the founder of the Maronite church and was destroyed by Justinian II in the 7th century – hundreds were put to death as heretics. The survivors of this persecution fled up to the mountains and across to the Qadisha Valley (see the Tripoli & the North chapter). Later on the monastery's caves were fortified by the Arabs, and you can see arrow slits carved into some of the entrances.

Getting There & Away If you don't have your own car, then you can hire a taxi in Hermel to take you there and back. A short tour of Deir Mar Maroun and the Hermel Pyramid and back to Hermel should cost about US$10.

Al-Jord Ecolodge الجرد

Jord is an Arabic word meaning a mountain area 'beyond the last villages'. Al-Jord is a community-based private company (☎/fax 01-336 820, ✆ info@aljord.com) offering a range of environmental activities centred on an ecolodge in one of Lebanon's most remote and stunningly beautiful areas: the mountains between Hermel, Akkar and Tripoli. From the lofty 500,000-sq-m site one can view the cedar forests of Wadi Jehannam and Fneideq, the summit of Qornet as-Sawda and, far below, the plain of Akkar and the shimmering Mediterranean. Check out their Web site (www.aljord.com).

The company is on a mission to bring prosperity to the area's depressed economy while at the same time preserving its environmental and cultural resources. The brainchild of two affable and well-educated young Beirutis, Clement Zakhia and Jean-Pierre Zahar, Al-Jord offers short and long hiking programs as well as mountain-biking, rock-climbing and spelunking. Educational activities providing insights into the history of local tribes are available, as is volunteer reforestation work and participation in local development programs.

The ecolodge consists of basic mountain huts inspired by local architecture and built from stone, brushwood and juniper. They sleep from five to 10 people and cost US$18 per person. Alternatively, you can try what is called an 'architectural tent' for US$13 per person or camp for US$4 to US$7 per person. Guests are picked up from one of two parking areas (one near Hermel, the other in Sir ed-Dinniye) in order to minimise vehicle damage to the hillsides.

The South

Subject to occupation and conflict long after the civil war was over, the southern part of Lebanon is less developed than the rest of the country. It was the scene of heavy fighting during the civil war, and the extreme south was only liberated from Israeli occupation at the end of May 2000, causing widespread jubilation in Lebanon. Although the 22-year occupation greatly contributed to the area's general degradation, the south's predominantly Shiite population has traditionally suffered neglect at the hands of Beirut's Maronite power brokers (one of the many underlying causes of the civil war). What this means for travellers is that that facilities such as hotels and restaurants are more scarce than in other areas of the country. Nevertheless, there is plenty to see. The coastal towns of Sidon and Tyre both have extensive medieval and ancient remains and, so far, a couple of relatively unspoiled beaches remain open to the public. Hotel options are limited, but the entire area is easily visited on day trips from Beirut. If you want to

Highlights

- Lunch in an Ottoman palace at Sidon's Rest House.
- Cross the causeway and stand on the ramparts of the fortified Sea Castle in Sidon's historic harbour.
- Learn why the ancients limped to the Temple of Echmoun when they needed to be cured.
- Imagine yourself as a charioteer in one of the world's largest hippodromes in Tyre.
- See where Jesus may have turned water into wine in Qana.
- Explore the rubble of medieval and modern Lebanon's most strategic hilltop at Beaufort Castle.

visit sites around the towns, and don't want to rent a car, it might be worth hiring a taxi for the day. You'll be looking at about US$50 from Beirut, slightly less from Sidon or Tyre.

SIDON (SAIDA)   صيدا

☎ 07

History

The ancient town of Sidon, or Saida, is the largest city in southern Lebanon and lies 45km south of Beirut. There is evidence that Sidon was settled as early as 4000 BC, although some sources claim that the area has been inhabited since 6800 BC. In the Old Testament, Sidon is referred to as 'the first born of Canaan'. The name may have originated from the town's possible founder, one Saidoune ibn Canaan, or it could come from the word for 'fishing' or 'hunting' (*sayd* in modern Arabic). Whether it beats out Tyre as the most ancient Phoenician city is likewise a subject of scholarly debate, but without doubt it was one of the most important Phoenician cities.

WARNING

During their 20-year occupation, the Israelis, their SLA allies and their various Lebanese opponents littered the occupied zone with landmines. As a result, the area remains full of unexploded ordnance. This is especially true in the least built-up areas, which are not a priority for mine-clearing. In the fortnight following the Israeli withdrawal, five Lebanese were killed and 33 seriously injured by these hidden killers. Do NOT wander off roads or even walk on paths in the area without being absolutely sure that the terrain is safe. At the time of writing the situation in the former occupied zone, close to the Israeli border, was in flux and permits were required to visit the area. These could be obtained through Major Mohammed Rammel at the Ministry of Defence in Yarze (☎ 01-424 043, fax 424 273).

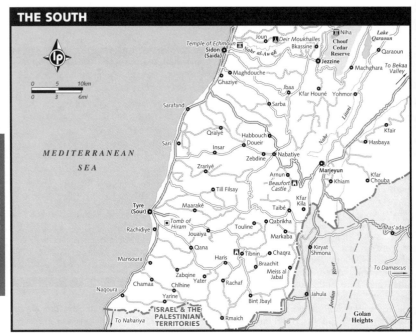

THE SOUTH

As early as the 14th and 15th centuries BC, Sidon had earned a reputation as a commercial centre. Trading links were particularly strong with Egypt, where the Tell al-Amarna tablets record correspondence between the Pharaoh Akhenaten (Amenophis IV) and the ruler of Sidon, Zimrida. The city gradually rose in prominence from the 12th to 10th centuries BC, when Phoenicia enjoyed relative peace. Much of its wealth came from trading murex, a mollusc that produced a highly valued purple dye (see the boxed text 'Murex' later in this chapter for more information). Geography helped, too: like many Phoenician cities, Sidon was built on a promontory with an offshore island. The island sheltered the harbour from storms and also provided a safe haven during times of war.

In common with the other Phoenician city-states, Sidon suffered from conquest and invasion numerous times during its history. In 1200 BC the Philistines destroyed the city and its fleet of trading ships, allowing Tyre to eclipse Sidon as the most important Phoenician centre. Although often under Tyre's control, or forced to pay tribute to the Assyrians, Sidon recovered its status as a trading centre, only to be destroyed in 675 BC by the Assyrian Esarhaddon.

The city's golden age came during the dominance of the Persian Empire (550–333 BC). The city was made the capital of the Fifth Province, which covered Syria, Palestine and Cyprus. Apart from the murex industry, Sidon became famous for its glass making which, at the time, was the best in the world. It was during this period that the Temple of Echmoun, about 2km to the northeast of the city, was built. Inscriptions found there reveal that Phoenician Sidon was built in two sections; the maritime city (Sidon Yam), and the upper part (Sidon Sadeh) which was built on the lower spurs of the Mt Lebanon Range, upwind from the noxious smell of the dye works.

The people of Sidon also became great shipbuilders and provided experienced sailors for the Persian fleet. The king of Sidon acted as admiral for the Persian fleet, which was successful in campaigns against the Egyptians in the 6th century BC, and later against the Greeks. This important role gave Sidon and the other Phoenician city-states a degree of independence over their Persian overlords. This lasted until the middle of the 4th century BC, when Phoenician rebellion, centred in Sidon, incurred the wrath of the Persians. Heading a huge army, King Artaxerxes Ochus, arrived to beat the

Sidonians into submission. According to the Greek historian, Diodorus, the Sidonians locked the city gates and set fire to the city rather than hand it over. More than 40,000 people died in the inferno. This weakened the city to such an extent that when Alexander the Great marched through the Middle East in 333 BC, the Sidonians were in no position to resist him. Sidon handed over power to the Greeks without a struggle.

Under the Greeks, Sidon enjoyed relative freedom and an advanced cultural life. Later the city came successively under the control of the Seleucids and the Ptolemies. In the

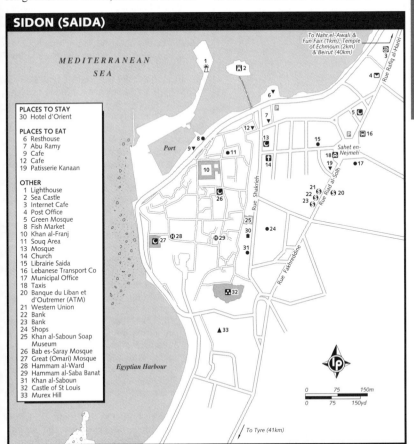

SIDON (SAIDA)

MEDITERRANEAN SEA

To Nahr el-Awali &
Fun Fair (1km), Temple
of Echmoun (2km)
& Beirut (40km)

Port

Sahet en-
Nejmeh

Egyptian Harbour

To Tyre (41km)

PLACES TO STAY
30 Hotel d'Orient

PLACES TO EAT
6 Resthouse
7 Abu Ramy
9 Cafe
12 Cafe
19 Patisserie Kanaan

OTHER
1 Lighthouse
2 Sea Castle
3 Internet Cafe
4 Post Office
5 Green Mosque
8 Fish Market
10 Khan al-Franj
11 Souq Area
13 Mosque
14 Church
15 Librairie Saida
16 Lebanese Transport Co
17 Municipal Office
18 Taxis
20 Banque du Liban et
    d'Outremer (ATM)
21 Western Union
22 Bank
23 Bank
24 Shops
25 Khan al-Saboun Soap
    Museum
26 Bab es-Saray Mosque
27 Great (Omari) Mosque
28 Hammam al-Ward
29 Hammam al-Saba Banat
31 Khan al-Saboun
32 Castle of St Louis
33 Murex Hill

0   75   150m
0   75   150yd

THE SOUTH

Murex

The famous purple dye of Phoenicia comes from the murex, a kind of mollusc, which grew in abundance in the coastal waters off Sidon and Tyre. There were in fact two kinds of mollusc used in the dye process: the murex and the buccinum. Both have a long sac or vein filled with a yellowish fluid that turns purple when exposed to light. The discovery of this natural source of purple dye made the fortunes of many merchants in Sidon and Tyre.

The origins of the discovery are lost, but a myth remains that the god Melkart was walking on the beach one day with his lover, a nymph called Tyrus, and his dog. The dog bit into one of the murex shells and its muzzle became stained with a purple dye. When she saw the beautiful colour, Tyrus demanded that Melkart make her a garment of purple. So Melkart gathered a quantity of the shellfish to dye a gown, which he presented to her.

This romantic tale hides the fact that the production of dye was a smelly, messy business that involved a great deal of hard work. The molluscs were gathered in deep water by dropping narrow-necked baskets baited with mussels and frog meat. Once harvested the shellfish were hauled off to dye pits where their sacs were removed, pulped and heated in huge lead vessels. All the extraneous matter was skimmed off and the resulting dye fixed.

The dye pits were placed downwind of the residential areas to avoid the noxious smell. With practice, the dyers could produce a variety of colours from pale pink to deep violet by mixing the murex and buccinum fluids in different quantities. The dye industry was on such a large scale that the molluscs were farmed to extinction.

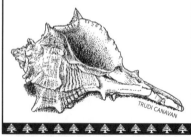

TRUDI CANAVAN

early days of the Roman Empire it formed a kind of republic with its own senate and its own minted coins. Augustus put an end to its independence and brought it under direct Roman rule. When St Paul visited Sidon on his journey from Caesarea to Rome in the 1st century AD, it had fallen into a decline although it was still commercially important.

During the Byzantine period it became the seat of a bishopric. It was during this time that the strong earthquake of AD 551 destroyed most of the cities in Phoenicia. Sidon came out of it better than most and became the home of Beirut's famous School of Law when that city was badly damaged. The following century was uneventful until the invasion and conquest by the Arabs in 667. The city took the Arabic name, Saida, and remained a wealthy centre, administered from Damascus.

In 1110 the city was besieged by Baldwin I, King of Jerusalem, and the Sidonians gave up after 47 days of resistance. In 1187 Saladin took the city and razed the ramparts to the ground in an attempt to make it useless as a Crusader base. It failed to deter them, however, and they recaptured it. Subsequent battles for control saw Sidon passed between the two sides as many as five times, each accompanied by widespread destruction, followed by rebuilding. It finally fell to the Mamluks after the fall of Acre in 1291.

In the 15th century Sidon's fortunes rose when it became one of the trading ports of Damascus. It flourished again in the 17th century under the rule of Fakhreddine (Fakhr ad-Din al-Maan II). He rebuilt and modernised parts of the city, including the Khan al-Franj (Inn of Foreigners). The city's prosperity was only temporary, however; in 1791, the Ottoman pasha of Acre, Ahmed Jazzar, drove the French from the town and Beirut took over as the centre of commerce with Europe. An earthquake in the 1830s, followed by bombardment during the Ottoman-European campaign to remove Bashir Shihab II, helped ensure the city's fall into relative obscurity.

In the early part of this century the area around Sidon was developed for agriculture, and fruit in particular remains the main crop. The oranges are said to be the original Jaffa variety, which is now grown extensively in Israel for export. The 1950s saw nascent industrial development, primarily centred around the terminus of the Trans Arabian Pipeline, but this all came to an end with the outbreak of the civil war. Sidon was fought over by the Palestinians, Syrians, Israelis and Hezbollah and Amal, and suffered greatly. In the postwar period, it has benefited from being the birth place of former prime minister Rafiq Hariri, who has used his eponymous foundation to channel huge amounts of money into reconstruction. Other wealthy Sidon financiers, such as the Audi family, are sponsoring restoration of the souqs.

Orientation

There is a main highway running north-south through the city. Near the northern end of the city, close to a mosque that sits between the Corniche and the main road north, is a square, Sahet en-Nejmeh, where the taxis and buses are based. The main road through town, Rue Riad al-Solh, is lined with shops, cafes and banks. The old part of the city with the port, Sea Castle and souqs are to the west of the main road, while the modern shopping centres and residential buildings are on the eastern side. If you are arriving from the north, you can easily spot the Sea Castle, which is the dominant feature of the city.

Information

Money Sidon's many banks, a couple with ATMs, are mainly clustered together on or near the main road, Rue Riad al-Solh, close to Sahet en-Nejmeh. In the old souqs are several moneychangers with reasonable rates.

Post & Communications The main post office and telephone bureau is a large white building on Rue Rafiq al-Hariri, north of Sahet en-Nejmeh. You can easily spot it by the huge antenna on the roof. Western Union on Rue Riad al-Solh acts as a private phone office and charges LL2000 per minute for overseas calls. It is open from 9 am to midnight.

Email & Internet Services There is an Internet cafe, PC Net, on the main road, north of Sahet en-Nejmeh. It is open from 10 am until midnight and charges LL3000 per hour.

Bookshop There is a small bookshop and stationers, Librairie Saida, on the road which runs west of the main square where the taxis stop. The books are mostly in Arabic, but it also has a fair selection of French and German magazines and local postcards.

Emergency The following Sidon telephone number may be useful in an emergency:

Ambulance   ☎ 722 532

Sea Castle

The Sea Castle (Qasr al-Bahr) sits on a small island, 80m offshore, that is reached on foot across a causeway that encloses the old fishing harbour. In the past, part of this was made of wood and could be removed to prevent enemies from entering the fortress.

The castle was originally the site of a Phoenician temple to Melkart, but later became a fortification. The structure you see today was built by the Crusaders as a defence from both sea and inland invaders after their recapture of Sidon from Saladin's successors, the Ayyubids, in 1228. It was hastily constructed from existing masonry when it was learned that the king of Germany, Frederick Barbarossa, would be arriving. Hence the Roman columns – you can still see sticking out from the foundations – which were placed transversally along the walls to strengthen the building. When the Mamluks finally drove out the Franks in 1291, they destroyed much of the building, but it was later rebuilt by Fakhreddine.

The building consists of two towers joined together by a wall. The northern tower, to the left of the entrance, is the best preserved. Rectangular in shape, it measures 21m by 17m and has a large vaulted room scattered with old carved capitals and rusting cannonballs. A winding staircase leads up to the roof (it is useful to have a torch here), where there is a small, domed, Ottoman-era mosque. From the roof there is a great view across the old city and fishing harbour. The right-hand tower is less well preserved and was built in two phases; the lower part dates to the Crusader period, while the upper level was built by the Mamluks, as testified by a marble inscription over a window looking into the interior hall.

In the clear, shallow water surrounding the castle you can see many broken columns of rose granite lying on the sea floor. Preliminary archaeological work carried out before the civil war showed extensive underwater remains off Sidon's coast, some dating back to the Persian period.

The castle is open from 9 am to 6 pm daily and entrance costs LL2000.

Khan al-Franj

Khan al-Franj, which literally means the 'Khan of the Foreigners', was the largest and best preserved of the many khans built by Fakhreddine during his reign in the 17th century and was donated to French traders in the Fakhreddine's drive to improve trading links with Europe. The khans were designed to store goods and house travelling merchants. They nearly all follow the same basic design: a large central courtyard with a fountain and covered arcades, used as stables and storage, and a galleried 2nd storey providing accommodation for merchants and travellers.

The Khan al-Franj was the principal khan in the 19th century and was the centre of economic activity in the city. It also housed the French consul and remains the property of the French government, as described on a marble slab at the building's entrance. Today its painstaking restoration, funded by the Hariri Foundation, is in its final stages. Once finished, the Khan will house a cultural centre, a tourist office and a museum. There is already one shop among the ground floor arcades: Anamel Saida (☎ 727 344) sells handicrafts and is open from 10 am to 3 pm every day except Sunday and Monday. The Khan is currently closed on Sunday.

Great Mosque

Facing the northern tip of the harbour is the Great (or Omari) Mosque. Originally a fortified building established in the 13th century

by the Knights Hospitaller, its sheer stone facade still has an air of impregnability when seen from the road running alongside the sea. A long, rectangular building with a sandstone minaret (rebuilt after its destruction during the 1982 Israeli invasion), it was converted to a mosque after the Crusaders were driven out of the Holy Land. The main prayer hall once housed the Church of St John of the Hospitallers and its original walls can still be seen. There are two entrances to the mosque: one down a maze of covered streets in the souqs, the other on the eastern side of the building (once the site of a palace built by Fakhreddine). Inside is a large courtyard surrounded on three sides by arched porticos and bordered on the fourth side by the prayer hall. There are two mihrabs on the southern wall of the prayer hall, with a modern minbar in-between. (See 'The Architecture of Lebanon' special section in the Facts about Lebanon chapter.)

Visitors are not exactly encouraged, but it is worth asking at the gate whether you can look around. Modest dress, including headscarves for women, is needed if you want to persuade the gatekeeper to let you in. Be sure to avoid prayer times.

Bab es-Saray Mosque

The Bab es-Saray Mosque dates back to 1201, making it the oldest mosque in the city. Located just east of the old Bab es-Saray, or Saray Gate, it also boasts the largest dome in Sidon and an enormous supporting column, made from black stone allegedly imported from Italy. The beautiful stonework has just been restored through a *waqf* (religious endowment). Covered heads (for women) and appropriate attire are necessary to enter. The mosque sits in the corner of a square, which has a pleasant cafe built on the site of the original *saray* (palace). If you look inside you can still see stone remnants of the old building. The square can be entered through the rear door of Khan al-Franj.

Souqs

The old covered souq of Sidon lies between the Sea Castle and the Castle of St Louis. This is the medieval heart of the city where,

CATHY LANIGAN

banon's literacy rate of over 90% is the highest in the Middle East.

BETHUNE CARMICHAEL

he smiling face of a drinks vendor in Baalbek

BETHUNE CARMICHAEL

Shade can be at a premium in a Beirut summer.

BRENDA TURNNIDGE

Men relaxing amid the bustle of the Tripoli souq

Tilling the terraces on the slopes to the west of the Bekaa Valley

Praying at Harissa's Virgin of Lebanon statue

Khan al-Franj (Inn of the Foreigners), Sidon

Sheepshearing in the Bekaa Valley

in labyrinthine alleyways, shopkeepers have their workshops and ply their trades in the same way they have done for centuries. Officially there are some 60 listed historic sites here; in reality, most of them, including several under preservation order, are ruins, either destroyed during the civil war, squatted in by refugees, or simply no longer used in their original capacity.

Scattered throughout the souqs are the coffee houses where men meet to smoke nargilehs (water pipes) and pass the afternoon. There is a huge number of pastry shops in the souqs where you can buy all manner of cakes and biscuits. The utterly delicious *sanioura* is a speciality of Sidon and is a light crumbly biscuit. The souqs are also famous for producing orange-blossom water.

Hammams

There are five *hammams*, or Turkish baths, in Sidon's old city, although only one is still functioning. Unfortunately, the city's grandest bathhouse, **Hammam al-Mir**, was partially destroyed by the Israelis, along with its mosaic-covered dome and marble floors. The survivor is **Hammam al-Ward**, beside the Grand Mosque. Built in 1721, the combination Italian/Ottoman style building is in a poor shape, but is still open for business. Hours and prices appear to be flexible, and

Bathing Ghosts

Sidon lore has it that the **Hammam al-Saba Banat** (Bathhouse of the Seven Girls), got its name from seven spirits that have haunted the bathhouse throughout its existence. Every night after the building was locked, locals reported hearing the clacking of hammam clogs across the marble floors, taps being opened and the sound of female voices. These were believed to belong to seven female *jinn*, or spirits, who would come and bathe in the hammam's seven stone basins in private. Nobody dared to disturb them and they appear to have disappeared with the last hammam customer. Unfortunately for thrill-seekers, the building now functions as a bakery.

you may have to hunt for the custodian, but the adjacent shopkeepers will help.

Khan al-Saboun Soap Museum

Although Tripoli may take credit for being the centre of the traditional soap-making industry, it is Sidon that has Lebanon's first museum dedicated to the craft. Located at the outer limit of Old Sidon in Khan al-Saboun, a 13th-century stone building that was adapted for use as a soap factory in the 19th century, it produced soap to meet the needs of the hammams in the town. Run by the Audi family – now among Lebanon's top bankers and businessmen – it fell into ruin when the family left the city in the latter half of the 20th century. Its beautiful restoration, funded by the family's charitable foundation, was all but complete at the time of writing.

The museum's curators have assembled all the accoutrements of soap making and the well laid out galleries and trilingual (Arabic, English, French) explanations take you through the entire soap-making process, from the massive stone tub where the raw ingredients were mixed together to the shaping and cutting of the still warm liquid. Towers of soap (ironically brought here from Tripoli) show how the finished product was dried before being packaged for sale.

Also interesting is a small but fascinating display of hammam accessories, including *saflin* (small seeds used as toothpicks) and *kiyaas hammam* (goat hair bags used as loofahs). The entrance to the museum is on Sharia al-Shakrieh, a small alleyway in the souq distinguishable by the number of restored, vaulted shops and workshops (also courtesy of the Audi Foundation). Mention the name Audi and most people will point you in the right direction. The museum has a small cafeteria, and a boutique selling handicrafts (presumably including soap) is due to open in the building. It exits on to Rue Moutrane, just along from the Hotel d'Orient (see Places to Stay).

Castle of St Louis

The ruins of this once-impressive castle stand on a mound to the south of town. The present structure dates back to the Crusaders, who built on the site of an earlier Fatimid fortress – as reflected in the local name, Qala'a al-Muizz or fortress of Al-Muizz, after the Fatimid caliph Al-Muizz li-din Allah, who fortified the site. The English/French name comes from Louis IX who rebuilt and then occupied the fortress when he retook Sidon from the Ayyubids in 1253. After the Arabs retook the city it was restored, but it later suffered at the hands of the Mamluks. This, coupled with centuries of pilfering of its large stones by locals, has left the structure in poor condition.

The hill on which the castle is situated is thought to have been the ancient acropolis of Sidon. Remains of a theatre have been uncovered here by archaeologists, but the site remains largely unexcavated. There is a low wall around the base of the hill and a locked gate. The site is usually unattended.

Murex Hill

Just south of the Castle of St Louis is an artificial hill about 100m high and 50m long, partially covered by a cemetery. This is Sidon's ancient garbage dump, largely formed from the crushed remains of hundreds of thousands of murex shells, the by-product of the city's famed dye. Traces of the shells can be seen on the embankment heading south from the castle.

Places to Stay

There is only one hotel in Sidon, the small *Hotel d'Orient* or *Nazel esh-Sharq* (☎ 720 364, Rue Shakrieh). Its six none-too-clean rooms and basic bathroom facilities only get a mention because there's nothing else in town. It is above a tiny baggage shop not far from the Muslim cemetery, and just along from the soap museum exit. Look for a painted banner/sign on the first floor. Doubles start at LL20,000, and prices drop according to whether there are three or four people in the room.

Places to Eat

Almost opposite the ticket office at the entrance to the Sea Castle, the *Abu Ramy* restaurant does a brisk trade in felafel sandwiches and other Lebanese fast-food sta-

ples. There are also lots of cheap cafes and *shwarma* stalls around Sahet en-Nejmeh as well as plenty of patisseries. Recommended for its famous pastries is the *Patisserie Kanaan* (☎ 720 271); the *Patisserie Abou Nawas* and *Patisserie Ramla* are also good.

The culinary highlight in town is without doubt the *Rest House* (☎ 722 469), a beautifully restored Ottoman khan, complete with vaulted ceilings and fine inlaid marble and stonework. The shaded garden terrace is on the edge of the sea and has a panoramic view of Sidon's seafront. Food here is traditional Lebanese, with good mezze and seafood. Expect to pay at least US$15 per person for a modest lunch of a few dips and a grill and salad, more if you indulge in wine or beer. You don't have to eat, though, and it is well worth dropping by for a drink.

Along the main road heading north is the far less beautiful and slightly cheaper *Palamera Pizzeria* which serves pizza, steak and, oddly, Chinese food for between US$5 to US$10.

Getting There & Around

The bus and service-taxi stands are on Sahet en-Nejmeh. Service taxis charge LL2500 to Beirut's Cola bus station and LL3000 to Tyre. The Lebanese Transport Company has an office on the square and buses run from here to Cola in Beirut every hour from 4.45 am until 8.30 pm. Tickets cost LL750. Buses to Tyre start at 6.30 am and run until 7 pm, also for LL750 (LL1000 return). Within town, service taxis cost LL1000; taxis LL5000. A private taxi to Echmoun and back will cost around LL8000. Alternatively, a one-way ride will cost LL5000 and you can walk back along the Nahr al-Awali and take your chances on finding a taxi on the highway.

AROUND SIDON
Temple of Echmoun معبد أشمون

This Phoenician temple is about 3km northeast of Sidon on the Nahr al-Awali. The whole area is filled with citrus orchards and the river banks are a favourite picnic spot with locals, although the garbage-strewn grass beside the river might deter others. The region has long been a fruit-growing area

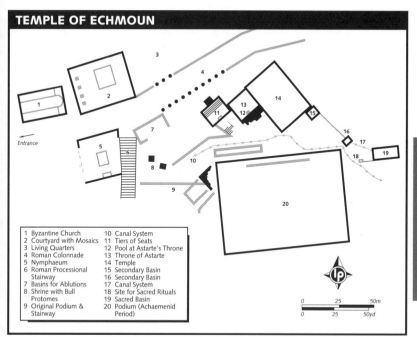

TEMPLE OF ECHMOUN

1 Byzantine Church
2 Courtyard with Mosaics
3 Living Quarters
4 Roman Colonnade
5 Nymphaeum
6 Roman Processional Stairway
7 Basins for Ablutions
8 Shrine with Bull Protomes
9 Original Podium & Stairway
10 Canal System
11 Tiers of Seats
12 Pool at Astarte's Throne
13 Throne of Astarte
14 Temple
15 Secondary Basin
16 Secondary Basin
17 Canal System
18 Site for Sacred Rituals
19 Sacred Basin
20 Podium (Achaemenid Period)

THE SOUTH

and the site of the temple is known as Boustan al-Sheikh (Garden of the Sheikh).

Echmoun was the principal god of the city of Sidon and was associated with healing. This is the only Phoenician site in Lebanon that has retained more than just its foundation walls, although it is in ruins and the lack of any explanations can be disappointing for nonexperts.

The temple complex was begun in the 7th century BC and the following centuries saw numerous additions to the basic building. Some of the buildings, such as the Roman colonnade and the Byzantine church and mosaics, are far later than the original Phoenician temple and are an indication of how long the site retained its importance as a place of pilgrimage.

The legendary story of Echmoun closely follows that of Tammuz and Adonis. Echmoun began as a mortal youth from Berytus (Beirut). The goddess Astarte fell in love with him; to escape from her, he mutilated himself and died. Not to be thwarted she brought him back to life in the form of a god, hence his story was linked to fertility and rebirth. He was still primarily a god of healing and is identified with the Greek Asklepios, the god of medicine, and the Roman Aesculapius. It is from the snake motif of Echmoun that we get the serpentine symbol of the medical profession. The idea of a serpent coiled around a staff was found on a gold plaque at Echmoun.

The look of the temple complex is reminiscent, on a much-reduced scale, of the terraced Persian site at Persepolis, an open-air sanctuary rather than enclosed in the Greek style. It has a nearby water source for the ritual ablutions. It was customary for people coming to the temple to ask for the god's help to bring a small statue with the name of the person who needed healing. Many of these votive statues depicted children and examples can be seen at the National Museum in Beirut.

Between the 6th and 4th centuries BC Sidon was known for its opulence, culture and industry. During this era, one of the rulers was Echmounazar II. His sarcophagus was discovered in 1858 and it had inscriptions on it relating that he and his mother, Amashtarte, built temples to the gods at Sidon including the Temple of Echmoun. The sarcophagus is now in the Louvre in Paris.

Detail of the sarcophagus of Echmounazar II which was discovered in 1858 near Sidon.

The temple built by Echmounazar II was rediscovered by archaeologists during the excavation of Boustan al-Sheikh earlier this century. It had been destroyed by an earthquake around the middle of the 4th century BC. Although the temple was never rebuilt, the site retained its reputation as a place of healing and some of the smaller buildings were restored and the later church built. It was used by both pagan and Christian pilgrims. The site remained popular until the 3rd century AD, though it was by that time in ruins.

As you enter the site, there is a colonnade of shops on the right which probably did a roaring trade selling souvenirs to pilgrims. On the left are the remains of a **Byzantine church** just past what was a large courtyard with some very faded 3rd century BC mosaics showing the seasons. On the right is a Roman processional stairway, which leads to the upper levels of the site. The stairway was added in the 1st century AD. Also on the right is a **nymphaeum** with a fountain and niches containing statues of the nymphs.

Further along on the right is one of the most interesting artefacts, the **Throne of Astarte** flanked by two sphinxes. The throne is carved from a solid block of granite in the Egyptian style. There is also a very worn frieze depicting a hunting scene.

The site has no formal opening times, although the gate is often closed at sunset, and there is no charge for entry. There is usually a soldier at the entrance taking care of the site. If you turn up on your own (not in a tour bus) don't be surprised if he accompanies you around the site. Independent visitors are a bit of a rarity.

Getting There & Away The site is within walking distance (about 30 minutes) of Sidon, although most of this is alongside the heavy traffic on the less-than-picturesque main coastal highway. Follow the highway north for about 3km and turn right at the signpost for the temple, just beside a small fair ground. This road follows the river bank and the site is about 2km further along. If you don't want to brave the fumes, you can catch a taxi Sahet en-Nejmeh in Sidon for LL5000 one way. To return by taxi, you will have to arrange to be picked up or ask the driver to wait (LL8000). You can also ask the Beirut – Sidon bus to drop you off at the Nahr al-Awali (Awali River) and walk on the road which runs alongside the river until you reach the temple.

Joun جون

Joun is a large village in the midst of olive plantations above the Nahr al-Awali. Its main claim to fame is that it was the home for many years of the famous woman traveller Lady Hester Stanhope. Before the war there was even a cafe named after her in the main square. See the boxed text 'Lady Hester Stanhope' (opposite) for more information on this eccentric colonial figure.

To reach her home, pass through the village and after about 2km turn left at the sign for the 'Stanhope Tyre Factory'(!). Follow the road, bearing right at any forks, and eventually you will find yourself at the ruins of her once-substantial house. Fifty metres to the south-west was her tomb, which lay in

Lady Hester Stanhope

The Middle East has always attracted intrepid women explorers and adventurers and Lady Hester Stanhope was one of the most extreme examples of the breed. She was born into an affluent but eccentric life in London in 1776, the daughter of the domineering Earl of Stanhope and Hester Pitt, sister of William Pitt, the future prime minister of England.

She grew up without a governess and later on a tutor engaged by her father was charged with high treason. She became close to her uncle, William Pitt, and when he became prime minister, she moved into 10 Downing Street and played political hostess. Her first love was Sir John Moore who took her favourite brother, James, to serve with him in Salamanca. They were both killed and when her uncle also died, Hester was homeless and broken hearted.

To forget her grief, Hester decided to travel abroad and took her personal physician, Dr Meryon, with her. He remained in her service for 28 years, even while she had a notorious affair with Ian Bruce. In typical colonial fashion, she and her retinue travelled the Middle East being treated like royalty. Her greatest moment of glory was riding into Palmyra in Syria on an Arab stallion at the head of her travelling procession. The Bedouin there later 'crowned' her 'Queen of the Desert'. Of this she wrote that she had charmed them so that 'they all became as humble as possible'. Such incidents cemented her fantasy that she was somehow a representative of the Arabs she so liked to dominate, and she began meddling in regional politics, much to the exasperation of rulers like Muhammed Ali, the Viceroy of Egypt, who complained that she caused him more trouble than the peoples of Palestine, Syria and Lebanon combined.

Her name was famous all over the Arab world by the time she came to Joun (north-east of Sidon). Having installed herself as a guest in the house of a Christian merchant, she announced that she liked the house so much that she would stay for the remainder of her days. When it became clear that she meant this literally, the merchant protested to the local emir, but Hester wrote directly to the sultan in Constantinople who wrote back 'Obey the Princess of Europe in everything'.

Once she possessed the Joun house, Lady Hester became increasingly eccentric, reportedly forsaking books for communing with the stars. Although greatly respected by local people, among whom she liberally distributed money until she bankrupted herself, she gradually became a recluse, only receiving a few European visitors who would wait at Sidon for word of whether she would see them. The poet Lamartine was one such visitor, as was the son of a childhood friend, Kinglake (author of *Eothen*). He reported that she was wearing a large turban of cashmere shawls and a flowing white robe and seemed to be quite alone in her oriental sitting rooms.

When she died in 1839, she was totally alone and in debt. The British consul had to be sent for to take care of her burial and her remains were hurriedly placed alongside those of a young officer in Napoleon's Imperial Guard – reputedly a former lover – in a grave behind her house.

the shade of an olive grove. However, the once simple step-pyramid grave was a casualty of the civil war and is now a hole in the ground with rubble strewn around. Still, her final resting-place remains a picturesque spot and is ideal for picnicking.

Deir Moukhalles (Saint Saviour's Monastery)

دير المخلّص

Local legend has it that this 18th century Greek Catholic monastery was built on the site of a miracle. As the story goes, a bishop was passing through the area when one of the priests in his entourage was accidentally shot in the stomach. The alarmed bishop reportedly exclaimed 'holy saviour,' at which the victim stood up and was found to be unhurt; the offending bullet had melted into a harmless flat disk. The bishop ordered that a monastery be built on the site. After being badly damaged in an earthquake in 1956 and abandoned during the civil war, the monastery was recently restored and has some fine icons.

Joun is about 15km north-east of Sidon and Deir Moukhalles is about 3km further east. They can be reached by taxi or private car. The taxi fare is around US$12 one way. There is little other traffic on this road so you will need to have the taxi wait or arrange to be collected.

Jezzine

جزّين

One of South Lebanon's most famous summer resorts, Jezzine sits 950m up on the western slopes of Jebel Niha, below one of the eastern Mediterranean's largest pine forests.

Known for its 40m-high waterfalls and cool summer temperatures, the town has a long history, although most architectural remains have gone. A more recent monument worth visiting, however, is the **Farid Serhal Palace**, an Ottoman-style building with lavish interiors and displays of antiquities.

In the valley below Jezzine is **Fakhreddine's Cave**, the cave where Fakhreddine, like his father before him, hid from the Ottomans. His father eventually died there but Fakhreddine was discovered and taken to Istanbul.

Service taxis from Sidon cost LL3000, taxis LL8000.

Sarafand

صرفند

☎ 07

Sarafand is the biblical Zarephath (also later known as Sarepta), which is famous for the miracle of Elijah who raised the widow's son from the dead and multiplied her olive oil and grain supplies (1 Kings 17). The ancient town was also mentioned in Egyptian and Assyrian texts. Apart from miracles, Sarafand was famed in ancient times for its glass-making (the word *seraph* means 'to melt' in Hebrew). Archaeological excavation before the civil war revealed that the site was first occupied in the middle of the second millennium BC, eventually becoming an important trading town. The original port extended for over 1km and enclosed three small bays, which are still used by local anglers as anchorages. Ruined Phoenician masonry of houses and cisterns is visible on the shore, and there are even the remains of ancient slipways used by Phoenician vessels.

During the Crusades, Sarepta, as it was then called, was a fairly large, fortified town. It was the seat of a bishopric and home to a Carmelite order. There was a church commemorating St Elijah in the centre of town, probably beneath the site of the Wadi al-Khader.

Modern Sarafand is 19km south of Sidon and is no longer a vital trading town, but a featureless village with a few restaurants built on the inland side of the main coastal road. Illegal construction and looting during the civil war have unfortunately destroyed many of the archaeological remains that were described by nineteenth century travellers in the vicinity. To see the traces of the old port, head down to the fishing harbour.

Places to Stay & Eat One of the few hotels in the south is in Sarafand. The **Mounis Hotel** (☎ 666 657, **@** fakihco@cyberia .net.lb) is built out on the water and is connected to the mainland by a causeway. It is clean and modern with double rooms costing US$50. Lunch and dinner are available in the hotel restaurant for about US$12.

Sarafand has spawned a collection of fish restaurants along the coast road, supplied by the local fishing industry. As with other seafood restaurants in Lebanon, they are not cheap and the fish is chosen by the customer and sold by weight. Allow from US$15 to US$20 per person for grilled fish and side dishes. A popular local favourite is *Fouad Ville* (☎ 722 442), on the Sidon side of town.

Getting There & Away Sarafand is on the main north-south highway and service taxis or buses can drop you here from either Beirut or Sidon. The service taxi fare from Sidon is LL2000.

TYRE (SOUR)   صور
☎ 07
History
Tyre's origins are lost to us. According to Herodotus, the city was already 2300 years old when he wrote his histories, which dates it back to approximately 2750 BC, around the time of the founding of the Temple of Melkart (Heracles) and the Canaanite invasions. The original founders are believed to have come from Sidon to establish a new city port.

Under the 18th (Egyptian) dynasty, Tyre fell under the supremacy of the pharaohs and from the 17th to 13th centuries BC benefited from Egypt's protection and prospered commercially.

Toward the end of the 2nd millennium BC, Tyre became a kingdom ruled at first by Abibaal. His son Hiram I ascended the throne in 969 BC and forged very close relations with the Hebrew kings Solomon and David. Hiram sent cedar wood and skilled workers to help construct the famed temple in Jerusalem, as well as large amounts of gold. In return he received a district in Galilee with 20 towns in it.

Under Hiram's reign, Tyre flourished. The original layout of the city was in two parts; an offshore island, which was the

THE SOUTH

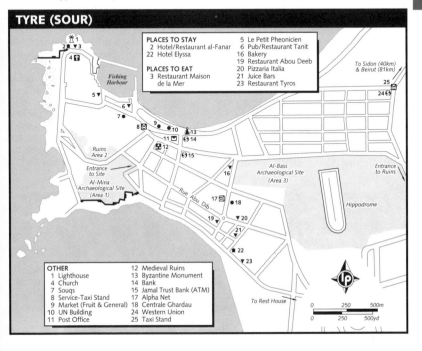

TYRE (SOUR)

PLACES TO STAY
2 Hotel/Restaurant al-Fanar
22 Hotel Elyssa

PLACES TO EAT
3 Restaurant Maison de la Mer

5 Le Petit Pheonicien
6 Pub/Restaurant Tanit
16 Bakery
19 Restaurant Abou Deeb
20 Pizzaria Italia
21 Juice Bars
23 Restaurant Tyros

To Sidon (40km) & Beirut (81km)

Fishing Harbour

Ruins Area 2

Entrance to Site
Al-Mina Archaeological Site (Area 1)

Rue Abu Dib

Al-Bass Archaeological Site (Area 3)

Entrance to Ruins

Hippodrome

To Rest House

OTHER
1 Lighthouse
4 Church
7 Souqs
8 Service-Taxi Stand
9 Market (Fruit & General)
10 UN Building
11 Post Office
12 Medieval Ruins
13 Byzantine Monument
14 Bank
15 Jamal Trust Bank (ATM)
17 Alpha Net
18 Centrale Ghardau
24 Western Union
25 Taxi Stand

0   250   500m
0   250   500yd

Hiram versus Solomon

Relations between King Hiram of Tyre and King Solomon of Israel were cordial but competitive. According to the annals of Tyre, there was a contest of wisdom between the two kings. They would each set riddles for the other. Whoever failed to guess correctly had to pay a fine. Wrong answers cost Hiram a fortune, but he eventually sharpened his wits and turned the tables on Solomon, winning back all he had lost and more.

older part of the city, and the overspill on the mainland. Hiram developed the island-city and used landfill to connect it to other small islands nearby, and to the mainland by a narrow causeway. According to the Bible, Hiram allied himself with King Solomon in developing trade with Arabia and North and East Africa. During his reign, the Phoenicians colonised Sicily and North Africa, which later became the off-shoot Carthaginian Empire. Such was Hiram's success that the Mediterranean Sea became known as 'the Tyrian Sea' and Tyre was the most important city on it.

After Hiram's 34-year reign ended, Tyre fell into bloody revolution, even as it continued to expand its trading links as far as the west coast of Africa and the south-east of Britain. The city paid tribute to the Assyrians but remained close to the Israelites and was ruled by a succession of kings. Perhaps the most famous woman of ancient Tyrian legend was Princess Elissa, also

known as Dido. She was embroiled in a plot to take power and, when it became clear that she'd failed, seized a fleet of ships and sailed for North Africa. She founded a new port on the ruins of Kambeh, which became known in time as Carthage, near modern-day Tunis. This became the seat of the Carthaginian empire.

The rise of Carthage gradually saw a corresponding fall in Tyre's fortunes. Weakened as a power, the Tyrians sued for peace when the Assyrians conquered the Levant and became their vassal state. When Assyria's power weakened, Tyre ceased to pay tribute and rebelled against their overlords. Assyrian attempts to keep their rebellious vassal in line led to periods of war throughout the 7th and 6th centuries BC.

With the fall of the Assyrians in 612 BC, Tyre was peaceably controlled by the Neo-Babylonians until 586 BC, when it once again rebelled, leading to a 13-year siege by the Babylonian king, Nebuchadnezzar. The inhabitants stood firm behind the high walls of the island-city and the siege failed.

The next in Tyre's long line of strongman-conquerors, was more successful than Nebuchadnezzar. Alexander the Great was out to conquer the known world following his defeat of the Persian army and, in 332 BC, he marched along coastal Phoenicia exacting tribute from all its city-states. In its time-honoured tradition, Tyre alone decided to resist. The city was thought to be impregnable, but upon arriving in 332 BC Alexander built a mole or breakwater in the sea to reach the city. This impressive feat

TRUDI CANAVAN

Detail of a sarcophagus found at Tyre, carved with a scene from Homer's *Illiad*

was carried out under a constant hail of missiles. At the same time on the mainland, Alexander's engineers were constructing huge mobile towers called *helepoleis*, which, at 20-storeys high, were the tallest siege towers ever used in the history of war. After seven months these great war machines lumbered across the mole and lowered the drawbridge, unleashing archers and artillery on the city.

Tyre fell after seven months and Alexander, enraged at the dogged resistance of the Tyrians which had caused heavy Greek losses, destroyed half the city. The city's 30,000 citizens were massacred or sold into slavery. This destruction heralded the domination of the Greeks in the Mediterranean.

Nevertheless, the city recovered from its devastation and, after a period of Seleucid rule following Alexander's death, became autonomous in 126 BC. In 64 BC, Tyre became a Roman province and later became the capital of the Roman province of Syria-Phoenicia.

Later Tyre became one of the first Lebanese towns to adopt Christianity and was the seat of an archbishopric with 14 bishoprics under its control. By the 4th century AD it had recovered some of its former splendour and a basilica was built on the site of the former temple of Melkart, probably using the much older stone in its construction. In the Byzantine period, flourishing silk, glass and purple-dyeing industries allowed the city to prosper.

The city was taken by the Arabs in 635, and its prosperity continued. The Umayyad caliph Mu'awiyah transformed the city into a naval base and it was from here that the first Arab fleet set sail to conquer Cyprus.

With the arrival of the Crusaders, Tyre's future was to become less assured. By paying tribute in 1099, the city avoided attack as the Crusaders marched on Jerusalem. It narrowly survived another Crusader encounter in 1111–12, when King Baldwin placed it under siege for nearly five months, finally giving up after his siege towers were engulfed in flames and some 2000 of his men were killed. Twelve years later it was not so lucky. People from other coastal cities had fled to Tyre

when the Crusaders started to take the Middle East in 1124. They felt safe behind Tyre's 'impregnable' walls. After a siege of five and a half months, Tyre's defences collapsed and the Christian army occupied the city and the surrounding fertile land.

The Crusaders rebuilt the defensive walls and Tyre remained in Crusader hands for 167 years, until the Mamluk army of Al-Malik al-Ashraf retook the city in 1291. Over time, the classical and early Christian remains were demolished and the worked stone reused in later buildings. The ports silted up and the mole which connected the island to the mainland became a sand bar; the city of Tyre became a peninsula which is now covered in modern buildings.

At the beginning of the 17th century Fakhreddine attempted to rebuild and revitalise Tyre, but without much success. Following the fall of the Ottoman Empire, Tyre was included in the French Mandate of Greater Lebanon, and then incorporated into the Lebanese republic.

Once the State of Israel was established in 1948, its position next to the closed border further marginalised the city, which was already sidelined by Beirut and Sidon. Along with the rest of the south it also suffered greatly during the civil war, and Israel's long occupation of the adjacent border area left the city depressed long after the 1991 ceasefire. Today, Tyre has a picturesque harbour adjoining a lively souq and is the administrative centre for a number of villages and towns, but much of the central area is surrounded by unplanned squatter settlements, and the feeling of prosperity found in many other postwar Lebanese cities is absent.

Orientation

Tyre lies on the coast with the former island part of the city jutting out into the sea to the west. To the north of the headland is the picturesque fishing harbour. The 'neck' of the peninsula is the wide sand bar which covers the old causeway. The modern shopping streets and residential district of Tyre are built over this land. On the eastern side of Tyre is the residential suburb of Al-Bass and the excavated Roman site.

Alexander the Great

Alexander was one of history's greatest military leaders. He was born in Pella, an ancient city of Macedonia in northern Greece in 356 BC. His father was Philip II of Macedonia and his mother was Olympia, a princess of Epirus. Alexander had an extraordinary and privileged upbringing; his tutor was Aristotle who gave him a knowledge of rhetoric and literature and a grounding in science, medicine and philosophy.

With the assassination of his father in 336 BC, Alexander became king of Macedonia. He set about disposing of his enemies and quelling rebellions. He razed Thebes to the ground as punishment for disloyalty, sparing only the temples and the house of the poet Pindar. Thebes' 30,000 citizens were enslaved. This immediately brought the other Greek states into submission.

After restoring order at home, Alexander turned his attention to the threat from Persia. After being elected commander of all the Greek forces at the congress of Corinth, he set out with 40,000 men in 334 BC. His three chief officers were Antigonus, Ptolemy and Seleucus; all became rulers of the empire after Alexander's death.

Alexander's first great victory against the Persians was near Troy where he attacked 40,000 Persian and Greek mercenaries. Alexander, according to tradition, only lost 110 men. After this, all of Asia submitted to him. When he encountered the main Persian army, led by Darius III, at Issus in northern Syria, he was greatly outnumbered but still scored a decisive victory. King Darius fled north, abandoning his family who Alexander treated with the respect due to a royal family.

After this turning point in his career, Alexander swept south conquering the Phoenician sea ports. Only Tyre was a real obstacle. The city was heavily defended and only submitted after a lengthy siege. Gaza was captured next and Alexander passed into Egypt where he was greeted as a deliverer. In 332 BC he founded the city of Alexandria at the mouth of the Nile which would later develop into the literary, scientific and commercial centre of the Greek world.

In 331 BC Alexander made his celebrated pilgrimage to the oracle at the Temple of Amun Ra, the Egyptian equivalent of Zeus. This is in the remote oasis of Siwa in the western desert. His quest was to be recognised as a son of Amun Ra and therefore a true ruler of Egypt. He came away satisfied,

Information

Money There is a bank on the Corniche, just in front of the Byzantine Monument. A block inland, on the corner of the street running perpendicular to the sea, is the Jamal Trust Bank, which has an ATM. There is a Western Union branch near the taxi stand on the road to Sidon.

Post & Communications The main post office and telephone bureau is at the western end of the harbour, not far from the lighthouse. There is a private phone office, Centrale Ghardau, opposite Alpha Net. They charge US$1 per minute for overseas calls.

Email & Internet Services Alpha Net is just north of the main roundabout on Rue Abu Dib and charges LL3000 per hour. It opens at 10 am and closes at 1 am.

Archaeological Sites

The main reason for visiting Tyre is to look at the **excavated ruins**. In 1979 Tyre was declared a World Heritage Site in the hope of halting the damage being done to archaeological remains by anarchic urban development and conflict. There are three sites within the city, Al-Mina, on the south side of the city, Al-Bass, on the original mainland section, and a medieval site in the centre off what was the island.

Al-Mina Archaeological Site In an impressive setting leading down to the ancient Egyptian harbour, Al-Mina (Area 1) incorporates remains of Roman and Byzantine Tyre. Upon entering, a double line of columns to the right is thought to be part of the **agora** or market place for the area. Further down is a long, **colonnaded road** lead-

Alexander the Great

SARAH JOLLY

and the seeds of the idea of his own divinity were sown. Then he turned northwards, reorganised his troops at Tyre, and headed for Babylon. Crossing the Tigris and Euphrates Rivers, he met Darius again and once again Alexander defeated the Persians at the Battle of Gaugamela in 331 BC. Darius fled, but was slain by two of his own generals.

Alexander plundered the treasuries of the Persians and burned their towns, finishing the destruction of the Persian Empire forever. He did not stop there and carried on eastwards, eventually conquering most of Central Asia and even parts of northern India. He achieved all this in just three years. He had grandiose plans for his new empire and dreamed of uniting the world. He founded many cities, often named after him, and his veteran troops colonised them, spreading Greek language and culture far and wide.

Shortly before his untimely death, he issued an order that he should be worshipped as a god in the Greek cities, an order which was ignored after his death. He died of a fever in Babylon in the spring of 323 BC, leaving no clear instructions for the administration of the empire. His generals fought over the spoils and ended up dividing the empire into three. Although his dream of a 'one world empire' died with him, he paved the way for the later Hellenistic Greek kingdoms and subsequently the Roman Empire.

---

ing directly to what was the southern harbour. The marble sections of the pavement date back to the Roman era, while the black and white mosaics are Byzantine. To the right of the road, below a modern cemetery, are the remains of an unusual, rectangular **arena**, with five rows of terraced seating cut in to limestone. In the centre was a pool that may have been used for some kind of spectator water sports. Water cisterns surround the arena.

Beside the arena, and covering the area heading south towards the harbour, was the settlement's residential quarter. The remains are of small rooms, some with mosaic paving.

Across the colonnaded main road is the ruin of an extensive Roman bathhouse. Measuring some 40m x 30m, the complex did not fare well during the civil war. However, you can still see the vaulted mud-brick

basement and there are several rows of stone disks, which were used to support a hypocaust or raised floor that would have been heated by hot air flowing underneath.

Heading down to the shore, if you look out to sea you will see what look like islands breaking the surface. These are, in fact, the remains of Phoenician jetties and Alexander the Great's breakwater.

The site is open from 7 am until sunset (7 pm in summer) and admission is LL5000.

Crusader Cathedral About a five-minute walk to the north of the Al-Mina site, the remains of the Holy Cross Cathedral are unfortunately fenced off and closed to the public. However, you can see the ruins from the road. Foundations and granite columns are all that remain of the 12th-century building, giving scant indication of its importance in Crusader

THE SOUTH

times. The King of Jerusalem was once crowned within its walls and the remains of the German king Frederick Barbarossa are reputed to be buried here. Beneath and around the cathedral is a network of Roman and Byzantine roads and other buildings, one of which may have been the original temple of Melkart, the ancient god of the city.

Al-Bass Archaeological Site Located on the land-ward side of Tyre, about 20 minutes on foot from the other sites, the enormous Al-Bass (or Area 3) site has some of the most impressive archaeological remains in Tyre. A colonnaded east-west road, possibly a continuation of the road at the Al-Mina site, takes you through a vast **Roman necropolis** containing dozens of highly decorated marble and stone sarcophagi. The more elaborate have reliefs depicting scenes from Greek mythology and Homeric epics. Most are from the 2nd and 3rd century AD, but some date back as far as the 2nd century BC, and there are Byzantine coffins from as late as the 6th century.

A huge, triple-bay **triumphal arch** stands further along the colonnaded street. Originally the gateway to the Roman town, it dates to the 2nd century AD. Behind it, to the south of the road, are traces of the city's old **aqueduct**, which brought water from Ras al-Ain, 6km south of Tyre. According to travellers' accounts, it was almost intact during the 19th-century. It did not fare so well in the 20th century, however.

Beyond the arch is the largest and the best-preserved **Roman hippodrome** in the world. The huge, partly reconstructed structure is 480m long and once seated some 20,000 spectators. It was used for very popular and dangerous chariot races, as seen in the movie *Ben Hur*. Each end of the long, narrow course was marked by a turning stone, called a *metae*, which you can still see. The tight, high-speed turns at the metae were the most exciting part of the race and often produced dramatic spills and collisions. Today, local Tyrians use the hippodrome as a jogging course.

The site is open from 7.30 am until sunset daily; admission is LL5000. The main entrance is on the main north-south highway, near the Palestinian camp of Al-Bass. There is another gate near the end of Rue Abu Dib, which is unstaffed but sometimes open.

Fishing Harbour & Souqs
Small, but bustling with activity, the fishing harbour is the most picturesque part of Tyre. Brightly coloured wooden boats, fishing nets and old-fashioned boat repair shops make for photo opportunities. There are also a number of fish restaurants and cafes overlooking the water that make a good vantage point for watching the scene.

Behind them, running from east to west, lie Tyre's Ottoman-era **souqs**, which aren't as extensive as those of Sidon and Tripoli, but are still interesting to wander around.

As you walk around the northern side of the harbour, you come to the city's **Christian quarter**, where there are six churches (one ruined), reflecting Lebanon's multitude of Christian denominations. They are surrounded by narrow, winding residential streets, some lined with old houses, and make for a pleasant wander. At the edge of the promontory, by the lighthouse, there are a couple of very pleasant restaurants and cafes with fantastic views over the sea.

Special Events
The **Tyre Festival** is held annually in late July/early August, and includes a mix of local and international singers, artists and musicians. A highlight of the festival is a spectacular laser display. For more specific details, contact the tourist office in Beirut or the festival organisers (cell ☎ 03-816 992).

Beaches
Just south of Tyre is one of Lebanon's rare public beaches. Reputedly clean, it is backed by trees and there are tented restaurants serving fish. Just take the road that heads south past the Rest House (see Places to Stay). After a few minutes you will see the beach to your right.

Places to Stay
There are no rock-bottom budget places in Tyre. One of the cheaper options is *Hotel/*

Restaurant Al-Fanar (☎ 741 111), right by the lighthouse (*al-fanar* is lighthouse in Arabic) in the Christian quarter. In a house that dates back several hundred years, it has a vaulted basement looks right out onto the sea. Unfortunately, the six rooms are in a modern addition and are uninspiring, if clean. Price depends on the number of people in a room, and ranges from US$20 to US$50 per person, including breakfast.

Also reasonably priced is the resolutely modern *Hotel Elyssa* (☎ 741 267), which is on the south side of the peninsula facing the sea. It has 40 rooms, all with bath, and a restaurant. Rooms cost US$35/55 for singles/doubles which includes breakfast and service. Lunch and dinner are a good deal at around LL10,000; a beer is LL3000.

If you follow the road south, the old government rest house has been transformed into the *Rest House* (☎ 740 677, cell 03-356 663, ✉ info@resthouse-thyr.com.lb), a four-star beach hotel. Most of the 30 rooms are for long-term stay, but some are held back for overnighters. There is a restaurant, bar, tearoom and shop as well as a good bathing beach. During the week, singles/doubles cost US$70/80 plus 16% service. At the weekend, prices may rise, depending on occupancy. All prices include breakfast and beach entrance. If you're not staying there, beach entrance costs US$10.

Just outside the northern entrance to Tyre, overlooking the Litani River near the village of Qasmieh, is the *Abu Dib Motel* (☎ cell 03-360 250). Quiet and comfortable, with a swimming pool and restaurant, rooms range from US$50 to US$100, including breakfast.

Places to Eat
There is a fair choice of restaurants in Tyre and, despite its reputation as a Shiite stronghold, alcohol is served at all but the budget options.

Tyre's cheap restaurants are mostly clustered on or around the roundabout on Rue Abu Dib. The *Restaurant Abou Deeb* dominates on the corner at the roundabout and serves reasonably priced Lebanese staples. Almost opposite is the *Pizzaria Italia*,

where pizzas start at LL4000. On the road heading north towards the Byzantine Monument is a large bakery that makes *man-aeesh* (a pizza snack topped with thyme and sesame seeds) and other specialties, as well as delicious bread. Back towards the southern side of the peninsula are a couple of juice bars that make for a change from the usual carbonated drinks.

Over by the lighthouse, there are two pleasant places to eat. *Al-Fanar* (☎ 741 111) has a cavernous dining room and a set menu that includes mezze, a main course with rice, a beer and fruit for US$15 per person. Next door, the *Restaurant Maison de la Mer* has fish by the kilo, as well as the usual mezze dishes for between LL3000 and LL5000. The treat here is the fabulous terrace in a quiet walled garden that is right beside the sea.

The harbour area also has a cluster of restaurants. The small and friendly *Pub/Restaurant Tanit* (☎ 740 987) is popular with UN soldiers stationed in Tyre. A grill and salad will cost you US$10 to US$15 and a beer is US$3. Nearby is *Le Petit Phoenician* (☎ 741 562), which was once owned by Pepe of the Byblos Fishing Club. Now it's a pleasant, checked-tablecloth type of place overlooking the harbour. It specialises in seafood which, like everywhere in Lebanon, increases the price of your meal dramatically. There is also a selection of mezze and grills. Expect to pay between US$15 and US$35 per person, depending on whether you order fish.

On the south side of the peninsula near Hotel Elyssa is *Restaurant Tyros* (☎ 741 027), which serves Lebanese food in a tent-like structure and is extremely popular with locals. A modest meal of mezze and a grill will cost about US$8.

Getting There & Away
The service-taxi stand in Tyre is about 50m before the port on the northern coastal road. Service taxis to and from Cola in Beirut cost LL6000; to Sidon, LL2000. The Lebanese Transport Company runs buses to Sidon from the taxi stand on the Sidon road for LL750. The buses run hourly starting at

THE SOUTH

6.30 am; the last one leaves at 7 pm. From Sidon you can stay on the bus to Beirut for another LL750.

AROUND TYRE
Tomb of Hiram   قبر أحيرام

At the 6km mark on the road to Qana is a huge limestone tomb with a large pyramid-shaped top, rising to an overall height of almost 6m. Although some scholars contend that it dates back to mid-way through the first millennium BC, most likely to the Persian period (550–330 BC), it is locally known as Qabr Hiram, and has traditionally been associated with Hiram, the famous king of Tyre who ruled some 500 years earlier.

Below the sarcophagus are large stone steps (now blocked) and a rock-cut cave that were first discovered by Renan, the French theologist and historian. When he started excavations at the foot of the tomb in the mid-19th century, he found an even earlier staircase, which connected to the mausoleum's foundations. There are other signs of tombs in the area as well as a sanctuary.

Qana   قانا

Qana is a small Shiite village 14km southeast of Tyre. Tragically catapulted into international consciousness in 1996 for the

massacre by Israel of civilians and UN soldiers sheltering at a base here (see the boxed text 'Bitter Wine from Grapes of Wrath'), the village is also at the centre of a scholarly debate as to whether it is in fact the biblical Cana, where Jesus performed his first miracle of turning water into wine. Until recently it was assumed that the Israeli village of Kefr Kenna was the site of biblical Cana, but the 4th-century historian, Eusebius seems to support the idea that Cana was near Sidon, as do the 3rd-century writings of St Jerome. Further proof for the claim is centred on early Christian **rock carvings** and a grotto about 1km outside the village. The worn carvings depict thirteen figures, said by proponents of the Qana-as-Cana position to be Jesus and his disciples. The cave, just below the carvings, could possibly be where he and his followers hid from persecution. Elsewhere in the village large basins have been excavated and are said to have contained the water that was transformed into wine. Without more definitive proof the debate will no doubt continue, but the site is worth a visit.

To reach the carvings, head down the steep path next to the school about 1km before reaching the village (if you're coming from the Tomb of Hiram). The spot is

---

Bitter Wine from Grapes of Wrath

By 1996 Israel had already occupied Lebanon for more than a decade with no appreciable gain. Hezbollah guerrillas continued their hit and run attacks on the occupying army, as well as launching sporadic rocket attacks into northern Israel. On April 11th of that year, Prime Minister Shimon Peres, under pressure to end the peace process after a wave of suicide bombings inside Israel, launched a 16-day air, artillery and naval attack dubbed 'Operation Grapes of Wrath'. Its stated objective was to wipe out Hezbollah bases throughout Lebanon. The intensity of the attack was such that an estimated 35,000 shells fell on Lebanese land, destroying infrastructure and damaging thousands of buildings.

On 18 April an estimated 800 people were sheltering from the fighting at the UN peace-keeping base in Qana. Nevertheless, the base was shelled, with several direct hits on an underground shelter that left 102 dead and a further 120 wounded. At the time, Israel maintained that Hezbollah guerillas had entered the base and that it hadn't known that there were civilians sheltering there. A UN investigation subsequently provided substantial evidence that this was unlikely and suggested that Israel had deliberately targeted the base.

There is now an official day of mourning on 18 April throughout Lebanon, and the site of the massacre, including the twisted wreckage of the shelter, has been turned into a memorial to the victims.

marked by a modern, white marble stone with black Arabic script. The track leads into a deep valley and it is a five-minute walk down to the grotto and carvings. To see inside the grotto you will need a torch. The site is not supervised so you can visit any time. The stone basins are between two back gardens of village houses and you will need to ask the villagers (who are usually only too happy to help) for directions, or get your taxi driver to show you.

Getting There & Away A service taxi from Tyre to Qana costs LL2000. Keep in mind that they aren't frequent. A taxi from Tyre is about LL7500, LL10,000 for a return trip. The memorial to the massacre victims is at the UN base, 2km beyond the town.

Tibnin تبنين

Twelve kilometres north-west of the town of Bint Jbayl is the town of Tibnin, famous in recent history as the birthplace of Amal leader Nabih Berri. Delving back slightly deeper into history, however, the town derives its fame for the Crusader castle that dominates the landscape. Built in 1104 by Hugues de Sain Omer, the governor of Tiberias, in preparation for the siege of Tyre, it was given the old French name of Le Toron, meaning high or isolated place. It fell to Saladin after the battle of Hittin in 1187, but was taken back by the Franks in 1229. The Mamluk sultan Beybars recaptured it again in 1266. The structure was added to and modified during Mamluk and Ottoman times, in particular by the 17th century governor of Acre, Zaher al-Omar. Ahmed al-Jazzar later destroyed much of the building. Much of the interior is still in ruins. Nevertheless, the castle still extends over an area of 2000 sq m and retains its outer fortified walls, on which extensive restoration work has been carried out in recent years. It also affords spectacular views of the surrounding area.

Beaufort Castle قلعة الشقيف

A symbol of the region's troubled politics and history, Beaufort Castle (Qala'at ash-Shaqif in Arabic) has been fought over by almost every invader to have passed through the area over the past 1000 years. Its commanding hilltop location, some 710m above sea level, gives superb panoramic views of the coast, northern Israel, Syria and the mountains to the north. The origins of the fortress are uncertain; some scholars argue that it was built in the Byzantine period and then restored and added to by the Arabs, who were later replaced by the Crusaders. It was captured from a local prince, Shehab ed-Din, in 1138 by the Fulk of Anjou, King of Jerusalem, who passed it to Sidon's Crusader overlords.

William of Tyre relates that after their 1192 defeat in Baniyas, Syria, many Crusaders took refuge in the castle, which was subsequently besieged by Saladin. He eventually took it by a ruse, persuading Renaud, Prince of Sayette, to leave the fortress for a meeting. The prince was then captured and tortured in front of his appalled men. Still, they did not give up and it took two years to starve them out. The castle changed sides several times over the following decades. At one point it was bought from a Sidonian prince by the Templars, who built a small fort called Château Neuf. The Mamluk sultan Beybars finally took it back in 1268.

In the 17th century, Fakhreddine saw the advantage of such a fortress in his revolt against the Ottomans, and restored the structure. However, it was besieged and partially destroyed when the pashas of Acre and Damascus sent forces against him.

Beaufort's strategic worth came into play again in the 1970s, when it was occupied by Palestinian guerrillas. It was then attacked and badly damaged by Israeli jets during the 1982 invasion. In one of those historical ironies that seem to be a Lebanese speciality, the Israelis proceeded to occupy the fortress for twenty years, modern Crusaders who, with their Christian allies, were surrounded by a hostile, largely Muslim local population. The historical parallels continued with their ultimate defeat by Hezbollah.

In its retreat in May 2000 the Israeli army blew up parts of the castle to destroy traces of their occupation, despite a specific request by the Lebanese government that they respect the integrity of the already ravaged historic site.

At the time of writing the castle had just been vacated by the Israelis and a Lebanese army barracks had taken its place. Concerns about possible structural weakness may lead to its closure until restoration work is carried out, but in principle it is open to the public and plans have been announced for a sound-and-light show, so check with the tourist office for the latest information.

Getting There & Away Beaufort is above the village of Arnun, 7km south-east of Nabatiye. A service taxi from Beirut to Nabatiye costs about LL4000; from Sidon LL2000. To get a taxi to Arnun, you'll be looking at about LL5000, one way.

Khiam
خيام

Khiam is the site of a notorious hilltop prison that belonged to Israel and its proxy army, the SLA, during the Israeli occupation of south Lebanon. When the Israeli army withdrew in May 2000, the SLA guards fled and the local population flooded in and rescued the 140 remaining prisoners. The jail was turned into an impromptu museum and memorial for its victims. Its appalling conditions make for a sobering visit.

Getting There and Away For the time being, the only way to get to Khiam is by taxi from Tyre. Expect to pay at least LL10,000 for the return trip.

Hasbaya
حاصبيا

Hasbaya is one of the principal towns on the sides of Jebel ash-Sheikh (Mt Hermon). Although the town's history goes back to antiquity, the oldest monuments here go back to Crusader times. When the Shihab family took over the area in the 18th century, they fortified the tower of the town's Crusader fort and turned it into an Italianate palace, a sort of miniature Beiteddine. Other noteworthy buildings in Hasbaya include a 13th-century mosque with a distinct hexagonal minaret.

Three kilometres outside town, on the road to Marjeyun, is Souq al-Khan. At a crossroads in the forest are the remains of an old khan where, according to local lore, Fakhreddine's son Ali was killed. These days it is the site of a popular weekly market, which is held every Tuesday.

There are infrequent service taxis between Sidon and Hasbaya for LL5000 each way. Taxis cost at least LL10,000 one way.

Language

ARABIC

Arabic is the official language of Lebanon. Though French is also spoken – and English is rapidly gaining ground – any effort to communicate with the locals in Arabic will be well rewarded. No matter how far off the mark your pronunciation or grammar might be, you'll often get the response (usually with a big smile): 'Ah, you speak Arabic very well!'. Greeting Lebanese officials with *salām alaykum* (peace be upon you), will often work wonders.

Learning a few basics for day-to-day travelling doesn't take long at all, but to master the complexities of Arabic would take years of consistent study. The whole issue is complicated by the differences between Classical Arabic (Fus-ha), its modern descendant MSA (Modern Standard Arabic) and regional dialects. The classical tongue is the language of the Quran and Arabic poetry of centuries past. For long it remained static, but in order to survive it had to adapt to change, and the result is more or less MSA, the common language of the press, radio and educated discourse. It is as close to a *lingua franca* (common language) as the Arab world comes, and is generally understood – if not always well spoken – across the Arab world.

As it happens, the spoken dialects of Lebanon are not too distant from MSA. For most outsiders trying to learn Arabic, the most frustrating element remains understanding the spoken language (wherever you are), there is virtually no written material to refer to for back up. Acquisition of MSA is a long-term investment: an esoteric argument flows back and forth about the relative merits of learning MSA first (and so perhaps having to wait some time before being able to communicate adequately with people in the street) or a dialect. All this will give you an inkling of why so few non-Arabs, or non-Muslims, embark on a study of the language.

Pronunciation

Pronunciation of Arabic can be tongue-tying for someone unfamiliar with the intonation and combination of sounds. Pronounce the transliterated words slowly and clearly.

This language guide should help, but bear in mind that the myriad rules governing pronunciation and vowel use are too extensive to be covered here.

Vowels

Technically, there are three long and three short vowels in Arabic. The reality is a little different, with local dialect and varying consonant combinations affecting their pronunciation. This is the case throughout the Arabic-speaking world. More like five short and five long vowels can be identified; in this guide we use all but the long 'o'.

a	as in 'had'
e	as in 'bet'
i	as in 'hit'
o	as in 'hot'
u	as in 'put'

A macron over a vowel indicates that the vowel has a long sound:

ā	as the 'a' in 'father'
ē	as the 'e' in 'heir'
ī	as the 'e' in 'ear', only softer
ū	as the 'oo' in 'food'

Consonants

Pronunciation for all Arabic consonants is covered in the alphabet table on the following page. Note that when double consonants occur in transliterations, both are pronounced. For example, *al-hammam* (toilet), is pronounced 'al-ham-mam'.

Other Sounds

Arabic has two sounds that are very tricky for non-Arabs to produce, the 'ayn and the

The Arabic Alphabet

Final	Medial	Initial	Alone	Transliteration	Pronunciation
ﺎ			ا	ā	as the 'a' in 'father'
ﺐ	ﺒ	ﺑ	ب	b	as in 'bet'
ﺖ	ﺘ	ﺗ	ت	t	as in 'ten' (but the tongue touches the teeth)
ﺚ	ﺜ	ﺛ	ث	th	as in 'thin'; also as 's' or 't'
ﺞ	ﺠ	ﺟ	ج	j	as in 'jet'; often also as the 's' in 'measure'
ﺢ	ﺤ	ﺣ	ح	H	a strongly whispered 'h', almost like a sigh of relief
ﺦ	ﺨ	ﺧ	خ	kh	a rougher sound than the 'ch' in Scottish *loch*
ﺪ			د	d	as in 'den' (but the tongue touches the teeth)
ﺬ			ذ	dh	as the 'th' in 'this'; also as 'd' or 'z'
ﺮ			ر	r	a rolled 'r', as in the Spanish word *caro*
ﺰ			ز	z	as in 'zip'
ﺲ	ﺴ	ﺳ	س	s	as in 'so', never as in 'wisdom'
ﺶ	ﺸ	ﺷ	ش	sh	as in 'ship'
ﺺ	ﺼ	ﺻ	ص	ṣ	emphatic 's' *
ﺾ	ﺿ	ﺿ	ض	ḍ	emphatic 'd' *
ﻂ	ﻄ	ﻃ	ط	ṭ	emphatic 't' *
ﻆ	ﻈ	ﻇ	ظ	ẓ	emphatic 'z' *
ﻊ	ﻌ	ﻋ	ع	'	the Arabic letter 'ayn; pronounce as a glottal stop – like the closing of the throat before saying 'Oh oh!' (see Other Sounds on p.241)
ﻎ	ﻐ	ﻏ	غ	gh	a guttural sound like Parisian 'r'
ﻒ	ﻔ	ﻓ	ف	f	as in 'far'
ﻖ	ﻘ	ﻗ	ق	q	a strongly guttural 'k' sound; often pronounced as a glottal stop
ﻚ	ﻜ	ﻛ	ك	k	as in 'king'
ﻞ	ﻠ	ﻟ	ل	l	as in 'lamb'
ﻢ	ﻤ	ﻣ	م	m	as in 'me'
ﻦ	ﻨ	ﻧ	ن	n	as in 'name'
ﻪ	ﻬ	ﻫ	ه	h	as in 'ham'
ﻮ			و	w	as in 'wet'; or
				ū	long, as the 'oo' on 'food'; or
				aw	as the 'ow' in 'how'
ﻲ	ﻴ	ﻳ	ي	y	as in 'yes'; or
				ī	as the 'e' in 'ear', only softer; or
				ay	as the 'y' in 'by' or as the 'ay' in 'way'

Vowels Not all Arabic vowel sounds are represented in the alphabet. See Pronunciation on p.241.

*Emphatic Consonants Emphatic consonants are similar to their nonemphatic counterparts but are pronounced with greater tension in the tongue and throat.

glottal stop. The letter 'ayn represents a sound with no English equivalent that comes even close. It is similar to the glottal stop (which is not actually represented in the alphabet) but the muscles at the back of the throat are gagged more forcefully – it has been described as the sound of someone being strangled. In many transliteration systems 'ayn is represented by an opening quotation mark, and the glottal stop by a closing quotation mark. To make the transliterations in this language guide (and throughout the rest of the book) easier to use, we have not distinguished between the glottal stop and the 'ayn, using the closing quotation mark to represent both sounds. You should find that Arabic speakers will still understand you.

Transliteration

It's worth noting here that transliteration from the Arabic script into English – or any other language for that matter – is at best an approximate science.

The presence of sounds unknown in European languages and the fact that the script is 'defective' (most vowels are not written) combine to make it nearly impossible to settle on one universally accepted method of transliteration. A wide variety of spellings is therefore possible for words when they appear in Latin script – and that goes for places and people's names as well.

The whole thing is further complicated by the wide variety of dialects and the

The Transliteration Dilemma

TE Lawrence, when asked by his publishers to clarify 'inconsistencies in the spelling of proper names' in *Seven Pillars of Wisdom* – his account of the Arab Revolt in WWI – wrote back:

'Arabic names won't go into English. There are some "scientific systems" of transliteration, helpful to people who know enough Arabic not to need helping, but a washout for the world. I spell my names anyhow, to show what rot the systems are.'

imaginative ideas Arabs themselves often have on appropriate spelling in, say, English (words spelt one way in Jordan may look very different again in Lebanon, with strong French influences); not even the most venerable of western Arabists have been able to come up with a satisfactory solution.

While striving to reflect the language as closely as possible and aiming at consistency, this book generally spells place, street and hotel names and the like as the locals have done. Don't be surprised if you come across several versions of the same thing.

Pronouns

I	*ana*
you	*inta* (m)/*inti* (f)
he	*huwa*
she	*hiyya*
we	*naHnu/neHna*
you	*ento*
they	*humma*

Greetings & Civilities

Arabs place great importance on civility and it's rare to see any interaction between people that doesn't begin with profuse greetings, enquiries into the other's health and other niceties.

Arabic greetings are more formal than in English and there is a reciprocal response to each. These sometimes vary slightly, depending on whether you're addressing a man or a woman. A simple encounter can become a drawn-out affair, with neither side wanting to be the one to put a halt to the stream of greetings and well-wishing. As an *ajnabi* (foreigner), you're not expected to know all the ins and outs, but if you come up with the right expression at the appropriate moment they'll love it.

The most common greeting is *salām alaykum* (peace be upon you), to which the correct reply is *wa aleikum as-salām* (and upon you be peace). If you get invited to a birthday celebration or are around for any of the big holidays, the common greeting is *kul sana wa intum bi-khīr* (I wish you well for the coming year).

After having a bath or shower, you will often hear people say to you *na'iman*, which roughly means 'heavenly' and boils down to an observation along the lines of 'nice and clean now, huh'.

Arrival in one piece is always something to be grateful for. Passengers will often be greeted with *il-Hamdu lillah al as-salāma* – 'thank God for your safe arrival'.

Hi.	*marHaba*
Hi. (response)	*marHabtain*
Hello.	*ahlan wa sahlan* or just *ahlan* (Welcome)
Hello. (response)	*ahlan fīk*

It's an important custom in Lebanon to ask after a person's or their family's health when greeting, eg, *kīf suHtak?* or *kīf essuHa?* (How is your health?), *kīf il'ayli?* (How is the family?). The response is *bikhēr il-Hamdu lillah*, (Well, thank you).

Goodbye.	*ma'a salāma* or *Allah ma'ak*
Good morning.	*sabaH al-khayr*
Good morning. (response)	*sabaH 'an-nūr*
Good evening.	*masa' al-khayr*
Good evening. (response)	*masa 'an-nūr*
Good night.	*tisbaH 'ala khayr*
Good night. (response)	*wa inta min ahlu*

Basics

Yes.	*aiwa/na'am*
Yeah.	*ay*
No.	*la*
Please. (request)	*min fadlak* (m)/ *min fadlik* (f) or *iza bitrīd* (m)/ *iza bitrīdi* (f)
Please. (polite)	*law samaHt* (m)/ *law samaHti* (f)
Please. (come in)	*tafaddal* (m)/ *tafaddali* (f)/ *tafaddalū* (pl)
Thank you.	*shukran*

Thank you very much.	*shukran ktīr*
You're welcome.	*'afwan* or *tikram/tikrami* (m/f)
Pardon/Excuse me.	*'afwan*
Sorry!	*āsif!*
No problem.	*mafi mushkili*
Never mind.	*ma'alesh*
Just a moment.	*laHza*
Congratulations!	*mabrouk!*

Small Talk

Questions like 'Is the bus coming?' or 'Will the bank be open later?' generally elicit the inevitable response: *in sha' Allah* – 'God willing' – an expression you'll hear over and over again. Another common one is *ma sha' Allah* – 'God's will be done' – sometimes a useful answer to probing questions about why you're not married yet.

How are you?	*kīf Hālak/Hālik?* (m/f)
How're you doing?	*kīfak/kīfik?* (m/f)
Fine.	*mnīH/mnīHa* (m/f)
What's your name?	*shu-ismak?* (m)/ *shu-ismik?* (f)
My name is ...	*ismi ...*
Pleased to meet you. (departing)	*tsharrafna*
Nice to meet you.	*tasharrafna* (lit: you honour us)
Where are you from?	*min wayn inta?*

I'm from ...	*ana min ...*
Australia	*ustrālya*
Canada	*kanada*
Europe	*oropa*
Japan	*yabān*
New Zealand	*nyu zīlanda*
South Africa	*afriqya el janubiya*
the USA	*amerka*

Are you married?	*inta mutajawwiz?* (m)/ *inti mutajawwiza?* (f)
Not yet.	*mesh Halla*
How old are you?	*shu 'amrak?* (m)/ *shu 'amrik?* (f)
I'm 20 years old.	*o'mri 'ashrīn sana*

I'm a student.   *ana tālib/tilmīz* (m)/
     ana tāliba/tilmīzi (f)
I'm a tourist.   *ana sa'iH* (m)/
     ana sa'iHa (f)
Do you like ...?   *inta bitHib?*
I like ...   *ana bHib ...* (m)/
     ana uHib ... (f)
I don't like ...   *ana ma bHib ...*

Language Difficulties

Do you speak   *bitiHki inglīzi?*
   English?
I understand.   *afham*
I don't understand.   *ma bifham*

I speak ...   *ana baHki ...*
   English   *inglīzi*
   French   *faransi*
   German   *almāni*

I speak a little   *ana beHki arabi*
   Arabic.   *shway*
I don't speak   *ana ma beHki arabi*
   Arabic.
I want an   *biddī mutarjem*
   interpreter.
Could you write   *mumkin tiktabhu, min*
   it down, please?   *fadlak?*
What does this   *shu yānī?*
   mean?
How do you say   *kīf t'ul ... bil'arabi?*
   ... in Arabic?

Getting Around

Where is ...?   *wayn ...?*
   airport   *al-maṭār*
   bus station   *maHaṭṭat al-baṣ*
   ticket office   *maktab at-tazākar*

What time does ...   *ay sā'a biyitla'/*
leave/arrive?   *biyuṣal ...?*
   aeroplane   *ṭīyara*
   (small) boat   *ash-shakhtūra*
   ferry/ship   *as-safina*
   bus   *al-baṣ*
   train   *al-qiṭār*

Which bus goes   *aya baṣ biyrūH*
to ...?   *'ala ...?*

I want to go to ...   *ana badeh rūh ala ...*
Does this bus go   *hal-baṣ biyrūH*
   to ...?   *'ala ...?*
How many buses   *kem baṣ biyrūH*
   per day go to ...?   *ben nahar ...?*
How long does   *kem sa'a ar-riHla?*
   the trip take?
Please tell me   *'umal ma'arūf illī*
   when we get to ...   *lamma nūsal la ...*
Stop here, please.   *wa'if hūn 'umal*
   ma'arūf
Please wait for me.   *'umal ma'arūf unturnī*
May I sit here?   *mumkin a'ūd hūn?*
May we sit here?   *mumkin ni'ūd hūn?*

1st class   *daraja ūla*
2nd class   *daraja tāni*
ticket   *at-tazākar*
to/from   *ila/min*

Where can I   *wayn fīni*
hire a ...?   *esta'jer ...?*
   bicycle   *'ajala/bisklēt*
   car   *sayyāra*
   motorcycle   *motosikl*
   tour guide   *ad-dalī as-siyāHi/*
   al-murshid as-siyāHi

Directions

How do I get to ...?   *kīf būsal ala ...?*
Can you show me   *mumkin tfajīni*
   (on the map)?   *('ala al-kharīṭa)?*

Signs		
ENTRY *dukhūl*	مدخل
EXIT *khurūj*	خروج
TOILETS (Men) *Hammam lirrijal*	حمام للرجال
TOILETS (Women) *Hammam linnisa'a*	حمام للنساء
HOSPITAL *mustashfa*	مستشفى
POLICE *shurta*	الشرطة
PROHIBITED *mamnu'u*	ممنوع

How many kilometres?	*kem kilometre?*
What ... is this?	*shū ... heyda?*
street/road	*ash-shāri*
village	*al-qarya/adaya'*

on the left	*'ala yasār/shimāl*
on the right	*'ala yamīn*
opposite	*muqābil*
straight ahead	*dughri*
at the next corner	*tanī zarūb/tanī mafraq*
this way	*min hon*
here/there	*hon/honīk*
in front of	*amām/iddām*
near	*qarīb*
far	*ba'īd*
north	*shimāl*
south	*junub*
east	*sharq*
west	*gharb*

Around Town

| I'm looking for ... | *ana abHath ...* |
| Where is the ...? | *wayn ...?* |

bank	*al-bank*
beach	*ash-shāti'/al-plāj/ al-baHr*
chemist/pharmacy	*as-saydaliyya*
city/town	*al-medīna*
city centre	*markaz al-medīna*
customs	*al-jumruk*
entrance	*ad-dukhūl/al-madkhal*
exchange office	*al-masref*
exit	*al-khurūj*
hotel	*al-funduq*
information	*isti'lāmāt*
market	*as-sūq*
mosque	*al-jāmi'/al-masjid*
museum	*al-matHaf*
old city	*al-medīna al-qadīma/ al-medīna l'atīqa*
passport & immi- gration office	*maktab al-jawazāt wa al-hijra*
police	*ash-shurṭa*
post office	*maktab al-barīd*
restaurant	*al-maṭa'am*
telephone office	*maktab at-telefon/ maktab al-hālef*

Emergencies

Help me!	*sā'idūnī!*
I'm sick.	*ana marīd* (m)/ *ana marīda* (f)
Call the police!	*ittuṣil bil bolīṣ!*
doctor	*duktūr/tabīb*
hospital	*al-mustash-fa*
police	*ash-shurta/al-bolīṣ*
Go away!	*rouh min hūn!*
Shame on you! (said by woman)	*istiHi a'la Hālak!*

| temple | *al-qala'a/al-ma'abad* |
| tourist office | *maktab as-siyaHa* |

I want to change ...	*baddī sarref ...*
money	*maṣāri*
travellers cheques	*shīket msefrīn*

What time does it open?	*aymta byeftaH?*
What time does it close?	*aymta bi sakkir?*
I'd like to make a telephone call.	*fini talfen 'omol mārūf*

Paperwork

date of birth	*tarīkh al-mīlad/-wilāda*
name	*ism*
nationality	*jensīya*
passport	*jawaz as-safar*
permit	*tasrīH*
place of birth	*makan al-mīlad/ -wilāda*
visa	*visa/ta'shira*

Accommodation

I'd like to book a ...	*biddī ehjuz ...*
Do you have a ...?	*fī ...?*
(cheap) room	*oda (rkhīsa)*
single room	*oda mufrada*
double room	*oda li shakhsayn*

for one night	*li leili waHde*
for two nights	*leiltayn*
May I see it?	*mumkin shūfa?*
It's very noisy/ dirty.	*ktīr a'jka/wiskha*

How much is it per person?	'addaysh li kul waHid?
How much is it per night?	'addaysh bel leili?
Where is the bathroom?	Wayn al-Hammam?
We're leaving today.	nihna musafirīn al-youm

address	al-'anwān
air-conditioning	kondishon/mūkayif
blanket	al-baṭāniyya/al-Hrēm
camp site	mukhayam
electricity	kahraba
hotel	funduq
hot water	mai sukhni
key	al-miftaH
manager	al-mudīr
shower	dūsh
soap	sabūn
toilet	twalet

Food

I'm hungry/thirsty.	ana ju'ān/aṭshān
What is this?	shu hāyda?
I'd like ...	bheb ...
Another ... please.	... waHid kamān, min fadlak

breakfast	al-fuṭūr/at-terwīqa
dinner	al-'ashā
food	al-akl
grocery store	al-mahal/al-baqāl
hot/cold	sokhon/bārid
lunch	al-ghada
restaurant	al-maṭ'am
set menu	tabak

Vegetarianism is a nonconcept in the Middle East. Even if you ask for meals without meat, you can be sure that any gravies, sauces etc will have been cooked with meat or animal fat. See Food in the Facts for the Visitor chapter for more information.

Shopping

Where can I buy ...?	wayn fīni eshtirī ...?
What is this?	shu hayda?

How much?	addaysh?
How many?	kim waHid?
How much is it?	bi addaysh?
That's too expensive.	hayda ktīr ghālī
Is there ...?	fī ...?
There isn't (any).	ma fī
May I look at it?	fīni etallā 'alaya?

chemist/pharmacy	farmashiya
laundry	ghasīl
market	sūq
newsagents	maktaba

big	kbīr
bigger	akbar
cheap	rkhīs
cheaper	arkhas
closed	musakkar
expensive	ghāli
money	al-fulūs/al-maṣāri
open	maftūH
small	ṣaghīr
smaller	aṣghar

Time & Date

What's the time?	addaysh essa'ā?
When?	matā/emta?
now	halla'
after	b'adēn
on time	al waket
early	bakkīr
late	mit'akhar
daily	kil youm
today	al-youm
tomorrow	bukra
day after tomorrow	ba'ad bukra
yesterday	imbārih
minute	daqīqa
hour	sā'a
day	youm
week	usbū'
month	shahr
year	sana
morning	soubeH
afternoon	ba'ad eḍohor
evening	massa
night	leil

Monday	*al-tenein*
Tuesday	*at-talāta*
Wednesday	*al-arba'a*
Thursday	*al-khamīs*
Friday	*al-jum'a*
Saturday	*as-sabt*
Sunday	*al-aHad*

Months

The Islamic year has 12 lunar months and is 11 days shorter than the Western (Gregorian) calendar, so important Muslim dates will fall 11 days earlier each (Western) year. There are two Gregorian calendars in use in the Arab world. In Egypt and westwards, the months have virtually the same names as in English (January is *yanāyir*, October is *octobir* and so on), but in Lebanon and eastwards, the names are quite different. Talking about, say, June as 'month six' is the easiest solution, but for the sake of completeness, the months from January are:

January	*kanūn ath-thani*
February	*shubāt*
March	*azār*
April	*nisān*
May	*ayyār*
June	*Huzayrān*
July	*tammūz*
August	*'āb*
September	*aylūl*
October	*tishrīn al-awal*
November	*tishrīn ath-thani*
December	*kānūn al-awal*

The Hejira months, too, have their own names:

1st	*MoHarram*
2nd	*Safar*
3rd	*Rabi' al-Awal*
4th	*Rabei ath-Thāni*
5th	*Jumāda al-Awal*
6th	*Jumāda al-Akhira*
7th	*Rajab*
8th	*Shaban*
9th	*Ramadan*
10th	*Shawwal*
11th	*Zuul-Qeda*
12th	*Zuul-Hijja*

Numbers

Arabic numerals are simple to learn and, unlike the written language, run from left to right. Pay attention to the order of the words in numbers from 21 to 99.

0	٠	*ṣifr*
1	١	*waHad*
2	٢	*itnein/tintein*
3	٣	*talāta*
4	٤	*arba'a*
5	٥	*khamsa*
6	٦	*sitta*
7	٧	*saba'a*
8	٨	*tmāni*
9	٩	*tis'a*
10	١٠	*'ashara*
11	١١	*Hid-'ash*
12	١٢	*itn-'ash*
13	١٣	*talat-'ash*
14	١٤	*arba'at-'ash*
15	١٥	*khamast-'ash*
16	١٦	*sitt-'ash*
17	١٧	*saba'at-'ash*
18	١٨	*tamant-'ash*
19	١٩	*tisa'at-'ash*
20	٢٠	*'ashrīn*
21	٢١	*waHid wa 'ashrīn*
22	٢٢	*itnein wa ashrīn*
30	٣٠	*talātīn*
40	٤٠	*'arba'īn*
50	٥٠	*khamsīn*
60	٦٠	*sitteen*
70	٧٠	*saba'īn*
80	٨٠	*tamanīn*
90	٩٠	*tis'īn*
100	١٠٠	*mia*
101	١٠١	*mia wa waHid*
200	٢٠٠	*mītein*
300	٣٠٠	*talāt mia*
1000	١٠٠٠	*alf*
2000	٢٠٠٠	*alfein*
3000	٣٠٠٠	*talāt-alaf*

Ordinal Numbers

first	*awal*
second	*tanī*
third	*talet*
fourth	*rabeh*
fifth	*khames*

Glossary

Abbasids – Baghdad-based successor dynasty to the *Umayyads*; ruled from AD 750 until the sack of Baghdad by the Mongols in 1258

ain – well, spring

Amal – Shiite militia turned political party

Amorites – Western Semitic people who emerged from the Syrian deserts around 2000 BC and influenced life in the cities of Mesopotamia and Phoenicia until 1600 BC

apse – semicircular recess for the altar in a church

Arab League – a league of 22 independent Arab states, formed in 1945, to further cultural, economic, military, political and social cooperation between the states

architrave – the lowest division of the *entablature*, extending from column to column; also the moulded frame around a door or window

Arz ar-Rab – 'Cedars of the Lord'; local name for small remaining group of old cedar trees near Bcharré

AUB – American University of Beirut

Ayyubids – an Egyptian-based dynasty founded by *Saladin*

bilad ish-Sham – the area of modern Syria, Lebanon and Palestine

bir – well

burj – tower

caliph – spiritual and temporal leader of Sunni Muslim community, or 'umma' (the institution of the caliphate was abolished in 1924)

capital – the uppermost part of a column, supporting the *entablature* or arch

caravanserai – see *khan*

cardo maximus – Roman main street, from north to south; see *decumanus maximus*

cella – inner part of temple that houses the statue of a god or goddess

centrale – government phone office

chador – one-piece head-to-toe black covering garment

Chalcolithic – period between the *Neolithic* and Bronze Ages in which there was an increase in urbanisation and trade and the occasional use of copper

cornice – the upper portion of the *entablature* in classical or Renaissance architecture

cuneiform – wedge-shaped characters of several different languages, including Babylonian

dabke – national Lebanese dance, an energetic folk dance

decumanus maximus – Roman main street from east to west; see *cardo maximus*

deir – monastery

donjon – castle keep or great tower

Druze – a religious sect based on Islamic teachings; followers are found mainly in Lebanon, with some in Syria and Israel

Eid al-Adha – Feast of Sacrifice marking the end of the pilgrimage to Mecca

Eid al-Fitr – Festival of Breaking the Fast celebrated at the end of *Ramadan*

emir – an independent ruler or chieftain; military commander or governor

entablature – the upper part of the classical order, comprising the *architrave*, *frieze* and *cornice*, supported by the colonnade

exedra – a room or outdoor area with seats used for discussions

ezan – call to prayer

Fakhreddine – Nationalist hero. Appointed by the Ottomans in 1590 to pacify the Druze, he unified the Mt Lebanon area. Also spelt Fakhr ad-Din.

Fatimids – a Shiite dynasty from North Africa who claimed to be descended from Fatima, daughter of Prophet Mohammed, and her husband Ali ibn-abi Talib

frieze – central part of the *entablature*

furn – oven

Green Line – line which divided Beirut's eastern (Christian) half from its western (Muslim) half

haj – pilgrimage to Mecca

hammam – Turkish-style bathhouse with sauna and massage

haram – the sacred area inside a mosque

Hejira – migration; usually refers to Mohammed's flight from Mecca in AD 622. It is also the name of the Islamic calendar.

Hezbollah – 'party of God'; radical Shiite political party. Its guerrilla arm was largely responsible for expelling Israel from the south of the country.

Hyksos – Semitic invaders from Western Asia, probaby Asia Minor (ie, Anatolia) who were famed for their horsemanship. They introduced the horse to Pharaonic Egypt and ruled there from 1720 to 1560 BC.

hypocaust – raised floor in Roman bathhouses, heated by circulating hot air beneath

iconostasis – screen with doors and icons set in tiers separating sanctuary from the nave in a church

iftar – breaking of the day's fast during *Ramadan*

imam – prayer leader in a mosque; Muslim cleric

Islamic Jihad – the armed wing of the *Hezbollah*

iwan – vaulted hall, opening onto a central court, usually in the *madrassa* of a mosque

jebel – mountain

jihad – literally 'striving in the way of the faith'; holy war

Kaaba – the rectangular structure at the centre of the grand mosque in Mecca (containing the black stone) around which *haj* pilgrims walk

khan – large inn enclosing a courtyard which provided accommodation for caravans; also known as caravanserai

kiyaas hammam – goat-hair bags used as loofahs

kursi – a wooden stand for holding the *Quran*

Lebanese Commuting Company (LCC) – private bus company

Lebanese Transport Company – private bus company

Levant – literally 'where the sun rises'; region of the Eastern Mediterranean from Egypt to Greece

madrassa – theological school

maktab amn al-aam – general security office

Mamluks – military class of ex-Turkish slaves established about AD 1250 who ruled much of Syria and Lebanon from Egypt and who remained in power in the latter until 1805

mar – saint

Maronite – Lebanese Christians who embrace the Monothelite Doctrine that Christ had two natures but only a single divine will

medina – old walled centre of any Islamic city

mezze – starters

mihrab – prayer niche in the wall of a mosque which indicates the direction of Mecca

minaret – tower of a mosque from which *ezan* is made

minbar – pulpit in a mosque

Mu'awiyah bin Abu Sufyan – (AD 661–750) Governor of Syria and founder of the *Umayyad* dynasty

muezzin – mosque official who, from the *minaret*, sings the *ezan* five times a day

murex – a kind of mollusc from which the famous purple dye of Tyre comes

mutasarrifa – an Ottoman administrative unit, eg, Mt Lebanon

nahr – river

nargileh – water pipe used to smoke tobacco

nave – central part of a church

nebaa – spring

Neolithic – literally 'new stone' age; period based on the development of stone tools and which witnessed the beginnings of domestication and urbanisation

OCFTC – Lebanese government bus company

Phalangist – member of a Lebanese Christian paramilitary organisation, founded in 1936

PLO – Palestinian Liberation Organization

Qala'at – castle or fortress
Quran – Holy book of Islam

rakats – cycles of prayer during which the *Quran* is read and bows and prostrations are performed
Ramadan – the Muslim month of fasting
ras – headland

Saladin – warlord who retook Jerusalem from the Crusaders; founder of the *Ayyubid* dynasty; also spelt Salah ad-Din
saray – palace
Seleucids – Royal dynasty (312–64 BC) whose rule extended from Thrace to India at its peak. It was founded by Seleucus, a Macedonian general in Alexander the Great's army.
serail – Ottoman palace; also spelt 'seraglio'
servees – service taxi

Sharia – Islamic law
Shiism – a branch of Islam which regards the prophet Mohammed's cousin Ali and his successors as the true leaders
SLA – South Lebanese Army
souq – market
stele(ae) – inscribed stone slab
sultan – the absolute ruler of a Muslim state
sumac – a reddish, lemony dried herb that is delicious on eggs and in salad
Sunni – main branch of Islam. Based on the words and acts of the Prophet Mohammed, with the *caliph* seen as the true successor.

Umayyads – first great dynasty of Arab Muslim rulers, based in Damascus

waqf – religious endowment

zaatar – thyme
zawiye – hospice and religious school

LONELY PLANET

You already know that Lonely Planet produces more than this one guidebook, but you might not be aware of the other products we have on this region. Here is a selection of titles that you may want to check out as well:

Jordan, Syria & Lebanon Travel Atlas
ISBN 0 86442 441 8
US$14.95 • UK£8.99 • 95FF

Middle East
ISBN 0 86442 701 8
US$24.95 • UK£14.99 • 180FF

French phrasebook
ISBN 0 86442 450 7
US$5.95 • UK£3.99 • 40FF

Istanbul to Cairo on a shoestring
ISBN 0 86442 749 2
US$16.95 • UK£10.99 • 130FF

Turkey
ISBN 0 86442 599 6
US$21.95 • UK£13.99 • 170FF

Egypt
ISBN 0 86442 677 1
US$19.95 • UK£12.99 • 160FF

Israel & the Palestinian Territories
ISBN 0 86442 691 7
US$17.95 • UK£11.99 • 140FF

Jordan
ISBN 0 86442 694 1
US$17.95 • UK£11.99 • 140FF

Syria
ISBN 0 86442 747 6
US$17.95 • UK£11.99 • 140FF

Available wherever books are sold

LONELY PLANET

ON THE ROAD

Travel Guides explore cities, regions and countries, and supply information on transport, restaurants and accommodation, covering all budgets. They come with reliable, easy-to-use maps, practical advice, cultural and historical facts and a rundown on attractions both on and off the beaten track. There are over 200 titles in this classic series, covering nearly every country in the world.

 Lonely Planet Upgrades extend the shelf life of existing travel guides by detailing any changes that may affect travel in a region since a book has been published. Upgrades can be downloaded for free from **www.lonelyplanet.com/upgrades**

For travellers with more time than money, **Shoestring** guides offer dependable, first-hand information with hundreds of detailed maps, plus insider tips for stretching money as far as possible. Covering entire continents in most cases, the six-volume shoestring guides are known around the world as 'backpackers bibles'.

For the discerning short-term visitor, **Condensed** guides highlight the best a destination has to offer in a full-colour, pocket-sized format designed for quick access. They include everything from top sights and walking tours to opinionated reviews of where to eat, stay, shop and have fun.

CitySync lets travellers use their Palm™ or Visor™ hand-held computers to guide them through a city with handy tips on transport, history, cultural life, major sights, and shopping and entertainment options. It can also quickly search and sort hundreds of reviews of hotels, restaurants and attractions, and pinpoint their location on scrollable street maps. CitySync can be downloaded from **www.citysync.com**

MAPS & ATLASES

Lonely Planet's **City Maps** feature downtown and metropolitan maps, as well as transit routes and walking tours. The maps come complete with an index of streets, a listing of sights and a plastic coat for extra durability.

Road Atlases are an essential navigation tool for serious travellers. Cross-referenced with the guidebooks, they also feature distance and climate charts and a complete site index.

ESSENTIALS

Read This First books help new travellers to hit the road with confidence. These invaluable predeparture guides give step-by-step advice on preparing for a trip, budgeting, arranging a visa, planning an itinerary and staying safe while still getting off the beaten track.

Healthy Travel pocket guides offer a regional rundown on disease hot spots and practical advice on predeparture health measures, staying well on the road and what to do in emergencies. The guides come with a user-friendly design and helpful diagrams and tables.

Lonely Planet's **Phrasebooks** cover the essential words and phrases travellers need when they're strangers in a strange land. They come in a pocket-sized format with colour tabs for quick reference, extensive vocabulary lists, easy-to-follow pronunciation keys and two-way dictionaries.

Miffed by blurry photos of the Taj Mahal? Tired of the classic 'top of the head cut off' shot? **Travel Photography: A Guide to Taking Better Pictures** will help you turn ordinary holiday snaps into striking images and give you the know-how to capture every scene, from frenetic festivals to peaceful beach sunrises.

Lonely Planet's **Travel Journal** is a lightweight but sturdy travel diary for jotting down all those on-the-road observations and significant travel moments. It comes with a handy time-zone wheel, world maps and useful travel information.

Lonely Planet's eKno is an all-in-one communication service developed especially for travellers. It offers low-cost international calls and free email and voicemail so that you can keep in touch while on the road. Check it out on **www.ekno.lonelyplanet.com**

FOOD & RESTAURANT GUIDES

Lonely Planet's **Out to Eat** guides recommend the brightest and best places to eat and drink in top international cities. These gourmet companions are arranged by neighbourhood, packed with dependable maps, garnished with scene-setting photos and served with quirky features.

For people who live to eat, drink and travel, **World Food** guides explore the culinary culture of each country. Entertaining and adventurous, each guide is packed with detail on staples and specialities, regional cuisine and local markets, as well as sumptuous recipes, comprehensive culinary dictionaries and lavish photos good enough to eat.

LONELY PLANET

OUTDOOR GUIDES

For those who believe the best way to see the world is on foot, Lonely Planet's **Walking Guides** detail everything from family strolls to difficult treks, with 'when to go and how to do it' advice supplemented by reliable maps and essential travel information.

Cycling Guides map a destination's best bike tours, long and short, in day-by-day detail. They contain all the information a cyclist needs, including advice on bike maintenance, places to eat and stay, innovative maps with detailed cues to the rides, and elevation charts.

The **Watching Wildlife** series is perfect for travellers who want authoritative information but don't want to tote a heavy field guide. Packed with advice on where, when and how to view a region's wildlife, each title features photos of over 300 species and contains engaging comments on the local flora and fauna.

With underwater colour photos throughout, **Pisces Books** explore the world's best diving and snorkelling areas. Each book contains listings of diving services and dive resorts, detailed information on depth, visibility and difficulty of dives, and a roundup of the marine life you're likely to see through your mask.

LONELY PLANET

Guides by Region

Lonely Planet is known worldwide for publishing practical, reliable and no-nonsense travel information in our guides and on our Web site. The Lonely Planet list covers just about every accessible part of the world. Currently there are 16 series: Travel guides, Shoestring guides, Condensed guides, Phrasebooks, Read This First, Healthy Travel, Walking guides, Cycling guides, Watching Wildlife guides, Pisces Diving & Snorkeling guides, City Maps, Road Atlases, Out to Eat, World Food, Journeys travel literature and Pictorials.

AFRICA Africa on a shoestring • Cairo • Cairo City Map • Cape Town • Cape Town City Map • East Africa • Egypt • Egyptian Arabic phrasebook • Ethiopia, Eritrea & Djibouti • Ethiopian (Amharic) phrasebook • The Gambia & Senegal • Healthy Travel Africa • Kenya • Malawi • Morocco • Moroccan Arabic phrasebook • Mozambique • Read This First: Africa • South Africa, Lesotho & Swaziland • Southern Africa • Southern Africa Road Atlas • Swahili phrasebook • Tanzania, Zanzibar & Pemba • Trekking in East Africa • Tunisia • Watching Wildlife East Africa • Watching Wildlife Southern Africa • West Africa • World Food Morocco • Zimbabwe, Botswana & Namibia
Travel Literature: Mali Blues: Traveling to an African Beat • The Rainbird: A Central African Journey • Songs to an African Sunset: A Zimbabwean Story

AUSTRALIA & THE PACIFIC Auckland • Australia • Australian phrasebook • Australia Road Atlas • Bush-walking in Australia •Cycling New Zealand • Fiji • Fijian phrasebook • Healthy Travel Australia, NZ and the Pacific • Islands of Australia's Great Barrier Reef • Melbourne • Melbourne City Map • Micronesia • New Cale-donia • New South Wales & the ACT • New Zealand • Northern Territory • Outback Australia • Out to Eat – Melbourne • Out to Eat – Sydney • Papua New Guinea • Pidgin phrasebook • Queensland • Rarotonga & the Cook Islands • Samoa • Solomon Islands • South Australia • South Pacific • South Pacific phrasebook • Sydney • Sydney City Map • Sydney Condensed • Tahiti & French Polynesia • Tasmania • Tonga • Tramping in New Zealand • Vanuatu • Victoria • Walking in Australia • Watching Wildlife Australia • Western Australia
Travel Literature: Islands in the Clouds: Travels in the Highlands of New Guinea • Kiwi Tracks: A New Zealand Journey • Sean & David's Long Drive

CENTRAL AMERICA & THE CARIBBEAN Bahamas, Turks & Caicos • Baja California • Bermuda • Central America on a shoestring • Costa Rica • Costa Rica Spanish phrasebook • Cuba • Dominican Republic & Haiti • Eastern Caribbean • Guatemala • Guatemala, Belize & Yucatán: La Ruta Maya • Healthy Travel Central & South America • Jamaica • Mexico • Mexico City • Panama • Puerto Rico • Read This First: Central & South America • World Food Mexico • Yucatán
Travel Literature: Green Dreams: Travels in Central America

EUROPE Amsterdam • Amsterdam City Map • Amsterdam Condensed • Andalucía • Austria • Baltic States phrasebook • Barcelona • Barcelona City Map • Berlin • Berlin City Map • Britain • British phrasebook • Brus-sels, Bruges & Antwerp • Brussels City Map • Budapest • Budapest City Map • Canary Islands • Central Europe • Central Europe phrasebook • Corfu & the Ionians • Corsica • Crete • Crete Condensed • Croatia • Cycling Britain • Cycling France • Cyprus • Czech & Slovak Republics • Denmark • Dublin • Dublin City Map • Eastern Europe • Eastern Europe phrasebook • Edinburgh • Estonia, Latvia & Lithuania • Europe on a shoestring • Finland • Florence • France • Frankfurt Condensed • French phrasebook • Georgia, Armenia & Azerbaijan • Germany • German phrasebook • Greece • Greek Islands • Greek phrasebook • Hungary • Iceland, Greenland & the Faroe Islands • Ireland • Istanbul • Italian phrasebook • Italy • Krakow • Lisbon • The Loire • London • London City Map • London Condensed • Madrid • Malta • Mediterranean Europe • Mediterranean Europe phrasebook • Moscow • Mozambique • Munich • the Netherlands • Norway • Out to Eat – London • Paris • Paris City Map • Paris Condensed • Poland • Portugal • Portuguese phrasebook • Prague • Prague City Map • Provence & the Côte d'Azur • Read This First: Europe • Romania & Moldova • Rome • Rome City Map • Russia, Ukraine & Belarus • Russian phrasebook • Scandinavian & Baltic Europe • Scandinavian Europe phrase-book • Scotland • Sicily • Slovenia • South-West France • Spain • Spanish phrasebook • St Petersburg • St Petersburg City Map • Sweden • Switzerland • Trekking in Spain • Tuscany • Ukrainian phrasebook • Venice • Vienna • Walking in Britain • Walking in France • Walking in Ireland • Walking in Italy • Walking in Spain • Walking in Switzerland • Western Europe • Western Europe phrasebook • World Food France • World Food Italy • World Food Spain
Travel Literature: Love and War in the Apennines • The Olive Grove: Travels in Greece • On the Shores of the Mediterranean • Round Ireland in Low Gear • A Small Place in Italy • After Yugoslavia

LONELY PLANET

Mail Order

Lonely Planet products are distributed worldwide. They are also available by mail order from Lonely Planet, so if you have difficulty finding a title please write to us. North and South American residents should write to 150 Linden St, Oakland, CA 94607, USA; European and African residents should write to 10a Spring Place, London NW5 3BH, UK; and residents of other countries to Locked Bag 1, Footscray, Victoria 3011, Australia.

INDIAN SUBCONTINENT Bangladesh • Bengali phrasebook • Bhutan • Delhi • Goa • Healthy Travel Asia & India • Hindi & Urdu phrasebook • India • Indian Himalaya • Karakoram Highway • Kerala • Mumbai (Bombay) • Nepal • Nepali phrasebook • Pakistan • Rajasthan • Read This First: Asia & India • South India • Sri Lanka • Sri Lanka phrasebook • Tibet • Tibetan phrasebook • Trekking in the Indian Himalaya • Trekking in the Karakoram & Hindukush • Trekking in the Nepal Himalaya
Travel Literature: The Age of Kali: Indian Travels and Encounters • Hello Goodnight: A Life of Goa • In Rajasthan • A Season in Heaven: True Tales from the Road to Kathmandu • Shopping for Buddhas • A Short Walk in the Hindu Kush • Slowly Down the Ganges

ISLANDS OF THE INDIAN OCEAN Madagascar & Comoros • Maldives • Mauritius, Réunion & Seychelles

MIDDLE EAST & CENTRAL ASIA Bahrain, Kuwait & Qatar • Central Asia • Central Asia phrasebook • Dubai • Hebrew phrasebook • Iran • Israel & the Palestinian Territories • Istanbul • Istanbul City Map • Istanbul to Cairo on a shoestring • Jerusalem • Jerusalem City Map • Jordan • Lebanon • Middle East • Oman & the United Arab Emirates • Syria • Turkey • Turkish phrasebook • World Food Turkey • Yemen
Travel Literature: Black on Black: Iran Revisited • The Gates of Damascus • Kingdom of the Film Stars: Journey into Jordan

NORTH AMERICA Alaska • Boston • Boston City Map • California & Nevada • California Condensed • Canada • Chicago • Chicago City Map • Deep South • Florida • Great Lakes • Hawaii • Hiking in Alaska • Hiking in the USA • Honolulu • Las Vegas • Los Angeles • Los Angeles City Map • Louisiana & The Deep South • Miami • Miami City Map • New England • New Orleans • New York City • New York City City Map • New York City Condensed • New York, New Jersey & Pennsylvania • Oahu • Out to Eat – San Francisco • Pacific Northwest • Puerto Rico • Rocky Mountains • San Francisco • San Francisco City Map • Seattle • Southwest • Texas • USA • USA phrasebook • Vancouver • Virginia & the Capital Region • Washington DC • Washington, DC City Map • World Food Deep South, USA • World Food New Orleans
Travel Literature: Caught Inside: A Surfer's Year on the California Coast • Drive Thru America

NORTH-EAST ASIA Beijing • Beijing City Map • Cantonese phrasebook • China • Hiking in Japan • Hong Kong • Hong Kong City Map • Hong Kong Condensed • Hong Kong, Macau & Guangzhou • Japan • Japanese phrasebook • Korea • Korean phrasebook • Kyoto • Mandarin phrasebook • Mongolia • Mongolian phrasebook • Seoul • Shanghai • South-West China • Taiwan • Tokyo
Travel Literature: In Xanadu: A Quest • Lost Japan

SOUTH AMERICA Argentina, Uruguay & Paraguay • Bolivia • Brazil • Brazilian phrasebook • Buenos Aires • Chile & Easter Island • Colombia • Ecuador & the Galapagos Islands • Healthy Travel Central & South America • Latin American Spanish phrasebook • Peru • Quechua phrasebook • Read This First: Central & South America • Rio de Janeiro • Rio de Janeiro City Map • Santiago • South America on a shoestring • Santiago • Trekking in the Patagonian Andes • Venezuela
Travel Literature: Full Circle: A South American Journey

SOUTH-EAST ASIA Bali & Lombok • Bangkok • Bangkok City Map • Burmese phrasebook • Cambodia • Hanoi • Healthy Travel Asia & India • Hill Tribes phrasebook • Ho Chi Minh City • Indonesia • Indonesian phrasebook • Indonesia's Eastern Islands • Jakarta • Java • Lao phrasebook • Laos • Malay phrasebook • Malaysia, Singapore & Brunei • Myanmar (Burma) • Philippines • Pilipino (Tagalog) phrasebook • Read This First: Asia & India • Singapore • Singapore City Map • South-East Asia on a shoestring • South-East Asia phrasebook • Thailand • Thailand's Islands & Beaches • Thailand, Vietnam, Laos & Cambodia Road Atlas • Thai phrasebook • Vietnam • Vietnamese phrasebook • World Food Thailand • World Food Vietnam

ALSO AVAILABLE: Antarctica • The Arctic • The Blue Man: Tales of Travel, Love and Coffee • Brief Encounters: Stories of Love, Sex & Travel • Chasing Rickshaws • The Last Grain Race • Lonely Planet Unpacked • Not the Only Planet: Science Fiction Travel Stories • Lonely Planet On the Edge • Sacred India • Travel with Children • Travel Photography: A Guide to Taking Better Pictures

OFF THE ROAD

Journeys, the travel literature series written by renowned travel authors, capture the spirit of a place or illuminate a culture with a journalist's attention to detail and a novelist's flair for words. These are tales to soak up while you're actually on the road or dip into as an at-home armchair indulgence.

The new range of lavishly illustrated **Pictorial** books is just the ticket for both travellers and dreamers. Off-beat tales and vivid photographs bring the adventure of travel to your doorstep long before the journey begins and long after it is over.

Lonely Planet **Videos** encourage the same independent, tough-minded approach as the guidebooks. Currently airing throughout the world, this award-winning series features innovative footage and an original soundtrack.

Yes, we know, work is tough, so do a little bit of deskside dreaming with the spiral-bound Lonely Planet **Diary**, the tearaway page-a-day **Day-to-Day Calendar** or a Lonely Planet **Wall Calendar**, filled with great photos from around the world.

TRAVELLERS NETWORK

Lonely Planet Online. Lonely Planet's award-winning Web site has insider information on hundreds of destinations, from Amsterdam to Zimbabwe, complete with interactive maps and relevant links. The site also offers the latest travel news, recent reports from travellers on the road, guidebook upgrades, a travel links site, an online book-buying option and a lively traveller's bulletin board. It can be viewed at **www.lonelyplanet.com** or AOL keyword: lp.

Planet Talk is a quarterly print newsletter, full of gossip, advice, anecdotes and author articles. It provides an antidote to the being-at-home blues and lets you plan and dream for the next trip. Contact the nearest Lonely Planet office for your free copy.

Comet, the free Lonely Planet newsletter, comes via email once a month. It's loaded with travel news, advice, dispatches from authors, travel competitions and letters from readers. To subscribe, click on the Comet subscription link on the front page of the Web site.

Index

Text

Bold indicates maps.

Bold indicates maps.

Boxed Text & Special Sections

MAP LEGEND

CITY ROUTES

Freeway	Freeway	Lane	Lane
Highway	Primary Road	Unsealed Road	Unsealed Road
Road	Secondary Road	Pedestrian Street	Pedestrian Street
Street	Street	Stepped Street	Stepped Street

REGIONAL ROUTES

Tollway, Freeway
Primary Road
Secondary Road
Minor Road

BOUNDARIES

International
Disputed
Fortified Wall

HYDROGRAPHY

River, Creek
Canal
Lake
Dry Lake; Salt Lake

TRANSPORT ROUTES & STATIONS

Train
Cable Car, Chairlift
Walking Trail
Path

AREA FEATURES

Building
Park, Gardens
Market
Sports Ground
Beach
Cemetery
Campus
Plaza

POPULATION SYMBOLS

✪ CAPITAL .... National Capital	● CITY .... City	● Village .... Village
	● Town .... Town	Urban Area

MAP SYMBOLS

■ .... Place to Stay	▼ .... Place to Eat	● .... Point of Interest

✈ Airport	✉ Embassy	⚱ Monument	Ruins
Bank	Fountain	Mosque	Ski Field
Border Crossing	Fuel	▲ Mountain	Taxi
Bus Stop	Hammam	Museum	Telephone
Bus Terminal	Hospital	National Park	Temple (Classical)
Castle	Internet Cafe	Parking	Theatre
Cave	Lighthouse	Police Station	Tomb
Chapel/Church	Lookout	Post Office	Tourist Information
Cinema	Monastery	Pub or Bar	Transport

Note: not all symbols displayed above appear in this book

LONELY PLANET OFFICES

Australia
Locked Bag 1, Footscray, Victoria 3011
☎ 03 9689 4666 fax 03 9689 6833
email: talk2us@lonelyplanet.com.au

UK
10a Spring Place, London NW5 3BH
☎ 020 7428 4800 fax 020 7428 4828
email: go@lonelyplanet.co.uk

USA
150 Linden St, Oakland, CA 94607
☎ 510 893 8555 TOLL FREE: 800 275 8555
fax 510 893 8572
email: info@lonelyplanet.com

France
1 rue du Dahomey, 75011 Paris
☎ 01 55 25 33 00 fax 01 55 25 33 01
email: bip@lonelyplanet.fr
www.lonelyplanet.fr

World Wide Web: www.lonelyplanet.com *or* AOL keyword: lp
Lonely Planet Images: lpi@lonelyplanet.com.au